MONETARY AND ECONOMIC POLICY PROBLEMS
BEFORE, DURING, AND AFTER THE GREAT WAR

Titles in the Liberty Fund Library of the Works of Ludwig von Mises

LUDWIG VON MISES

Selected Writings of Ludwig von Mises

Monetary and Economic Policy Problems Before, During, and After the Great War

 Edited and with an Introduction by
Richard M. Ebeling

LIBERTY FUND   *Indianapolis*

This 2012 Liberty Fund edition is published by arrangement with
Hillsdale College. Introduction, editorial additions, and translation
© 2012 by Hillsdale College.

Original materials used for the translations that appear in the present
edition are © by the estate of Ludwig von Mises and are used by
permission.

Frontispiece used courtesy of Richard M. Ebeling and Bettina Bien
Greaves.

C   1   2   3   4   5   6   7   8   9   10
P   1   2   3   4   5   6   7   8   9   10

Library of Congress Cataloging-in-Publication Data

Von Mises, Ludwig, 1881–1973.
Monetary, fiscal, and economic policy problems before,
during, and after the Great War/edited and with an introduction by
Richard M. Ebeling.
    p.   cm.   (Selected writings of Ludwig von Mises; 1)
Includes bibliographical references and index.
ISBN 978-0-86597-832-4 (hbk.: alk. paper)
ISBN 978-0-86597-833-1 (pbk.: alk. paper)
    1. Austria—Economic policy   2. Austria—Economic conditions—
To 1918.   3. Austria—Economic conditions—1918–1945.   4. Monetary
policy—Austria—History—20th century.   5. Fiscal policy—Austria—
History—20th century.   I. Ebeling, Richard M.   II. Title.
    HC265.V664 2011
    330.9436'044—dc23   2011041366

Liberty Fund, Inc.
8335 Allison Pointe Trail, Suite 300
Indianapolis, Indiana 46250-1684

CONTENTS

ACKNOWLEDGMENTS

This volume, like the other two in this series, was made possible by the continuing support of Hillsdale College, which arranged for the translations of virtually all the articles, essays, and lectures contained in the volume. I would like to particularly thank Dr. Larry Arnn, Hillsdale College president, and Mr. Mike Harner, chief staff officer and assistant to the president at Hillsdale College. I am especially grateful for their patience and encouragement in my bringing the *Selected Writings of Ludwig von Mises* project to a close with the publication of this, the last of the three volumes in the series.

The primary translators of the articles in this volume were the late Dr. Herbert Izzo and Dr. Rebecca Garber, with individual pieces translated by Wolfgang Grassl, Mary M. Custer, and Andrew Swift. To all of them I extend my most sincere thanks for making my work as editor that much easier. Dr. Izzo, an expert in both Romance and Germanic languages, had helped in the translation of many of the pieces that also appeared in volume 2 of these *Selected Works*. He was also a valued friend who deeply believed in the ideas of liberty, and whom I greatly miss.

The project would have never begun if former Hillsdale College president Dr. George Roche (1935–2006) had not immediately thrown the complete support of the college behind the work after my wife, Anna, and I discovered in 1996 that Mises's "lost papers" that had been looted by the Nazis from his Vienna apartment in 1938 had survived the war, and were preserved in a former secret Soviet archive in Moscow, Russia. He and Mr. John Cervini, Hillsdale College director for development, promptly arranged the financial support for Anna and me to travel to Moscow in October 1996 to obtain photocopies of virtually the entire collection of 10,000 pages of material.

I also owe a deep debt of gratitude to Liberty Fund of Indianapolis for enthusiastically expressing an interest in publishing a large selection of these recovered documents and other related papers and essays in the three-volume set that is now, finally, in print. I particularly wish to thank Alan Russell and Chris Talley, who are senior officers at Liberty Fund, and Manuel Ayau, Leonard Liggio, and Giancarlo Ibarguen, who serve on Liberty Fund's board of directors, all of whom I have known for many years, and whose friendship and support I greatly appreciate. I also owe a sincere thanks to Mr. Dan Kirklin of Liberty Fund, who has very helpfully assisted in the final editing process for this volume.

I would be remiss if I did not also mention Ludwig von Mises's widow, Margit (1890–1993), who took me under her wing when I was a graduate student in New York many years ago, sharing her knowledge about her husband and the old Vienna before the Second World War, as well as encouraging my interest in her husband's work. Margit kindly introduced me to her daughter, Gitta Sereny, who shared her knowledge and memories of her stepfather, Ludwig von Mises. Gitta and her husband, Donald Honeyman, graciously gave of their time during several trips that Anna and I made to London, where they live.

I also owe thanks to Bettina Bien Greaves, who for many years worked at the Foundation for Economic Education (FEE) in Irvington, New York. Already when I was an undergraduate in the 1970s, Bettina was sharing with me hard-to-get articles by Mises, and was the first one who told me about how the Nazis had plundered Mises's apartment in Vienna and had taken away his papers, manuscripts, and other personal and family documents, many of which have now seen the light of day in these *Selected Writings*.

As I have said in acknowledgments in the previous volumes in this series, my greatest debt is to my wife, Anna. It was through her friends and contacts in her native city of Moscow that we were able to gain entrée to that former secret archive and acquire copies of the "lost papers." She first organized the papers in a logical and systematic way when we returned to Hillsdale College, and has assisted me in every step of the process leading to their publication. She was especially helpful in the preparation of this volume in doing much of the research for the editor's footnotes that are included in the chapters.

But most important, she has never wavered in her support and insistence that I bring the project to a successful conclusion. Her love and companionship have made everything that I do meaningful and worthwhile.

PREFACE

This three-volume set of the *Selected Writings of Ludwig von Mises* has been published in reverse chronological order. The current volume, the last prepared in the series, in fact, is devoted to some of the earliest of Mises's writings on a variety of economic issues. They mostly cover monetary, fiscal, and general economic policy matters in the Austro-Hungarian Empire before and during the First World War, with additional articles that Mises wrote in the postwar period that had not been included in volume 2. An appendix to the present volume includes a talk that Mises delivered at his private seminar, which would meet in his office at the Vienna Chamber of Commerce, in the spring of 1934 on the methodology of the social sciences, before he moved to Geneva, Switzerland; and the curriculum vitae that his great-grandfather prepared for the Habsburg Emperor in 1881 as part of his ennoblement that gave him and his heirs the hereditary title of "Edler von."

It is in the second volume of the *Selected Writings* (2002), *Between the Two World Wars: Monetary Disorder, Interventionism, Socialism, and the Great Depression*, that the reader will find a large collection of Mises's many articles and policy pieces from the 1920s and 1930s dealing with the Great Austrian Inflation, fiscal and regulatory mismanagement by the government, and the negative effects of numerous forms of government intervention and controls before and during the Great Depression. The volume also includes critiques of socialist central planning and his defense of *praxeology*, the science of human action.

The third volume of the *Selected Writings* (2000), *The Political Economy of International Reform and Reconstruction*, focuses on Mises's writings mostly from the first half of the 1940s. In the midst of the Second World War, Mises lectured and wrote on the pressing issues of how Europe, small nations, and underdeveloped countries could recover from war and poverty and start on the path to economic renewal and prosperity.

Each volume begins with an introduction in which I try to explain the historical context in which Mises wrote the pieces in that particular volume. I have also tried to assist the reader with footnotes explaining some of the ideas, persons, events, or geographical locations to which Mises refers in the text.

This project developed out of the discovery of the "lost papers" of Ludwig von Mises in a formerly secret KGB archive in Moscow, Russia, in 1996. Looted by the Gestapo from Mises's Vienna apartment in March 1938 shortly after the Nazi annexation of Austria into the German Third Reich, they ended up among a huge cache of stolen documents, papers, and archival collections that the Nazis had plundered from all over occupied Europe. At the end of the Second World War the entire cache, including Mises's papers, was captured by the Soviet Red Army in a small town in western Czechoslovakia. After being informed about what had been captured, Stalin instructed that it all be brought to Moscow and that a secret archive be built to house it. For half a century, only the Soviet secret police and the Soviet Ministry of Foreign Affairs had access to the collections in this archive.

In the introduction to volume 2 in these *Selected Writings of Ludwig von Mises*, I describe in detail how my wife and I came to find out about this archive and the existence of Mises's papers among them, amounting to about 10,000 pages of material. In October 1996, we journeyed to Moscow and spent about two weeks carefully going through the entire collection of Mises's papers. We returned to the United States with photocopies of virtually the entire collection, which includes Mises's correspondence, unpublished manuscripts, published articles, policy memoranda prepared during the years when he worked for the Vienna Chamber of Commerce, material relating to his teaching at the University of Vienna and his famous private seminar, and his military service during the First World War. Many of the articles, policy memoranda, essays, and speeches that were found among Mises's "lost papers" have been included in this series, especially in volumes 1 and 2 of his *Selected Writings*.

Shortly after the discovery of the "lost papers" was announced, Liberty Fund contacted Hillsdale College and me about the possibility of publishing a selection of these and some of Mises's related essays, lectures, and articles covering the period from before the First World War to the 1940s during the Second World War. I most happily accepted Liberty Fund's kind offer to serve as editor of the translations (mostly from German) and to prepare the volumes for publication.

It has been a labor of love that has ended up taking far longer to complete than I had expected. A good part of the delay in finishing the last of these volumes was due to a five-year "distraction" during which I served as the president of the Foundation for Economic Education (FEE) from 2003 to 2008. But my return to the "calmer" life of academia has permitted me to finally finish the task.

Ludwig von Mises is most famous for his great works on monetary theory, socialist central planning, the general theory of the market process, and the methodology of the social sciences, the leading ones, of course, being *The Theory of Money and Credit*; *Socialism: An Economic and Sociological Analysis*; *Liberalism*; *Critique of Interventionism*; *Epistemological Problems of Economics*; *Bureaucracy*; *Omnipotent Government*; *Human Action: A Treatise on Economics*; *Theory and History*; and *The Ultimate Foundations of Economic Science*.

But what the *Selected Writings of Ludwig von Mises*, in general, bring out is the "unknown Mises," if you will. Not the Mises of grand economic theory and sweeping political economy, or the fundamental problems of human action. Here, instead, is Mises as applied economist, detailed policy analyst, and economic policy problem-solver in the detailed reality of the many pressing public policy issues that confronted the old Austro-Hungarian Empire and the new Austrian Republic in the aftermath of the Great War, and then the need for reconstruction and economic reform after the Second World War.

For those who have sometimes asked, "Well, but how do you apply Austrian economics to the 'real world' of public policy?" here is the answer by the economist who was considered the most original, thoroughgoing, and uncompromising member of the Austrian School in the twentieth century!

Indeed, it can be argued that it was having to grapple with the intricacies of these types of everyday economic policy issues during a time of great, and sometimes cataclysmic, change in the Europe and the Austria of the first half of the twentieth century that helped to guide and form Mises's thinking on those wider and more general problems for which he is most famous.

The *Selected Writings of Ludwig von Mises* provide an insight into and a better understanding of the first two-thirds of Mises's long and productive life as a professional economist in a way that has not been available before. It also brings into English translation for the first time the vast majority of his practical economic policy writings from this, in many ways his most prolific, period before he left war-ravaged Europe in 1940 to make a new home and career for himself in the United States.

INTRODUCTION

The articles and lectures included in this volume by the Austrian economist Ludwig von Mises were written in the years before, during, and after the Great War of 1914–18, as the First World War used to be called. They focus on the monetary, fiscal, and general economic policy problems of, first, the Austro-Hungarian Empire and, then, the new postwar Austrian Republic after the dismantling of the Habsburg Monarchy.

For those who may be familiar with Mises's more theoretical works on various themes of monetary theory and policy,[1] comparative economic systems—capitalism, socialism, and interventionism[2]—the general nature and workings of the market economy, or the methodology and philosophy of the social sciences,[3] most of these articles and lectures (like the ones in volume 2 and 3 in this series)[4] offer a different

1. Ludwig von Mises, *The Theory of Money and Credit* (Indianapolis: Liberty Fund, 3rd rev. ed., [1924; 1953] 1981) and "Monetary Stabilization and Cyclical Policy," (1928) in *The Causes of the Economic Crisis, and Other Essays Before and After the Great Depression* (Auburn, Ala.: Ludwig von Mises Institute, 2006), pp. 53–153.

2. Ludwig von Mises, *Socialism: An Economic and Sociological Analysis* (Indianapolis: Liberty Fund, [1951] 1981), *Liberalism: The Classical Tradition* (Indianapolis: Liberty Fund, [1927] 2005), *Critique of Interventionism* (Irvington-on-Hudson, N.Y.: Foundation for Economic Education, [1929] 1996), *Interventionism: An Economic Analysis* (Irvington-on-Hudson, N.Y.: Foundation for Economic Education, [1940] 1996), *Bureaucracy* (Indianapolis: Liberty Fund, [1944] 2007), and *Planning for Freedom, and Other Essays* (Indianapolis: Liberty Fund, [1951] 2008).

3. Ludwig von Mises, *Epistemological Problems of Economics* (New York: New York University Press, [1933] 1981), *Human Action: A Treatise on Economics* (Indianapolis: Liberty Fund, [1949; 4th rev. ed. 1966] 2007), *Theory and History: An Interpretation of Social and Economic Evolution* (Indianapolis: Liberty Fund, [1957] 2005), and *The Ultimate Foundation of Economic Science* (Indianapolis: Liberty Fund, [1962] 2006).

4. Richard M. Ebeling, ed., *Selected Writings of Ludwig von Mises*, vol. 2, *Between the Two World Wars: Monetary Disorder, Interventionism, Socialism, and the Great Depression* (Indianapolis: Liberty Fund, 2002); *Selected Writings of Ludwig von Mises*, vol. 3, *The Political Economy of International Reform and Reconstruction* (Indianapolis: Liberty Fund, 2000).

perspective on Mises as an applied economist. Here is not the broad theorist concerned, often, with stepping back from the particular details of specific historical circumstances to investigate and evaluate the essential and universal properties of human action; or the institutional prerequisites for economic calculation and the rational allocation of resources among competing ends; or the relationships between time preference, investment time horizons, monetary expansion, and the sequential stages of the business cycle.[5]

Instead, these essays investigate and analyze the historical and institutional workings of the pre–World War I monetary system of the Austro-Hungarian Empire, and the issues surrounding legal specie redemption for the banknotes of the Austro-Hungarian Bank; the politics behind the establishment of the gold standard in Austria-Hungary; the growing fiscal imbalances developing in the Habsburg Empire due to the patterns of government spending and taxing policies in the first decade of the twentieth century; and the reasons behind the economic crisis that hit Austria-Hungary in the years immediately before the start of the Great War. Here, too, we see Mises analyzing during the war the motives behind German and Austro-Hungarian trade policy, the impact and significance of emigration from Austria, the effects from the monetary inflation used to fund the government's war expenditures, and the pros and cons of financing those war expenditures through taxation versus borrowing by the issuance of war bonds.

After the war, Mises explains the distorting effects from the new Austrian government's control and rationing of foreign exchange for imports and exports; the impact on the Austrian foreign exchange rate of monetary expansion to finance the government's huge deficit spending; a specific policy agenda to bring the country's financial house back into order, and the need for cooperation from both businesses and labor unions if this was to be achieved without Austria's currency collapsing into hyperinflation; the claims that holders of banknotes of the old Austro-Hungarian Bank could make on the new Austrian National

---

5. On Mises's life and contributions to economics in general and the philosophy of freedom, see Richard M. Ebeling, "A Rational Economist in an Irrational Age: Ludwig von Mises," in *Austrian Economics and the Political Economy of Freedom* (Northampton, Mass.: Edward Elgar, 2003), pp. 61–100, and *Political Economy, Public Policy, and Monetary Economics: Ludwig von Mises and the Austrian Tradition* (London: Routledge, 2010); also, Murray N. Rothbard, *Ludwig von Mises: Scholar, Creator, Hero* (Auburn, Ala.: Ludwig von Mises Institute, 1988); Israel M. Kirzner, *Ludwig von Mises* (Wilmington, Del.: ISI Books, 2001); and Jörg Guido Hülsmann, *Mises: The Last Knight of Liberalism* (Auburn, Ala.: Ludwig von Mises Institute, 2007).

Bank in the postwar period; Austria's fiscal problems in the period after the end of the inflation; and the lessons for banking reform after the collapse of several banks in 1931.

Ludwig von Mises became immersed in these issues because he had to earn a living outside the Austrian academic arena. University teaching appointments were few and far between in Austria both before and after the First World War, even though Mises was clearly qualified for such a position.[6] His only formal relationship with the University of Vienna, after graduating in 1906 with a doctoral degree in jurisprudence,[7] was as a *privatdozent* (an unsalaried lecturer), which permitted him the privilege of offering seminars during the academic year. Mises offered such a seminar almost every term from 1913 to 1934 (except for most of the time during the Great War). He was promoted to professor extraordinary in May 1918, but this was a purely honorific title that was still unsalaried and with a nominal "tenure" as a professor in this status.[8]

However, from 1920 until the spring of 1934, Mises organized and chaired a *privatseminar* (private seminar) of interested scholars in the fields of economics, history, sociology, political science, and philosophy. It met twice a month between October and June on Friday evenings at 7 p.m. at his office at the Vienna Chamber of Commerce. The private seminar came to an end when Mises accepted a full-time teaching position at the Graduate Institute of International Studies in Geneva, Switzerland, as professor of international economic relations beginning in autumn 1934.[9]

6. For Friedrich A. Hayek's explanation for Mises's failure to obtain a formal academic position, see Peter G. Klein, ed., *The Collected Works of F. A. Hayek*, vol. 4, *The Fortunes of Liberalism: Essays on Austrian Economics and the Ideal of Freedom* (Chicago: University of Chicago Press, 1992), pp. 127–28. While anti-Semitism may have played a part in Mises's not being offered a position at the University of Vienna, Hayek believed that it was mostly due to Mises's uncompromising and outspoken criticism of socialism when the intellectual community of Vienna was heavily dominated by the Left.

7. Training as an economist was received through the faculty of law at the University of Vienna.

8. He was also permitted to serve as a chair on dissertation committees and was regularly called upon as a faculty participant at graduate student oral defenses of theses. For example, the book by Fritz Machlup on the gold-exchange standard that Mises discusses in Chapter 22 of this volume was Machlup's dissertation under Mises's supervision at the University of Vienna. He was also on the faculty committee that questioned Alfred Schutz, later internationally known as a sociologist and phenomenological philosopher, when he defended his thesis at the University of Vienna.

9. See Appendix A in this volume for Mises's last paper presented at his private seminar, "Maxims for the Discussion of the Methodological Problems of the Social Sciences," in March 1934.

Because an academic career was closed off to him, from 1909 to 1934 Mises made his living as an economic advisor and policy analyst for the Vienna Chamber of Commerce, Crafts, and Industry. First hired as an assistant for the drafting of documents, in 1910 he was promoted to deputy secretary. When he returned from active duty in the First World War, he was made "first secretary" at the Chamber, responsible for matters relating to a wide variety of areas including monetary and fiscal affairs, trade and financial issues, and administrative and constitutional law.

He developed and refined his skills as an economist having to deal with the everyday practical affairs and policy issues of the Austria of his time. He had to master and maintain a thorough and extremely detailed knowledge of the Austrian economy and the impact of Austrian government policy on the industrial, commercial, and monetary and fiscal affairs of the country.[10] As Mises expressed it years later in his *Memoirs:*

> My job with the *Handelskammer* [the Chamber of Commerce] greatly expanded my horizons. That I now have the material for a social and economic history of the downfall of the Austrian civilization readily at hand is to a great degree the result of the studying that was required of me to be able to carry on with my work in the *Handelskammer.* Travels that led me to all parts of old Austria-Hungary from 1912–1914 taught me much in particular. In visiting the centers of industry, my intent was to become acquainted with the industrial situation in view of the renewal of customs and trade relations with Hungary, and the adoption of new, autonomous tariffs and trade treaties.
>
> The main thrust of my job with the *Handelskammer* was not dealing with commercial questions, but those pertaining to finance, currency, credit, and tax policy. In addition, I was given special assignments on

Many of those who participated in the seminar recalled in later years that they considered it to be one of the most rewarding and challenging intellectual experiences of their lives because of the consistent quality of the papers delivered and the discussions that followed. For accounts of the seminar by some of the participants, see Ludwig von Mises, *Memoirs* (Auburn, Ala.: Ludwig von Mises Institute, [1940] 2009), pp. 81–83, and the recollections of other members of the seminar in the appendix to Margit von Mises, *My Years with Ludwig von Mises,* 2nd ed. (Cedar Falls, Iowa: Center for Futures Education, 1984), pp. 201–10.

10. For a detailed discussion of Mises's policy writings and work at the Vienna Chamber of Commerce in the interwar period, see Richard M. Ebeling, "The Economist as the Historian of Decline: Ludwig von Mises and Austria Between the Two World Wars," in *Political Economy, Public Policy, and Monetary Economics,* pp. 88–140. For many of Mises's articles and Chamber of Commerce policy pieces during the 1920s and 1930s, see Richard M. Ebeling, ed., *Selected Writings of Ludwig von Mises,* vol. 2, *Between the Two World Wars: Monetary Disorder, Interventionism, Socialism, and the Great Depression.*

an ongoing basis. From the time of the armistice until the signing of the Peace Agreement of Saint Germain [in September 1919] I was the consultant on financial questions to the Foreign Office. Later, when the terms of the peace treaty were put into effect, I was in charge of the office concerned with the prewar debt. In this capacity I had numerous dealings with the representatives of our former enemies. I was the Austrian delegate to the international *Handelskammer* [the International Chamber of Commerce] and a member of many international commissions and committees, whose insoluble task it was to facilitate the peaceful exchange of goods and services in a world pervaded by national hatred and the precursors of genocide.[11]

At a relatively early age Mises seems to have formulated in his mind a rather comprehensive classical liberal worldview of the social order. His experience in the role of applied economist clearly left its mark and influenced his understanding of the effects that government intervention could have on the effective functioning of a modern market economy. To appreciate this, and the writings included in his volume, it is necessary to take a glance at the political and economic environment of the old Austro-Hungarian Empire and the Austrian monetary system as it developed in the nineteenth century.

The Habsburg Monarchy and the Austro-Hungarian Empire[12]

The House of Habsburg, which came to rule a vast empire for nearly eight hundred years, had its origin in the thirteenth century. Through

---

11. Ludwig von Mises, *Memoirs*, pp. 63–64; also see, on Mises's work at the Chamber, Alexander Hörtlehner, "Ludwig von Mises und die österreichissche Handelskammerorganisation" ["Ludwig von Mises and the Chamber of Commerce"], *Wirtschaftspolitische Blatter*, no. 28 (1981), pp. 140–50.

12. The following summary of the history of the Habsburg Empire is drawn from Henry Wickham Steed, *The Hapsburg Monarchy* (New York: Howard Fertig, [1914] 1969); Oscar Jaszi, *The Dissolution of the Habsburg Monarchy* (Chicago: University of Chicago Press, 1929); A. J. P. Taylor, *The Habsburg Monarchy, 1809–1918: A History of the Austrian Empire and Austria-Hungary* (Chicago: University of Chicago Press, [1948] 1976); Arthur J. May, *The Hapsburg Monarchy, 1867–1918* (Cambridge: Harvard University Press, 1951); Arthur J. May, *The Passing of the Hapsburg Monarchy, 1914–1918* (Philadelphia: University of Pennsylvania Press, 1966); Robert A. Kann, *The Multinational Empire: Nationalism and National Reform in the Habsburg Monarchy, 1848–1918*, 2 vols. (New York: Columbia University Press, 1950); Robert A. Kann, *A History of the Habsburg Empire, 1526–1918* (Berkeley: University of California Press, 1974); Hans Kohn, *The Habsburg Empire, 1804–1918* (New York: D. Van Nostrand, 1961); Edward Crankshaw, *The Fall of the House of Habsburg* (New York: The Viking Press, 1963); C. A. Macartney, *The Habsburg Empire, 1790–1918* (New York: Macmillan, 1969); Gordon Brook-Shepherd, *The Austrians: A Thousand-Year Odyssey* (New York: Carroll & Graf, 1996); and Robin Okey, *The Habsburg Monarchy: From Enlightenment to Eclipse* (New York: St. Martin's Press, 2001).

a series of royal marriages, treaties, and some conquests, the Habsburg Monarchy gained control over a large territory in Central and Eastern Europe, and for a period of time large areas in Western Europe as well, including Spain, parts of modern-day France, Italy, Germany, and Switzerland, and what later became Holland, Belgium, and Luxemburg. From the thirteenth century to the middle of the nineteenth century, the Habsburgs also nominally headed the Holy Roman Empire, or its later, loose German Confederation.

It was during this time, when the Habsburgs were beginning to dominate so much of Europe, that Emperor Frederick III (1415–93) had inscribed on official buildings the five vowels, A E I O U, which he interpreted as "Alles Erdreich Ist Österreich Untertan" ("All the earth is subject to Austria"), or in Latin, "Austriae Est Imperare Orbi Universo" ("Austria must rule the universe").[13]

The Habsburgs ruled as absolute monarchs. But under the influence of the Age of Enlightenment and the early phase of the French Revolution, Empress Maria Theresa (1717–70) and then her sons, Joseph II (1740–90) and Leopold II (1747–92), attempted to introduce various forward-looking reforms while retaining the principle of absolutism. The dark turn taken in the French Revolution and the rise of Napoleon to power shifted the monarchy back in a far more conservative direction under Francis II (1768–1835). With Napoleon's victories over the German states, the Holy Roman Empire was dissolved and Francis II declared himself emperor of Austria in 1804.

As one of the final victors over the French after Napoleon's defeat in Russia in 1812, the Habsburg Empire in Central and Eastern Europe was consolidated following the Congress of Vienna in 1815 as one contiguous territory that by the 1880s incorporated what are today Austria, Hungary, the Czech Republic, Slovakia, Slovenia, Croatia, Bosnia, and large parts of Italy, Poland, Ukraine, and Romania.

In the years just preceding the First World War, the Austro-Hungarian Empire covered a territory of about 415,000 square miles and included within its borders a dozen or so national and linguistic groups, including Germans, Hungarians, Czechs, Slovaks, Croatians, Romanians, Italians, Poles, Bulgarians, Serbians, Slovenians, and Ruthenians. Out of a population of 50 million the Germans and Hungar-

---

13. See Hans Kohn, "The Problem of Central Europe: The Legacy of the Habsburgs," in *Not by Arms Alone: Essays on Our Time* (Cambridge: Harvard University Press, 1940), pp. 43–64.

ians each numbered about 10 million, with the remaining 30 million made up of these other groups.

Europe of the nineteenth century experienced a relentless battle between four powerful ideas: monarchical absolutism, political and economic liberalism, integral nationalism, and revolutionary socialism. Absolutism insisted upon the divine rights of kings to rule without restraint; liberalism demanded the recognition of individual liberty, representative and limited constitutional government, and freedom of private enterprise from state control; integral nationalism (by the middle decades of the nineteenth century) increasingly insisted upon the unification and political independence of peoples sharing a common language, culture, and history, and finally a common ethnicity or race;[14] and socialism called for the overthrow of private property, nationalization of the means of production, and greater economic and social equality by either violent or democratic methods. All four of these ideological forces were at work in the Habsburg Monarchy until the end of the Austro-Hungarian Empire in the ruins of the First World War.

The French Revolution of February 1848 reverberated across much of Europe, including in the Austrian Empire. Within days and weeks of the uprising in Paris, students on the streets of Vienna demanded constitutional change, and the Italians and Hungarians were in open revolt against their Habsburg rulers. By the end of 1849, however, the Italians and Hungarians had been crushed (the latter through the intervention of the Russian Imperial Army), and Habsburg rule was once more imposed with especial ruthlessness against the Hungarians.

At first reforms were promised to the Austrian liberals, with a constitution promised in July 1848. And when eighteen-year-old Francis Joseph (1830–1916) assumed the throne upon the abdication of his uncle, Ferdinand I (1793–1875), in December 1848, the new emperor gave his support to the constitutional changes.[15] Almost immediately, however,

---

14. On the development and evolution of the nationalist idea in the nineteenth century, see G. P. Gooch, *Nationalism* (New York: Harcourt Brace & Howe, 1920); Carlton J. H. Hayes, *The Historical Evolution of Modern Nationalism* (New York: Richard R. Smith, 1931); Walter Sulzbach, *National Consciousness* (Washington, D.C.: American Council on Public Affairs, 1934); Frederick Hertz, *Nationality in History and Politics* (New York: Oxford University Press, 1944); Hans Kohn, *Nationalism: Its Meaning and History* (Princeton, N.J.: D. Van Nostrand, 1955) and *Nationalism and Realism: 1852–1879* (Princeton, N.J.: D. Van Nostrand, 1968).

15. On the life and reign of Francis Joseph, who ruled over the empire for sixty-eight years, see Joseph Redlich, *Emperor Francis Joseph of Austria* (New York: Macmillan, 1929); and Alan

he reversed himself and insisted upon the reassertion of absolutist authority. What Francis Joseph had inherited from his ruling ancestors was a belief in "his divine right of unlimited monarchical power," tempered with the idea "that his rule must, before all, produce the best possible results for the peoples of his realm. . . . Yet, up to the end he did not doubt that his empire, composed of so many different races and lands, could be governed successfully only by a hereditary monarch and according to his absolute will."[16] Thus, he could not make concessions that would have undermined his absolute rule in the name of caring for the well-being of his subjects.

Neither could he completely concede to the increasing nationalist sentiments of the diverse peoples in his large realm without also abdicating his responsibility as that benevolent ruler. Many Austrian liberals who lived a good portion of their lives under the reign of Francis Joseph believed that he twice missed the opportunity to successfully transform his multinational empire into a federal domain that might have reconciled the conflicting interests and demands of the national groups under his rule. The ideal of these liberals from the middle of the nineteenth century to the First World War had been what some of them called "the Austrian idea." If a federal structure of government could have been set up in which each of these peoples had wide political and social autonomy within their own lands while sharing a common bond of economic freedom and civil liberties, the Habsburg Monarchy could have created on a larger and far grander scale what had been formed in the Swiss confederation with its reconciliation and harmony among its French-, German-, and Italian-speaking citizens.[17]

Francis Joseph's rejection of constitutional reforms and the reimposition of central authority over the Italians, Hungarians, and his Slav

---

Palmer, *Twilight of the Habsburgs: The Life and Times of Emperor Francis Joseph* (New York: Grove Press, 1994).

16. Joseph Redlich, "The End of the House of Austria," *Foreign Affairs* (July 1, 1930), p. 605; see also Kohn, *The Habsburg Empire, 1804–1918*, p. 49: "Like a good eighteenth century monarch, [Francis Joseph] regarded himself as the first servant of the nation, but he identified the nation with himself and his dynasty. He worked indefatigably for the good of his people, but they were *his* people and he interpreted what was good for them."

17. On the mutual benefits to be derived from a state that incorporates a variety of different national groups, see the classic essay by Lord Acton, "Nationality," (1862) in J. Rufus Fears, ed., *Selected Writings of Lord Acton*, vol. 1, *Essays in the History of Liberty* (Indianapolis: Liberty Fund, 1985), pp. 409–33; for a contrary view as to why such a Swiss-type solution to the nationalist tensions of the Austro-Hungarian Empire was not feasible, see Benedetto Croce, *History of Europe in the Nineteenth Century* (New York: Harcourt, Brace, 1933), pp. 181–86.

subjects in 1848–49 was the first chance lost for any such reconciliation. The second lost opportunity occurred following his defeat at the hands of the Prussians in 1866, when Bismarck pushed Austria out of the German Confederation. Fearful of the Hungarians taking advantage of the empire's postwar weakness to claim full independence through another violent uprising, Francis Joseph agreed to the *Ausgleich,* the "Compromise," of 1867 that transformed the Austrian Empire into the Austro-Hungarian Empire. While Francis Joseph remained emperor of both halves of his domain, Hungary became widely independent in many of its domestic affairs. Only a common customs and monetary system and a shared military and foreign policy completely linked Hungary to the Austrian "Crownlands" directly ruled by Francis Joseph's government in Vienna.[18]

As Hans Kohn, one of the twentieth century's leading experts on the history and philosophy of nationalism, who had grown up under the rule of Francis Joseph in Prague, explained, "In the Compromise with the Hungarian nobility in 1867, the aspirations of the Czechs, Slovaks, Serbs, Croats, and Romanians, who in large majority were then still loyal to the dynasty, were sacrificed for the purpose of winning the assent of the Magyars to a common foreign and military policy on the part of what now became the Dual Monarchy."[19] Indeed, at first, several leading Czech and Hungarian nationalist leaders believed that the flowering of their people's cultural and linguistic identities could best flourish in the wider setting of a multinational Habsburg Empire. But as the nineteenth century progressed this sentiment shifted into a belief that only national independence could secure these goals.

A far more liberal-minded voice in the Habsburg family was Francis Joseph's son, Crown Prince Rudolf (1858–89), the heir to the throne. Among his personal tutors had been Carl Menger (1840–1921), the founder of the Austrian School of economics. Under Menger's guidance, Crown Prince Rudolf had become well versed in the free trade and relatively laissez-faire ideas of the Classical economists.[20] Menger

18. The Habsburg "Crownlands" directly under the emperor's authority were made up of the territory of present-day Austria, Bohemia, and Moravia (the present-day Czech Republic), Galicia and Bukovina (now part of western Ukraine), Slovenia, Dalmatia (along part of the Adriatic seacoast), and southern Tyrol (now part of northern Italy); Bosnia was ruled as a separate administrative entity.

19. Hans Kohn, "The Viability of the Habsburg Monarchy," *Slavic Review* (March 1963), p. 38.

20. See Erich W. Streissler and Monika Streissler, eds., *Carl Menger's Lectures to Crown Prince Rudolf of Austria* (Northampton, Mass.: Edward Elgar, 1994).

also had coauthored with Rudolf a scathing criticism of the Austrian nobility, who were accused of having lost their sense of social duty and, instead, had escaped into frivolous court intrigues, pointless social entertainments, and financial irresponsibility. It was a clear call for recognition of and respect for the middle-class values of enterprise, frugality, and personal responsibility. The bourgeois virtues needed to replace the anachronistic role of the aristocracy in society, who had lost their way in the pretensions of power and lure of wasteful pleasures.[21] But whatever influence the crown prince might have had on the course of events in Austria-Hungary was cut short by his suicide in 1889 at his hunting lodge at Mayerling.[22]

The particularly nationalist imperialism of the Hungarians against the other peoples under their control was not the only problem as the nineteenth century progressed in terms of growing antagonism among the subject peoples in the Dual Monarchy. The German-Austrians, also, increasingly became defensive and antagonistic toward the rising nationalist aspirations of the Czechs, Poles, Slovenians, and others in the Crownlands, as well as the growing demands of the Hungarians for independence.

As Hans Kohn pointed out, "The spread of democracy, literacy, and economic well-being in the western half of the monarchy after 1867 strengthened the non-German nationalities there at the expense of the Germans. The result was that many Germans in the monarchy lost their faith in an Austrian idea as much as many Slavs and other non-Germanic peoples did. . . . By the end of the nineteenth century many Austrian Germans looked to the Prussian German Reich as their real home and venerated [Otto von] Bismarck."[23]

Looking back at the events that brought about the demise of the Habsburg Empire in the immediate aftermath of the First World War, Ludwig von Mises explained why many German-Austrians turned against liberalism as a foundation for the preservation of the monarchy and

---

21. Crown Prince Rudolf and Carl Menger, "The Austrian Nobility and Its Constitutional Vocation: A Warning to Aristocratic Youth," (1878) in Eugene N. Anderson, Stanley J. Pinceti, and Donald J. Siegler, eds., *Europe in the Nineteenth Century, a Documentary Analysis of Change and Conflict*, vol. 2, 1870–1914 (Indianapolis: Bobbs-Merrill, 1961), pp. 78–101.

22. See Richard Barkeley, *The Road to Mayerling: The Life and Death of Crown Prince Rudolph of Austria* (New York: Macmillan, 1958); and Judith Listowel, *A Habsburg Tragedy: Crown Prince Rudolph* (New York: Dorset Press, 1978). Rudolph's domestic liberalism, however, was combined with support for Austrian foreign policy imperialism; see Robert A. Kann, *The Multinational Empire*, vol. 2, pp. 181–87.

23. "Viability of the Habsburg Monarchy," p. 39.

the Austro-Hungarian state. Over the centuries German-Austrian settlers had made their homes in the eastern reaches of the empire. They brought with them the German language, culture, literature, commercial knowledge, and knowhow. They viewed themselves as a "civilizing force" among the lesser-advanced nationalities, especially among the Slavic peoples. Indeed, many of these subject peoples became acculturated into German-Austrian life, since the latter was the dominant group; the German language in particular became the venue for social and economic advancement. But as literacy and national consciousness awakened among these other peoples in the nineteenth century, loyalties to and identification with German-Austria and the Habsburg dynasty were replaced with a growing allegiance and sense of belonging to their own ethnic and linguistic groups.

Furthermore, these peoples had higher birth rates than the Germans living among them. Cities and towns that had been settled and predominantly populated by Germans for centuries became increasingly Czech or Hungarian or Polish or Romanian or Slovenian communities. German-Austrians found themselves shrinking minorities in lands that they had long considered to be their own politically, culturally, and commercially. This was especially true in the Czech lands with Prague at the center.

As the nineteenth century progressed, German-Austrians discovered that adherence to liberal principles of representative government and full individual and cultural equality before the law meant the demise of the German communities sprinkled across the Habsburg domains. For many German-Austrian liberals the choice was between a liberalism that would logically mean the decentralization and possible eventual breakup of the empire along nationalist lines, or advocacy of centralized political control, monarchical dictate when required, and subversion of democratic aspirations among the non-German peoples.

The first course meant the eventual loss of German political and cultural domination in the non-German lands; the second meant holding onto both political and cultural power as long as possible in the non-German areas of the empire, but only by increasingly alienating the other subject peoples. As Mises explained, part of the German-Austrian tragedy was that national and linguistic imperialism won over liberal idealism.[24]

---

24. Ludwig von Mises, *Nation, State, and Economy: Contributions to the Politics and History of Our Time* (Indianapolis: Liberty Fund, [1919] 2006), pp. 88–109.

What enabled the Habsburg Empire to endure for fifty years after the establishment of the Dual Monarchy in 1867 was the constitutional order that had been implemented at the same time as the *Ausgleich* (or "Compromise"). The Constitution of 1867, which accompanied the creation of "Austria-Hungary," was imbued with the spirit of the classical liberal ideas that were then at their zenith in Europe.[25] Every subject of the Habsburg emperor was guaranteed freedom of religion, language, association, profession, and occupation, and could appeal to a special higher court of law if a violation of these rights had occurred. Any subject might live wherever he chose throughout the emperor's domain. Private property was secure, and relatively free trade prevailed within the boundaries of the empire, though protectionist barriers to international trade not only continued but grew in various ways in the last decades of the nineteenth and first decade of the twentieth centuries.[26]

The economic free trade zone that made up the Austro-Hungarian Empire fostered significant economic development beginning in and especially after the 1880s, though very far from matching the economic progress in Western Europe or in Imperial Germany after 1871.[27] However, various forms of government controls and regulations began to be domestically superimposed on the society, including the nationalization of the railways, starting in the 1880s. As a result, the remain-

25. See Kohn, *The Habsburg Empire, 1804–1918*, p. 72: "Amidst all the controversies and upheavals caused by the growing conflict of nationalities and by the vain search for an Austrian idea, the Austrian Constitution of December 31, 1867, which was a document of mid-century liberalism, remained in force for over half a century." The Fundamental Law Concerning the General Rights of Citizens from the Austrian Constitution of 1867 may be found at http://www.h-net.org/~habsweb/sourcetexts.auscon.htm. However, see Robert S. Wistrich, *The Jews of Vienna in the Age of Franz Joseph* (New York: Oxford University Press, 1989), p. 151: "[Adolf] Fischof put his finger on the central contradiction of the 1867 Constitution—that Austria-Hungary was a multinational state masquerading under liberal German hegemony as a nation-state on the Western European model. It had a dual personality, liberal with regards to the rights of the individual but oppressive in its relation to the Slav nationalities who were treated as 'servant peoples.'" Adolf Fischof (1816–93) was a prominent figure in the Austrian Revolution of 1848, and an outspoken liberal in support of autonomy for the various subject nationalities in the Austro-Hungarian Empire.

26. In 1867, for example, the Lower Austrian Chamber of Commerce located in Vienna declared, "The state has fulfilled its task if it removes all obstacles to the free, orderly activity of its citizens. Everything else is achieved by the considerateness and benevolence of the factory owners and above all by the personal efforts and thriftiness of the workers." See Okey, *Habsburg Monarchy*, p. 206.

27. See David Good, *The Economic Rise of the Habsburg Empire, 1750–1914* (Berkeley: University of California Press, 1984).

ing history of the monarchy was one of liberal freedoms introduced in 1867 being undermined by nationalist discord, periods of rule by central government decree, and the continuation or introduction of interventionist policies that merely intensified the antagonisms among the subject peoples. As A. J. P. Taylor explained:

> In another way, the Austrian state suffered from its strength: it never had its range of activity cut down during a successful period of *laissez-faire*, and therefore the openings for national conflict were far greater. There were no private schools or hospitals, no independent universities; and the state, in its infinite paternalism, performed a variety of services from veterinary surgery to the inspecting of buildings. The appointment of every schoolteacher, of every railway porter, of every hospital doctor, of every tax collector, was a signal of national struggle. Besides, private industry looked to the state for aid from tariffs and subsidies; these, in every country, produce "log-rolling," and nationalism offered an added lever with which to shift the logs. German industries demanded state aid to preserve their privileged position; Czech industries demanded state aid to redress the inequalities of the past. The first generation of national rivals had been the products of universities and fought for appointments at the highest professional level; their disputes concerned only a few hundred state jobs. The generation that followed them was the result of universal elementary education and fought for the trivial state employment that existed in every village; hence, the more popular national conflicts at the end of the century.[28]

In spite of all this, and the international tensions and foreign policy fiascos that would eventually plunge Austria-Hungary and the rest of Europe into the calamitous cauldron of conflict in 1914, the Habsburg Monarchy succeeded in generating a cosmopolitan culture, especially in Vienna, that brought all the subject peoples together and fostered an inspiring and flourishing world of the arts, music, literature, philosophy, the humanities, and the sciences.[29]

It gave many who lived in the postwar period of rising totalitarianism in the 1920s and 1930s a deep nostalgia for what seemed a far more

28. *The Habsburg Monarchy, 1809–1918*, p. 173.
29. See William M. Johnson, *The Austrian Mind: An Intellectual and Social History, 1848–1938* (Berkeley: University of California Press, 1972); Allan Janik and Stephen Toulmin, *Wittgenstein's Vienna* (Chicago: Ivan R. Dee, 1973); Carl E. Schorske, *Fin-de-Siècle Vienna: Politics and Culture* (New York: Alfred A. Knopf, 1980); Hilde Spiel, *Vienna's Golden Autumn, 1866–1938* (New York: Weidenfeld & Nicolson, 1987); Paul Hofmann, *The Viennese: Splendor, Twilight, and Exile* (New York: Doubleday, 1988).

civilized and humane epoch in turn-of-the-century Vienna. One voice that attempted to capture this "lost world" was that of Stefan Zweig (1881–1942), a renowned Austrian novelist and essayist who fled Vienna in 1934 and committed suicide in Brazil during the Second World War out of despair for all that was happening in the European world that he had known. In his posthumous work *The World of Yesterday*, he said:

> One lived well and easily and without cares in that old Vienna. . . . "Live and let live" was the famous Viennese motto, which today still seems to me more humane than all the categorical imperatives, and it maintained itself throughout all classes. Rich and poor, Czechs and Germans, Jews and Christians, lived peaceably together in spite of occasional chafing, and even the political and social movements were free of the terrible hatred which has penetrated the arteries of our time as a poisonous residue of the First World War. In the old Austria they still strove chivalrously, they abused each other in the news and in the parliament, but at the conclusion of their ciceronian tirades the selfsame representatives sat down together in friendship with a glass of beer or a cup of coffee, and called each other Du [the "familiar" in the German language]. . . . The hatred of country for country, of nation for nation, of one table for another, did not yet jump at one daily from the newspaper, it did not divide people from people and nations from nations; not yet had every herd and mass feeling become so disgustingly powerful in public life as today. Freedom in one's personal affairs, which is no longer considered comprehensible, was taken for granted. One did not look down upon tolerance as one does today as weakness and softness, but rather praised it as an ethical force. . . . For the genius of Vienna—a specifically musical one—was always that it harmonized all the national and lingual contrasts. Its culture was a synthesis of all Western cultures. Whoever lived there and worked there felt himself free of all confinement and prejudice.[30]

For Zweig, thinking back on that bygone paradise, "It was sweet to live here, in this atmosphere of spiritual conciliation, and subconsciously every citizen became supernational, cosmopolitan, a citizen of the world."[31]

It was, of course, only an illusion. That twilight of the liberal era in the old Austro-Hungarian Empire about which Zweig was so nostalgic

---

30. Stefan Zweig, *The World of Yesterday* (New York: Viking Press, 1943), pp. 24–25.
31. Ibid., p. 13; see also Richard M. Ebeling, "1914 and the World We Lost," *The Freeman: Ideas on Liberty* (June 2004), pp. 2–3.

had never been as pure and perfect as his mind recalled it. It was certainly true that liberal ideals had been established in the Constitution of 1867, and that they were implemented and enforced for the most part, especially in the Crownlands more directly under Emperor Francis Joseph's imperial authority. But beneath the surface of tolerance, civility, and cosmopolitanism were all the undercurrents of racial and nationalist bigotry, economic collectivism, and political authoritarianism that poured forth like destructive lava from an exploding volcano during and in the aftermath of the First World War.

The Austrian Monetary System, 1867–1914[32]

A leading theme of Mises's articles in the first part of this volume concerns the reasons for and the resistance to the full implementation of a gold standard in Austria-Hungary. His arguments in these essays can be better understood against the backdrop of Austria's monetary policies and experiences during the nineteenth century leading up to the currency reform act of 1892.

The story of the Austrian currency in the late eighteenth century and the first two-thirds of the nineteenth century is one of almost continual financial mismanagement. The government would debase the currency to cover its expenses, then make promises to put its budget on a sound footing, only to see another crisis arise requiring once again turning the handle on the monetary printing press.[33]

The Austrian government made several experiments with state-

32. Part of the discussion in this section draws upon Richard M. Ebeling, "Austria-Hungary's Economic Policies in the Twilight of the 'Liberal' Era: Ludwig von Mises' Writings on Monetary and Fiscal Policy," in *Political Economy, Public Policy, and Monetary Economics: Ludwig von Mises and the Austrian Tradition*, pp. 57–87.

33. The following brief account of the history of the Austrian currency is primarily taken from Charles A. Conant, *A History of Modern Banks of Issue*, 5th ed. (New York: G. P. Putnam's Sons, 1915), pp. 219–50; J. Laurence Laughlin, *History of Bimetallism in the United States* (New York: Appleton, 1898), pp. 189–97, 331–37; Robert Zuckerkandl, "The Austro-Hungarian Bank," in *Banking in Russia, Austro-Hungary, the Netherlands, and Japan* (Washington, D.C.: Government Printing Office, 1911), pp. 55–118. Also, specifically on the currency reform of 1892 and its implementation, "The Gold Standard in Austria" [Translation of the Report of the Special Currency Commission to the Upper House of the Austrian Parliament], *Quarterly Journal of Economics* (January 1893), pp. 225–54; "Reform of the Currency in Austria-Hungary," *Journal of the Royal Statistical Society* (June 1892), pp. 333–39; Friedrich von Wieser, "Resumption of Specie Payments in Austria-Hungary," *Journal of Political Economy* (June 1893), pp. 380–405; and Wesley C. Mitchell, "Resumption of Specie Payments in Austria-Hungary," *Journal of Political Economy* (December 1898), pp. 106–13.

chartered banks in the 1700s. But each of these banks soon collapsed or was closed due to lack of public confidence following large quantities of paper monies being issued to cover government expenditures. These expenditures reached huge proportions during the long years of war between the Austrian Empire and first Revolutionary and then Napoleonic France.

Between 1797 and 1811, the supply of government paper money increased from 74,200,000 florins to 1,064,000,000 florins, yielding a fourteen-fold increase over this period. Not surprisingly, whereas the price of silver coin expressed in paper money was 118 in 1800, it rose to 203 by 1807, then to 500 by 1810, and reached 1,200 by 1811.

The government announced its intention in 1811 to stop the printing presses and issue a new currency that would be converted at the ratio of five old florins for one new florin, with the total amount of paper money in circulation to be reduced to 212,800,000 florins. But the renewal of the war with Napoleon in 1812 resulted in the new currency being increased to 678,716,000 florins by 1816, a near tripling of the "reformed" currency in five years.

With the final defeat of Napoleon, the Austrian government announced that it would use a portion of the war reparations being paid by France to retire about 131,829,900 florins from circulation, leaving the paper money supply outstanding at around 546,886,000 florins. This process was assisted with the establishment of a new National Bank of Austria, with the Bank withdrawing government paper money in circulation in exchange for its own banknotes, until by early 1848, the total currency supply in circulation had been reduced to 241,240,000 florins; that is, there was an almost two-thirds reduction in the paper money supply over a thirty-year period. The National Bank, in February 1848, had silver reserves of about 65,000,000 florins, or, an approximate 25 percent specie cover for its outstanding currency in circulation.

But all of these monetary reforms began to unravel with the outbreak of the revolution of 1848, especially the Hungarian revolt against Austrian rule. Within days, panic runs on the National Bank reduced its silver reserves to 35,023,000 florins, a 53 percent loss in specie. The Austrian government suspended silver redemption and banned the exporting of silver and gold. Putting down the revolution forced the government to again borrow heavily from the National Bank. As a result, confidence in the Bank fell so low that in 1849 the government publicly promised to stop borrowing and cease increasing the currency.

But the process started again in a few years with Austria's military mobilization during the Crimean War, and then its wars against Italian nationalists and their French ally in a vain attempt to maintain control of portions of northern Italy. In 1850 government indebtedness to the National Bank had stood at 205,300,000 florins. With the Crimean War of 1854, the government's debt increased to 294,200,000 florins. It was reduced to 145,700,000 florins by 1859. But the start of the Italian campaigns that year pushed it up again to 285,800,000 florins, along with a renewed suspension of specie payments as the public wished to redeem the paper currency representing the value of this enlarged debt.

In 1863, an attempt was made, once again, to introduce a currency reform—the Plener Act—this time along the lines of Britain's Peel's Bank Act of 1844. But Austria's disastrous war with Prussia in 1866 pushed the supply of paper money in circulation from 80,000,000 florins before the conflict to 300,000,000 florins at its end.

The Compromise of 1867 that formally created the Austro-Hungarian Empire granted Hungary its own parliament, government, and domestic budget. It established a customs union and a common military and foreign policy between the two parts of the Habsburg domain, and a monetary union with the Austrian National Bank retaining its monopoly of note issue throughout Francis Joseph's domain. Some of the Hungarian liberals had advocated a system of competitive note-issuing private banks in place of the National Bank, but secret agreements between the emperor's government and the Hungarian nobility eliminated this as an option.

On July 1, 1878, the Austrian National Bank was transformed into the Austro-Hungarian Bank. The emperor, under joint nomination of the Austrian and Hungarian parliaments, appointed its governor. He was assisted by two vice-governors—one Austrian and the other Hungarian—appointed by the respective governments. The Bank's operating privileges were renewed in 1887, 1899, and 1910, with few substantial changes in their detail.

Formally, from 1816, Austria had been on a silver standard. But as we saw, the Austrian National Bank maintained unofficial specie redemption only for limited periods of time, soon interrupted usually by another war crisis requiring currency expansion to fund the government's expenditures.

The paper currency florin, not surprisingly, traded at a significant discount against the silver coin florin. Between 1848 and 1870, this discount was never less than about 14 percent and was often between 20 and 23 percent. But restrictions on note issuance under the operating rules of the Bank limited the expansion of the supply of banknotes. The provisions of the 1863 Bank Act limited the circulation of "uncovered" florins to 200,000,000. Any amount above that had to be covered by gold or silver coin or bullion. Any additional "uncovered" banknote issuance was subject to a penalty tax against the Bank of 5 percent.

With many of the major governments of Europe and North America establishing or reestablishing their economies on a gold basis in place of silver in the 1870s, the world price of silver began to fall.[34] After the Austro-Prussian War of 1866, the government's pressures on the Bank to fund deficits were greatly reduced, and the Bank could more or less follow the rules against uncovered note issuance. As a result, the paper florin's discount relative to silver disappeared by 1878. Silver began to flow into Austria-Hungary in such quantities that the Bank was instructed by the government to end the free minting of silver.

As a result, the paper florin actually rose to a premium against silver. As Friedrich von Wieser expressed it, "Silver had become of less value than paper!"[35] In addition, the florin was significantly appreciating in value against gold. The price in paper florins for 100 gold florins between 1887 and 1892 was:

Average for the year	Austrian florin notes
1887	125.25
1888	122.87
1889	118.58
1890	115.48
1891	115.83

The major monetary issue, therefore, during these years was to bring a halt to any further increase in the value of the Austrian paper currency. In February 1892, the Austrian and Hungarian governments invited a group of professional and academic experts to meet and address a set of questions relating to whether a gold standard should be

34. For example, following the Franco-Prussian War of 1870–71, the German Empire was proclaimed, unifying under Prussian leadership the various German states and principalities. In 1871 and 1873, legislation was passed formally putting Imperial Germany on the gold standard. See *The Reichbank, 1876–1900* (Washington, D.C.: Government Printing Office, 1910).
35. "Resumption of Specie Payments," p. 386.

adopted; if so, should it be monometallic or partly bimetallic with silver; what should be the status of government notes in circulation; how should the conversion from the existing florin to a gold standard be undertaken; and what monetary unit should be chosen?

Some of the most illustrious people in the field were brought together to offer their views and opinions on these questions. Thirty years later Ludwig von Mises described them in the following manner:

> From March 8 to March 17, 1892, the government-convened Currency Inquiry Commission met in Vienna. The chairman was Finance Minister [Emil] Steinbach; beside him stood the memorable Eugen von Böhm-Bawerk, as section head. Thirty-six experts appeared before the commission to answer five questions that were posed by the government. No Austrian was left off the list of participants at the inquiry who had anything of importance to say on currency matters. Along with Carl Menger, the founder of the Austrian School of economics, there was Wilhelm von Lucam, the highly honored longtime secretary general of the Austro-Hungarian Bank; Moriz Benedikt, the publisher of *Neue Freie Presse* [New Free Press]; Theodor Thaussig, the spiritual leader of the Viennese banking world; and Theodor Hertzka, the well-known writer on monetary matters and social policy. The thick quarto volume that makes up the stenographic minutes of the inquiry remains today a source for the best ideas on all matters relating to monetary policy.[36]

Virtually all of the participants spoke in favor of Austria's adoption of a gold standard. Menger, for example, at one point said: "Gold is the money of advanced nations in the modern age. No other money can provide the convenience of a gold currency in our age of rapid and massive commodity exchanges. Silver has become a troublesome tool of trade. Even paper money must yield to gold when it comes to monetary convenience in everyday life. . . . Moreover, under present conditions only a gold currency constitutes hard money. Neither a bank note and treasury note nor a silver certificate can take the place of gold, especially in moments of crisis."[37]

---

36. "The Austrian Currency Problem Thirty Years Ago and Today," Chapter 19, in the present volume.

37. Quoted in Hans Sennholz, "The Monetary Writings of Carl Menger," in Llewellyn H. Rockwell, ed., *The Gold Standard: Perspectives in the Austrian School* (Auburn, Ala.: The Ludwig von Mises Institute, [1985] 1992), p. 26; see also Günther Chaloupek, "Carl Menger's Contributions to the Austrian Currency Debate (1892) and His Theory of Money" (paper presented to the 7th ESHET Conference, Paris, France, January 30–February 1, 2003).

Later summarizing the work of the commission, Wieser supported the adoption of the gold standard in colorful language:

> Money is like speech; it is a means of intercourse. He who would have dealings with others must speak their language, however irrational he may find it. Language is rational by the very fact that it is intelligible to others, and more rational in proportion as it is intelligible to more people or to all. There can no more be an independent money system than independent speech; indeed, the more universal character of money, as compared with language, appears in this, that while a national language has its justification and significance in the intercourse of the world, there is no place for a national monetary system in the world's intercourse. If Europe errs in adopting gold, we must still, for good or evil, join Europe in her error, and we shall thus receive less injury than if we insist on being "rational" all by ourselves.[38]

The Currency Commission, in its official report to the Upper House of the Austrian Parliament, was no less adamant that gold, and only gold, was the recognized and essential international money. For that reason Austria-Hungary needed to adopt gold as the nation's standard if it was to successfully participate in the commerce and trade of the world.[39]

The commission proposed and the government accepted that the monetary unit would be renamed the *krone* (the crown), with the new crown being equal to one-half the replaced florin. Standard coins would be gold pieces of ten and twenty crowns, each one being of 900 parts gold to 100 parts copper. The twenty-crown coin would have a full weight of 6.775067 grams, and a fine weight of 6.09756 grams. In 1892 an exchange rate for the crown was fixed at 1.05 Swiss francs and 0.8505 German marks.

Silver was kept as a secondary medium of exchange of limited legal tender status for smaller transactions. Government paper money was temporarily kept in circulation up to a certain maximum, but with the expectation of its eventual retirement. For the transition to a full gold standard with legally mandated redemption of banknotes for specie, it was expected that the Austro-Hungarian Bank would continue to accumulate sufficient supplies of gold until at an unspecified date formal redemption would be instituted.

---

38. Wieser, "Resumption of Specie Payments," pp. 387–88.
39. "Gold Standard in Austria," p. 230.

An obligation to redeem crowns for gold was, in fact, never made into law. Yet from 1896 and most certainly after 1900 up until the outbreak of the war in 1914, the Austro-Hungarian Bank acted as if it now had that obligation and did pay in gold for its banknotes presented for redemption. Indeed, the oversight of this "shadow" gold standard (as it was called) by the Austro-Hungarian Bank, with maintenance of the exchange rate within a margin not much off the "gold points," was praised by authorities at the time as an exemplary case of a highly successful "managed currency."[40]

Ludwig von Mises's Writings on Monetary and Fiscal Policy Before the Great War

Ludwig von Mises's earliest writings on monetary and fiscal policy were published between 1907 and 1914,[41] and focused on these currency reform and related issues. He devoted a chapter in his *Memoirs* to explaining the background behind some of these articles.[42] He details his frustrations when the articles resulted in his coming face-to-face for the first time with opposition by government officials to reasonable and publicly endorsed policies due to political corruption and misappropriation of "secret" slush funds that would be threatened by implementing a fully convertible gold standard.

But he does not go into very great detail about the content of these early essays. They may be grouped under two headings. The first consists of articles concerning the political pressures that finally led to putting Austria formally on the path of a gold standard in 1892, and the reasons for the resistance and delay in legally establishing gold convertibility up to the beginning of World War I. The second group deals with fiscal extravagance and the regulatory and redistributive intrusiveness of the Austro-Hungarian government, which was leading the

---

40. More recently, the Austro-Hungarian Bank's exchange rate policy has been praised as an example of successful "target zone" management of an exchange rate band; see Marc Flandreau and John Komlos, "Target Zone in History and Theory: Lessons from an Austro-Hungarian Experiment (1896–1914)," Discussion Paper no. 18 (July 2003), Department of Economics, University of Munich, Germany.

The "gold points" represented the upper and lower limits of fluctuations of a country's foreign exchange value under the gold standard, beyond which it would be profitable to either export gold out of or import gold into that country.

41. Mises was between twenty-six and thirty-two years of age when he wrote these articles.

42. Mises, *Memoirs*, pp. 33–42.

country to a potential financial and economic crisis. Even if the events of the war had not intervened to accelerate the process that culminated in an end to the nearly eight-hundred-year reign of the Habsburgs, the growth of the interventionist state was weakening the foundations of the country.

The earliest of these essays is "The Political-Economic Motives of the Austrian Currency Reform." It is primarily an analysis of the changing factors influencing various interest groups that finally led to a sufficient coalition of these interests endorsing the move toward a gold standard. It highlights the fact that a major shift in economic policy is often dependent upon the vagaries of unique historical events, without which such a change might never have the chance to be implemented.[43]

From 1872 to 1887, the Austrian currency had been depreciating on the foreign exchange market. Many of the agricultural and manufacturing interests in both Austria and Hungary did not object to this trend, since it reduced foreign competition by raising the costs of imports and worked to make Austrian goods more competitive in other countries. But beginning in 1887, the currency began to appreciate, and continued to do so until 1891. The same interests that were quite happy living with a currency losing value were extremely anxious with an appreciating currency that lowered the costs of imports and raised the costs of Austrian exports.

By the time the Austrian Currency Commission was convened in 1892, all the leading manufacturing, agricultural, and financial interests had agreed behind the scenes on the necessity for currency reform to bring the appreciation of the Austrian florin to a halt. And they all concurred on the desirability for Austria-Hungary to establish a gold standard, while they initially argued over the particular rate of exchange at which the new currency—the crown—would be stabilized.

Mises's essay reads partly as what, today, would be considered a "public choice" analysis of the special-interest politicking that often guides

---

43. For example, the Classical economist Henry Fawcett argued in *Free Trade and Protection* (London: Macmillan, 1878), pp. 17–47, that if not for the great famine due to the failure of many of the crops and therefore such a large portion of the population in England and Ireland simultaneously threatened with starvation in the winter of 1845–46, the pressure for the unilateral repeal of agricultural protectionism (the Corn Laws) might never have occurred. It was unlikely that the same passion for a radical change to free trade would have been stimulated by the existing industrial and manufacturing protectionism that affected only different diverse and limited subgroups of the consuming public.

public policy. It brings out how a concentrated benefit to a wide array of interest groups served to generate a consensus on a significant institutional change in the existing monetary system. It also demonstrates how the costs or burdens imposed on a variety of smaller interest groups—particularly creditors and a number of medium-sized businesses who gained from currency appreciation, and conservatives who opposed a gold standard on ideological grounds—could be outweighed and outmaneuvered into being unable to prevent the monetary reform.

But at first, the Austro-Hungarian Bank was not legally compelled to redeem its notes for specie (gold). Its initial task was to prevent any further appreciation of the new crown from its formal foreign exchange rate. It was not given any direct instruction to prevent any renewed depreciation, if it were to occur. This, too, was consistent with the dynamics of the coalition of interest groups that had opposed any further increase in the value of the currency, but had not objected to the earlier years of currency depreciation.

But after 1896, the Austro-Hungarian Bank had accumulated enough gold and foreign exchange that it could assure the stability of the Austrian crown's foreign exchange rate within both the upper and lower ends of the gold points, and in fact kept it within less than one percent of the parity rate most of the time. And after 1900, the Bank was redeeming and issuing its notes for gold as well as for foreign exchange on an unofficial de facto basis, while still not legally required to follow a policy of specie redemption.

This was the context in which Mises wrote four of the essays in this volume: "The Problem of Legal Resumption of Specie Payments in Austria-Hungary," "The Foreign Exchange Policy of the Austro-Hungarian Bank," "On the Problem of Legal Resumption of Specie Payments in Austria-Hungary," and "The Fourth Issuing Right of the Austro-Hungarian Bank."

Mises's argument was that nothing was keeping the Austro-Hungarian Bank from now being given the legal obligation to redeem gold on demand for its banknotes, and thus formally joining the international community of gold standard nations. He insisted that this would immediately raise the creditworthiness of debt issued by the Austrian and Hungarian governments on foreign markets, and therefore lower the costs of borrowing from international creditors. It would also improve global confidence in Austria-Hungary as a developing nation desirous of attracting foreign investment and lower the cost of international capital for Austrian entrepreneurs.

Opponents of formal specie redemption argued that requiring the Austro-Hungarian Bank to redeem gold would risk a large hemorrhage of specie reserves at any time an international crisis induced holders of crown notes to transfer their liquid capital out of the country. If during such an international crisis other central banks were to raise interest rates to protect their gold reserves from the danger of capital flight, the Austro-Hungarian Bank would be compelled to also raise its interest rate to prevent loss of its own gold reserves. Domestic manufacturing and commerce would then find that the cost of capital was held captive to the uncontrollable market forces of international finance. Domestic interest rates could experience swings that would carry negative effects for business within the country, merely to counteract speculators who wished to move gold in and out of the country to take advantage of interest rate spreads that had nothing to do with the legitimate needs of the import and export trade to facilitate international transactions. These critics argued that it was far better to maintain the present system of de facto specie payments, which gave the Austro-Hungarian Bank the latitude and liberty to, at any time, refuse gold or foreign exchange redemption for its notes to shelter the domestic economy from unnecessary and destabilizing interest rate changes.

Mises counterargued in these articles that since the 1860s, first the old Austrian National Bank and then its successor, the Austro-Hungarian Bank, had had legal authority to hold a sizable portion of its reserves against notes outstanding (even when official redemption was not imposed) in foreign bills of exchange, foreign currency, and other foreign-denominated assets that were, themselves, redeemable abroad in specie money. In other words, the Austrian central bank operated on the basis of a gold-exchange standard rather than a full gold standard. Through this method the Austro-Hungarian Bank was able to earn a significant interest income from its reserve holdings instead of letting its gold sit idle in the Bank's vaults. At the same time, these foreign earnings not only went to the Bank's stockholders, but were shared by law with the Austrian and Hungarian governments, thus reducing what otherwise might have been higher taxes to cover government expenditures.

For a long time the Bank already had been utilizing its holdings of foreign exchange and other foreign-denominated assets precisely to

substitute for having to meet every demand with an actual gold outflow. This not only was an effective tool for meeting "legitimate" needs
for specie in international transactions, but served to counteract speculative demands for gold or foreign exchange to keep the crown's foreign
exchange rate within the gold points, beyond which it would become
profitable to export or import gold.

Furthermore, the Austro-Hungarian Bank did, in fact, export gold
at times of international crisis, as well as on a regular basis. In normal times it exported gold precisely to replenish its stock of foreign
exchange, foreign bills of exchange, and other foreign-denominated
assets redeemable in specie abroad to maintain a supply sufficient to
cover its international dealings and obligations. And during international financial crises it consciously exported gold to markets in Germany, Great Britain, and France to help alleviate the pressure for gold
abroad, and at the same time earned a handsome return when gold
prices were high. By supplying gold to foreign markets at such times,
it also reduced the need to raise interest rates at home since the gold
exports reduced the need for other central banks to raise their interest
rates to protect their own gold reserves.

Finally, even while not legally obligated to redeem its notes for specie, the Austro-Hungarian Bank used its discount rate when it deemed
it necessary to dampen the demand for both gold and other foreign-
denominated assets among its reserves on the part of "speculators"
and any others. Thus the Bank was already doing all the things that it
would be required to do or could do under formal specie redemption
to both maintain the official parity rate and preserve its gold reserves
from undesired withdrawals. From any of the critics' perspectives, no
case could be reasonably made against the Austro-Hungarian government's legislatively enacting the final completion of the currency reform process that had begun in 1892.

So why did the Austrian and Hungarian governments never pass
legislation establishing formal specie redemption on the part of the
Austro-Hungarian Bank? Mises gave no fully satisfactory answer in
these articles, which were all published in respected scholarly journals
of the time. However, in his *Memoirs* Mises explained that behind the
scenes the opposition to formal convertibility was partly because a portion of the rather large funds earned from foreign exchange dealings
by the Austro-Hungarian Bank were hidden away in a secret account
from which senior political and ministerial officials could draw for

various "off the books" purposes, including influencing public opinion through the media. He learned about this special fund from Eugen von Böhm-Bawerk (1851–1914),[44] the internationally renowned Austrian economist and Mises's mentor, who told him about it off the record. Böhm-Bawerk was disgusted by the whole business and frustrated that even when he was finance minister (1900–1904), he had not been able to abolish the fund. A good part of the opposition and anger expressed against Mises's defense of legal convertibility was the fear by those accessing these special funds that this source of money would dry up under the more transparent accounting procedures that would come with legal redemption.[45]

In his 1909 article "The Problem of Legal Resumption of Specie Payments in Austria-Hungary," Mises did point out that one reason behind the opposition to legal convertibility was the resistance of the Hungarians. They wanted to weaken the power of the joint Austro-Hungarian Bank as a way to continue their drive for independence from the Habsburg Monarchy. Since the Compromise of 1867,

> Hungarian politics have ceaselessly endeavored to loosen the common bonds that connect that country to Austria. The achievement of economic autonomy from Austria has appeared as an especially important goal for Hungarian policy as a preliminary step leading to political independence. The national rebirth of the non-Magyar peoples of Hungary—Germans, Serbo-Croatians, Romanians, Ruthenians, and Slovaks—will, however, pull the rug out from under these endeavors and contribute to the strengthening of the national ideal of Greater Austria. At the moment, however, Hungarian policy is still determined by the views of the Magyar nobility, and the power of the government rests in the hands of the intransigent Independence Party.

The nationalistic "rebirth" of these peoples under the often oppressive control of the Hungarians did not strengthen the "national ideal of Greater Austria"—that "Austrian idea" of a harmonious multinational empire under the reign of the Habsburgs—that Mises assumed and clearly hoped would triumph. Instead, the appeal of nationalism over individual liberty and liberalism that had been developing throughout

---

44. For a short biography of Böhm-Bawerk and his contributions to Austrian economics and service as Austro-Hungarian minister of finance, see Richard M. Ebeling, "Eugen von Böhm-Bawerk: A Sesquicentennial Appreciation," *Ideas on Liberty* (February 2001), pp. 36–41.

45. Mises, *Memoirs*, pp. 37–39.

the empire for decades finally contributed to the death of the Habsburg dynasty in 1918.[46]

But if the centrifugal forces of nationalism were pulling the empire apart from within, it was also being undermined by the fiscal cost and growth of the state. This was the second theme in Mises's policy writings before the First World War, in two essays: "Financial Reform in Austria" and "Disturbances in the Economic Life of the Austro-Hungarian Monarchy During the Years 1912–13."

After having its financial house in order for almost twenty years, Mises pointed out, the Austrian government was now threatening the fiscal stability of the society with increasing expenditures, rising taxes, and budget deficits. Government spending was likely to significantly grow in future years partly due to the expenses of maintaining costly military forces in an environment of an international arms race. The other major factor at work on the spending side of the government's ledger were social welfare expenditures that the Austrian authorities were taking on, and which would only grow in the years ahead. Already in the preceding ten years, government spending had increased by over 53 percent, and over the same decade the cost of funding the government's debt had increased by nearly 20 percent. The cost of financing many of the ministries was exploding; the nationalized railway system was running large deficits that had to be covered from other government funding sources; and the Austrian Crownlands were managed with a three-layered bureaucratic system of administrators at the national, provincial, and municipal levels, each with its own rules, regu-

---

46. Almost fifteen years after the First World War, Mises still regretted the failure of the "Austrian idea," referring to "the attempts which were made to find some means of ensuring the amity of the various peoples that constituted the Empire. These efforts, which met with the approval of some of the most intelligent and noble spirits of the time, aimed not only at the maintenance of the Habsburg dynasty; they were informed by the idea that an entirely satisfactory solution of the struggles of the different nationalities could not be found simply in a dismemberment of the Empire. The fact is that a large area of the old Empire was inhabited by people of different languages, living together without geographical separation. For these territories, which are the cradle of all struggles between the nationalities, a system of peaceful cooperation could be more easily found within the framework of a big empire than by giving to every nationality a separate sovereignty. Events since the armistice, both political and economic, prove *ex post* the soundness of the attempts to transform the Habsburg Monarchy into a kind of Eastern European League of Nations." See Ludwig von Mises, review of "Die letzten Jahrzehnte einer Grossmacht. Menschen, Völker und Probleme des Habsburg-Reichs," by Rudolph Sieghart in *Economica* (November 1932) p. 477.

lations, and taxing authorities—and often in contradiction with each other.

To cover these expenditures, a wide variety of taxes were being increased, including inheritance taxes, sales and excise taxes, and income and corporate taxes. They frequently were manipulated to shift the incidence of the tax burden away from the agricultural and rural areas of Austria onto the shoulders of the urban populations and especially onto industry and manufacturing. In addition, the finance ministry wanted to implement legislation giving the government the authority to examine the books of businesses and industries. Mises observed that "Austrian entrepreneurs rightly see in this arrangement an intensification of the harassment that the authorities display toward them." Although the tax rates and burdens that Mises analyzes and criticizes seem by today's higher and more intrusive fiscal standards to be part of that bygone, idyllic world of limited government liberalism before the First World War, they all represented significant increases at the time, and all pointed in a dangerous direction for the future.

What Mises also found most disturbing in the coalition of political forces raising taxes and shifting them onto industry and the urban areas was a clear ideological bias against modern capitalist society. There were conservative and rural interests who wished for a return to the preindustrial era, Mises claimed, and were using their preponderant representation in the Austrian parliament to place roadblocks in the way of modernization, and delay if not stop the economic development of the country.

The economic crisis in Austria-Hungary in 1912 and 1913, Mises argued, showed that fiscal irresponsibility was pervasive in both the government and the private sector. Everywhere consumption spending was growing at the expense of savings, while everyone did all in their power to avoid work. Government expenditures were expanding and eating away at the hard-won wealth and capital accumulation of previous years as a result of government deficit spending. But the private sector was no more frugal than government. In every walk of Austrian life, people attempted to live beyond their means. Everyone lived on credit that depended upon the illusion that debts accumulating on the books of retailers and wholesalers eventually could be repaid. Retailers extended credit to their customers; wholesalers extended credit to retailers; and the financial institutions extended credit to the wholesalers, manufacturers, and merchants.

It was a financial game of musical chairs in which everyone through-out the entire chain of production and sales appeared to be prosperous and profitable only because of the claims on the books against others up and down the payment structure of the economy. A serious default anywhere along the line could set off repercussions that would threaten the entire financial system. And precisely because of this, whenever anyone failed to pay even a fraction of the balances owed, the lines of credit were extended further to put off the inevitable day of reckoning and keep the illusions going.

The financial crisis of 1912–13, Mises explained, had been par-tially that day of reckoning in which the financial system was found to be built on sand. Mises could only hope that some lessons would be learned: that consumption needed to be based on production, and debts undertaken needed to be repaid through savings, work, and in-vestment. He feared that the lessons had not been learned. Within a matter of months after writing in early 1914 his analysis of the causes and consequences of this crisis, Austria-Hungary was plunged into a far more disastrous crisis from which it would not survive as a political entity.

In two pieces written in 1913, "The General Rise in Prices in the Light of Economic Theory" and "On Rising Prices and Purchasing Power Policies," Mises had attempted to explain the monetary mecha-nism by which increases in the supply of money and credit bring about a general rise in prices. Mises develops part of the argument that he had formulated in 1912, in *The Theory of Money and Credit*,[47] that the period of inflation through which Austria-Hungary and much of the world was passing was due to the expansion of credit by the banking system in the form of fiduciary media. The latter, in Mises's terminol-ogy, are money substitutes in the form of banknotes and checking de-posits that are claims against specie currency held as reserves by the central bank and other lending institutions. However, such fiduciary media may be of two sorts: those that Mises calls "commodity credit," which is fully backed by bank reserves, and "circulation credit," which is only partially backed by reserves in the banking system. It is the frac-tional reserve basis behind a growing amount of the fiduciary media in circulation, Mises insists, that is the real cause of price inflation and the business cycle. Creating and lending unbacked fiduciary media at

47. Pp. 261–366.

artificially lowered rates of interest produces an imbalance between savings and investment that leads to an unsustainable boom, which finally has to end in an economic downturn and a period of readjustment in the market.[48]

But Mises suggested that another influence was generating a general rise in prices, which he argued was caused by the nature of monetary transactions in an increasingly complex market order. In a developed market with multistaged processes of production, in which producers no longer meet face-to-face with their ultimate consumers, each seller must fix his prices on the basis of his expectations about what he thinks buyers further down the production chain may be willing to pay. This expectation about what his buyer will be willing to pay, in turn, influences the price he will be willing to pay to the producer or wholesaler from whom he purchases goods.

To the extent that such a seller expects that his buyer may be willing to pay more, he then will be willing to pay prices to those who sell to him that he otherwise might consider too high. Thus, Mises argued, a dynamic is set in motion that results in a continuing rise in prices throughout the various sectors of the economy in a certain temporal sequence. For example, trade unions may demand wages higher than employers consider the workers' labor to be worth. But if those employers are confident that they can pass on the cost of paying higher money wages to those to whom they sell their products, they acquiesce in money wage demands that would otherwise be unjustifiable. At the same time, the higher real wages that those workers hope to obtain through an increase in their money wages will be eroded as prices of finished goods continue to rise in the economy due to this general inflationary process throughout the market. What trade unions might consider their demonstrated capacity to improve the real wages of workers was illusionary, since over time any temporary gains would be washed out by the general rise in prices. In the long run workers

48. For a detailed exposition of Mises's "Austrian" theory of the business cycle, see Richard M. Ebeling, "The Austrian Economists and the Keynesian Revolution: The Great Depression and the Economics of the Short-Run," in *Political Economy, Public Policy, and Monetary Economics: Ludwig von Mises and the Austrian Tradition*, pp. 203–72; "Two Variations of the Austrian Monetary Theme: Ludwig von Mises and Joseph A. Schumpeter on the Business Cycle," in ibid., pp. 273–301; and "Money, Economic Fluctuations, Expectations and Period Analysis: The Austrian and Swedish Economists in the Interwar Period," in ibid., pp. 302–31. Also, Richard M. Ebeling, "Ludwig von Mises and the Gold Standard," in *Austrian Economics and the Political Economy of Freedom*, pp. 136–58.

could not obtain real wages in excess of the value of their marginal product.

Mises went as far as to say that nothing really could be done about this inherent price-increasing process; he even suggested that it was indicative of a dynamic and growing economy in which constant shifts in supply and demand and the conditions and methods of production required pricing decisions to be made on the basis of expectations under inescapable uncertain future market conditions. Mises concluded that the fact that the economy was not static, and therefore not more fully predictable, was a reason for optimism that these changing economic circumstances were bringing about improvements all the time.

What is missing in this part of Mises's analysis is any clear link with either a prior or simultaneous increase in the supply of money and fiduciary media that permits this price-inflationary process to continue, or an indication that the process implies an increase in the velocity of money that would allow the same number of market transactions to be facilitated at rising prices. As he formulated it in these two articles, his argument seems to represent a version of what in the post–World War II period became known as cost-push inflation.[49]

War Financing, Inflation, and the Goals of International Trade Policy

When war broke out in summer 1914, Mises's artillery reserve unit was called up for active duty. For part of the next four years he sometimes saw intense action on the eastern front against the Russian Army. However, in 1918, during the last year of the war, Mises was assigned to work in various consulting capacities for the Austrian High Command in Vienna. And for a short time he served in Austrian-occupied Ukraine involved with currency matters.[50]

In 1916, he published "On the Goals of Trade Policy," in which he presents a clear analysis of the gains from division of labor and international trade. But Mises goes on to explain that what motivated nations such as Germany and Austria-Hungary was a particular dilemma. For

---

49. See Fritz Machlup, "Another View of Cost-Push and Demand-Pull Inflation," (1960) in *Essays on Economic Semantics* (New Brunswick, N.J.: Transaction Books, [1963] 1991), pp. 241–68; also, Gottfried Haberler, *Inflation: Its Causes and Cures* (Washington, D.C.: American Enterprise Institute, 1966), pp. 65–78, and *Economic Growth and Stability* (Los Angeles: Nash Publishing, 1974), pp. 99–116.

50. For a thorough discussion of Mises's wartime activities, see Hülsmann, *Mises: The Last Knight*, pp. 257–98.

these relatively overpopulated countries in Europe, the greater economic opportunities in foreign countries resulted in emigration that meant a loss of manpower both for future wars and as part of the workforce during peace as well as at times of international conflict. Also, in the cultural struggles between countries, emigration meant a loss of part of a nation's human heritage, since over time many such emigrants were absorbed into the culture and language of the host nation.

Thus, in countries like Germany and Austria-Hungary the task was to develop policies that would raise the living standards and opportunities in the homeland to reduce the incentive to leave and be "lost" to the fatherland. The nationalist trade method rejected free trade and erected protectionist barriers to artificially raise prices and secure domestic employments for the population. Alternatively, such a country could attempt territorial expansion into surrounding areas to gain the land and resources that would overcome the too densely populated condition within the pattern of existing political boundaries in which, for example, Germany was currently confined. One other method was to acquire colonies abroad to which emigrants could move while retaining their cultural identity and political allegiance to the fatherland.

Writing at a time of war, Mises carefully emphasized that these political trade policy goals were in the long run incompatible with the economic forces of an increasingly global market society. These forces were constantly working to guide both labor and capital to where their productive capacity was most highly valued, which inevitably would result in redistributions of people around the world to reflect their most optimal employments in the international division of labor. In the long run, the logic and incentives of the market would transcend the political goals of nationalist ideology.

In "Remarks Concerning the Problem of Emigration," a memorandum that Mises prepared in 1918 for the Austrian government commission to which he was assigned in Vienna, he suggested a variety of domestic policies that would reduce the incentive for workers to leave Austria. These included making more farmland available out of existing larger estates for the benefit of small landholders who currently could not support their families on the properties they owned. It would be useful for the government and private associations to assist seasonal migrant labor in finding more attractive wage and work condition opportunities abroad, thus increasing the likelihood they would return home to a country that cared about their well-being. It was also necessary to reduce the burden and inconveniences of compulsory military service that too often induced some workers employed abroad to not come home.

Also in the summer of 1918, Mises delivered a public lecture, "On Paying for the Costs of War and War Loans." He praised the military successes of Austria's armed forces in its fight against the Allied Powers and the industrial efficiencies of Austrian business that had provided the manufacturing wherewithal for, Austria to do so well, even in the face of Allied blockades that cut Austria off from foreign sources of supply. But production had to be paid for, and the issue arose of whether the government's war costs should be covered by taxation or debt.

Mises reminded his listeners that borrowing did not enable the current generation to shift any part of the costs of war to a future generation. Current consumption could only come out of current production, and this applied no less to consumption of finished goods designed for and used in war. Whether the war was financed by taxes or borrowing, the citizenry paid for it today by forgoing all that could have been produced and used, if not for the war. Mises also explained to his audience what today is often referred to as the Ricardian equivalence theorem, named after British economist David Ricardo (1772–1823). In his 1820 essay, "Funding System," Ricardo argued that all that the borrowing option entailed was a decision whether to be taxed more in the present or more in the future, since all that was borrowed now would have to be paid back at a later date through future taxes; therefore in terms of their financial burden the two funding methods can be shown to be equivalent, under specified conditions. Ricardo, however, also pointed out that due to people's perceptions and evaluations of costs in the present versus the future, they were rarely equivalent in their minds.[51]

But Mises raised a different point in favor of certain benefits to debt financing for the government's war expenditures. First, many who would not have the liquid assets to pay lump-sum wartime taxes would either have to sell off less liquid properties to pay their tax obligation, or would have to borrow the required sum to pay the tax. In the first case, a sizable number of citizens might have to liquidate properties more or less all at the same time to improve their cash positions, which would put exceptional downward pressure on the market prices of those as-

51. Ricardo, "Funding System," (1820) in Piero Sraffa, ed., *The Works and Correspondence of David Ricardo*, vol. 4, *Pamphlets and Papers, 1815–1823* (Cambridge: Cambridge University Press, 1951), pp. 149–200, especially pp. 186–87.

sets. This would impose a financial loss on those forced to sell these properties and assets to the benefit of those who were able to buy them at prices that would not have been so abnormally low if not for the war and need for ready cash to pay the tax obligation. Second, to the extent that some citizens would need to borrow to cover their wartime tax payments, the private individual's creditworthiness undoubtedly would be much lower than the government's. As a consequence, these private individuals would have to pay a noticeably higher interest rate than that at which the government could finance its borrowing. Thus, the interest burden from government borrowing to be paid for out of future taxes would be less for the citizenry than the financial cost of their having to borrow money in the present to cover all the costs of war through current taxation.[52] Hence it was both patriotic and cost-efficient for those listening to Mises's presentation to buy war bonds in support of the war effort.

Finally, in "Inflation," another lecture delivered in the late summer of 1918, Mises explained the impact of the government's financing a large amount of its war expenditures through monetary expansion. First, all creditors who had failed to anticipate the resulting depreciation in the value of the Austrian crown are paid back in money possessing less purchasing power than when the loan was issued. This might seem to be a desirable side effect, since clearly the debtor gains by paying back his loan in depreciated crowns, especially if it is "the poor" who are the predominant debtor group. But it was worth recalling, Mises said, that in modern society the debtors were most often businesses that had borrowed to cover investment costs, while the creditors were middle-class citizens, widows and orphans, civil servants, and members of the lower-income working class who had put their savings into the financial institutions that did the lending. Hence, Mises pointed out, in this debtor-creditor relationship, under inflation the "rich" benefited at the expense of the middle class and the "poor."

Some saw the benefit from inflation in that it also reduced the real value of the government's accumulating debt, thus reducing the "real" cost of the war. At the same time, rising money incomes and profits in the private sector due to inflation meant that the government gained higher tax revenues in money terms. On the other hand, to the ex-

---

52. See also Ludwig von Mises, *Nation, State, and Economy: Contributions to the Politics and History of Our Time* (Indianapolis: Liberty Fund, [1919] 2006), pp. 136–42.

tent to which the government had covered part of its debt with foreign borrowing denominated in another currency, the falling value of the crown on the foreign exchange market due to inflation increased the amount of crowns the government had to pay to meet its foreign financial obligations. Also, some taxes were fixed at a specified level, so in this instance the taxpayer gained in real terms during inflation while the government lost. Furthermore, the worse and more continuing the inflation, the more reluctant citizens would be to buy war bonds and other government debt instruments, thus increasing the difficulties of financing the war other than through inflation. Thus, from a variety of perspectives, inflation was a dangerous and undesirable method of covering the costs of war, since it undermined the real wealth of the middle class and those in the working class who saved in an attempt to improve their position in society.

After War: Hyperinflation and Fiscal Mismanagement in the New Austria[53]

In October and November 1918, the Austro-Hungarian Empire began to disintegrate as various national groups began to break away and declare their independence, most notably the Czechs and Slovaks, who joined in creating their own country, then the Hungarians, who were then followed by the Serbs, Croats, Slovenians, and Bosnians, who formed a new Yugoslavia. The Romanians soon began to incorporate Transylvania within their borders, and Italy seized south Tyrol and the port of Trieste. Galicia became a battleground between the Poles, the Ukrainians, and the Russian Bolsheviks in the next few years.

In what was declared the new state of German-Austria a coalition government was formed between the Social Democrats, the Christian Socialists, and the Nationalist Party. Almost immediately, they began a campaign of expensive food subsidies for the urban population at controlled prices, compulsory requisitioning of agricultural goods from the rural parts of the country, foreign exchange controls on all imports and exports at an artificial rate of exchange, a vast array of social wel-

---

53. See Richard M. Ebeling, "The Economist as the Historian of Decline: Ludwig von Mises and Austria Between the Two World Wars," in *Political Economy, Public Policy, and Monetary Economics: Ludwig von Mises and the Austrian Tradition,* especially pp. 92–100, for a detailed account of the political and economic situation in Austria in the years following the end of the First World War.

fare programs, and the use of the monetary printing press to finance it all. By the middle of 1919 and then into 1920 and 1921, serious inflation had degenerated into hyperinflation. [54]

Mises's articles "Monetary Devaluation and the National Budget" and "For the Reintroduction of Normal Stock Market Practices in Foreign Exchange Dealings" explained that the foreign exchange rate was a market-created price that could not be simply fixed and manipulated by the state. The value of any one currency in terms of another was ultimately a reflection of each currency's purchasing power. Guided by the "law of one price," the market tendency was to establish the exchange rate at that point at which the attractiveness of buying some quantity of a good in either country was the same. Setting the exchange rate at some level other than the market-determined rate merely meant that it was artificially fixed at too dear or too cheap a price. In the face of the currency shortages that the exchange control resulted in, the government then commanded that all foreign exchange earnings be sold to the Austrian Exchange Control Authority at the fixed rate, with the government bureaucracy now determining the rationing of it to both importers and exporters.

Prohibiting normal foreign exchange dealings merely drove transactions underground into the black market, and prevented the functioning of those institutional arrangements through which individuals can hedge against uncertain fluctuations in the foreign exchange rate by utilizing a legal futures market. Instead, the inflationary environment, with limited legal avenues to "take cover" against the effects of a depreciating currency, meant that more and more people were shifting into the use of foreign monies in domestic Austrian business transactions. The foreign exchange controls needed to be abolished, and the printing presses needed to be brought to a halt if a monetary disaster was to be averted.

The fundamental cause for Austria's problems was that it was in the stranglehold of the socialist idea, with all of its negative consequences. This was the theme in two pieces by Mises: "The Austrian Problem" and "The Social Democratic Agrarian Program." The socialists were

---

54. For a brief history of the inflation in Austria during and after the First World War and its disastrous consequences, see Richard M. Ebeling, "The Great Austrian Inflation," *The Freeman: Ideas on Liberty* (April 2006), pp. 2–3; also, Richard M. Ebeling, "The Lasting Legacies of World War I: Big Government, Paper Money and Inflation," *Economic Education Bulletin*, vol. 48, no. 11 (Great Barrington, Mass.: American Institute for Economic Research, November 2008), for accounts of the hyperinflations in both Germany and Austria.

determined to control and spend their way into the destruction of the country. Under this administration, taxes and inflation ate away at the accumulated wealth of the past and hindered any capital formation in the present. They demagogically promised wealth while causing waste by nationalizing and regulating industries that ended up suffering losses that needed to be paid for through even more inflation. Their agricultural agenda was to do with the rural economy the same harm they were doing with industry and manufacturing in the cities.

What was to be done? In February 1921, Mises presented the outline of a plan in answer to the question, "How Can Austria Be Saved?" The first order of business was to stop the monetary printing presses. But this could be done only if the costly food subsidies were eliminated and the nationalized industries were reprivatized to end the huge expenses to cover their deficits, so the national budget once again could be brought into balance. Foreign exchange controls had to be abolished with a free market in all currency dealings. At the same time, the value of the Austrian crown had to be stabilized once the central bank had stopped issuing paper money and the depreciation of the currency was brought to a halt. All domestic regulations and controls inhibiting free commerce among the various provinces of Austria had to be lifted, and free trade had to be reintroduced in all forms of foreign trade. This was the path to a revitalized and prosperous Austria.

A sound monetary system was unlikely if the governments of those new states that had formerly been part of the Austro-Hungarian Empire looted the assets of a reconstructed Austrian central bank. Thus, in "The Claims of Note Holders upon Liquidation of the Bank," published in February 1921, Mises argued against those who asserted that those other governments had a right to a portion of the old Austro-Hungarian Bank's gold reserves. Under the Treaty of Saint-Germain, which had ended the war between Austria and the Allied Powers, the successor states were obligated to redeem the old crown notes on their territories for their own respective currencies. The old Austro-Hungarian Bank notes were then to be turned over to the new Austrian central bank, which would take them out of circulation. Mises argued that everyone knew that the huge expansion of banknotes to fund the government's war expenses were backed by nothing, and certainly not by whatever gold may have remained in the central bank's vaults. To demand anything else would be to plunder the gold and other assets upon which a reconstituted Austrian monetary system would be built.

Mises observed in an article early in 1922, "The Austrian Currency Problem Thirty Years Ago and Today," that the key to ending Austria's problems was stopping inflation. Thirty years earlier, in 1892, the task had been to stabilize a currency that was appreciating in value. The task in 1922 was to bring a halt to its depreciation. But the method was the same: link the currency to gold and do not manipulate its quantity in circulation.

As the situation worsened, Mises put together a proposal on behalf of the Vienna Chamber of Commerce for "The Restoration of Austria's Economic Situation," which was submitted to other trade and labor union associations in the country to devise a way to bring an end to the government budget deficits as a prelude to stopping the inflation. In a nutshell, Mises recommended the establishment of price indexation throughout the economy. Already government expenditure levels were automatically adjusted in line with a cost-of-living index. Now the same arrangement had to be set up for government revenues. Otherwise nominal expenditures would keep growing while nominal tax revenues would always lag behind, never leading to an end to the deficits. Incomes, profits, and wages and prices all had to be indexed to the market value of gold. This would continually adjust government tax revenues to government expenditures. It would mean that government nationalized sectors, such as the railway system, would have their prices rise in tandem with the average rate of depreciation of the currency reflected in its link to the price of gold, which would help to reduce their losses and maybe even earn a profit from transit fees for cargos passing through Austria. At the same time, gold indexation would assist in keeping the wages and salaries of many workers rising to maintain a certain real value of their income.

Mises emphasized that such an indexation policy was desirable not only due to questions of equity in a period of rapid depreciation and the need to bring the government's budget better into balance. It was also needed because inflation distorted the very essence of a money-using economy: the ability for economic calculation to reasonably estimate profit and loss, and relative profitability of alternative lines of production. Price and wage indexation linked to the price of gold would help to reduce the miscalculations that inflation caused, and which often resulted in capital consumption. This measure, Mises stated, was meant to be a transition method to bring stability to the Austrian economy, or, as he concluded, "We must make up our minds to return from the extravagant intoxication of spending 'billions' to the sober, more modest financial figures of a smaller state. The object of the proposed plan is to avoid a sudden and disastrous collapse."

The inflation *was* brought to a halt in late 1922 and early 1923 with the financial assistance and supervisorial oversight of the League of Nations. In 1925, in "The Gold-Exchange Standard," Mises pointed out that while Austria and a number of other countries were moving back to a gold-backed currency, it was not a full gold standard system. Most countries did not have large amounts of actual gold reserves, and gold coins were nowhere in circulation. Instead, their monetary systems (like that under the old Austro-Hungarian Bank) were gold-exchange standards, under which most reserves were held in other countries in the forms of financial assets that were, in principle, redeemable in gold in those other countries. The entire system depended upon at least a few countries, like the United States at that time, being willing to serve as ultimate gold reserve redeemers. Mises thought that this was only a shadow of the type of real gold-backed system that could assure noninflationary stability to the various countries of the world.

In 1926, Mises had spent three months traveling in the United States. When he returned he delivered the talk "America and the Reconstruction of the European Economy." Any further European recovery from the effects of the Great War could not count upon American political or economic leadership. Both manufacturing and agricultural interests in the United States were heavily protectionist and therefore resistant to imports. This, in turn, made it difficult for Europeans to find markets for their goods or to earn the dollars to pay back their wartime loans to America. While the United States was a creditor nation with the means to invest in Europe, money would not be given away but would depend on the profitability of such investments. Thus Europe would have to rely upon itself if it was to continue to overcome the legacy of the war.

Mises pointed out the difficulty for such stable recovery and growth in a summary he presented in 1928, "The Currency and Finances of the Federal State of Austria." Five years after the end to Austria's inflation, the currency was on a relatively sound basis. A new schilling had replaced the old crown and was fixed at a specific value in terms of gold. The rules under which the new Austrian National Bank operated made it difficult for it to serve as a means to finance the expenses of the government.

However, the fiscal affairs of the nation were far from sound. The government was still running budget deficits, but all of it was due to cost overruns in the nationalized sectors of the economy, especially the railway system and the lumber industry in the nationalized forest system. Financial pressures were placed on the federal authority because of the tax and related transfers to the provincial governments, which were all overlaid with bureaucratic regulatory structures and mismanagement. And in Vienna, where the Social Democrats controlled the municipal government, the financial extravagance on public projects was exceptionally large. For domestic growth and international competitiveness, Austria had to make its economy more productive. Cutting wasteful government and radically reducing taxes was the only avenue to a prosperous future for Austria.

When the Great Depression began in the early 1930s, the banking system was badly shaken. The collapse in May 1931 of the Austrian bank, Credit-Anstalt, in particular, sent shock waves throughout the financial markets. Shortly afterward, Mises wrote "The Economic Crisis and Lessons for Banking Policy." In his eyes, the banking systems in Germany and Austria had two weaknesses. First, too many banks had become financially entangled with the industrial corporations to whom they lent. In fact, they often had become major shareholders in the very companies whose financial status they were supposed to oversee with a critical eye in terms of continuing creditworthiness. Instead, they unsoundly extended more credit to companies they should have pulled back from because their own balance sheets were too closely linked to the illusion of their continuing profitability. Finally the situation imploded, taking the banks down with those companies.

Second, those same banks had poorly managed the term structure of their investment portfolios. They lent long, while being liable for depositor withdrawals on demand. In other words, they had become caught in the system of fractional reserve banking, in which the amount of claims payable on demand far exceeded their available cash reserves to meet depositor liabilities.

The banking crisis, as far as Mises was concerned, was not the end of capitalism, but showed the need to reorganize the way banks managed their liabilities and investments after the crisis had passed. Sounder banking principles in a market economy were the avenue to avoid similar crises in the future.

Interventionism, Collectivism, and Their Ideological Roots

In the 1920s, one of the contributions for which Mises was most famous was his theory of government intervention. In 1930, he published "The Economic System of Interventionism," a brief summary of his critique of this practice, with particular emphasis on the deleterious effects from all forms of control over prices. While various forms of production regulations had the tendency to reduce productivity, price controls were a far more directly harmful type of intervention. They inevitably distorted the relationship between supply and demand, artificially generated either shortages or surpluses, and deflected production from those avenues most likely to satisfy consumer demand. They also had a tendency to spread out to more and more sectors of the economy, as the government imposed similar controls on other markets and industries in a vain attempt to compensate for the imbalances the earlier price controls had created. If followed to their logical conclusion, such price controls led to a fully planned economy through piecemeal interventions imposed one after another.

Where did all this lead? In "Economic Order and the Political System" (1936), Mises pointed out that in the eighteenth and early nineteenth centuries, political democracy, civil liberty, and economic freedom had grown hand in hand. But in the second half of the nineteenth century the idea had taken hold that political democracy and personal freedom could be preserved even if the government increasingly intervened in and controlled the economic affairs of the citizenry in the name of social justice and socialist planning.

What the twentieth century was showing, however, was that political democracy and individual freedom could not last long when government planning increasingly replaces the market economy. Economic planning means planning people's lives, and people must then conform in all their affairs to what the plan dictates. In countries like Soviet Russia, fascist Italy, or National Socialist (Nazi) Germany even the appearance of preserving democratic and personal liberties had been discarded and the reality of where planning leads could be most clearly seen. This was the crossroads that now confronted the remaining relatively free and democratic societies in the West: freedom or planning.

More than twenty years later, in 1959, Mises offered "Remarks Concerning the Ideological Roots of the Monetary Catastrophe of 1923," when hyperinflation had brought Germany to the edge of total eco-

nomic collapse. He reflected back to when he was a young man before the First World War, during the years when he wrote those early
pieces on the gold standard and had only just published *The Theory
of Money and Credit*. He had attended the meetings of the *Verein für
Sozialpolitik* (Society for Social Policy), the leading and most influential social science association in the German-speaking world, which
was dominated by members of the German Historical School. Here
he came face-to-face with the enemies of economic liberalism, who
rejected most of economic theory in the name of a historically based
approach to social analysis, on the basis of which they rationalized aggressive nationalistic conclusions, all leading to an eventual war. They
had contempt for the Austrian economists and ridiculed the idea that
there were "laws of economics" that should stand in the way of markets
and money being controlled by the state. These were the thinkers who
were the harbingers of many of the disasters of the twentieth century.
Their aggressive nationalism had led to two world wars; their belief
in the interventionist state had cultivated the coming of the planned
and regulated society; and their confidence that money and its value
were creatures of the state had fostered the inflations of the twentieth
century.

And though Mises did not point it out, many of these German
thinkers laid the ideological groundwork for the mass murder of millions at the hands of the National Socialists, including the destruction of six million Jews. Indeed, it was because of such ideas and their
consequences that Mises himself was forced to flee a Nazi-dominated
Europe and find sanctuary in America in the midst of the Second
World War.

Leaving Europe for America had not been an easy decision for
Mises. Indeed, he said in a letter to Friedrich A. Hayek in May 1940,
as he was approaching his departure from Switzerland for the United
States, "The decision to leave is truly difficult. For me, it represents saying good-bye to a life which I have always lived, it is for me an 'adieu'
to a Europe which is about to disappear forever."[55]

It is only appropriate, therefore, that before concluding this introduction we should take a look at Mises's Jewish family roots in the old
Habsburg Empire and how the fate of the Austrian Jews led to a man

---

55. Letter from Mises to Hayek, May 22, 1940, Geneva, Switzerland, Hayek Papers, Hoover
Institution archives; the original letter is in German.

like Mises having to say good-bye to the life and world in which he made his career and won his reputation as one of the leading economists of his time, and his having to make a new start at the age of fifty-eight in the New World.

Liberating Liberalism and the Austrian Jews[56]

Ludwig von Mises was born on September 29, 1881, into a prominent Jewish family in Lemberg (Lvov in present-day Ukraine), the capital of the Austrian Crownland of Galicia, far to the east of Vienna and near the border with the Russian Empire. In the last decades of the nineteenth century, more than 50 percent of the population of some parts of Galicia was Jewish, with the center of Jewish life and culture being in Lemberg.[57]

The documents that Ludwig von Mises's great-grandfather, Mayer Rachmiel Mises (1801–91), prepared as background for his ennoblement by the Austrian emperor, Francis Joseph, in mid-1881 (just a few months before Ludwig was born), record the history of the Mises family in Lemberg going back to the 1700s. Mayer's father, Fischel Mises, had been a wholesaler and real estate owner who had received permission to live and conduct business in the "restricted district" reserved for non-Jews. At the age of eighteen, Mayer married a daughter of Hirsch Halberstamm, the leading Russian-German export trader in the Galician city of Brody.

Mayer took over the family business following his father's death and also served for twenty-five years as a commissioner in the commercial court of Lemberg. For a time he also was on the city council and was a full member of the Lemberg Chamber of Commerce. He also was a cofounder of the Lemberg Savings Bank, and later was a member of the board of the Lemberg branch of the Austrian National Bank. He also was one of the founders of the Cracow-Lemberg railway line. In addition, he was a founder of a Jewish orphanage, a reform school, a secondary education school, a charitable institution for infant orphans, and a library in the Jewish community. Some of these charities were

---

56. Part of this section draws upon Richard M. Ebeling, "Ludwig von Mises and the Vienna of His Time," in *Political Economy, Public Policy, and Monetary Economics: Ludwig von Mises and the Austrian Tradition*, pp. 36–56.

57. See William O. McCagg Jr., *A History of Habsburg Jews, 1670–1918* (Bloomington: Indiana University Press, 1989), pp. 105–22, 181–200.

begun with funds provided by Mayer for their endowment. Indeed, it was for his service to the emperor as a leader of the Jewish community in Lemberg that Mayer Mises, great-grandfather of Ludwig von Mises, was ennobled.

Mayer's oldest son, Abraham Oscar Mises, ran the Vienna office of the family business until he was appointed in 1860 the director of the Lemberg branch of the Credit-Anstalt bank. Abraham also was the director of the Galician Carl-Ludwig Railroad. His other son, Hirsch Mises, was a partner in and a director of the Halberstamm and Nirenstein banking company.[58]

It is perhaps because of the family's connection with the railroad business that Hirsch Mises's son, Arthur Edler von Mises, took up civil engineering with a degree from the Zurich Polytechnic in Switzerland, and then worked for the Lemberg-Czernowitz Railroad Company. Arthur married Adele Landau, the granddaughter of Moses Kallir and the grandniece of Mayer Kallir, a prominent Jewish merchant family in the city of Brody. Arthur and Adele had three sons, of whom Ludwig was the oldest. His brother, Richard, became an internationally renowned mathematician who later taught at Harvard University. The third child died at an early age.

Members of the Mises family also were devout practitioners of their Jewish faith. The vast majority of the Galician Jews were Hasidic, with all the religious customs and rituals that entailed. But the Mises family was part of that movement in the Jewish community devoted to theological and cultural reform, and participated in the liberal-oriented political activities that were attempted in nineteenth-century Galicia. As a small boy, Ludwig would have heard and spoken Yiddish, Polish, and German, and studied Hebrew in preparation for his bar mitzvah.

Ludwig's father, Arthur, like many of his generation, chose to leave Galicia and make his life and career in the secular and German cultural world of Vienna, where he accepted a civil servant's position with the Austrian Ministry of Railways. But from the documents among

58. See Appendix B in the present volume for a translation of Mayer Rachmiel Mises's short curriculum vitae that he submitted in June 1881 to the office of the Austrian emperor, Francis Joseph, as part of the legal process for ennoblement and the bestowing of the honorific and hereditary title of "Edler von." He was ennobled on April 30, 1881, with the ennoblement document issued on July 13, 1881. Ludwig von Mises is not mentioned at the end of the document among Mayer Rachmiel Mises's great-grandchildren because Ludwig's birth would not occur until September.

Ludwig von Mises's "lost papers" found in the Moscow archives,[59] it is clear that his mother maintained ties to her birthplace, contributing money to several charities in Brody, including a Jewish orphanage. In Vienna in the 1890s, Arthur was an active member of the Israelite Community's Board, a focal point for Jewish cultural and political life in the Austrian capital.[60]

Until the early and middle decades of the nineteenth century, Jews throughout many parts of Europe were denied civil liberties, often being severely restricted in their economic freedom, and, especially in Eastern Europe, confined to certain geographical areas. In the 1820s it was still not permitted for Jews to unrestrictedly live and work in Vienna; this required the special permission of the emperor.[61] Commercial and civil liberation of the Austrian Jews occurred only in the aftermath of the Revolution of 1848, and most especially with the new constitution of 1867, which created the Austro-Hungarian Dual Monarchy following Austria's defeat in its 1866 war with Prussia. The spirit and content of the 1867 constitution, which remained the fundamental law of the empire until the collapse of Austria-Hungary in 1918, reflected the classical liberal ideas of the time. Every subject of the emperor was secure in his life and private property; freedom of speech and the press was guaranteed; freedom of occupation and enterprise was permitted; all religious faiths were respected and allowed to be practiced; freedom of movement and residence within the empire was a guaranteed right; and all national groups were declared to have equal status before the law.

No group within the Austro-Hungarian Empire took as much advantage of the new liberal environment as the Jews. In the early decades of the nineteenth century a transformation had begun among the Jewish community in Galicia. Reformers arose arguing for a revision in

59. See Richard M. Ebeling, "Mission to Moscow: The Mystery of the 'Lost Papers' of Ludwig von Mises," *Notes from FEE* (July 2004), pp. 1–3, http://www.fee.org/pdf/notes/NFF_0704.pdf; also, for a more detailed account, see Richard M. Ebeling, introduction to *Selected Writings of Ludwig von Mises*, vol. 2, pp. xv–xx.

60. Robert S. Wistrich, *The Jews of Vienna in the Age of Franz Joseph*, p. 165.

61. On the history of the Jews in the Austro-Hungarian Empire, see Wistrich, *Jews of Vienna*; McCagg, *A History of Habsburg Jews, 1670–1918*; Steven Beller, *Vienna and the Jews, 1867–1938: A Cultural History* (Cambridge, Mass.: Cambridge University Press, 1989); George E. Berkley, *Vienna and Its Jews: The Tragedy of Success, 1880s–1980s* (Lanham, Md.: Madison Books, 1988); and Max Grunwald, *History of the Jews in Vienna* (Philadelphia: Jewish Publication Society of America, 1936).

the practices and customs of Orthodox Jewry. Jews needed to enter the modern world and to secularize in terms of dress, manner, attitudes, and culture. The faith had to be stripped of its medieval characteristics and ritualism. Jews should immerse themselves in the German language and German culture. All things "German" were distinguished as representing freedom and progress.[62]

With the freedoms of the 1867 constitution, Austrian and especially Galician Jews began a cultural as well as a geographical migration. In 1869, Jews made up about 6 percent of the population of Vienna. By the 1890s, when the young Ludwig von Mises moved to Vienna from Lemberg with his family, Jews made up 12 percent of the Vienna population. In District I, the center of the city where the Mises family lived, Jews made up over 20 percent of the population. In the neighboring District II, the Jews made up over 30 percent.[63]

But in the late nineteenth and early twentieth centuries, there was a stark contrast between these two districts of the city. In the central District I, the vast majority of the Jewish population had attempted to assimilate with their non-Jewish neighbors in dress, manners, and cultural outlook. In District II, bordering on the Danube, on the other hand, the Jewish residents were more likely to have retained their Hasidic practices and orthodox manners, including their traditional dress. It was the visible difference of these Jews, who often had more recently arrived from Galicia, which so revolted the young Adolf Hitler—who was shocked, and wondered how people acting and appearing as they did could ever be considered "real Germans." They seemed such an obviously alien element in Hitler's eyes.[64]

62. This transformation of the Jewish communities in Central and Eastern Europe, especially in the German-speaking lands, is usually associated with the influence of Moses Mendelssohn, beginning in the middle of the eighteenth century. See Marvin Lowenthal, *The Jews of Germany: A Story of 16 Centuries* (Philadelphia: The Jewish Publication Society of America, 1938), pp. 197–216; Ruth Gay, *The Jews of Germany: A Historical Portrait* (New Haven, Conn.: Yale University Press, 1992), pp. 98–117; Nachum T. Gidal, *Jews in Germany: From Roman Times to the Weimar Republic* (Köln, Germany: Könemann Verlagsgesellschaft mbH, 1998), pp. 118–23; Amos Elon, *The Pity of It All: A History of the Jews in Germany, 1743–1933* (New York: Metropolitan Books, 2002), pp. 1–64.

63. On the demographics of the Jewish community in Vienna, see Marsha L. Rozenblit, *The Jews of Vienna, 1867–1914: Assimilation and Identity* (Albany, N.Y.: State University of New York Press, 1983).

64. Adolf Hitler, *Mein Kampf* (Boston: Houghton Mifflin, [1925] 1943), p. 56: "Once as I was walking through the Inner City [of Vienna before the First World War] I suddenly encountered an apparition in a black caftan and black hair locks. Is this a Jew? was my first thought. For, to be sure, they had not looked like that in Linz. I observed the man furtively and cautiously, but

The characteristic mark of most of the Jews who migrated to Vienna (and other large cities of the empire such as Budapest or Prague) was their desire and drive for assimilation; in many ways they tried to be more German than the German-Austrians.[65] The Czechs, the Hungarians, and the Slavs, on the other hand, often were still focused on their traditional ways; the Hungarians in particular were suspicious of the Enlightenment, civil liberties, and equality—these threatened their dominance over the subject peoples in their portions of the empire (the Slovaks, Romanians, and Croats). To constrain the Hungarians, the emperor increasingly put the Czechs, Poles, and Slavs under direct imperial administration on an equal legal footing with the German-Austrians. For the Jews, Austrian imperial policy meant the end of official prejudice and legal restrictions, and a securing of civil rights and educational opportunities.[66] Their continuing and generally steadfast loyalty to the Habsburgs, however, led many of the other nationalities to be suspicious and anti-Semitic as the years went by. The Jews were viewed as apologists and blind supporters of the Habsburg emperor, without whose indulgence and protection the Jews might have been kept within the ghetto walls.[67]

Civil liberties and practically unrestrained commercial and profes-

---

the longer I stared at this foreign face, scrutinizing feature after feature, the more the first question assumed a new form: Is this a German?"

65. On the parallel process of Jewish assimilation and resistance from non-Jews in Prague and Bohemia, see the autobiographical recollections of this period in Hans Kohn, *Living in a World Revolution: My Encounters with History* (New York: Trident Press, 1964), pp. 1–46.

66. Habsburg enlightenment was more advanced in many ways than that of the German government. For example, before the First World War it was virtually impossible for a Jew to be commissioned as an officer in the German Army, no matter what his qualifications and merit. On the other hand, Jews were accepted as officers in the Austrian Army with no similar prejudice, and that is what enabled Ludwig von Mises to be commissioned as a reserve officer in the Austrian Army as a young man, and serve with distinction in the First World War on the Russian front. See Wistrich, *Jews of Vienna*, pp. 174–75:

In striking contrast to the Prussian regiments, there was no deliberate exclusion of Jewish officers and anti-Semitism was not officially tolerated. Indeed, anti-Semitism appears to have been notably weaker in the army than in many other sectors of Austrian society in spite of persistent nationalist agitation and the fact that most officers were Roman Catholic Germans. . . . In this supranational institution *par excellence* which was loyal to the Emperor and the dynasty alone, Jews were by and large treated on equal terms with other ethnic and religious groups. The army could simply not tolerate open racial or religious discrimination which would only undermine morale and patriotic motivation.

67. On the perception of the Jews before the First World War by the various nationalities of the Austro-Hungarian Empire, including the Austrian-Germans, see Henry W. Steed, *The Hapsburg Monarchy*, pp. 145–94.

sional opportunity soon saw the Jews rise to prominence in a wide array of areas of Viennese life.[68] By the beginning of the twentieth century more than 50 percent of the lawyers and medical doctors in Vienna were Jewish. The leading liberal and socialist newspapers in the capital were either owned or edited by those of Jewish descent, including the *New Free Press*, the Viennese newspaper for which Mises often wrote in the 1920s and 1930s. The membership of the journalists' association in Vienna was more than 50 percent Jewish. At the University of Vienna, in 1910, professors of Jewish descent constituted 37 percent of the law faculty, 51 percent of the medical faculty, and 21 percent of the philosophy faculty. At the time Mises attended the university in the first decade of the twentieth century almost 21 percent of the student body was Jewish. The proportion of Jews in literature, theater, music, and the arts was equally pronounced.[69]

The main avenue for social and professional advancement was education in the gymnasium system—the high school system in the German-speaking world. But the gymnasium education not only offered a path to higher education and a university degree for many Jews, it also was an avenue for acculturation and assimilation into European and especially German culture. For example, Mises and his fellow student Hans Kelsen (who later became an internationally renowned philosopher of law and the author of the 1920 constitution of the Republic of Austria) attended the *Akademisches Gymnasium* in the center of Vienna. It was meant for students preparing for the university and professional careers. Here a wide liberal arts education was acquired, with mandatory courses in Latin, Greek, German language and literature, history, geography, mathematics, physics, and religion, with electives in either French or English—Mises selected French. At the core of the curriculum was the study of the ancient Greek and Roman classics. Mises and other Jewish students at the *Akademisches Gymnasium*, as a part of their religion training, had courses in Hebrew.[70]

According to memoirs written by people who attended the *Akademisches Gymnasium* in the 1880s and 1890s, most of the students ridi-

68. See Jerry Z. Muller, *The Mind and the Market: Capitalism in Modern European Thought* (New York: Alfred A. Knopf, 2002), pp. 350–52.
69. On the occupational demographics, see Rozenblit, *Jews of Vienna*, pp. 47–70; Beller, *Vienna and the Jews*, pp. 165–87.
70. On the Vienna gymnasiums, and Jewish assimilation and social and economic advancement, see Rozenblit, *Jews of Vienna*, pp. 99–126; Beller, *Vienna and the Jews*, pp. 49–70.

culed the religion classes as "superstition." The Greek and Roman classics were considered literary avenues for entering the mainstream of
modern European and Western culture. And while it was not assigned,
the students absorbed on their own contemporary writings in history,
social criticism, literature, and the sciences as their way to integrate
themselves into modern and "progressive" society.[71]

In the 1890s, during Mises's time at the *Akademisches Gymnasium*,
44 percent of the student body was Jewish. But there were some gymnasiums at which Jewish admission was informally restricted. For example, the Maria Theresa Academy of Knights in Vienna was reserved
for the children of the nobility and senior officials. Joseph Schumpeter
attended it in the 1890s, but only because his stepfather was a lieuten-
ant field marshal. No matter what his academic qualification, Mises
would have had virtually no chance to be accepted there. Thus clusters
of these gymnasiums were clearly closed to Jews, even if they were con-
verts to Christianity, while other clusters represented the high schools
where middle-class Jewish businessmen, professionals, and civil servants sent their children.[72]

But for all their assimilationist strivings—their conscious attempts to
be German-Austrians in thought, philosophy, outlook, and manner—
the Jews remained distinct and separate. Not only was this because they
belonged to schools, professions, and occupations in which they as Jews
were concentrated, but because non-Jewish German-Austrians viewed
them as separate and distinct. However eloquent and perfect their German in literature and the spoken word, no matter how contributing
they were to the improvement of Viennese society and culture, most
non-Jewish Viennese considered these to be Jewish contributions to
and influences on German-Austrian corners of cultural life.[73]

Name, family history, gossip, and mannerisms made it clear to most

71. See Arthur Schnitzler, *My Youth in Vienna* (New York: Holt, Rinehart and Winston, 1970),
for a rich memoir on the *Akademisches Gymnasium* in Vienna a few years before Mises attended as a student. Also see the fascinating account of Viennese gymnasium life during this
time in Zweig, *The World of Yesterday*, pp. 28–66.
72. On the Maria Theresa Academy of Knights in Vienna during the time when Schumpeter
attended, see Robert Loring Allen, *Opening Doors: The Life and Work of Joseph Schumpeter*,
vol. 1 (Brunswick, N.J.: Transaction Books, 1991), pp. 18–22; and Richard Swedberg, *Schumpeter: A Biography* (Princeton: Princeton University Press, 1991), pp. 10–12.
73. In 1897, a prominent Jewish liberal political figure pointed out in a Vienna newspaper the
German-Austrian attitude to the attempt by many Jews to fully integrate themselves into Austrian life: "When you consider the way the poor Jews strive to gain your favor in the ranks of the
Germans, how they try to accumulate the treasures of German culture, how they work in the

people who were Jewish and who were not. The wide and pronounced success of so many Viennese Jews made non-Jews conscious of their preponderance and presence in many visible walks of life. This success also served as the breeding ground for anti-Semitism.[74]

In the Habsburg domain, part of this anti-Semitism was fed by conservative and reactionary forces in society who often resented the emperor's diminishment or abolition of the privileges, favors, and status of the Catholic Church and the traditional landed aristocracy. The high proportion of Austrian Jews involved in liberal or socialist politics made them targets of the conservatives who said they were carriers of modernity, with its presumption of civil equality, unrestrained market competition, and a secularization that was said to be anti-Christian and therefore immoral and decadent. Preservation and restoration of traditional and Christian society, it was claimed, required opposition to and elimination of the Jewish influence on society. Jews were the rootless "peddlers" who undermined traditional occupations and ways of earning a living, as well as the established social order of things. They pursued profit. Honor, custom, and faith were willingly traded away by them for a few pieces of gold, it was said. Craft associations became leading voices of anti-Semitism, especially when economic hard times required small craftsmen and businessmen to go hat in hand to Jewish bankers for borrowed sums to tide them over.[75]

sciences, some perhaps dying young as a result—and still all the thanks they get is that they are not even accepted as human beings." Quoted in Beller, *Vienna and the Jews*, p. 163.

74. On the nature and evolution of anti-Semitism in Germany and Austria, see Peter G. J. Pulzer, *The Rise of Political Anti-Semitism in Germany and Austria* (New York: John Wiley, 1964); and Bruce F. Pauley, *From Prejudice to Persecution: A History of Austrian Anti-Semitism* (Chapel Hill: University of North Carolina Press, 1992).

75. That the real target behind much of the anti-Semitism in Germany and Austria was economic liberalism has been suggested by Frederick Hertz, *Nationality in History and Politics*, p. 403: "It was rightly felt by many that the real object of [anti-Semitic attacks such as those by the German historian Heinrich von Treitschke] was not the Jews, but liberalism, and that the Jews were only used as a means for working up public opinion against its fundamental principles." Similarly, Hans Kohn, *Prophets and Peoples: Studies in Nineteenth Century Nationalism* (New York: Macmillan, 1946), pp. 124–25: "Treitschke's words, 'The Jews are our misfortune,' served as a rallying banner for the German anti-Semitic movements for the next sixty years. Though the Jews were the immediate goal of the agitation, it ultimately aimed at the liberalism that had brought about Jewish emancipation. Treitschke hated the liberal middle-class society of the West and despised its concern for trade, prosperity and peace. . . . In view of the apparent decay of the Western world through liberalism and individualism, only the German mind with its deeper insight and its higher morality could regenerate the world." See also F. A. Hayek, *The Road to Serfdom* (Chicago: University of Chicago Press, [1944] 2005), p. 161:

In Germany and Austria the Jew had come to be regarded as the representative of capitalism because a traditional dislike of large classes of the population for commercial pursuits

German nationalism also was a vehicle for growing anti-Jewish sentiment. The paradox here is that in the 1860s and 1870s a sizable number of Jewish intellectuals were founders and leaders in the Austrian and German nationalist movements. German culture and society were viewed as representing the universal values of reason, science, justice, and openness in both thought and deed. German culture and political predominance within the Austro-Hungarian Empire restrained the backward-looking forces of darkness—the Hungarian, Czech, and Slavic threats. At the same time, German culture in Central Europe offered rays of enlightenment in the regions of Eastern Europe.

Mises estimated that before the Second World War, Jews made up 50 percent of the business community in Central Europe and 90 percent of the business community in Eastern Europe.[76] Indeed, in *Omnipotent Government* he asserted that in Eastern Europe "modern civilization was predominantly an achievement of Jews."[77] What the Jews in these parts of Europe introduced and represented, at least in their own minds, was the enlightened German mind, with its culture and institutions. But to those other nationalities being introduced to and "threatened" by this German cultural influence, it was perceived as being Jewish as much as German—a dominating, imperial, and "foreign" culture.

At the same time, in both Germany and German-Austria, the Jews in the forefront of the Pan-German nationalist movements were viewed as interlopers by many of the Christian German nationalists. As a consequence, there emerged in the second half of the nineteenth century

had left these more readily accessible to a group that was practically excluded from the more highly esteemed occupations. It is the old story of the alien race being admitted only to the less respected trades, and then being hated still more for practicing them. The fact that German anti-Semitism and anti-capitalism spring from the same root is of great importance for the understanding of what has happened there, but this is rarely grasped by foreign observers.

And Fritz Stern, *The Politics of Cultural Despair: A Study in the Rise of Germanic Ideology* (Berkeley: University of California Press, 1961), pp. 142–43: "Of course, the Jews favored liberalism, secularism, and capitalism. Where else but in the cities, in the free professions, in an open society, could they escape from the restrictions and prejudices that lingered on from the closed, feudal society of an earlier era? They were, and in a sense had to be, the promoters and profiteers of modernity, and for this . . . [many Germans] could not forgive the Jews."

76. Ludwig von Mises, "Postwar Economic Reconstruction of Europe," (1940) in Richard M. Ebeling, ed., *Selected Writings of Ludwig von Mises*, vol. 3, *The Political Economy of International Reform and Reconstruction*, p. 27.

77. Ludwig von Mises, *Omnipotent Government: The Rise of the Total State and Total War* (New Haven: Yale University Press, 1944), p. 185.

rationalizations to justify the rejection of Jewish participation in the cause of German nationalism and culture. First, it was said that only Christians and the Christian faith were consistent with true German life and culture. But when a significant number of German and Austrian Jews converted to Christianity, it still was found not to be enough. Now it was claimed that to be a true German it was not sufficient to be a convert to Christianity. "Germanness" was a culture, an attitude toward life, and a certain sense of belonging to the Volk community.

As a growing number of Jews immersed themselves in all things German—language, philosophy, literature, dress, and manner—it was found, again, not to be enough. Really to be a German was to share a common ancestry, a heritage of a common blood lineage.[78] This was one barrier the German and Austrian Jews could not overcome. In the emergence of racial anti-Semitism in the 1880s and 1890s, there were laid the seeds of the "final solution."

In Vienna, Karl Lueger, who was mayor of the capital city in the first decade of the twentieth century and a leader of the Christian Social Party, represented the spirit of anti-Semitism. He insisted that only "fat Jews" could weather the storm of capitalist competition. Anti-Semitism, Lueger said, "is not an explosion of brutality, but the cry of oppressed Christian people for help from church and state."[79] He blended anti-Semitism with social-left reforms, which included civil service and municipal government restrictions on Jewish access to city jobs or contracts. On the other hand, when Lueger was challenged as to why he had Jewish friends and political associates, he replied, "I decide who is a Jew."[80]

But in spite of the presence and growth of anti-Semitic attitudes in

78. This attitude was expressed, as one example, during the 1930s by the ardent National Socialist Adolf Bertels, who said of Heinrich Heine (possibly, after Goethe, the greatest German writer of the nineteenth century) that "however well he handles the German language and German poetical forms, however much he knows the German way of life, it is impossible for a Jew to be a German." Quoted in Alistair Hamilton, *The Appeal of Fascism: A Study of Intellectuals and Fascism, 1919–1945* (London: Anthony Blond, 1971), p. 109.

79. Quoted in J. Sydney Jones, *Hitler in Vienna, 1907–1913: Clues to the Future* (New York: Cooper Square Press, 2002), p. 155.

80. Ibid., p. 157; also, Berkley, *Vienna and Its Jews*, pp. 103–11; on the history of the Christian Social movement with its blending of anti-Semitism, anticapitalism, and socialism, and Lueger's role and participation in it, see John W. Boyer, *Political Radicalism in Late Imperial Vienna: Origins of the Christian Social Movement, 1848–1897* (Chicago: University of Chicago Press, 1981) and *Culture and Political Crisis in Vienna: Christian Socialism in Power, 1897–1918* (Chicago: University of Chicago Press, 1995).

the late nineteenth and early twentieth centuries in Austria in general and Vienna in particular, Mises's seeming lack of attention to his own Jewish family background or any hint of the impact of anti-Semitism around him—there were anti-Jewish student riots at the University of Vienna during the years when he was a student there around the turn of the century—was in fact not uncommon.[81] One can read Stefan Zweig's fascinating account of everyday life in the Vienna of this time and have the distinct impression that anti-Semitic attitudes or municipal government policy were virtually nonexistent.

Yet many invisible walls characterized the circles in which people moved in Viennese society both before and after the First World War. Traditional or Orthodox Jews lived and worked within a world of their own in the city.[82] Secular and assimilated Jews, like Ludwig von Mises and Hans Kelsen, moved in circles of both Jews and non-Jews, but even the nonreligious and German-acculturated Jews clustered together. A review of the list of participants in Mises's famous private seminar in Vienna, for example, shows a high proportion of Jews.[83] And even after Mises had moved to Geneva, Switzerland, in 1934, his agenda books for this time show that many of his social engagements were with other Jews residing in or visiting that country.

The end of the nineteenth and the beginning of the twentieth century saw the eclipse of liberalism in Austria and the rise of socialism in its place, centered in the political ascendancy of the Social Democratic Party. A sizable number of Jews were prominent in the Austrian socialist movement; they were anticapitalist and viewed the entrepreneurial segment of the society as exploiters and economic oppressors. The capitalist class would be swept away in the transformation to socialism, including the Jewish capitalists in the "ruling class." Most of the Jews in the socialist movement not only were secular and considered themselves harbingers of the worker's world to come; they were contemptuously opposed to cultural and religious Judaism as well.[84]

81. Mises barely mentions anti-Semitic sentiments in Austria in his *Memoirs*, and devotes time to a detailed discussion of it only in *Omnipotent Government*, pp. 169–92, written during the Second World War. For a discussion of Mises's critique of anti-Semitism, see Richard M. Ebeling, "Ludwig von Mises and the Vienna of His Time," especially pp. 43–49.
82. Harriet Pass Freidenreich, *Jewish Politics in Vienna, 1918–1938* (Bloomington: Indiana University Press, 1991), p. 138.
83. Mises, *Memoirs*, p. 83.
84. See Robert S. Wistrich, *Socialism and the Jews* (East Brunswick, N.J.: Associated University Presses, 1982).

These three political movements in Austria and Vienna when Mises was a young man—conservatism, German nationalism, and radical socialism—were, each for its own reasons, enemies of liberal society, opponents of free-market capitalism, and therefore threats to the ideas and occupations of those middle class, or "bourgeois," walks of life heavily populated by the Jews of Austria and Vienna.

The history of Austrian Jewry during this time is a story of triumph and tragedy. The winds of nineteenth-century liberalism freed the Austrian Jewish community, both internally and externally. Internally, the liberal idea pried open Orthodox Jewish society in places such as Austrian Galicia. It heralded reason over ritual; greater individualism over religious collectivism; open-minded modernity over the strictures of traditionalism. Externally, it freed the Jewish community from legal and political restraints and restrictions. The right of freedom of trade, occupation, and profession opened wide many opportunities for social improvement, economic betterment, and political acceptance.[85]

Within two generations this transformed Austrian Jewish society. And that same span of time saw the rise of many Jews to social and economic prominence, with greater political tolerance than ever known before. If these two liberating forces had not been at work, there would not have been Ludwig von Mises—the economist, the political and social philosopher, and the notable public figure and policy analyst in Austria both before and between the two world wars.

At the same time, these two liberating forces set the stage for the tragedy of the German and Austrian Jews. Their very successes in the arts and the sciences, in academia, and in commerce fostered the animosity and resentment of those less successful in the arenas of intellectual, cultural, and commercial competition. It set loose the emotion of envy, the terror of failure, and the psychological search for scapegoats and excuses. It ended at the gates to the Nazi death camps.

---

85. Many of the Jews in Germany and Austria understood the connection between economic liberalism and individual opportunity that had enabled so many in the Jewish community to prosper in spite of anti-Semitic sentiments. Thus, for example, in 1897, Emil Lehmann, head of the Dresden Jewish community, argued against the Social Democrats, "In the Mosaic teaching the ideals of justice and equality before the law find their substantiation just as envy and hatred—which the Social Democrats share with the anti-Semites—receives the sharpest condemnation. Thou shalt not covet! Other demands contrary to civilization such as the abolition of the family, State education of children, etc. etc., which are desired by the Social Democrats, are firmly rejected in the Ten Commandments." Quoted in Wistrich, *Socialism and the Jews*, p. 69.

In Mises's case and for many others it meant leaving the country of their birth and seeking refuge in other lands. Among those who left before or immediately after Germany's annexation of Austria were many members of the Austrian School of economics or Mises's private seminar circle (both Jews and non-Jews): Martha Steffy Browne, Gottfried Haberler, Friedrich A. Hayek, Felix Kaufmann, Fritz Machlup, Ilse Mintz, Oscar Morgenstern, Paul N. Rosenstein-Rodan, Alfred Schutz, and Erich Voegelin, to name just a few.

Mises had departed in autumn 1934 for a teaching position at the Graduate Institute of International Studies in Geneva, when it was clear that the collectivist darkness was starting to fall over the center of Europe. He made a new life for himself after 1940 in the United States, like many of his Austrian colleagues and friends, where the spirit of freedom was not yet in the same shadow of tyranny as in their native Austria. America, for them, was still a land where Austrian Jews such as Mises could breathe the air of liberty.

He continued to explain and defend the principles and ideals of classical liberalism and the free market in his new home in America until his death on October 10, 1973, at the age of 92.

Richard M. Ebeling
Professor of Economics
Northwood University

June 2011

MONETARY AND ECONOMIC POLICY PROBLEMS
BEFORE, DURING, AND AFTER THE GREAT WAR

PART 1

Austro-Hungarian Monetary and Fiscal Policy Issues Before the First World War

CHAPTER 1

The Political-Economic Motives
of the Austrian Currency Reform[1]

I

The fact that from the middle of 1888, changes in the value of the Austrian currency had taken on a pattern disadvantageous to domestic production gave a direct impetus for the reform of the Austro-Hungarian monetary system, a reform that had been dragging on for decades before this.

The price of 100 florins in gold (250 francs) amounted, on average for the year 1872, to 110.37 Austrian paper florins and increased, beginning with this year (with a small interruption), up to 125.23 Austrian paper florins as the average for 1887. From then on, it began to decline. It amounted to:

Valued in Austrian florins	Average for the year
122.87	1888
118.58	1889
115.48	1890
115.83	1891

A widely held view, which met with little opposition, held that these increases in value of the Austrian currency were neither incidental nor temporary phenomena; in fact, they could be traced back to serious, economic causes. There was a perceived agreement that the fall in the agio[2] would not come to an end by itself: indeed, it would continue at an increased rate in future years if a change in the currency did not oc-

1. [This article originally appeared in German in the *Zeitschrift für Volkswirtschaft, Sozialpolitik und Verwaltung*, vol. 16 (1907).—Ed.]
2. [Agio is the rate at which a currency may be exchanged on the foreign currency market. —Ed.]

cur at the appropriate time. This view found its most ardent supporter in Hertzka,[3] who articulated that opinion in the investigations of the currency commission. If the monarchy persisted with a nonconvertible currency, the florin would continue to increase in value until finally it would equal the gold value of the pound sterling by the end of the nineteenth century.[4] Most of the individuals who had their say during the proceedings of the currency commission shared this view; Minister of Finance Steinbach[5] repeatedly expressed a similar opinion, for example, in the session of the House of Representatives on July 14, 1892. The generally widespread belief in the continuing "improvement" in the value of the Austrian currency was one of the most effective motives for the accelerated initiation of a reform of the currency.[6]

The majority saw the most important reason behind the increase in the value of the currency in the fact that there was a legal limit on the maximum quantity of state notes in circulation and a suspension of silver coinage for private uses. This meant that within the monarchy increases in the quantity of the currency could no longer match increases in the demand for currency. This argument, which was an application of the quantity theory to Austrian circumstances, primarily relied upon the fact that the quantity of currency in circulation within the monarchy remained considerably below the quantity in circulation in other countries.

According to O. Haupt, the currency in circulation within the Austro-Hungarian Monarchy amounted to 779 million florins at the end of 1885, which represented a per capita circulation of 20.10 fl. In the most important countries, the per capita money in circulation at the end of 1885, in francs, was [25 shown opposite—Ed.].

Austria was ranked twelfth place with respect to the relative size of the monetary system. However, this factor alone does not absolutely

3. [Theodor Hertzka (1845–1924), an Austrian economist and journalist. In 1879 he founded the *Wiener Allgemeine Zeitung*, which he edited until 1886.—Ed.]

4. See *Stenographische Protokolle . . . der Währungsenquetekommission* [The Stenographic Protocols of the Commission for the Currency Inquiry] (Vienna, 1892), p. 96.

5. [Emil Steinbach (1846–1907), Austrian economist, jurist, and politician. In 1891–93 served as minister of finance and in 1904–7 as president of the Supreme Court of Justice. He had a decisive influence on social legislation, supported the extension of the right to vote, implemented a currency reform, and reorganized the system of personal taxation.—Ed.]

6. See Carl Menger, *Der Übergang zur Goldwährung* [The Transition to the Gold Standard] (Vienna, 1892), pp. 10ff.

France	234.80
Netherlands	148.70
United States	112.90
Belgium	102.50
Great Britain	98.55
Germany	91.05
Spain	86.70
Switzerland	77.70
Denmark	77.20
Portugal	74.50
Italy	58.30
Austro-Hungary	41.25
Sweden	36.90
Rumania	32.20
Norway	29.80
Russia	27.55[7]

justify the conclusion that Austro-Hungary's money in circulation failed to correspond to the demand for it. It is obvious that those Western countries where capitalistic development had advanced far ahead of the Danube Empire had a larger demand for money. In addition, it is not surprising that Italy had a larger quantity of money in circulation than was in the Austro-Hungarian Monarchy, considering that in 1885 Italy was experiencing a period of growing paper money inflation and an increasing agio. It is equally inappropriate to compare the monarchy's circumstances with those in Spain and Portugal.

The proponents of the quantity theory laid the primary responsibility on the fact that the Austro-Hungarian monetary system lacked the possibility for a currency expansion starting in 1879, and in a certain sense already beginning in 1867.

Admittedly, an increase in the monarchy's monetary gold reserves was practically excluded. Because gold was not a part of the Austrian currency system, it could only be employed (aside from its use for the payment of customs duties and in some business transactions) as a backing for the notes issued by the Austrian-Hungarian National Bank. However, due to the decline in the price of silver, the Austro-Hungarian Bank could not increase its gold reserves without incurring

7. Compare *Statistische Tabellen zur Währungsfrage der österreichisch-ungarischen Monarchie* [The Statistical Tables Relating to the Currency Question in the Austro-Hungarian Monarchy] compiled in the Imperial and Royal Finance Ministry (Vienna, 1892), tables 169–71.

a loss; in the period from December 31, 1877, to August 10, 1892, these reserves grew by a mere 401.65 kg.[8]

Since the abolishment of silver coinage for private uses in the spring of 1879, silver face-value coins were minted only for government uses. In the years 1884–91, silver face-value coins were minted at an average annual value of 7 million florins. The entire amount of silver face-value coins minted between 1876 and 1891 amounted to 226.6 million florins. The Austro-Hungarian Bank's silver holdings increased from 66.6 million florins at the end of 1875 to up to 166.7 million florins at the end of 1891.

The legal limitation on state notes in circulation to 312 million florins was a particular characteristic of the Austrian monetary constitution, under which the quantity of short-term, interest-bearing treasury bills in circulation, and the sum of state notes and interest-bearing treasury bills was prohibited from exceeding a combined amount of 412 million florins. Within this limit, however, the decrease in the quantity of Saltworks notes[9] was replaced with an increase in the circulation of state notes. The possibility always existed for satisfying the increasing demand for currency in circulation within this limit through an expansion of state notes in circulation. And beginning in 1888 we see a constant increase in the quantity of these notes in circulation. The entire state note circulation amounted to:

Million florins	At the end of the year
336.8	1888
357.2	1889
370.4	1890
378.8	1891

Although until the fourth privilege of the Austro-Hungarian Bank went into effect the quantity of notes in circulation not backed by precious metals was strictly limited to 200 million, the number of banknotes in circulation increased from 247 million florins at the end of 1867 to 391 million florins at the end of 1887. The system adopted in the Austro-Hungarian Bank's fourth privilege of an indirect limita-

8. See Mecenseffy, *Bericht über den Goldbesitz der österreichisch-ungarischen Bank* [Report on the Gold Held by the Austro-Hungarian Bank] (Vienna, 1897), p. 15.
9. ["Saltworks Notes" (*Salinenscheine*) were short-term, interest-earning Austrian treasury bills.—Ed.]

tion offered a freer scope to the expansion of notes in circulation. It amounted to:[10]

Average for the year	Tax-free note limitation	Notes in circulation	Tax-free bank-note reserves
	Millions of Austrian florins		
1888	433	385	49
1889	443	399	43
1890	449	416	33
1891	453	421	32

The entire paper money in circulation (state- and banknotes) amounted to:

Millions of Austrian florins	At the end of the year
762.5	1888
834.0	1889

This corresponded to a total increase of 71.5 million and an average annual increase of 23.8 million florins. That this increase in the quantity of paper money in circulation did not lag behind the increasing demand for it, or at least not far behind, is shown by a comparison of the numbers from the period after the inauguration of the currency reform. Since then, it is generally accepted that the increase in currency in circulation completely satisfied the needs of business. The monarchy's money in circulation amounted to:

Million crowns	At the end of the year
1728.0	1892
2279.1	1904

This represents a total increase of 551 million and an average annual increase of 45.9 million crowns. The average annual increase of money in circulation was thus not larger in the period after 1892 than it was in the years immediately preceding that year.

In light of these facts, the claim that Austrian currency in circulation lacked the possibility for expansion cannot be maintained. However, to conclude that the increase in the currency in circulation satisfied

10. *Statistische Tabellen zur Währungsfrage der österreichisch-ungarischen Monarchie*, p. 145.

the developing and increasing demand for it would be equally invalid. Such a conclusion would be prohibited because the statistical evidence is completely lacking for determining what were the required amounts of currency in circulation. Irrespective of this, however, even with the presumption of a domestic contraction, a direct causal relationship between such a contraction and an increase in the international value of the currency could not be determined.

It must be acknowledged that as the domestic currency in circulation becomes scarcer, this initially leads to a contraction of credit and an increase in the cost of borrowing, and has the further result of bringing about a fall in the prices of goods. It is obvious, however, that such a drop in prices can be only for those goods that cannot be exported. A decline in the prices of these goods in terms of the domestic currency will not result in foreigners offering higher prices for bonds on the Viennese market. This could be brought about only by a reduction in the prices of exported goods. This could occur only if as a result of the fall in other domestic prices the production of exported goods increased to such an extent that their prices fell due to their increase in supply. The increase in the rate of exchange that would result, however, as a consequence of this increased supply of exportable goods could be neither considerable nor of significant duration, because the decline in their prices would be transferred to the global market within a short period of time. Then any motive that foreigners would have to offer higher prices for Austrian bonds would slip away.[11]

It is not possible, given the current underdeveloped state of monetary theory and the lack of statistical data, to arrive at any certain conclusions about what influence the limit on increases in currency in circulation may have had on the value of money through its impact on the prices of goods. In other respects, the impact on the foreign exchange rate due to the limit on the maximum quantity of state notes in circulation and the administrative suspension of silver coinage can be determined with certainty: in fact, it was a means of securing the credit of the monarchy. The strictness with which the two governments of Austria-Hungary followed the conservative rules of its currency policy reestablished trust in the two financial administrations' fulfillment of its monetary obligations, especially after this had been severely shaken

11. Compare Heyn, "Das Steigen des Rupienkurses nach Aufhebung der indischen Silberwährung" [The Rise in the Value of the Rupee Following the Repeal of the Indian Silver Currency], *Jahrbücher für Nationalökonomie und Statistik*, vol. 28, especially pp. 176ff.

both domestically and abroad by the events of 1797–1866. The danger of an inflationary increase in the supply of paper money, much like the danger of a return to a silver-backed currency, retreated into the distance.

The improvement in the creditworthiness of the currency went hand in hand with the strengthened creditworthiness of the government bonds. This was considerably influenced by the gradual disappearance of the threat of war, which had risked the peaceful development of our fatherland since the Congress of Berlin.[12]

Without a doubt, a war with one of the Great Powers would have forced Austria to resort to a new issue of paper money emissions, to renewed borrowing through the issuing of premium bonds, and perhaps also to a reduction in bond coupon payments, which would have destroyed the national credit for a long time.

The average annual rate of Austrian 4 percent gold bonds on the Berlin exchange rose from 61.05 percent in 1877 to 93.50 percent in 1886. Following a downturn in 1877 to 89.67 percent (during the Bulgarian Question),[13] the upward movement continued. The annual average amounted to:

90.46%	in 1888
94.09%	in 1889
95.12%	in 1890
95.69%	in 1891
104.55%	in 1897

The rate for Hungarian gold bonds was increasing as well. The rate of return on the 6 percent gold bond amounted to (calculated accord-

12. [The Congress of Berlin (1878) was a meeting of the political leaders of European Great Powers and the Ottoman Empire in the wake of the Russo-Turkish War of 1877–78, in order to reorganize the countries of the Balkans. Otto von Bismarck, who led the congress, undertook to balance the distinct interests of Britain, Russia, and Austria-Hungary. However, differences between Russia and Austria-Hungary only intensified, as did the nationality question in the Balkans.—Ed.]

13. [As a result of the Russo-Turkish War of 1877–78, Bulgaria regained independence after four hundred years of Turkish rule. Fearful of a Bulgarian uprising in 1876, the Turkish military put down suspected resistance, and in the process killed an estimated 12,000 to 15,000 Bulgarians. This massacre of unarmed civilians created an international uproar against Turkish rule in this part of the Balkans. This led first to a war between the Turkish Empire and Serbia and Montenegro, and then in 1877 to war between Imperial Russia and the Turkish Empire that finally led to a truce in the face of Russian victories on the battlefields, and the settlement in the Congress of Berlin in 1878.—Ed.]

ing to the average annual rate) 7.9 percent in 1877, and that of the 4 percent gold bond amounted to 4.4 percent in 1891.[14]

As long as the concern continued regarding peace in Europe, speculation countered an increase in the note value. Out of fear of a decline in the Austrian currency, investors avoided accumulating large amounts in Austrian cash assets and preferred to deposit their liquid assets in gold bills of exchange. The disappearance of the risk of war allowed such a speculative collecting of gold exchanges to appear superfluous, and the pressure that the domestic speculative demand for gold had exerted on the currency market dropped off.[15]

If one item in the monarchy's balance of payments improved in this way, other entries show a favorable pattern as well.

The Austro-Hungarian trade balance for imports and exports amounted to:

In the years	Excess imports	Excess exports
	Millions of Austrian florins	
1869–1873	475.7	—
1874–1878	—	151.7
1879–1883	—	532.3
1884–1888	—	652.5

The excess exports in the import-export trade amounted to:

Millions of Austrian florins	In the year
114.2	1885
159.4	1886
104.3	1887
195.7	1888
177.0	1889
160.7	1890
173.8	1891

Starting in 1889, Austro-Hungarian investments began to immigrate back from abroad. The unfavorable effect that a capital migration of this type is able to exert on the balance of payments, and through this on the bond rate, was alleviated by the fact that new government borrowing by both governments had practically come to a halt in 1889. The domestic demands for investment were extensive enough to take

14. See *Deutsche Übersetzung der von dem königlichen ungarischen Finanzministerium der für den 8. März 1892 einberufenen Valutaenquete vorgelegten statistischen und synoptischen Tabellen* (Budapest, 1891), p. 115.

15. See Benedikt's articles in the *Neue Freie Presse*, August 24 and September 14, 1890.

up the funds flowing back into the country without disturbing the currency or bond markets.[16]

According to Sax,[17] the positive balance in the balance of payments amounted to:

57 million Austrian florins	in 1889
40 million Austrian florins	in 1890
54 million Austrian florins	in 1891

The favorable pattern of the balance of payments explains the general improvement in the Austrian currency in the four-year period that began in the summer of 1888. The exceptionally low rate for foreign bonds in the third quarter of 1890 can be traced back to a particular cause: the Sherman Act of July 14, 1890.[18]

Since the Bland-Allison Act (February 28, 1878),[19] agitation by silver proponents in the United States had decreased and, following a break of several years, only resumed in 1889 with new vigor. The movement's goal was the freeing of silver coinage; however, all that the silver proponents were able to achieve was the Sherman Act of July 14, 1890. An unparalleled bull market speculation was linked to the American agitation. The silver price in London was quoted at:

42 ⅝ d.	on Oct. 1, 1889
49 ½ d.	on Jul. 14, 1890
51 ¼ d.	on Aug. 13, 1890 (treasury began silver purchases)
54 ⅝ d.	on Sept. 3 and 4, 1890 (highest price)

These bull market movements influenced the Viennese foreign exchange and currency markets. The German Reichsmark was quoted on the Vienna exchange at:

57.32½ fl.	on Jul. 1, 1890
56.75 fl.	on Aug. 1, 1890
55.80 fl.	on Aug. 18, 1890
54.37 fl.	on Sept. 2, 1890 (lowest price)

16. See Emil Sax's article in the *Neue Freie Presse*, July 28, 1894.

17. *Neue Freie Presse*, July 28 and August 2, 1894.

18. [The Sherman Silver Purchase Act that was passed on July 14, 1890, required the United States Treasury to purchase 4.5 million ounces of silver bullion every month, making it the second-largest buyer in the world, after the government of India, at the time. The act was repealed in 1893.—Ed.]

19. [The Bland-Allison Act of 1878 required the U.S. Treasury to purchase between $2 million and $4 million of silver bullion per month. It was replaced by the Sherman Act of 1890.—Ed.]

As an aside, it should be noted that circumstances similar to these, which had caused the improvement in the Austrian currency, also drove up the price of the ruble. In this case as well, favorable balance of payments, political quiet both domestically and abroad, and the silver bull market of 1890 were of primary importance. The quote for 100 credit rubles on the Berlin exchange was:

162.25 marks	on Mar. 7, 1888
216.40 marks	on Oct. 1, 1888
219.40 marks	on Jan. 1, 1890
262.30 marks	on Sept. 15, 1890
238.00 marks	on Dec. 1, 1890

II

The decrease in the agio placed the currency question, which had been dealt with only tepidly for years, back on the agenda.

It is true that, following the unfavorable events of 1848/49 and 1859, the financial administration immediately and energetically tackled the organization of the subverted monetary system; it aimed with vigor and skill at eliminating the forced exchange after the Prussian War, which wrecked the large-scale plans of the elder Plener[20] in the same fashion that the French War a few years previously had destroyed similar endeavors by Bruck.[21] No serious steps for reforming the currency were undertaken for a long time. The cause for this conspicuous inactivity in the area of currency policy, which contrasted so sharply with the bustling activity of the previous epoch, was not simply the difficulty and complexity that the international currency problem had developed into since the continuous drop in the price of silver. It was, rather, that the project for reforming the currency was absolutely unpopular in Austria, and even more so in Hungary. One could only imagine an implementation of currency reform by means of depressing the so-called

20. [Ignaz von Plener (1810–1908) was a prominent Austrian statesman who initiated what became known as Plener's Bank Act of 1863, which was modeled after Great Britain's Peel's Bank Act of 1844 that restricted the issuance of banknotes to the amount of gold reserves at a fixed rate of redemption.—Ed.]

21. [Karl Ludwig Baron Bruck (1798–1860) was Austrian minister of commerce and public works from 1848 to 1851. As minister of finance from 1855 to 1860, he attempted to introduce a series of fiscal and monetary reforms that failed due to the Austrian war to retain its Italian provinces beginning in 1857. Unjustly blamed for Austria's financial difficulties, he resigned as finance minister and committed suicide the next day. He was officially declared innocent of all wrongdoing in his ministerial position one month after his death.—Ed.]

agio[22] until it disappeared completely. The fast drop of the agio, which had occurred in the first half of the 1860s as a result of the currency reform endeavors, was still an uncomfortable memory for all manufacturers. The fact that the situation had changed essentially since 1879, and that a return of the so-called gold agio at parity to the customary exchange rate for Austria was not possible, was not easy to recognize at the beginning, especially because the designation of the twenty-franc coin as an eight-florin coin gave ample cause for errors.

With the depreciation of the currency in the period 1872–87, the agrarian and industrial manufacturers both capitalized in the same manner. The increasing agio functioned like a protective tariff against the import of foreign manufactured goods, and assisted the export of domestic products like an export premium, and also benefited the debtors. Under such circumstances, support for currency reform plans could not be counted on from the industrial or agricultural circles.

The falling agio affected primarily those who had taken advantage of the previous increases. While the prices on the global market remained unchanged, the foreign exchange rate on the Viennese market dropped, and the exporter who had received 50 fl., 6¾ krona (crowns) for 100 francs in February 1887 received only 44 fl., 54½ krona in September 1890. The farmer received 10 percent less for his produce than two years previously, but taxes and mortgage interest had to be paid at the old levels.

Up until spring 1890, hope had been placed on an early backlash. The summer of the same year brought such expectations to an end. As soon as the recognition began to spread that the increase in the value of the currency was not based on temporary circumstances, and when it would stop could not be predicted, the demand for currency reform became general. In the first half of September 1890, the Austro-Hungarian Export Association dispatched a call to its members, in which it advocated for action in favor of currency reform. Rallies in favor occurred in all corners of the empire.[23] In the general media, propaganda for reform was heard.

Particularly characteristic was the reversal of opinion in Hungary. Hungary had raised constant, fervent resistance to the Austrian cur-

22. About the applicability of the term "agio" at all to the Austrian currency circumstances prior to 1892, see Spitzmüller, "Die österreichisch-ungarische Währungsreform," *Zeitschrift für Volkswirtschaft, Sozialpolitik und Verwaltung* 11, p. 342, note 1.
23. See Dorns, *Volkswirtschaftliche Wochenschrift*, September 11 and 18, and October 2, 1890.

rency reform plans, and delivered a decisive veto in November 1884 to the proposals by Austrian Finance Minister Dunajewski.[24] Now, however, Hungary ardently advocated for reform. Of primary importance in this decision were the agricultural interests, particularly those of the wheat exporters; a further drop in the foreign exchange should be prevented at all costs. Therefore, the Hungarian Finance Ministry began to buy gold foreign exchange in November 1890, in order to exert pressure on the rate of the paper florin. Over the course of a few months, the Hungarian treasury had acquired about 45 million florins in gold exchange, and the desired result had not failed to occur.[25]

Along with the agrarian motives, however, which allowed Hungary to call for currency reform as a method to stop the "improvement" of the currency, other motives were also present. For forty years, Hungary's politics had only one goal: the achievement of economic independence as a precursor to political independence. In the introduction of the gold currency and the implementation of specie payments, those in Budapest saw their most secure means of financially freeing themselves from the Viennese banks, increasing the prestige of Hungarian national credit abroad, and acquiring the means from international capital that were necessary for economic war with Austria.

Since 1890, hardly a single voice has been raised in Hungary against currency reform. With unique unity, the entire nation followed the political rallying cry pronounced by Alexander Wekerle,[26] the most knowledgeable Magyar in monetary-related areas: truly an example of political discipline worthy of awe.[27]

With the reversal of opinion in Hungary, the fate of currency reform was decided. Since October 1890, no one doubted any longer that the currency reform would be tackled as soon as possible, and it was just as certain that the currency's rate of exchange would be higher than

---

24. See *Neue Freie Presse*, November 22, 1884.

25. See Sax, *Neue Freie Presse*, August 2, 1894, and Carl Menger in the preface to Lorini, *La questione della Valuta in Austria-Ungheria* (Torino, 1893), p. xix and notes.

26. [Alexander Santor Wekerle (1848–1921), Hungarian statesman, who served several terms as Hungarian minister of finance and prime minister. Improved the financial position of the country, carried out the conversion of the state loans, and succeeded, for the first time in Hungarian history, in avoiding a budget deficit. In October 1918 declared Hungarian independence, which brought about his dismissal from office by Austro-Hungarian Emperor Karl I.—Ed.]

27. The credit for winning public opinion in Hungary in support of currency regulation is due to the future Minister President Count Stephan Tisza, who caused a text about the reform of the currency to appear in the Magyar language in 1891.

the exchange rate prevailing on the market at that time. The following comparison shows how quickly and correctly the Viennese banking circles grasped the new situation.

On October 2, 1890, Wekerle announced in his exposé the early realization of the currency draft (which was, however, delayed as a result of the Baring Crisis).[28] On October 6, he met in Vienna in order to confer with Dunajewski about currency reform. Under the influence of this news, the currency rate soared. German Reichsmarks were quoted on the Viennese market at:

55 fl. 10 kr.	on Oct. 1
55 fl. 52½ kr.	on Oct. 4 (Sat.)
56 fl. 30 kr.	on Oct. 6 (Mon.)
57 fl. 00 kr.	on Oct. 7

III

The question has to be asked, whether the belief in the continuing improvement of the Austrian currency, and in the general pervasiveness of which belief we detect the main reason for the swift tackling of currency reform, was not based on an error.

It must be noted in advance, however, that even if this question were to be answered affirmatively, one would not be justified thereby in accusing the initiators of currency reform of lacking foresight. Ignoring the fact that a continuation had been presumed to be highly probable of all of those circumstances that had affected the favorable pattern of the balance of payments since 1888, no one in Europe could predict around 1892 which direction the silver question would take in the United States. The majority by which the House of Representatives had voted against the freeing of silver coinage numbered:

131 votes	in 1878
37 votes	in 1887
17 votes	in 1890
7 votes	in 1891[29]

28. [The Panic of 1890 was an acute depression precipitated by the near insolvency of the Baring Brothers bank in London due to poor investments in Argentina. The Bank of England finally bailed out the Baring Brothers. The panic was associated with call money reaching an astonishing 45 percent and a slump in the international commodities market.—Ed.]

29. See Prager, *Die Währungsfrage in den Vereinigten Staaten von Nordamerika* (Stuttgart, 1897), pp. 306, 383.

One had to come to terms, therefore, with the fact that soon the silver proponents would achieve their goal, which they had pursued for years with an enormous energy. What result this would have for the foreign exchange rate was learned in the summer of 1890.

An examination of the exchange rates shows that the favorable pattern of the monarchy's balance of payments has been maintained in the fifteen years that have elapsed since the beginning of the currency reform. In 1893–96, however, the exchange rate showed an unfavorable character: in fall 1893, the agio temporarily reached a level of more than 6.5 percent compared with the "relation" established in the Act of '92. This formation of the agio was traced back to the chance coincidence of a series of unfavorable circumstances.[30] Since 1896, the agio has indeed disappeared and, since this time, the exchange rates have maintained parity on average with limited fluctuations. For more than a decade, the monarchy has enjoyed, in this manner, a currency that is stable in value compared with foreign countries.

The means by which this goal was achieved, the well-known foreign exchange policy of the Austro-Hungarian Bank, was made feasible only by the favorable pattern of the balance of payments. Lotz remarked quite correctly, "the Bank can issue exchange only for as long as they can buy foreign exchange, even at a sacrifice. Foreign exchange, however, can only be obtained as long as the Austrian economy possesses foreign receivables or can acquire them through the sales of goods or securities. As long as a country can do this, then gold impoverishment due to an actual specie system absolutely need not be feared again."[31] The well-known appraisals by the Austrian Finance Ministry about the monarchy's balance of payments yield the statistical proof for the correctness of this statement.

The great advantages that the Bank's (justifiably praised) foreign exchange policy brought to the economy do not lie, as the naïve layman's view perceives whenever he hears talk of suspended specie payments, in the fact that it frees Austria from the actual fulfillment of its international obligations, but rather in the fact that it gives the Bank the possibility of separating so-called legitimate requests for gold from illegitimate ones. In this fashion, it was possible to keep the bank rate in Vienna lower than that in Berlin and London; what this means,

30. See Spitzmüller, ibid., pp. 498ff. Then Kalkmann, *Wiener staatswissenschaftlichen Studien,* vol. I, p. 3.
31. See Lotz, "G. F. Knapps neue Geldtheorie," *Schmollers Jahrbuch* 30, p. 360.

however, does not require any further explanation. It should be noted in passing that the necessity of dealing differently with speculative demand for gold to exploit the difference in the discount rates than with demand by importers has demonstrated itself elsewhere. The Bank of France does not require a gold premium if it is brought proof that the bearer of the notes presented for redemption requires the gold for the import of foreign raw materials. The German Reichsbank and the Bank of England also only hand over gold coins for export at a weight 2–3 per mill lighter than the newly minted coins.

Just like the German and English gold currency policy and the French gold premium, the Austrian foreign exchange policy is possible only through the monarchy's favorable balance of payments. That the favorable balance of payments can be established only by increasing external debt through the export of investments is not relevant. The only deciding circumstance, above all, is that the balance of payments is positive. If this were not the case, then the Bank could not sell enough foreign exchange and would have to introduce an agio immediately.

In the past decade, there have been repeated periods in which the foreign exchange rate has been below parity. Gold imports into Austria then took place, and the Bank accepted the gold. In 1901, for example, gold stockpiles of approximately 153 million crowns flowed into the Bank in this manner. The import of gold from abroad continued each time until the foreign exchange rate again had approximated parity as closely as possible, so that additional gold imports were no longer profitable. Under the hegemony of the old Austrian currency system, such gold imports would not have occurred, and this impossibility would have led to an increase in the value of the currency.

If the country had adhered to the nonconvertible currency, then a lack in circulating media of exchange in domestic commerce would have made itself felt soon as well. Even if it is not possible to say something specific about the increase in demand for circulating media of exchange, it remains that the swift (at least for Austrian circumstances) economic development of recent years has broadened this demand to a considerable degree. If this demand for circulating media of exchange were not being correspondingly satisfied (and that that satisfaction was realized was only made possible by the new currency acts), then without doubt, credit reductions and, as a result of them, critical occurrences would have arisen.

The experiences of the last fifteen years confirm the correctness of that theory that a continuing "improvement" awaited the Austrian paper currency.

IV

The increase in the value of the Austrian currency reduced agricultural and manufacturers' income, and increased the capitalists' income. The owners of bonds payable in paper or silver saw the value of the debt owed to them constantly increase, and it was understood that they could not be enthusiastic about a currency reform that cut off their hope of additional increases in the value of money.

Nevertheless, the opposition that currency reform found in these circles was powerless, primarily because it lacked even the appearance of a legal foundation. The owners of paper and silver bonds, even of state bonds, had no claim that the country should allow the favorable situation of the monetary system to continue unchanged for their interests alone. The country would have committed no breach of law with regard to them, even if it had freed silver minting again.

The sharp protests that some foreign news media raised against the planned currency stabilization were accorded little importance, because foreign ownership in Austrian investments included only the smallest portions in securities paying interest in silver or in notes, the vast majority of which, however, were paid interest in gold. However, even on the part of the majority of domestic owners of bonds payable in silver or notes, a boisterous opposition was not to be expected. Their standpoint was represented in the currency inquiry commission solely by the secretary general of the First Austrian Savings Bank, Mr. Nava. In the course of parliamentary discussions, hardly any voice had been raised on the part of these doubtless affected interests.

It is surprising, but not inexplicable, that the markets and the banks were not only not opponents of currency reform, but, on the contrary, they exerted so much effort for this cause that those not involved would have acquired the impression that the currency change was primarily in the interests of this circle. The Christian Social Party repeatedly pointed out that high finance decisively advocated for reform.

This opinion of the monetary institutions cannot be traced directly back to the interest that they had in the development of industry and agriculture. Such considerations may well have played a role; however, they were not pivotal by any means. Much more decisive was the fact that, since the Crash of 1873, the banking business in Austria had not really prospered.[32] Issuance of securities practically slumbered. In Cisleithanien [Austria], it amounted to:

| | | Capital of the stock corporations | |
| | | Excl. the railway companies | Incl. the railway companies |
At the end of the year	Number of stock corporations	In million florins Austrian valuation	
1878	460	627.7	1,447.1
1892	453	692.6	1,562.1

From 1883 to 1892, only one joint-stock bank was established in the kingdoms and states represented in the state council: the exchange society "Merkur" opened in Vienna in 1887 with capital of 1.2 million florins, which had increased to 1.8 million in 1891. Even two decades after the great speculative crisis, the entire practice of founding institutions still stood under the shadow of a critical breakdown.

Even the bond business had lost its importance since equilibrium had been restored in the state budget. Beginning in 1889, the issuing of new state securities had come to a stop in both halves of the kingdom. The continuing nationalization of the railways withdrew a broad field of activity from private capital.[33] The connection between the banks and industry was quite weak, the proceeds from running a business had not assumed the position in the banks' balance sheets that they enjoy today, and deposit banking was still in its infancy. It was therefore only natural for the banks to link large expectations to currency reform. In spite of this, it could be predicted that this would impact the foreign exchange business, because they promised substantial profits from the issuing of currency certificates and from the acquisition of gold for both governments, and hoped that the simultaneously enacted conversion of the 5 percent bond securities would enliven interest in dividend stocks.

32. [The Panic of 1873, which affected financial markets on both sides of the Atlantic, especially in the United States and Germany, broke out in Austria on May 9, 1873, with a crash of the Vienna stock exchange. This was followed by a series of major bank failures in Austria-Hungary, from which the Austrian financial sector only slowly recovered.—Ed.]

33. [In 1884, the Austrian government founded the Imperial General Directorate of the State Railways and began to nationalize the private railway companies. By 1914, out of about 23,000 kilometers of railway track in the Austrian Crownlands, the government owned and operated nearly 19,000 kilometers of it, or around 82 percent.—Ed.]

The prospect for large profits that could be made here appeared more appealing to the financial circles than the always doubtful increase in capital bonds. Contributing to this position may have been the fact that the assets of the large capitalists, the bankers and those personalities who directed the policy of the large banking institutions, were predominantly invested in dividend securities and less so in fixed-income-bearing bonds, so that their interests were more closely related to those of the manufacturers than those of the capitalists. The medium and smaller capitalists, mostly owners of public bonds, mortgage creditors, and investors in savings banks, did not have the possibility of effectively representing their endangered interests, because they did not have friends in the media nor in the parliament.

Among the opponents of currency reform that arose in parliament and in the media, the supporters of bimetallism earn a certain respect because two of the most distinguished leaders of the international bimetallism party, Eduard Sueß and Josef Neuwirt, appeared at their head. However, their efforts had to be limited to preventing the implementation of a gold currency in such a way that it would not prevent a possible future transition to a double currency. One could not speak about an implementation of bimetallism in Austria-Hungary alone; it was predictable that the monarchy by itself would not be able to establish a legal exchange rate between the two currency metals and that, under such circumstances, the transition to a double currency would be tantamount to a return to a pure silver currency.[34]

The primary argument of the bimetallists—the increase in the value of gold since 1873 and its counterpart, the general depression in the price of goods—was completely without effect in Austria, because the value of Austrian paper money experienced greater increases than that of international gold money. The political-economic interests demanded that a currency comparable to that in the Western European nations be established as soon as possible; this pushed into the background for the foreseeable future the demand for a money possessing an invariant purchasing power.

It can only be ascribed to the lack of clarity dominating the problem of the currency system that very few supporters of the international

---

34. Compare Karl Menger, "Die Valutaregulierung in Österreich-Ungarn," *Jahrbücher für Nationalökonomie und Statistik*, 3, p. 643.

double currency were to be found among the Austrian agriculturists and their close circles. The farmers in countries that had gold currencies were supporters of bimetallism, whose introduction would have meant a decrease in the purchasing power of money. For the monarchy, however, affiliation with an international bimetallism system, which was conceivable only because of the traditional exchange ratio of 1:15.5, would have increased the value of money. "For a country with a gold currency, the transition to bimetallism means a price increase, for Austria, on the other hand, a *direct* and *initial* drop in prices," explained the expert Benedikt in the currency inquiry, because the Austrian seller would initially receive the old amount for his export articles abroad, while those same articles would have a lower value domestically.[35]

With growing enlightenment about questions of currency policy, the number of bimetallists melted down. There were no supporters of a pure silver currency; this was understandable, since the fluctuations in the price of silver and the fear of a fast rise in value of the white metal if the silver proponents were victorious in North America had given the direct impulse for tackling currency reform in the first place.

One cannot gain a true picture of the position on the currency question held by the individual classes of citizens and interested groups from the reports of the parliamentary sessions or from the news media. Purely political considerations stepped into the foreground and pushed economic opinions into the background. The Croatian and the Young Czech representatives raised fervid opposition to the draft of the reform, because the motto and crest on the coins of the crown currency did not accommodate their constitutional claims. Otherwise, the Czech representatives declared themselves to be completely and fundamentally in agreement with a transition to a gold currency. It is significant for this type of opposition that a few years later their leader, Kaizl,[36] when finance minister, cooperated in the continuation of the reform efforts in a distinguished manner.

---

35. Compare *Sten. Protokolle*, p. 18; in addition, Lotz, *Schmollers Jahrbuch* 16, pp. 1255–56.
36. [Josef Kaizl (1854–1901) was appointed to a teaching position in 1879 at Charles University in Prague, and professor of political economy in 1883. He was a leader of the Young Czech movement that wanted greater Czech autonomy in the Austro-Hungarian Empire in the 1890s. He served as Austrian finance minister in 1898–99, the highest position ever held by a Czech in the Austrian government.—Ed.]

V

The currency reform met a truly serious and boisterous opposition in the then small, but active, Christian Social Party.

The gold currency was generally viewed with mistrust in the camp of the conservative parties. "The currency reform," opined Wilhelm Freiherr von Berger, was designed "in the interests of international commerce and international competition, that is, the global economy."[37] He continues, "our limited standpoint allows us to observe humanity in regard to its economic interests as members of naturally and historically determined economic areas; we see grave dangers for these economic interests from a gold currency that appears suitable for assisting the global economy; this is even ignoring for the moment that our monetary system will be abandoned to international gold speculation and exposed to all of the disadvantages associated with the circulation of an international currency." The advantage from the introduction of a gold currency was "mostly for those elements that believe they have an interest in the development and construction of the global economy, and these are big industry and the large mobile funds." These two are, by their nature, "cosmopolitan and international." On the other hand, "the rightly understood interests of all working classes of the truly producing people" depend "on the development of the fatherland as an autonomous national economic state, as an autonomous national customs and commercial area."[38]

The uncertain stance of the conservative parties regarding the currency question can be traced partially back to the fact that there were only a few men in their ranks who were capable of making an independent judgment about the difficult and complex problems of the monetary system. They included among their supporters many distinguished agriculturists, several merchants and industrial magnates, but hardly any banking experts, and their scientific party members had consistently dealt more with questions about agricultural and social policy than with policies about the monetary and credit systems. Even a man like Rudolf Meyer[39] considered the usual arguments of the bimetallists

---

37. Compare Berger, "Zur Währungs- und Valutaregulierungsfrage," *Monatsschrift für christliche Sozialreform* 13 (1890): 117.

38. Ibid., p. 118.

39. [Dr. Rudolf Meyer (1839–99), a German social historian and economist. He was forced to leave Germany because of a highly critical book against Bismarck and took refuge in Austria, where he soon became the inspirer of the Catholic party and the advocate of Catholic socialism. In 1881 he emigrated to the United States and then to Canada, but he returned to Austria

from gold currency countries to be applicable to the Austrian circumstances, and had nothing to say about the difficulties that arose for Austrian manufacturing from the sinking of the agio.[40]

Only the events on the foreign exchange market since 1888 and their consequences for agriculture have convinced the conservatives, little by little, that maintaining their opposition to the gold currency was out of place. Finance Minister Steinbach sought out the individual party clubs from the House of Representatives in May and June 1892 and issued explanations to the representatives about all of the important points of the currency question. Indeed, he succeeded in dispelling the misgivings of the agrarian supportive parties, and in winning the Polish Club and the Hohenwart Club, the two most powerful conservative, religious groups in the House, for the draft.

Only the Christian Social Party fought the draft reform proposal with great energy. They were not open even to the necessity of currency reform, and with good reason, as they primarily represented small manufacturing interests. The small manufacturer indeed had less to suffer under a decline in the foreign exchange rate, because he generally did not export anything; he was squeezed by a lack of capital and a lack of credit. The friends of "the little guy" opined that both could be traced back to the lack of circulating media of exchange and considered the most certain assistance to lie in the increase of the nation's money supply, best achieved through a "moderate" increase in state notes, and eventually through increasing the annual silver minting also, which, however, would be undertaken only for the state budget. The strongest attacks from this side targeted the government's intention of initiating the currency reform by borrowing a large amount of gold, the proceeds from which the state notes would be redeemed. At least it had to admit, it was claimed, that as a result the tax burdens would be increased and any possible tax reductions would be postponed.

All of these arguments, which had been brought forward by inflationists from all countries and at all times, were accepted by the friends of "our fathers' paper florin" to defend their standpoint.[41] The weapons

in 1889. He had established personal contacts with Karl Marx, and in the last decade of his life he wrote for the Marxist newspaper *Neue Zeit.*—Ed.]

40. See R. Meyer, *Zur Valutafrage* (Vienna, 1894); *Der Kapitalismus fin de siècle* (Vienna, Leipzig, 1894), pp. 357ff.

41. See in particular Schober, *Die Valutafrage* (Vienna, 1888) *Sonderausgabe des Zentrallblatt für die Gewerbegenossenschaften Österreichs* I; idem, *Die Valutaregulierung in Österreich* (Vienna, 1892); Mosser, *Zur Torheit der Goldwährung und der Valutaregulierung* (Triest,

with which these battles were fought were not always genteel; opponents did not lack for suspicions of and insults toward the "liberal, usurious, capitalistic, national economy." The objective accomplishments, in contrast, could hardly assert a claim for a serious respect; because even if one accepted all of the inflationist arguments and wanted to admit that "increasing the media of exchange in circulation means welfare and earthly happiness, decreasing misery by the same amount,"[42] a series of important considerations remain against the practical implementation of these plans.

When Prince Alois Liechtenstein[43] recommended "a rational, moderate inflation accommodating the needs of production but not anticipating them by too much,"[44] or Schober desired that the nation might equip the economy "with a sufficiently large amount of non-dwindling money,"[45] there was still nothing that could be learned about the goals and methods of a future monetary system policy.

Only Josef Ritter von Neupauer formulated a certain suggestion. Based on chartalist theory,[46] he supported maintaining the paper currency; he even wanted to replace the silver florin with notes. Money is, namely, "that which the state declares it to be." The purchasing power of money is dependent upon its quantity, its velocity of circulation, and the monetary requirements within its geographical area of use. The currency reform, with its transition to specie circulation, was not only squandering the people's capital, but also was fraught with disadvantages, since it would deprive the government of its ability to influence the value of money by increasing or decreasing the amount of media

1889); Neupauer, *Die Schäden und Gefahren der Valutaregulierung für die Staatsfinanzen, die Volkswirtschaft und die Kriegsbereitschaft* (Vienna, 1892); Gruber, *Nationales oder internationales Geld. Die Quintessenz der Währungsfrage* (Vienna, 1892); Schlesinger, *Gefahr im Verzuge. Gewinn 100 Millionen Kronen auf Kosten des Volkes* (Vienna, 1894); idem, *Volksgeld, Befreiung der Völker und Staaten aus den Klauen der Hochfinanz* (Vienna, 1896); idem, *1250 Millionen Kronen Volksgeschenk zur Erbauung von "k. k. Volksbahnen"* (Vienna, 1900).

42. See R. Meyer, *Kapitalismus*, p. 387.

43. [Prince Alois Liechtenstein (1850–1920), member of the Liechtenstein ruling family and radical member of the Austrian Christian social coalition. Served for a total of twenty years in the Austrian parliament as one of the leaders of the conservative clerical party and deputy of the peasants of Hartleb who above all demanded an abbreviation of compulsory school attendance.—Ed.]

44. Session in the House of Representatives, July 15, 1892.

45. See Schober, *Valutaregulierung*, p. 7.

46. [Chartalism called for a fiat, or paper, money system, under which new money is created through government spending. The word is derived from the Latin *charta*, meaning token or ticket.—Ed.]

of exchange in circulation. Indeed, money must not be *capriciously* increasable. "The natural obstacle to the increase in hard currency," however, can "be substituted by legal obstacles to the increase in state paper money under public control." One merely had to detect "an ideal measure of value" that would underlie economic policy. For this ideal measure, however, Neupauer proposed the relative market price of gold for Austrian currency notes. The legislature would have to ascertain a standard price for the yellow metal and decree "by how much the state administration would have to approximate this standard price and counterbalance fluctuations above or below a certain point by regulating the amount of money in circulation."[47]

It should be noted that if Neupauer's proposal had been adopted, which boils down to a type of calculation in terms of gold, the monarchy would have been unable to avoid the effects from a change in the price of gold, whether it were a devaluation due to production exceeding demand, or a rise in its price due to insufficient production. It is inconceivable why Neupauer did not want to endorse the free minting of gold coins according to parity at the standard price. This would offer a secure means against all increases in the international price of gold for the currency, and would place only low costs on the economy, if the circulation of state notes were retained at its entire amount. The primary failure in the Neupauer project, which it shares with all other inflationist proposals, by the way, is the lack of any clear observable indicator for measuring increases in the value of gold. Neupauer carefully skirts another obstacle with which similar proposals usually collide: we mean the difficulty of detecting a reliable criterion for an insufficiently supported demand for currency. Because he starts with the tacit understanding that all other states will retain specie in circulation, a benchmark for the value of the paper currency results directly from its international appraisal. The goal of monetary policy for maintaining the value of money becomes maintaining its parity with a foreign currency; however, the methods that lead to this goal will remain obscure for now. No one can say what effect an increase in the media of exchange by a certain amount is capable of generating. Even Neupauer had to concede this, since he says there might be "by way of a test, a successive increase in media of exchange to be placed in circulation." The economy, however, is not a suitable object for tests.

---

47. See Neupauer, *Schäden and Gefahren*, pp. 1, 3, 25–26.

It should be assumed with all probability that even the news that a potential increase in the state note circulation was impending (albeit only under legally determined preconditions) would have forced down the price for Austrian money further than would have appeared healthy even to many of the friends of "cheap money." To what steps would the moderate inflationists then turn? It could have easily come about that the increasing agio would have gone hand in hand with insufficient supply of money in circulation.

The mistrust within market circles and among the broadest classes of the population against any new issuance of notes would have been completely justified. Once such a basis for influencing the value of the currency had been accepted, who could have assured that the agricultural and bourgeois interests (that have prevailed for a quarter century in our politics) would not have soon been pushing for an endless progression on the way to inflation. Where would this have led, if Josef Schlesinger's[48] People's Money fantasy had become law?

A rational and feasible monetary policy can only make preservation of the stability of the currency's exchange rate its goal; in the first place, the only means to adhere to this is to maintain specie in circulation, and under the current circumstances this means keeping gold in circulation. Every attempt to promote a single interest group through selective changes in the value of money must inherently fail, ignoring all other reasons, because the economic effects of this kind of measure are only temporary; in order to maintain those effects there would have to be a continuing increase of the notes. This could, however, end in no other way than with a complete devaluation of the money in circulation.[49]

VI

The power relationships between the parties concerned with monetary policy at the time of tackling currency reform were generally in favor of the introduction of a gold currency. Unimportant in number and influence were those who advocated the maintenance of the current monetary system, because they expected a continuing increase in the value of money. To wit, these were solely the possessors of monetary

48. [Josef Schlesinger (1831–1901) was an Austrian scientist, philosopher of science, and politician who championed paper money and its expansion as a means to prosperity.—Ed.]
49. See also Helfferich, *Geld und Banken* (Leipzig, 1903), vol. 1, pp. 528ff.

claims. All other interest groups desired a change in the currency that would offer, at a minimum, a halt to the continuing "improvements" of the value of the currency; all manufacturers belonged to this group, and also the workers and employees, whose interests here went hand in hand with those of their employers. Even high finance, which had substantial words to say about currency questions, was found to be on this side. Admittedly, the opponents of the current currency system were not united in their views about the structure of a future system. However, the efforts to create a "national," inflationist monetary system were completely futile.

Voices that spoke for the adoption of a gold-backed currency included those speaking for trade and manufacturing interests, and also those voices supporting the gold currency doctrine, the tenet starting from Lord Liverpool's theory,[50] developed further by Bamberger[51] and Soetbeer,[52] and which remained unshakably standing despite all of the bimetallist attacks. They found solely in the yellow metal a suitable basis for the currency system of a cultured people.

Thus, the question of implementing a metallic currency was already decided before the actual discussions about the reform project had even begun, and general interest had already turned to the so-called relation. This was the point where the parties' differences most vehemently collided. One ascribed the greatest economic importance to the gold content of the future monetary unit. All investigations about the economic goals and the results of the reform began with the question of the parity exchange relationship.

The importance of the question—whether the new florins would be

---

50. [Robert Banks Jenkinson, Second Earl of Liverpool (1770–1828), served as British prime minister for thirty years, leading Britain into an era of unparalleled economic and national triumph. A follower of Adam Smith and steadfast defender of sound economic principles and a specie standard, Lord Liverpool strongly opposed the possibility of maintaining a paper money.—Ed.]

51. [Ludwig Bamberger (1823–99), a German economist and publicist, a leading authority on currency problems in Germany. Originally a radical, he became a moderate liberal in Bismarck's Germany, and in 1871 he entered the Reichstag as a National Liberal. He advocated the standardization of the German coinage, adoption of the gold standard, and establishment of the Reichsbank. He supported Bismarck's outlawing of the Socialist Party and attempts to nationalize the railways, but he opposed Bismarck's policy of protective tariffs, state socialism, and colonial expansion.—Ed.]

52. [Adolf Soetbeer (1814–92), a German economist and a secretary of the Hamburg Chamber of Commerce, ranked as the leading defender of the pure gold standard, the adoption of which by Germany was brought about largely through his efforts. He wrote numerous monographs and pamphlets defending the cause of gold monometallism.—Ed.]

minted lighter or heavier—was neither to be denied nor underestimated. If one had selected, instead of the parity set by law in August at a base of 2 francs, 10 centimes, a lighter florin of approximately 2 francs or a heavier florin of approximately 2 francs, 50 centimes (the known proposals that were made about the value of the florin fluctuated within these boundaries), this certainly would have exerted a deep and enduring effect on the entire economic system of the monarchy, and the results of such a revolutionary change to the value of money would only have been settled much later. However, there could be no discussion of such a drastic "reform" of the value of the Austrian currency.

The proposals receiving serious consideration for the future exchange value of the currency did not deviate more greatly from each other than the actual fluctuations of the exchange rate on the Viennese market during times of intense movement within a few months or even weeks. That the exchange rate resulting from the currency reform would not essentially depart from 119 was considered to be agreed upon by market circles already one and a half years prior to the introduction of the draft reform in the State Council; and, indeed, it was this fact that constantly pinched the currency rate beginning in fall 1890, far more so than the much discussed gold purchases by the Hungarian government. Also, the apparent difference between average market price and current price, which played a large role in the publicized debates about the draft, lost its importance upon closer examination, particularly if one took into consideration that the difference between these two prices became ever smaller and completely disappeared on the day of the introduction of the draft in the two parliaments, which can certainly be traced back to the activities of currency speculation.

The belief that lay behind the excessive emphasis on the importance of the "relation" in agricultural circles and among commercial manufacturers and the scientific discussions about the currency question (the suspense with which the market followed the battle between the light and heavy florins requires no further explanation) was that the value of money in domestic commerce would not, or would not immediately, change according to the change in the value of the currency on the global market. Or, in other words, it was considered possible, with the transfer to the new currency system, to "eternalize" the currency differential between the Austrian currency and those of the gold currency countries. This view is based, however, on an error. Sooner or later, the prices of all domestic goods and services will adjust to the change in value of money, and the advantages that a devalued currency offers to production, and the obstacles that an overvalued one sets against production, will disappear. This is because the agio as such does not function as an export premium or as a protective tariff; rather, it is merely the *increasing* agio, or inversely only the *decreasing* agio, not the low agio in itself, that is able to check exports and boost imports.

The importance of currency policy in relation to currency reform did not lie in the higher or lower "relation," but rather in that the monarchy converted from a monetary system with a currency that was increasing in value compared with the currencies of the economic Great Powers, to a monetary system with a currency that was stable abroad.

The Act of August 2, 1892, admittedly only arrested the increase in the value of the Austrian currency. Since August 11, 1892, the day that it came into effect, the value of the Austrian florin (2 crowns) essentially cannot rise above the value of 2 francs, 10 centimes or 1 mark, 70.12 pfennig. In contrast, no legal barricade was placed against a decrease in the value of money. This should become impossible in the future due to the implementation of specie payments, which was considered by the creators of the reform act to be its conclusion.

It is certain that the implementation of specie payments was initially postponed only because for its assurance sufficient provisions, most notably the accumulation of a correspondingly large stockpile of precious metal in the bank's vaults, were necessary, and a favorable configuration of circumstances on the international currency markets had to be awaited. However, it also appeared just as certain that, precisely due to the fact that only a further increase in the value of money had been made provisionally impossible by the adoption of the draft reform, the chance of a possible decrease in the value of money, if one might even discuss such a thing, by contrast remained open, and had assisted in the victory of the reform project. By agreeing to currency reform, the friends of "cheap money" sacrificed nothing and won a great deal: the establishment of an upper limit to the value of money.

The further fate of currency reform admittedly has turned out differently than even the most highly informed circles could have predicted in 1892. After the events on the international currency market in 1893 and 1896 had placed the success of currency reform in doubt, the foreign exchange policy of the Austro-Hungarian Bank, inaugurated in 1896, established the stability of the currency, including a lower limit. It should be noted, however, that this bank policy, initially suggested in 1894 by the then Austrian Finance Minister Ernst von Plener,[53] resulted absolutely from the initiative of governmental agencies that were accommodating the desires of the business world. Up until now, it had undergone neither an exhaustive parliamentary criticism nor a corresponding appraisal from the political parties.

Only through the bank's intervention on the foreign exchange market was the stabilization of the price of the Austrian currency achieved on both ends, and thereby the currency question was solved for the monarchy. Whether specie payments are to be implemented or not is a question of expediency and of the discount policy, in which currency policy considerations play only a limited role. No rational person on this or the other side of the Leitha[54] would advocate today against the gold currency.

---

53. [Ernst von Plener (1841–1923), an Austrian statesman, a prominent member of the Constitutional party and one of the leaders of the German classical liberals. In 1893–95 served as Austrian minister of finance.—Ed.]

54. [The Leitha, a river in Central Europe that is approximately 180 km. long, was part of the Austrian-Hungarian border until 1921. "Beyond the Leitha" was the Viennese colloquial term for Hungary, while "on this side of the Leitha" meant the region around Vienna, that is, Austria.—Ed.]

CHAPTER 2

The Problem of Legal Resumption
of Specie Payments in Austria-Hungary[1]

I
Process of Currency Regulation Since 1892

The currency reform that began in Austria-Hungary in 1892, and for whose introduction great material sacrifices were required by the two halves of the empire, still awaits formal conclusion through the legal resumption of specie payments. At the present time, the lawful money of the monarchy remains a paper currency. The Austro-Hungarian Bank is still relieved of the obligation to redeem its notes in specie, a legal status that remains indefinitely in force.

Admittedly, the experts believe that Austria-Hungary would be quite capable of completing the transition to a gold currency, and that the Austro-Hungarian Bank would be able to comply with all of the obligations that would arise from the legal resumption of specie payments.

Nevertheless, the desire to complete this great reform is small in both Austria and Hungary (as can be seen in the most recently concluded Bank inquiry), and there is no lack of voices that speak out against the legal resumption of specie payments. The present monetary regime, which might be described as a paper currency with gold reserves for foreign exchange transactions, or as a Bank-supported paper currency, would have its "temporary" character transformed into the permanent monetary system of the monarchy. The establishment of this fundamentally different monetary system is claimed to have its rationale in the monetary systems existing in other European countries. The arguments for this system are important enough that they deserve a detailed analysis.

1. The present work was completed at the beginning of December 1908. [This article originally appeared in German in the *Jahrbuch für Gesetzgebung, Verwaltung und Volkswirtschaft (Schmollers Jahrbuch)*, vol. 33, no. 3 (1909).—Ed.].

Up until the second half of the 1880s, manufacturers in Austria-Hungary had adjusted themselves to a paper currency, following the ending of a silver-backed currency for private transactions. The value of the Austrian currency was accepted to be in continuous decline in relation to the currencies of other countries on a gold standard. The price of 100 florins in gold (250 francs) in 1872 was, on average, 110.37 Austrian paper florins; beginning that year (with a small interruption), it continued to go up to 125.23 Austrian paper florins in 1887. Both agricultural and industrial producers benefited from this deterioration in the exchange rate. The increase in the foreign exchange rate at the Viennese bourse functioned like a protective tariff on the import of foreign manufactured items and served as an export premium for domestic products sold abroad; it also benefited borrowers at the expense of creditors. Under these circumstances, plans for monetary reform could not depend on much support from either the industrial or agricultural sectors.

The situation reversed itself beginning in 1888, and the value of the Austrian currency began to increase (the price for 100 florins in gold amounted to an average of only 115.48 Austrian paper florins in 1890). Suddenly the manufacturers and exporters who were harmed by the higher valuation of the currency understandably became supporters of the monetary reform that they had fought for years. In general, the belief was widely held that the increase in the exchange rate that began in 1888 was most likely neither a coincidental nor temporary event; instead, it could be traced back to deeper economic causes. There was considerable agreement that the fall in the agio would not stop of its own accord; indeed, it would continue at an increasing rate in the years ahead if a change in the currency was not introduced in a timely manner.

This view was completely justified. The general economic and political situation produced a continuous improvement in the monarchy's balance of payments, and as a result the foreign demand for Austrian exchange was increasing and the Austrian demand for foreign exchange was decreasing. At the time, there was absolutely no indication that this relationship would change in the years ahead.

The adoption of gold as a basis for the Austro-Hungarian monetary system appeared to be the most suitable way to prevent any further increase in the exchange rate, even though up to that time gold had never been used in the Austrian monetary system. To completely stop any further declines in the foreign exchange rate on the Viennese bourse, the answer was to legally bring the paper florin into a fixed relationship with gold and to obligate the Austro-Hungarian Bank to exchange all amounts of gold offered for banknotes at that rate. This was the approach taken by the legislature. Beginning on August 11, 1892, the effective date of the new exchange rate law, the value of one Austrian florin (2 crowns expressed in the new denomination) essentially could not increase above the value of 2 francs, 10 centimes or 1 mark, 70.1 pfennig.

It was, however, just as important to limit any fluctuation in the value of the Austrian currency at the lower range of the exchange rate. Even if the Christian Social Party (which at that time was rather small and not strong enough to push through all of their demands) had vigorously resisted every step taken to prevent an inflationary bias, the two governments and the majorities of both parliaments were in agreement: the fixing of the international value of the Austro-Hungarian exchange rate was necessary to completely eliminate the speculative activities that had come about as a result of the continuing fluctuations in the exchange rate. The most effective method for achieving this goal would be an immediate transition to a gold standard. Moreover, another positive factor behind the currency reform was the opportunity to improve the international creditworthiness of both halves of the monarchy; Western foreign countries had complete confidence only in nations that were on a gold standard.

There was no clear provision in the Monetary Reform Act of August 2, 1892, detailing the transition to a gold-backed currency. Such a provision would have had little meaning, since the transition to a gold-backed currency required extensive and costly preparations, and could be completed only at a later date. The task had to be approached, therefore, with the greatest caution in order to prevent a disaster similar to the one that occurred a little earlier in Italy, which had delayed the establishment of a fixed exchange rate. Thus the final transition to a gold currency was, in fact, put off; however, continuous efforts were being applied in preparation for it.

Initially, the state notes were taken out of circulation at a fixed rate of exchange. This happened in the following manner: gold proceeds from a large government bond issue were transferred to the Austro-Hungarian Bank, so the Bank could redeem the notes on behalf of the state. However, the redemption of the state notes did not initially take place in exchange for gold; they were redeemed through the issuing of banknotes, of silver florins that up until then had been held as reserves in the vaults of the Bank, and of five-crown and one-crown coins. Even today, the silver florins are face-value coins, just like the earlier German Taler; in contrast, the five-crown and one-crown coins are token coins, and no one is obligated in private transactions to accept in payment more than 250 crowns of the first type or 50 crowns of the second type. Provisionally, the gold remained in the Bank as backing for the notes, with the proviso, however, that at a later point in time the gold would enter into circulation in place of a large portion of the banknotes.

Banknotes took the place of the irredeemable state notes at a fixed rate of exchange. From then and up to the present the Bank's notes are irredeemable at a fixed rate of exchange. The great progress lay in the fact, however, that under the provisions of the statutes of the Bank, the banknotes were backed by gold and were negotiable, while the state notes had no backing. In addition, it should be mentioned that the gold reserves of the Bank were considerably increased through purchases from private importers as well. The reserves amounted to 1,099.3 million crowns on December 31, 1907, and were at that time exceeded in size only by the gold reserves held by the Bank of France and by the Russian State Bank.[2]

The only type of currency that currently stands in the way of the introduction of the pure, gold-backed currency, as it would be represented in Bamberger's ideal,[3] is the silver florin, whose minting had been reserved for the government after 1879 and which has been discontinued since 1892. As has already been mentioned, the silver florin is still a legal, face-value coin; however, it is no longer of great importance. At the end of 1904, the monarchy's entire inventory amounted to 336 million crowns in silver florins, according to estimates by the Austrian Finance Ministry. Due to the agreed-upon minting of an additional 64 million crowns in five-crown coins, which already had been partially implemented, the amount has decreased to 272 million crowns. The increasing demand for the monarchy's token coins should

2. About the course and the motives of the entire reform, see Spitzmüller, "Die österreichisch-ungarische Währungsreform," *Zeitschrift für Volkswirtschaft, Sozialpolitik und Verwaltung*, vol. 11, pp. 337ff., 496ff.; Mises, "The Political-Economic Motives of the Austrian Currency Reform," Chapter 1 in this volume; Knapp, *Staatliche Theorie des Geldes* (Leipzig, 1905), pp. 377ff.
3. [See Chapter 1, "The Political-Economic Motives of the Austrian Currency Reform," footnote 51.—Ed.]

be able to absorb this remaining amount in at least two decades, even at a modest increase in the token coins. Any threat to the gold-backed currency is thus not to be feared from this corner.

Incidentally, the silver florin has been slowly withdrawn from circulation since the beginning of 1908, and they are being accumulated in the Bank's vaults. At the end of October 1908, with the minting of the new five-crown coins currently under way, the entire sum of silver florins may have amounted to slightly more than 300 million crowns, of which 285 million were held by the Bank, with the remaining 15 million being in circulation.[4]

During the summer and autumn of 1892, the foreign exchange rate corresponded fairly closely to the underlying parity of the currency's exchange rate (100 Austrian florins = 170.1215 marks); indeed, it even dropped substantially below this rate for intermittent periods. Toward the end of the year it began to increase, and this unfavorable relationship continued for the next two years. An agio emerged in relation to the ratio established in the law of August 2, 1892, that temporarily even reached 6.5 percent.

The reason behind this unexpected drop in the value of the Austrian currency, whose continuing increase in value had been viewed as something to be prevented, was due to, as Kalkmann has conclusively shown,[5] the simultaneous financial squeeze on the international monetary market. In 1892, when the rate of interest was low for the English, Dutch, and Germans, they had loaned money to the Austrians and bought Austrian notes. As a result of the Australian crisis in May 1893,[6] the interest rate rose in London and then in Berlin and Amsterdam as well; the English, Dutch, and German investors now sought to pull their monies out of Austria as quickly as possible. They sent to Vienna the Austrian notes that they had in their possession and demanded payment. Since this could almost only take place through remittance of gold, the price of gold rose immediately and significantly on the Viennese bourse in line with the increase in the London private discount rate. The high discount rate on the foreign stock markets depressed the

---

4. See *Der österreichische Volkswirt*, Oct. 31, 1908.
5. See Kalkmann, *Die Entwertung der österreichischen Valuta und ihre Ursachen* (Freiburg i.B., 1899), pp. 1ff.; "Die Diskont- und Devisenpolitik der österreichisch-ungarischen Bank (1892–1902)," *Zeitschrift für Volkswirtschaft, Sozialpolitik und Verwaltung* 12, pp. 463ff.
6. [A speculative bubble in the Australian property market in the 1880s finally started to burst when the Federal Bank of Australia "failed" in January 1893. In May of that year, eleven commercial banks suspended trading, leading to a severe financial crisis.—Ed.]

prices of Austrian and Hungarian investments even more, and caused a large reverse flow of funds that at the same time contributed to the decline of the exchange rate.

The devaluation of the Austrian currency in 1893 was only one link in a long chain of events that occurred as part of the effects on Europe from the Australian and American crises. The government, however, was not guilt-free, insofar as it entered the Western currency markets and aggravated the strain on them at the most unfavorable moment imaginable; that is to say, by issuing 100 million florins in gold bonds and by withdrawing gold assets from abroad.

The government of the Dual Monarchy would have had to undertake two measures in order to prevent the increasing agio. The first measure would have been the release of gold or gold exchange at the parity ratio fixed by the law of 1892. However, the Ministry of Finance was against this, being afraid that this would result in the loss of the gold reserves after those reserves had only recently been regained through great sacrifice. Furthermore, the outcome would have been in doubt. In spring 1893, the Austrian Credit-Anstalt for Commerce and Industry repeatedly made large amounts of foreign exchange available to the market, but without any noticeable effect. The attempted lending of foreign exchange by the Austro-Hungarian Bank had just as little effect.

A satisfactory outcome could have resulted only if the Bank had followed an energetic interest rate policy. However, that would have been impossible because the two governments, influenced more by political considerations than by economic ones, attempted to keep the rate of interest low, and by lending large amounts of money, they tried to create an artificial quantity of credit on the markets. On August 2, 1893, the Bank of England increased its discount rate from 2.5 percent to 3 percent; on August 9, from 3 percent to 4 percent; and on August 23, from 4 percent to 5 percent. While doing so, it announced that additional increases in the discount rate would be forthcoming, and soon rumors circulated that it would not balk at increasing its official discount rate to 10 percent, if the outflows of gold did not end soon. The German Reichsbank had already increased its official discount rate to 5 percent on August 11, and it was officially announced in Berlin that the Reichsbank planned to align its discount rate in accordance with London in order to protect its gold reserves. The Austro-Hungarian Bank, however, persisted with its discount rate at 4 percent, even though the agio on the Austrian currency was constantly increasing and already equaled 5 percent by mid-August; as late as September 27, the Hungarian finance minister, Weckerle, spoke out in parliament against any increase in the discount rate. Only on October 5, when the decline in the currency's value was already very noticeable on Western markets, did the Bank increase the discount rate to 5 percent.

The definite improvement in international currency markets allowed even the Austrian foreign exchange rate to soon rise again. On November 9, 1893, the London foreign exchange rate achieved its highest level on the Viennese bourse, reaching 127.65. This rate marked a devaluation of 6.3 percent compared with the new parity of 120.087. Over the course of November, the agio fell extremely fast. After the London foreign exchange rate had fallen again to almost 125.00 on December 19, and then temporarily increased to 126.00 on February 1, 1894, it fell slowly but fairly constantly throughout 1894 and 1895. On October 17, 1895, for the first time again, the foreign exchange rate stood at parity.

From that point onward, the foreign exchange rates followed a less extreme trend. Since 1896, they have diverged no further from the parity ratio than would be the case following the legal resumption of specie payments. The small deviations from parity that could arise would be within the two gold points, that is, considering the costs of transporting gold coins, the wear and tear on the weight of coins circulating within the country's borders, the costs of minting, and the loss of interest income during their minting and transportation.

Arithmetic Mean of the Average Deviation of the Currency Rate of the Most Important Foreign Exchange Rates Recorded at the Viennese Bourse from the Parity Ratio, Represented in Percent Values (+ over, – under the parity ratio).[7]

Year	Berlin	Paris	London	Arithmetic mean
1892	−0.5	−0.5	−0.6	−0.5
1893	+3.2	+3.2	+3.1	+3.2
1894	+4.0	+4.1	+3.8	+4.0
1895	+1.4	+1.5	+1.5	+1.5
1896	+0.1	+0.2	+0.1	+0.1

7. See Zuckerkandl, "Österreichisch-Ungarische Bank," *Handwörterbuch der Staatswissenschaften*, 3rd ed., vol. II, p. 450, and the statistical sources cited there. [Robert Zuckerkandl, "The Austro-Hungarian Bank," translated in *Banking in Russia, Austria-Hungary, the Netherlands, and Japan* (Washington, D.C.: Government Printing Office, 1911), pp. 55–118.—Ed.]

Year	Berlin	Paris	London	Arithmetic mean
1897	−0.1	−0.1	−0.4	−0.2
1898	+0.1	−0.1	+0.2	+0.1
1899	+0.3	+0.4	+0.4	+0.4
1900	+0.6	+1.1	+0.8	+0.8
1901	−0.2	+0.1	−0.2	−0.1
1902	−0.3	+0.1	−0.2	−0.1
1903	−0.3	0	−0.3	−0.2
1904	−0.3	0	−0.2	−0.2
1905	−0.174	+0.229	−0.040	+0.005
1906	−0.146	+0.296	+0.095	+0.082
1907	+0.019	+0.437	+0.309	+0.255

From these numbers, it can be seen without a doubt that, since 1896, the Austrian currency has been able to match any of the European gold currencies in terms of the stability of its value.

As a result of the apparently successful achievement of a stable intercurrency exchange rate, which was the intended purpose of the currency reform, the two governments brought forward a bill before both parliaments in spring 1903 that had as its purpose the legal resumption of specie payments as the "crown" (as it was called) to the efforts for monetary reform. Because of the major political crisis that soon broke out, the bill never came up for parliamentary consideration, let alone for final passage. In the meantime, the proposals brought forward by the previous liberal government had become totally meaningless in the face of the complete change in the Hungarian government, and as a result, Austrian Minister Beck formally withdrew the bill on July 7, 1906.

Throughout this time, public opinion in Austria had remained negative toward the proposal. Of considerable importance were the opinions of the Industrial Council and the statements made by the Chambers of Commerce and Industry in Vienna and Brünn.[8] These views were summarized and detailed in a series of newspaper articles. At the present time, it can be said with good reason that opposition to the legal resumption of specie payments and the reasons for taking this position are shared by all of the major Austrian political parties.[9] Even

8. See *Verhandlungen und Beschlüsse des Industrierates*, issue 9, "Die Aufnahme der Barzahlungen" (Vienna, 1905), pp. 1ff.; *Sitzungsberichte der Handels- und Gewerbekammer für das Erzherzogtum Österreich unter den Enns*, 1903 (Sitzung vom 12. Mai 1903 und Beilage Nr. 6); *Verhandlungen der Handels- und Gewerbekammer in Brünn* (Beilage Nr. 2 zum Protokoll der Sitzung vom 9. November 1903).

9. See *Neue Freie Presse*, July 18, 1907 (report about the explanations offered by the representatives of the German National Party, the Christian Social Party, and the Polish Club Party in

the government appears to have aligned itself with this view, having abandoned its previous position and claiming to have found a theoretical support for this view in Knapp's *Staatlicher Theorie des Geldes* [The State Theory of Money].[10]

The legal resumption of specie payments is said to be too risky, in view of the uncertainty of future events on the international currency market and the unsettled political situation at home. Its only purpose, it is claimed, is to assure the stability of the foreign exchange rate, which has already been achieved without legalized specie redemption due to the Austro-Hungarian Bank's foreign exchange policy. The legal introduction of specie payments would require the Bank to resort to more frequent and larger increases in the discount rate in order to protect its gold reserves. This would drive up the cost of borrowing, which would in turn put obstacles in the way of manufacturing. The relatively low discount rate in Austria was made possible only by the fact that the Bank was not obligated to redeem its notes. Even in times of great tension on the international currency markets, the Bank could keep the interest rate appropriately low, because it did not have to fear that its gold reserves would be withdrawn for the purpose of being sent abroad when the price of gold made it seem right to do so.

A critical examination of these views must attempt, above all, to determine the fundamentals of the Bank's foreign exchange policy.

II
The Position of the Austro-Hungarian Bank on the Currency and Foreign Exchange Markets

The foundation of the currency reform activities of the Austro-Hungarian Bank is based on the near total concentration of the gold reserves of the monarchy within the Bank, along with foreign gold reserves in possession of the Bank.

---

the budget committee of the House of Representatives); about the position of the Social Democrats, see *Arbeiter-Zeitung*, October 23, 1907.

10. [Georg Friedrich Knapp (1842–1926) made his reputation as a statistician specializing in mortality problems. He also wrote on the history of German agriculture in the eastern territories. He was considered a leading member of a group known as the "Socialists of the Chair," who advocated state socialism under imperial paternalism in Germany before the First World War. In 1905, Knapp published *The State Theory of Money*, in which he argued that the selection, use, and value of money were matters of government regulation, independent of the market. For a summary and an insightful critical analysis of Knapp's argument, see Edwin Cannan's review of *The State Theory of Money* in *Economica* (June 1925), pp. 212–16.—Ed.]

The gold reserves of the Austro-Hungarian Bank amounted to:

Millions of crowns	At the end of the year
919.6	1900
1,116.1	1901
1,107.3	1902
1,109.5	1903
1,153.0	1904
1,074.1	1905
1,112.2	1906
1,099.1	1907

In comparison with these gold reserves, which as was mentioned are exceeded in amount in Europe only by those held by the Bank of France and the Russian Central Bank, the amount of gold still freely in circulation does not add up to very much.

The designers of the reform of 1892, which was in most respects modeled after the German monetary system, planned for a fairly wide circulation of gold inside the domestic economy. According to their plan, small transactions would be handled by silver, nickel, and bronze token coins, and medium-size transactions by face-value gold coins, while banknotes would be used only for large transactions, insofar as these could not be replaced through improved uses of checks, bank transfers, and the clearing mechanism. Accordingly, in Article 82 of the Bank Statutes, which were changed by an imperial decree on September 21, 1899, a provision was added that banknotes were not to be allowed in amounts smaller than 50 crowns. The issuing of twenty-crown notes would be permitted only until the time of the legal resumption of specie payments. On the other hand, the issuance of ten-crown notes to a maximum amount of 160 million crowns was also planned for the period following the introduction of specie payments. These latter notes could not be seen, however, as banknotes in the usual sense; it would be more correct to designate them as gold certificates because they had to be fully backed at all times by gold.[11]

The time was seemingly drawing near in 1901 when the Bank would be prepared to resume legal redemption in gold, since it was already doing so, on demand, though not as yet so obligated. In anticipation of this, the Bank began to issue ten- and twenty-crown gold coins at the end of August 1901, since at the time of legal resumption all smaller

11. See *Die neuen Valuta- und Bankgesetze*, edition and notes by Calligaris (Vienna, 1901), pp. 121ff., 324ff., 347f.

notes up to 20 crowns were supposed to be removed from circulation. It was thought that the twenty-crown notes could more easily be taken out of circulation if this was done at the same time that they were replaced with gold coins. In addition, as the population became accustomed to the use of gold coins, it would be easier to determine what the actual demand for them would be throughout the empire. Another way of determining the demand for them would be by simply determining the amount of twenty-crown notes in circulation. Concerns were expressed, however, about the amounts that might be needed to meet the demands in the rural areas due to a fear that the population there might hoard the gold coins. As was soon demonstrated, concerns of this type were completely unfounded.

To the great surprise of the government and the Bank, the public's opinion about the gold coins turned out to be quite negative. It had been expected that the population would greet the appearance of a gold currency with jubilation and see in it a demonstration of the success of the currency reform. Instead, the people who had grown to adulthood under the reign of paper money found the use of gold coins to be uncomfortable. The five-crown coins, silver florins, and one-crown coins, which had been placed in circulation after 1892, could be kept in circulation only because the one- and five-florin state notes had been withdrawn at the same time. Everyone who received the gold coins in payment attempted to exchange them for notes as quickly as they could, so the gold soon flowed back into the Bank.[12]

National Gold Crown Coins Placed in Circulation by the Austro-Hungarian Bank[13]

In the period from		Disbursed	Returned to bank	Remained in circulation
			Millions of crowns	
Aug. 24 to Dec. 31	1901	61.1	5.6	55.5
	1902	192.3	114.5	133.3
	1903	162.2	136.5	159.0
Jan. 1 to	1904	256.2	204.8	210.4
Dec. 31	1905	481.3	400.5	291.2
	1906	256.6	292.6	255.2
	1907	206.7	227.1	234.8

12. See *Jahresbericht der Wiener Börsenkammer für 1901* (Vienna, 1902), pp. 78f.
13. See Zuckerkandl, op. cit., p. 450.

Additionally, a smaller amount of 10 million crowns was placed in circulation by the Hungarian government by the end of March 1903.

At the beginning of 1908, therefore, there was at most 234.8 million crowns in circulation (ignoring the insignificant amounts placed in circulation by the Hungarian government, and about which no particulars are available). Considering the stability of the foreign exchange rate, it may be assumed that the coins in circulation did not flow out of the country in any considerable amount. On the other hand, it is certain that a large portion of the coins remained in the coffers of the government and in the vaults of the large banking institutions, and so on.

The actual amount in circulation, therefore, is thus found to be considerably lower than the maximum cited above. Even this smaller amount of gold was kept in circulation by artificial methods, with the exchequer trying to make its payments in small amounts of gold, often against the desire of the recipients. It is worth noting that, as was stressed in the 1903 report on guidelines for implementing specie payments, "recently the circulation of twenty-crown coins has been decidedly in decline, while the circulation of ten-crown coins has shown a fairly sustained increase. This leads to the conclusion that in view of the undeniable public distaste for using gold coins, the issuing of ten-crown notes that was set at 160 million crowns by an imperial decree on September 21, 1899, has turned out to be too low given the demand for notes of this denomination."[14] Bilinski came to the same conclusion when he referred, in particular, to the use of ten-crown coins in industrial areas.[15]

In the 1903 draft proposing the legal resumption of specie payments, the government completely dropped the position it had maintained up to that point concerning the denomination of notes and withdrew its opposition to the issuance of smaller notes. Paragraph 2 of the draft gave the Bank the right to issue ten- and twenty-crown banknotes, even after the legal resumption of specie payments; however, this was done with different regulations concerning the backing of these notes. These notes were to be completely backed by precious metals up to

14. See *Beilagen 1718 zu den stenographischen Protokollen des Abgeordnetenhauses*, 17th session, 1903, p. 4.
15. See Bilinski, "On International Payments," lecture in the special session of the 4th Polish judicial and political economics conference in Krakow on October 2, 1906, translated from the Polish, p. 6. (This important essay, which is not available in print, was made available to me by the secretary general of the Austro-Hungarian Bank in the most considerate manner.)

an amount of 400 million crowns; for any quantity in circulation that exceeded this amount, the same regulations would apply as those for other notes issued by the Bank that were backed by gold.

Thus, in a very short time, the government's view on the question of the size of the denomination of notes and, therefore, on the question of how much gold would actually be in circulation had undergone a surprising change. It would be incorrect to assert that this reversal primarily was due to the experience of what happened after the gold coins had been placed in circulation. Similar experiences are to be found in other countries, without this leading to a change in government policy. Most recently in Russia, though gold coins were initially rejected, they were still forced on commercial transactions.[16]

Over the years, the Austrian government has not objected to imposing great inconveniences on the market if it was seen as furthering an important, or allegedly important, public interest. The relatively minor inconvenience that the citizenry experienced due to their unfamiliarity with gold coins would have been easy for them to get over. It is probably more accurate to say that the Finance Ministry had, in the meantime, discovered the great economic impact that is inherent in the concentration of the national gold reserves in the central bank. The reports about the reasons behind reform policy decisions offer many clues in this direction; on the other hand, the practices of the Bank and the exchequer to constantly try to put gold into circulation appear oddly in contrast with that.

The monarchy's gold reserves for foreign exchange were not concentrated to the same degree as the gold reserves in the Bank's possession; the monarchy still had control of large amounts in foreign exchange and other assets held in foreign accounts.

After the Austro-Hungarian Bank had acquired large amounts in foreign exchange, the Statute of 1862 (Plener's Bank Act) formally granted it a qualification in paragraph 20: "for the maintenance of a corresponding ratio between its holdings of the precious metals (coined and uncoined gold and silver) and the banknotes in circulation, it may buy or sell foreign exchange at locations abroad." However, only the edict circulated by the Ministry of Finance on October 30, 1868, in fulfillment of the law of June 30, 1868, gave the Bank permission to include negotiable foreign exchange as backing for the Bank's notes. In the cri-

16. See Claus, *Das russische Bankwesen* (Leipzig, 1908), pp. 41, 141.

sis during summer 1870, the Bank provisionally was granted the authority to include in its portfolio foreign exchange along with the precious metal as backing for notes in circulation.

In Article 111 of the 1887 Bank Statute, the Bank was, in general, permitted "for as long as the fixed exchange of state notes is not abolished in both parts of the Dual Monarchy, to include as part of their specie reserves any foreign exchange (up to a maximum amount of 30 million florins) that are held in locations abroad, and which are legally payable in a currency backed by the precious metals." The purpose of this regulation was to transform a part of the Bank's holdings of precious metals into interest-earning assets, and, thus, increase the stock dividends of the Bank and the portion of the Bank's profits that went to the state.[17]

Under Article 111 of the Bank Statute of September 21, 1899 (which is still in effect) the Bank is permitted, for as long as its obligation to redeem its notes in legal hard currency is suspended, to include as part of its specie reserves any foreign exchange and *foreign notes* (up to a maximum amount of 60 million crowns) that are held in locations abroad, and which are legally payable in a currency backed by precious metals equivalent to gold.

The Bank is further allowed under Article 56k of the statute to buy and sell, in addition to foreign exchange at locations abroad, the acquisition of which had already been previously permitted, the following: checks at locations abroad; foreign notes and additional foreign exchange not denominated in crowns that may be bought domestically; also to issue checks and money orders at locations abroad; to undertake debt collections abroad and to make payments on foreign accounts; and *to maintain sufficient funds abroad for the conduct of these activities.* In addition, the Bank was authorized by Article 65, No. 4, to provide at locations abroad foreign exchange having a maturity of a maximum of six months (exactly analogous to foreign exchange held domestically), insofar as it—except for the maturity date—matches requirements for foreign exchange available for discount. The legal status of including negotiable and foreign banknotes redeemable in gold was included under Article 84. All of these provisions are separate from the suspension of specie payments; and paragraph 3 of the 1903 draft would have

---

17. See Mecenseffy, *Die Verwaltung der österreichisch-ungarischen Bank 1886–1895* (Vienna, 1896), p. 5.

permitted the inclusion of foreign exchange (up to a maximum of 60 million crowns) as part of the Bank's precious metal reserves after the legal resumption of specie payments.

Even though the Bank was allowed to acquire foreign exchange in this manner, long before the initiation of the currency reform, it made little use of it.

Up to 1887, the Bank was limited to the amount of 200 million florin notes that it could put into circulation under Plener's Bank Act, which was modeled after Peel's Bank Act.[18] This limit on the Bank's ability to issue notes not backed by the precious metals required the Bank to reduce its foreign exchange holdings because the growth in domestic market transactions resulted in an increasing demand for notes. Thus, due to the actual and anticipated domestic demand for notes, which had to be backed by gold, the Bank's foreign exchange holdings were repeatedly, and almost completely, liquidated, particularly after 1882.[19] At the end of 1882, for example, foreign exchange holdings amounted to only 95,981 florins.

On average, the foreign exchange holdings of the Bank at the end of each year amounted to:[20]

In the period	Millions of florins Austrian currency
1859–70	18.652
1871–77	7.890
1878–87	8.960
1888–91	23.698

Prior to 1892, the Bank's foreign exchange holdings did not have an important role in matters relating to monetary policy. After the end to the unrestricted minting of silver coins in 1879, the Austrian currency became a floating currency, with its value linked neither to the price of a precious metal nor to a foreign currency. Neither gold nor for-

18. [Peel's Bank Act of July 1844 divided the Bank of England into two parts: a Note Issuing Department and a Banking Department. The Issuing Department was restricted in the quantity of banknotes it could issue on the basis of the government debt (a maximum of fourteen hundred pounds), and notes beyond this had to be fully covered on the basis of additional deposits of gold coin or gold or silver bullion.—Ed.]

19. See Leonhardt, *Die Verwaltung der österreichisch-ungarischen Bank 1878–1885* (Vienna, 1886), pp. 39, 74f.

20. See *Statistische Tabellen zur Währungsfrage der österreichisch-ungarischen Monarchie* (Vienna, 1892), p. 128.

eign exchange redeemable in gold could be obtained from the Austro-Hungarian Bank. The Bank's operations in relation to its foreign exchange portfolio were limited to the exchange of short-term paper for long-term paper. Attempts to influence the currency exchange rate by selling off foreign exchange at a particular price failed completely. Doubtless any similar attempt would have led to a similar failure; the relative insignificance of the foreign exchange holdings would have certainly frustrated all such attempts.

The currency reform of 1892 did not initially bring about a change in the Bank's policies. It was only the unfavorable structure of the foreign exchange rates for the Austrian currency in 1893 and 1894 that resulted in both the Austrian and Hungarian governments approaching the Bank at the beginning of 1894, with the initiative originating with Ernst von Plener, who was then Austrian minister of finance. They declared that it was particularly important that, so as to assure that "the legitimate needs of business could regularly depend upon the Bank's assistance, that the Bank assign the greatest possible expansion to their dealings of foreign exchange and currencies, and make whatever adjustments necessary so a portion of its reserves might be used for the execution of foreign currency transactions."[21]

After it was repeated not much later, the Bank met this request in the most generous way. Beginning in 1896, the Bank began to focus its interest on the foreign exchange market to a much greater extent. Making use of the ordinances in the new Bank Statute, beginning in 1900 the Bank acquired other foreign assets in its revolving accounts in other countries, in addition to its holdings of foreign exchange.

On the basis of the public records, it is possible only to a limited extent to present a quantitative summary of the Bank's dealings in foreign exchange. The Bank provides no data about its holdings of foreign exchange and other foreign financial assets separate from its precious metal reserves; these are often simply covered under the entry "other activities." We, therefore, have to limit ourselves to quoting the few numbers that are spread out through a number of different publications. However, these numbers are sufficient to offer a picture of how significant a part these foreign exchange holdings played in the Bank's business.[22]

---

21. See XV. regelmäßige Jahressitzung der Generalsammlung der österreichisch-ungarischen Bank am 25. Februar 1894 (Vienna, 1894), pp. xvii, xxi.
22. See Zuckerkandl, op. cit., pp. 449ff.—Frankfurter Zeitung, May 17, 1908, names the different sources, in particular the financial journal Kompaß and the Tabellen zur Währungsstatistik published by the Royal and Imperial Finance Ministry.

The Bank's holdings in foreign exchange and assets amounted to:[23]

105.0 million crowns	on Dec. 31, 1900
249.8 million crowns	on Dec. 31, 1901
317.4 million crowns	on Dec. 31, 1902
326.7 million crowns	on Dec. 31, 1903
274.6 million crowns	on Dec. 31, 1904
226.3 million crowns	on Dec. 31, 1905
258.5 million crowns	on Jun. 30, 1906

The following data are available about the Bank's dealings in gold and foreign exchange:

	1	2	3		4
			Currency, exchanges, and other foreign receivables attained through transactions		Volume (sales and purchases) of currency and exchanges[24] through trades
	Purchase of gold bars and foreign gold coins according to tariff	Purchase of currency, exchanges, and other foreign receivables	a) Via sales	b) Via loans	
In the year	In millions of crowns				
1892	80.7	275.1	275.3	—	?[25]
1893	—	305.8	252.6	61.3	40.5
1894	—	356.5	278.7	71.0	90.4
1895	—	309.7	239.0	67.8	309.0
1896	32.2	500.2	486.8	94.6	400.2
1897	138.8	875.0	773.6	127.0	556.6
1898	0.2	709.2	643.6	138.4	536.0
1899	—	744.6	616.8	115.0	617.0
1900	—	698.9	533.0	123.1	514.7
1901	153.0	936.4	801.3	72.4	772.3
1902	102.1	913.9	798.4	147.2	1076.8
1903	61.2	1123.4	809.0	317.4	1155.8
1904	66.7	1081.2	868.3	313.7	997.2

An idea about the size of these transactions can be gained from a memorandum issued by the Bank's governor, Dr. von Bilinski. On one day, December 12, 1903, the volume of transactions undertaken by

23. See Bilinski, op. cit., p. 7.
24. Trades for the purpose of renewing the foreign exchange portfolio are contained in the entries listed in columns 2 and 3a.
25. Prior to 1898, no particular notations were made about this; the volumes pertaining to this (purchase and sales) are recorded in the numbers contained in columns 2 and 3a.

the foreign exchange department of the Bank amounted to a total of 71,901,000 crowns, in the amounts: 203,500 British pounds; 41,876,355 German marks; 18,527,333 French francs; and 196,000 Dutch florins.

The Bank's profits from its dealings in foreign currencies and exchange are correspondingly understood to have constantly increased. They amounted to:

Million crowns	In the year	Million crowns	In the year
0.745	1892	2.321	1900
0.538	1893	2.411	1901
0.414	1894	3.367	1902
0.316	1895	5.200	1903
0.499	1896	5.998	1904
1.330	1897	4.269	1905
1.379	1898	4.350	1906
1.482	1899	5.733	1907

By an intensive cultivation of its transactions in foreign exchange, the Bank succeeded in gradually attaining the dominant position on the Vienna foreign exchange market. The trade in foreign currency and exchange conducted by the major banks in Vienna, which had been a rich source of income for them, fell into an inexorable decline. In 1895 the earnings of just the Credit Anstalt, the Bankverein, and the Länderbank together (the three largest banks) amounted to 2.67 million crowns, but in 1907 it came to no more than 1.39 million crowns.

Of particular importance for the development of the Bank's foreign exchange dealings was the transfer of all the government's gold supplies to the Bank. Up until 1901, the government had deposited its gold revenues, most of them from customs duties, with Viennese investment banks for a low rate of interest. In exchange, these Viennese investment banks were under the obligation to furnish the necessary sums for foreign payments at the same low terms to both the Austrian and Hungarian governments. These transactions were quite lucrative for the banks, but not for the treasury in general. The government's foreign payments on particular dates for bond coupon redemption constantly exceeded its receipts in actual gold, and therefore it was forced to make considerable purchases of foreign exchange to cover these expenditures. For obvious reasons, the foreign exchange rate on exactly these days is quoted above parity, and for this reason the banks could count on a high price from the state's coffers. This disadvantage carried even more weight because this offered the banks the possibility of thwarting the discount policy of the central bank. Those clauses in the Bank's statutes that allowed it to have interest-earning deposits as well as to handle certain types of coinage and liquid assets (in notes or coin) in foreign currencies (Articles 75 and 111) provided the prerequisites for the central bank to take over the official administration of the government's gold, which it did in 1901.[26]

In this way, the Austro-Hungarian Bank gradually gained a preeminent position on the foreign exchange and currency markets. The vast majority of the country's gold reserves, as well as a large portion of the foreign currency and other short-term receivables that the monarchy had to have abroad, were now available to the Bank. The majority of all foreign payments took place through the Bank's mediation. Through this method an enormous power was concentrated in the hands of the Bank, which it employed in the defense of its specie reserves for the good of the entire economy.

III
The De Facto Resumption of Specie Payments

The discussion concerning the economic impact of Austria-Hungary's currency policy is, therefore, often directed along the wrong channels, so there is frequently a complete misunderstanding about the nature of the actual circumstances at the present time. From a formal, legal perspective that focuses on the literal letter of the law, it is constantly pointed out that specie payments are still suspended within the monarchy. And from a purely legal point of view, it cannot be disputed that the Austro-Hungarian Bank remains exempt from meeting any obligation of redeeming on demand its notes for legal coinage in the precious metals. But we consider this legal fact to be of secondary importance.

From the economic perspective, the suspension of specie payments has no importance, because for twelve years the Bank has made no use of this legal clause; not for a single day has it barricaded itself behind Article 111. The Bank has been prepared at all times to issue gold and gold-backed foreign exchange, checks, and so on to anyone who was in a position to transfer to the Bank the equivalent value in its notes or other Austrian payment instruments. Therefore, no further particu-

26. See Bilinski, op. cit., pp. 8ff.; Zuckerkandl, op. cit., pp. 441ff.

lar explanation is required for explaining the stability of the foreign exchange rates since 1896. *De facto, if not legally, Austro-Hungary is currently a gold-standard country.*[27] For this reason, any increase in the price for foreign exchange on the Viennese bourse that would be above the upper gold point is already impossible, because the Bank constantly supplies foreign exchange at a lower rate.[28]

Looked at in this way, it is unimportant that the Austro-Hungarian Bank primarily, but not exclusively, issues foreign exchange and checks backed by gold, instead of actually exporting gold like other central banks. In no way does this indicate the Bank's desire to step back from its voluntarily assumed obligation to make specie payments. In fact, the opposite is true, since the Bank issues foreign exchange below the gold point, making it more advantageous to receive and to provide these instruments instead of any actual gold.

The Bank also has not viewed its supply of gold as a *noli me tangere* [an untouchable item], but rather has willingly placed it at the service of the business world. The Bank has exported gold as often as this has been considered necessary to replenish any reduction in its reserves of foreign assets, and receives an equivalent value in foreign exchange or other assets at its various branches, which it can then control by the issuing of checks.

Equally irrelevant is the fact that, in general, it is not possible to

27. One actually has to designate the Austrian currency as a "limping" gold standard, because the silver florin is currently still the face-value coin. However, the Austro-Hungarian Bank never attempted to conduct a gold premium policy following the French, particularly since this amount will be reduced in the coming months by 28 million crowns by the further minting of five-crown coins.

28. Because in the following pages, an "upper gold point" is repeatedly discussed, this requires a more detailed explication. As long as the Bank prevented the exporting of gold by issuing foreign exchange, the upper gold point had no practical meaning; this will not change even after the legal resumption of specie payments in gold, unless the Bank completely abandons the foreign exchange policy that it currently follows. Because a precise, theoretical determination of the upper gold point is difficult to establish, the Bank, which requires a guideline for issuing its foreign exchange, used as a rule of thumb to always issue foreign exchange at a price that was closer to parity, as this was defined by the variations in the exchange rates in Berlin and London. By following this rule, it developed that the fluctuations in the foreign exchange rates were milder in Vienna than in the countries with specie payments. See Landmann, "Die währungspolitischen Aufgaben der schweizerischen Nationalbank," *Schweizerische Blätter für Wirtschafts- und Sozialpolitik*, vol. 15, pp. 307ff. A statistical review of the large amount of material available might provide interesting details; however, hardly anything would be changed as a result.

know in Vienna at what price the Bank will be ready to supply foreign exchange. It is no different in Berlin and London; even there no one can know at what price foreign exchange will be demanded the next day, and the only constant is that the gold points form the limits for any fluctuations in the foreign exchange rates. Exactly the same is the case in Vienna: the lower boundary of the exchange rate is determined already by the legal obligation of the Bank to redeem every kilogram of gold offered to it at the rate of 3,280 crowns (less the minting fee of two crowns); the upper boundary may not be legally fixed, but for all practical purposes it has been set at a rate lower than the upper gold point, as shown by the fact that the Bank never refuses to supply gold or foreign exchange below that upper point.

Admittedly, one could argue that while the Bank does indeed at this time *voluntarily* supply foreign exchange below the gold point, it, however, *does not have* to do so and could refuse to at any time; or it could refuse to supply it at lower prices, or at least it could refuse to issue it to certain individuals such as well-known arbitrage dealers. Whoever makes this claim, however, would only demonstrate his limited knowledge of the politics and economics of the situation. Under the current rules, the Bank could not introduce a change of such importance as refusing or restricting the supplying of foreign exchange against the wishes of both governments. No minister would give his agreement to this step without a very pressing need. Nor could there be a shift away from the Bank's current policy of exporting gold on demand, until all other means were found to be ineffective at stemming an outflow of gold.

The Bank would no more thoughtlessly resort to such a drastic measure as discontinuing gold payments than would any of the other countries that are legally required to make such specie payments. The impact on the market would be the same as the suspension of specie payments in any of the gold-standard countries. The immediate effect on the currency market from doing so, and, through this, its effect on annuities rates and other securities, would be devastating, to say nothing of the deeper, more long-term effects on the entire economy from a new agio emerging for a period of time.

Legally, it may very well be the case that specie payments are currently made voluntarily by the Bank only because they could be discontinued under tacit agreement with the government; whereas after legal resumption of specie payments, a law or at least an imperial emergency decree with the temporary force of law would be required for specie payments to be stopped. From an economic perspective, however, the voluntary nature of specie redemption does not really exist, because the historical precedent of making such payments leaves no choice other than requiring the legal introduction of specie payments.

The domestic and foreign stock exchanges, as well as the banking world in general, have been accustomed to the current situation for a long time; and understanding the nuanced reality of this aspect of public life in the country, these markets have assigned the same value to the currency of the Austro-Hungarian Monarchy as they do to other gold-standard countries.

In these circumstances, the legal resumption of specie payments, as both governments requested it in the spring of 1903, represents nothing more than a legal formality. It would mean only that the law recognized an already existing situation; the economic reality of specie payments that now already exists would be made into the permanent rule by a formal legal adoption of a gold standard. For quite some time now, specie payments have already been implemented for all practical purposes, with banknotes being fully redeemable.[29]

The secretary general of the Austro-Hungarian Bank, Hofrat von Pranger, therefore, justifiably asserted in a session of the General Council on April 2, 1903, shortly after the introduction of the guidelines, that as far as the Bank is concerned, questions connected with the introduction of specie payments had already been decided. Whether or not the Bank was legally obligated to redeem its notes for a precious metal was no longer a deciding factor in the Bank's behavior as guardian of the currency. The Bank would take exactly the same measures in the defense of the currency *after* the legal resumption of specie payments as it took currently, if the necessity for a defense of the currency were to occur.[30] The Bank does not currently refuse to pay gold upon demand for domestic use or for foreign transactions, and nothing will be changed by a legal provision. Austro-Hungary thus currently makes specie payments in practice, if not as a legal obligation.

It is therefore unnecessary to ask how it has been possible for the Austrian currency to have so stable a value since 1896, since this appears to be sufficiently explained by the policy of *de facto* specie pay-

29. See *Neue Freie Presse*, April 1, 1903.
30. See *Abendblatt der Neuen Freien Presse*, April 2, 1903.

ments. Instead, it should be asked, what has made it possible for the monarchy to resume specie payments and to maintain them up to the present day?

The answer is found in the extensive account given by the Austrian Finance Ministry about the monarchy's balance of payments, which is the only one currently available in the entire statistical literature.[31] It shows that the balance of payments was "positive" even when this was achieved only by a considerable export of investments. Therefore, the Austrian economy constantly had sufficient foreign exchange available in order to meticulously meet any foreign demands.

The generally favorable pattern of the balance of payments naturally does not exclude the fact that for longer or shorter periods of time there temporarily has been an unfavorable exchange rate. A particularly severe disruption of this type was caused by the widely discussed devaluation of the Austrian currency in 1893. The agio appeared for the last time toward the end of 1895: since 1896 it has been completely gone. Is this an indication, perhaps, that since 1896 there has not even been a temporary need to export gold to cover a momentary deficit in the balance of payments?

Most certainly not. Even after 1896, the monarchy's balance of payments—and this occurs in all countries, even in the wealthier ones— has repeatedly shown a deficit. However, the Austro-Hungarian Bank had changed its policy method in the meantime: it had learned to conduct a discount policy and indeed to conduct it as vigorously as the circumstances required: that is, the Bank would increase its discount rate to bring about an improvement in the balance of payments. In addition, the Bank has every time supplied gold and foreign exchange for export whenever required. This was made possible due to the large precious metal reserves and the stockpile of gold-backed currency that the Bank had accumulated over time.[32]

The change in the Bank's activities, which it completed during 1896 without any fanfare, remained unnoticed by the public for a long period of time. Only gradually have people begun to recognize its importance, and it has still not yet entered everyone's awareness that with the actual resumption of specie payments, the great task of the currency

31. See *Tabellen zur Währungsstatistik*, 2nd ed., pt. II, pp. 213ff.; Gruber, "Bericht betreffend eine Statistik der internationalen Zahlungbilanz," *Internationale statistische Institut X. Session* (London, 1905); Fellner, *Die Zahlungsbilanz Ungarns* (Vienna, 1908), pp. 1ff.
32. See Kalkmann, op. cit., pp. 42ff.; Herz, op. cit., pp. 493ff.

reform has been fully successful with only its formal adoption still remaining to be completed.

IV
The Alleged Advantages of Suspended Specie Payments for the Currency Market

The difference between *legal* and *practical* specie payments, which we have just developed, is not covered by the distinction between *compulsory* and *de facto* specie payments that is widely used in discussions about the Austrian currency. Compulsory specie payments, according to this distinction, mean the regulations governing the monetary system that would come into effect following, for example, the adoption and implementation of the specie payment guidelines of 1903; that is, a monetary constitution that legally obligates the Bank to redeem its notes for specie. In contrast, the present arrangement of de facto specie payments is one in which the Bank has the authority to redeem its notes, but is not under the obligation to do so.[33]

Indeed, the Bank does redeem them voluntarily, but the fact that this occurs only *voluntarily*, it is said, carries a weight of great importance. That is to say, this enables the Bank at any time to refuse to export gold and, in this manner, to protect its specie holdings and the currency during periods of rising interest rates on the international currency markets without having to implement a reciprocally spiraling hike in the discount rate. The expectation that the Bank may not pay in gold frightens away those who would desire to acquire foreign payment instruments merely to invest abroad at higher rates of interest; as a result, such individuals do not apply to the Bank for redemption, and thus the Bank does not have to actually refuse such demands for specie payment.

On the other hand, those with legitimate commercial claims for specie payments in order to import goods, as well as the demands by large bond debtors (countries, provinces, municipalities, private railways, mortgage banks, etc.) who need to redeem coupons that are reaching maturity can count on the Bank meeting their demands at any time.

---

33. The linguistic usage is quite fluid. Many understand the placement of gold coins in circulation beginning in 1901 to be part of the de facto system of specie payments. We hold ourselves to the designations applied in the best journalistic works about the Austrian currency.

The entire economy, it is said, enjoys the advantages of a currency that is internationally stable in value at a low discount rate.

The Bank's "active" foreign exchange policy consists in its refusal to provide to other banks the financial instruments that they may wish to export to invest abroad at more favorable interest rates than those available domestically. An increase in the foreign exchange rate above an acceptable level does not take place in spite of the Bank's refusal to supply foreign exchange for short-term investment abroad. At a slightly higher foreign exchange rate the demand for foreign exchange stops of its own accord, because from these bankers' point of view the low likelihood of being able to gain from the interest rate arbitrage does not justify the risk of a loss on the foreign exchange. Thus, under our current currency arrangement, the Bank does not face the problem of having to completely match the interest rate policies being followed in other countries, under the fear that other banks would drive up the exchange rate and withdraw gold in an attempt to capitalize on the interest rate differentials. It does not have to copy every increase in interest rates abroad with no concern for whether or not this would place an undue strain on the domestic credit market. It will be different after the introduction of legal specie payments. Then every banker will be in a position to present banknotes for redemption and claim as much gold from the central bank as he wants to send abroad in order to capitalize on the higher interests prevailing there. The Bank will see its foreign currency portfolio increase and its gold reserves decrease; and, since the Bank will have to offer a rate of interest sufficiently high to stop the flow of gold abroad, the higher rate of interest will at the same time raise the cost of borrowing for the entire domestic economy. Therefore, the benefit received by the entire domestic business community from a low rate of interest will have to be sacrificed for the private economic advantage of the financial sector.[34]

It is believed that the validity of this argument may be seen especially in the events on the currency markets during the tensions in 1906 and 1907. During this time, the Austro-Hungarian Bank in fact succeeded in defending its gold reserves with an interest rate that did not rise above 6 percent, while at the same time the bank rate in London

34. See "Barzahlungen und Währungspolitik," *Die Zeit*, September 25, 1907; see, in addition, "Die Devisenpolitik der Bank," *Die Zeit*, August 23, 1907; Riedl, "Fakultative oder obligatorische Barzahlung," *Neues Wiener Tageblatt*, July 14, 1907; Müller, *Die Frage der Barzahlungen im Lichte der Knappschen Geldtheorie* (Vienna, 1908), pp. 41ff.; and finally, the texts cited on pages 37 and 38 in footnotes 7 and 8.

Comparative Table of Bank Discounts

Year	Austro-Hungarian Bank			German Reichsbank			Bank of England			Bank of France		
	Avg.	Max.	Min.	Avg.	Max.	Min.	Avg.	Max.	Min.	Avg.	Max.	Min.
1892	4.02	5	4	3.20	4	3	2.52	3½	2	2.69	3	2½
1893	4.24	5	4	4.06	5	3	3.05	5	2½	2.50	2½	2½
1894	4.08	5	4	3.12	5	3	2.12	3	2	2.50	2½	2½
1895	4.30	5	4	3.14	4	3	2.00	2	2	2.20	2½	2
1896	4.09	5	4	3.66	5	3	2.48	4	2	2.00	2	2
1897	4.06	4	4	3.81	5	3	2.63	4	2	2.00	2	2
1898	4.16	5	4	4.27	6	3	3.24	4	2½	2.20	3	2
1899	5.04	6	4½	5.04	7	4	3.74	6	3	3.06	4½	3
1900	4.58	5½	4½	5.33	7	5	3.96	6	3	3.25	4½	3
1901	4.08	4½	4	4.10	5	3½	3.72	5	3	3.00	3	3
1902	3.55	4	3½	3.32	4	3	3.32	4	3	3.00	3	3
1903	3.50	3½	3½	3.84	4	3½	3.75	4	3	3.00	3	3
1904	3.50	3½	3½	4.84	5	4	3.64	4	3	3.00	3	3
1905	3.70	4½	3½	3.82	6	3	3.01	4	2½	3.00	3	3
1906	4.33	4½	4	5.15	7	4½	4.27	6	3½	3.00	3	3
1907	4.89	6	4½	6.03	7½	5½	4.93	7	4	3.46	4	3

amounted to 7 percent and in Berlin to even 7.5 percent. If, like the other European central banks, the Austro-Hungarian Bank were solely dependent on its discount policy for a defense of the currency, it would definitely have had to take refuge in a higher interest rate in order to prevent an outflow of gold. And because Austro-Hungary is a debtor country, the interest rate would have to have been even higher here than abroad in order to get creditors to defer making their claims.

If we compare the discount rate of the Austro-Hungarian Bank with that of the German Reichsbank in 1898, the result is that the average rate in Berlin was higher than in Vienna; only in 1899 was the average rate the same for both banks, and throughout 1902, with some exceptions, the average rate in Vienna was not quite a quarter of a percent higher than in Berlin. In 1903, 1904, and 1907, the bank rate in Vienna was also lower on average than the rate in London; this difference amounted to a quarter of a percent in 1903 and was negligible in 1907. One must, however, keep in mind that the Bank of England discounted below its official interest rate, while the Austro-Hungarian Bank has not done this for many years. A comparison with the French situation, with respect to the particular position of the Parisian currency market, does not show anything of significance.

Of particular note is the great stability of the Austro-Hungarian Bank's discount rate. It never climbed as high as that of the German and English central banks, and it also never fell as low. In the sixteen years from 1892 up to and including 1907, the Bank of England changed its discount rate seventy-four times; the German Reichsbank did so fifty-seven times; the Austro-Hungarian Bank, twenty-one times; and the Bank of France, ten times.

For the movements of international precious metals, however, it is the market discount rate, not the Bank's discount rate, that is decisive. The leading position on the currency markets definitely centers on the private discount rate.

Comparative Table of the Private Discount Rate
for Three-Month Bills (according to the annual
average)

Year	Vienna	Berlin	Paris	London
1892	3.66	1.81	1.75	1.33
1893	3.73	3.17	2.25	1.67
1894	3.58	1.74	1.63	1.70
1895	4.34	2.01	1.92	0.81

(*Continued*)

Year	Vienna	Berlin	Paris	London
1896	3.85	3.04	1.75	1.52
1897	3.69	3.08	1.90	1.87
1898	3.94	3.55	2.12	2.65
1899	4.75	4.44	2.96	3.29
1900	4.34	4.40	3.17	3.70
1901	3.65	3.06	2.41	3.18
1902	2.71	2.18	2.36	2.98
1903	3.01	3.01	2.73	3.40
1904	3.15	3.14	2.18	2.70
1905	3.25	2.85	2.42	2.66
1906	4.12	4.04	2.72	4.01
1907	4.68	5.12	3.37	3.37

A comparison of the market discount rates immediately gives a different view than that given by the Bank's discount rate. It is seen that the interest rate on the open market in Vienna consistently remained above that in Berlin; even 1900 and 1907 (crisis years in Germany) and 1903 were not exceptions to this. In general, the Viennese private discount rate was similarly above the London rate; only in 1902 and 1903 did the interest rate in London exceed that in Vienna. It is self-evident that Vienna also had a higher private discount rate than in Paris.

This structure of interest rates on the open market naturally does not exclude the fact that sometimes the rate in Vienna temporarily stood considerably below the rates in foreign countries. This was most clearly observed during the critical events in the last quarter of 1907.

Private Discount Rate for Three-Month Bills in the Last Quarter of 1907

Monthly Average	Vienna	Berlin	London	Paris
October	4.965	4.907	4.456	3.375
November	5.280	6.620	6.535	3.880
December	5.728	7.068	5.853	4.000

It can be seen that sometimes even the private discount rate in Vienna sank below that in the Berlin and London markets, and that the Austro-Hungarian Bank's discount rate was in general lower than that of the German Reichsbank, and even temporarily lower than that of the Bank of England.

The predominant explanation that the Bank could follow this interest rate policy due to the peculiarities of the Austrian currency system is totally unjustified.

Above all, it is not the case that the Austro-Hungarian Bank "*simply* refused to export foreign exchange and gold, when it considered this as only serving the purpose of facilitating foreign investments."[35] The Bank's conduct was a far cry from this explanation. Whenever it seemed advisable under the circumstances, the Bank sent gold abroad. If the domestic currency requirements were temporarily low and the Bank's gold holdings relatively high, the Bank would trade a portion of its gold reserves for interest-earning foreign exchange, rather than have the gold reserves remain in its vaults earning no interest. During extremely stressful times on the international currency markets, such gold exports by the Bank take on increased importance, because they help alleviate the situation on the international currency markets and therefore directly bring about an improvement on the domestic currency market.

This naturally assumes that domestic claims made on the Bank are sufficiently low that the gold does not have to be held, even under the most stringent observation of the regulations relating to gold reserves. Even putting aside the specific regulations concerning gold backing for the ten-crown notes and a portion of the banknotes that replaced the state notes, up to now the total notes in circulation have been far below the Bank's authorized maximum limit of two and a half times the precious metal reserves (holdings in gold in domestic and foreign coins as well as bars, silver florins, token coins, and foreign exchange up to a maximum of 60 million crowns), even during times of heaviest demand, and are predicted to remain even lower in the years to come.

The only concern is if the Bank, due to gold exported abroad, runs the risk of exceeding its tax-free limit of 400 million crown notes in circulation. Every increase in notes above this limit imposes a 5 percent tax on the Bank; if the interest rate earned by the Bank does not exceed 5 percent, it suffers a loss from issuing these notes. The income earned from gold exported to foreign markets can, under certain circumstances, completely cancel out these losses. The Bank's concern over this statutory regulation disappears as soon as its discount rate rises to 5 percent or higher, which is usually the rule in times of great financial distress.

The correct policy for the Bank, then, in these circumstances, is to send gold abroad in trade for interest-earning foreign exchange. The

---

35. See "Die Devisenpolitik der Bank."

general economic advantage joins the private economic gain of the bank stockholders and the state treasury, both of whom are keenly interested in the profitability of the Bank. Thus, the gold sent abroad helps to mitigate the rise in the price of gold on foreign exchange markets and at the same time reduces the demands made on the Bank by those at home who want to send gold abroad in order to profit from the higher interest rates. Because the difference between Viennese and foreign interest rates becomes smaller than it would have been without the Bank's gold exports, the incentive to acquire foreign currency or to export gold is lessened. In essence, this is exactly the same policy repeatedly followed by the Bank of France. The assistance that the Bank of England received from its French sister institution during the Baring Crisis and in autumn 1907 had its basis primarily in the discount policy followed in Paris. France most effectively protected its liquid assets and its relatively low interest rate simply by making its gold available abroad. The gold holdings of the Bank of France are enormous, and the Bank is not obligated by any legal clauses to maintain a particular ratio of currency to gold backing. It can, therefore, easily do without a large amount of gold and, like the Austro-Hungarian Bank, come to the assistance of foreign markets at critical moments.

By exporting gold, however, the Austro-Hungarian Bank increases its holdings of foreign exchange and other foreign assets. It is thus in a position to sell foreign exchange to those capitalists who want to send gold abroad, and can sell it at a price which always lies below the upper gold point. In this case, therefore, it never comes to an actual export of gold through private hands. The entire transaction peters out through foreign exchange passing into private hands out of the Bank's portfolio. The effect on the domestic currency market, however, is the same as an actual export of gold. Notes flow back into the Bank and the market rate rises.

Foreign central bank disclosures about the transfer of the precious metals indicate the international gold transactions that have already occurred. The situation is not as simple in reference to the Austro-Hungarian Bank. In general, the Bank's foreign exchange activities can be documented only through movements in "other assets" on the Bank's balance sheet. If the accrual of "other assets" corresponds to a decrease in gold reserves, then it can be construed from this that the Bank exported gold and acquired foreign receivables in exchange for it. A decrease of "other assets" can indicate any number of activities. If it corresponds to an increase in the "foreign exchange reserves," that is, those foreign exchange assets that are calculated as part of the gold reserves, then this can be considered to be a purely accounting operation, under which long-term foreign exchange that has come to be qualified as part of the foreign exchange reserves has been added to the precious metals account. It is also conceivable that the Bank has applied foreign exchange to its asset accounts with its corresponding banks. If with a decrease of "other assets" there occurs no corresponding increase in its precious metal holdings or in its foreign exchange reserves, then one must conclude that there occurred a transfer of foreign exchange and checks to the private sector, which has to be considered as a decrease in the circulation of notes.

The Bank avoids the need for supplying gold for export; however, since the voluntary introduction of specie payments that took place in 1896, it has never refused to supply foreign exchange below the upper gold point. It is possible, therefore, that requests for the surrender of actual gold never reach the Bank because, in these circumstances, it is cheaper to export foreign exchange than it is to export actual gold. For the Bank alone, with its large, non-interest-bearing reserve of gold, the export of gold is lucrative at any time, because it thereby exchanges uninvested capital for interest-bearing capital; for other capitalists, only an increase in the foreign exchange rate above the upper gold point creates an incentive for an actual export of gold. As soon as the Bank observes the emergence of a speculative demand for foreign exchange, it immediately increases the discount rate in order to defend its foreign exchange holdings and, therefore, its gold reserves. The Austrian situation differs from the mechanism of the international movement of precious metals as illustrated by Goschen[36] only in that the export of gold and the trade in foreign exchange are concentrated in the hands of the Bank.[37]

As long as the Bank monopolizes the gold trade and the foreign exchange rate does not reach the upper gold point, the Bank has a preeminent though not a dominating position on the foreign exchange market. The Bank encounters competition from other banks, and therefore

36. [Viscount Goschen, *The Theory of the Foreign Exchange*, 3rd ed. (London: Effingham Wilson, 1919). George Goschen, First Viscount Goschen (1831–1907), was a prominent British liberal who later switched to the Conservative Party. He served at various times as vice president of the Board of Trade, paymaster-general, president of the Poor Law Board, First Lord of the Admiralty, and as a director of the Bank of England. His book on the workings of the foreign exchange market is still considered a classic on the mechanisms of international exchange.—Ed.]

37. See Bilinski, op. cit., p. 3.

has to direct its foreign exchange sales according to market prices. The foreign exchange rates on the Viennese bourse are subject to the same determining forces as the Berlin or London markets. The rates cannot fall below the lower gold point, because otherwise it would be more lucrative to acquire gold and deposit it in the Bank; and it cannot rise above the upper gold point, because the Bank then seeks to counteract the dwindling supply of foreign exchange by the timely export of gold. This is the core of the Bank's foreign exchange policy: always to hold in readiness a sufficient reserve of foreign exchange, even if actual gold would have to be exported for this purpose.

Thus, it would be a complete misconception of the Bank's actual activities to assert that it refused to release foreign exchange when it concerned speculative demands for arbitrage rather than the satisfying of "legitimate" needs of business. It should be incidentally noted that it would be extremely difficult to make such a clear distinction between legitimate and illegitimate demands for foreign exchange, which would be necessary for such a different handling of the two. There are certain types of demands for means of payment in global commerce that could become exceedingly disruptive for the foreign exchange rate, but which nevertheless cannot be considered to be illegitimate: for example, the demand for foreign exchange to make payments for investments purchased abroad (even possibly speculative ones) that are flowing back to the domestic market. These backflows, however, appear regularly as soon as a persistent scarcity of money exists abroad.

The rates for Austrian as well as Hungarian bonds may remain relatively higher on the domestic market, due to the strong demand of domestic private banks, savings banks, and primarily the postal savings bank to meet their capital requirements by switching into fixed-interest-earning assets, when dividends on stocks are low or nonexistent.

A drop in the rate of Austro-Hungarian investments in the foreign markets does not generally generate a subsequent and corresponding drop on the Viennese and Budapest markets, therefore, because the domestic credit institutions purchased these assets and then sought to sell them to the broader public. Any difficulties created for the (doubtless speculative) acquisition of those financial instruments flowing back to the domestic market would shake the trust in the stability of their rate of return and increase the cost of credit far more strongly and more persistently than would ever be caused by temporary increases in the discount rate.

It should, incidentally, not be denied that the Austrian Ministry of Finance possesses an entire series of powerful instruments that it could use to prevent the large financial institutions from speculatively acquiring foreign currencies. We completely disregard the fact that at every Austrian credit-issuing institution a functionary of the Finance Ministry is appointed as presiding commissioner, to whom the task falls of overseeing that institution's financial conduct; and that at two major Viennese banks the director (governor) was appointed by the crown.

However, it is far more important that over the last twenty-five years legislation has been passed that, more or less, has brought every type of economic activity under the unrestricted discretion of state oversight. This is not the place to provide more details about this oversight, or to demonstrate how Austria has turned away from political-economic individualism faster and more effectively than have other European countries. For anyone desiring to place obstacles in the way of a bank or an industrial enterprise in which a bank is interested, there is no more suitable method than this state oversight, including its desire to export gold. We do not want to claim that any such actions against the exportation of gold have ever occurred. On the contrary, as we will demonstrate later, we think that the banks themselves have never demonstrated the intention of sending gold abroad as a monetary investment, because there have existed within the borders of the monarchy opportunities for more profitable uses of their capital. Thus, there has not been the need for initiating threats or making appeals to their patriotism.

However, in the exceptional case that an Austrian bank still had the intention of loaning a large sum abroad—perhaps in order to come to the assistance of one of its own foreign subsidiary institutions or of a closely associated enterprise—the Austro-Hungarian Bank still has an effective weapon on hand in order to prevent this type of undesired gold export. The Bank is the ultimate source for monetary instruments within the country, and all other banks are obligated to maintain good relations with it, because they have to retain the possibility of re-discounting their portfolios with the central bank. Under these circumstances, a nod by the central bank is sufficient to bring an end to any demand for foreign exchange. The source for the closing off of this demand is neither the legal suspension of specie payments nor any related circumstance; rather it lies in the fear of possible countermeasures on the part of the central bank. The Bank's position of power on the currency market would not be in the least weakened by the legal resumption of specie payments. It is generally known that the German Reichsbank, which is obligated by law to make specie payments, successfully uses similar methods to prevent the export of gold.

At the moment that the Bank actually absolutely refused to supply foreign exchange, or supplied it only below the upper gold point, whether for everyone or only for gold exporters, or indeed at the moment the possibility even existed that the Bank would plan or seriously consider doing it, the foreign exchange rate would skyrocket. The agio would experience a substantial height, because the demand for foreign exchange would rise to a significant magnitude given the available supply. The domestic currency market would be gripped by panic; foreigners who have deposited their monies in Austria and Hungary would forcefully attempt to withdraw them; on the foreign stock markets, a massive offering of Austrian and Hungarian investments would emerge at falling prices; and the monarchy would face the choice of either quietly observing the fall in the rates on investment or would have to at least temporarily buy them up and pay for the securities that were flowing back into the country. In addition, there would then arise a domestic demand for gold-backed currency on the part of those who wanted to cover, on a timely basis, foreign payments that were coming due at a later date.

A refusal by the Bank to supply gold would have the same effect, then, as a serious economic crisis or an impending political and military disaster. The effect on the bourse would be the same as the suspension of specie payments in a country legally obligated to pay them.

It should also be emphasized, again, that the Bank does not even remotely consider refusing to supply foreign exchange and checks abroad, and it is determined even in serious times of crisis to continue actual specie payments for as long as it is absolutely possible; this is no different from the central banks of England and France, and the German Reichsbank. In this endeavor, the Bank can count on the vigorous support of the state and the approval of the entire business community. How firmly the market trusted the Bank's willingness and ability to pay specie was seen in the difficult days of November 1907; during that time and in spite of many difficulties the thought that the Bank would discontinue the delivery of foreign exchange was not considered even for an instant.

The often-heard claim that the Bank maintains the stability of the foreign exchange rate through the abolition of speculation should also receive a few words. The Bank, it is said, appears on the foreign exchange market as a supremely powerful counterforce that has paralyzed speculators who have an interest in frequent and severe price fluctuations. We are confronted here with that widespread and amateur view that tries to connect all adverse and apparently inexplicable market events back to speculative activity. On the one hand, reference is made to the well-known legal and criminal prohibitions against arbitrage. On the other hand, it is asserted that the Bank does not completely suppress foreign exchange speculation, but instead limits it to a narrow band between the two gold points. However, the Bank accomplishes this by no means other than by actual specie payments, identical, for example, to the actions of the Bank of England. If the initial assertion is accepted, then it also would be necessary to say that the Bank of England prevents an increase in the foreign exchange rates on the London market by consciously engaging in counterspeculation by, at any time, supplying gold at a fixed price.

Thus, it cannot be claimed that the relative low Viennese currency rate is connected to the fact that the Bank is not obligated to make specie payments. The Bank does not make use of its right to refuse redemption on demand, and could not do so without the greatest damage to the stability of the foreign exchange rate. The entire doctrine of the alleged advantages from merely de facto specie payments that are not obligatory under the law to secure a lower level of interest rates, is nothing more than a repetition of the old theory of "isolated" countries that lack currencies backed by precious metals, a theory that has been repeatedly disproved, most recently by Kalkmann.[38]

During the era of paper money the assertion was made that the international money market could not influence the Austrian currency, because its value was independent of foreign currencies, and therefore the monarchy could not be negatively affected by any outflow of specie. The conclusion was made that it was not necessary for the Austro-Hungarian Bank to align its discount rate to those set by Western European central banks. Since the country already had to bear all the disadvantages of a paper currency, it could at least benefit from the one

38. See Kalkmann, op. cit., p. 48.

advantage of its monetary isolation: the ability to adjust the interest rate to reflect the country's domestic needs and conditions, with only the most cursory consideration to external circumstances.

Wilhelm von Lucam, the long-serving secretary general of the Austro-Hungarian Bank,[39] had already fought this error for a generation and argued the following proposition: the Bank can do nothing with its discount policy that would be forbidden to a bank making specie payments, and is not prevented from doing anything that is obligatory to such a bank.[40] He did not succeed in convincing his opponents. Similarly unsuccessful were the events of 1879–87 and 1893–94, during which the lack of an active discount policy led to a marked increase in the agio.

We have demonstrated that even today, the low bank discount rate in Vienna cannot be explained in this way. We must attempt to find another explanation for the evident fact that the Austro-Hungarian Bank actually makes specie payments and can maintain an interest rate lower than the central bank of the much richer German Empire.

V

The Discount Rate in Austro-Hungary in Relation to Foreign Discount Rates

Any theory that sees in the legal suspension of specie payments an explanation for the advantageous level of the discount rate in Austria-Hungary starts with the assumption that the interest rate in a debtor country like the Austro-Hungarian Monarchy necessarily must be higher than in creditor countries like England, Germany, France, and Holland. An incentive for foreigners to acquire Austro-Hungarian investments has to be created, and the most reliable way of doing so is by offering a higher rate of interest.

39. [Wilhelm von Lucam (1820–1900) was the secretary general of the Austrian National Bank in the mid-1800s, at the time when the growth of joint-stock banks confronted the central bank with an increasingly difficult task: to secure sufficient liquidity and to prevent an inflationary expansion of the money supply with a limited range of policy instruments. The very close and personal contact between managers of the central bank and leading participants of the Viennese financial center made an informal agreement in critical situations easier. However, when disagreements among the managers of the central bank arose, it was occasionally necessary to push through resolutions that had not been agreed upon unanimously. The words of Wilhelm von Lucam exerted great influence in that small circle of businessmen who dominated the Viennese money and capital market.—Ed.]

40. See Lucam, *Die österreichische Nationalbank während der Dauer des dritten Privilegiums* (Vienna, 1876), pp. 66ff.

The validity of this statement for the capital market, that is, the market for long-term investments, cannot be doubted. Austria-Hungary, in fact, is in debt to foreign countries to a very large extent. According to reports issued by the Austrian Ministry of Finance about the monarchy's balance of payments, foreign holdings of Austrian, Hungarian, and Bosnian securities at the end of 1903 amounted to 9,809 million crowns, compared with Austrian holdings of foreign securities of only 600–700 million crowns. The interest rate for long-term investments is also considerably higher in the monarchy than it is abroad. This is generally so well known that a closer statistical proof seems unnecessary. We will therefore content ourselves with a comparison of the market prices of German imperial bonds with Austrian crown bonds.

Average for the year	Market price of the Austrian 4% crown bond on the Viennese bourse	Profit ratio in percent	Market price of the German 3% imperial bond on the Berliner bourse	Profit ratio in percent
1903	100.74	3.97	91.49	3.27
1904	99.70	4.01	90.02	3.33
1905	100.34	3.99	90.08	3.33
1906	99.56	4.02	87.73	3.42
1907	97.54	4.10	84.15	3.56

A comparison of the bond prices of different countries is reliable up to a certain point. The legal formalities under which public bonds are issued internationally and their technical financial structure have become more uniform in various countries over the last several decades, so the cost of credit offers a benchmark for the differences in their marketability. This is not true of observed differences in central bank discount rates. It has been pointed out that individual central banks have not imposed similar standards for determining the quality of the bills of exchange to be discounted, neither concerning the term of the bond nor regarding the type of their accrual and the number of necessary signatures. Attention has also occasionally turned to the central banks' private rate and the treatment given to those applying for discount based on momentary fluctuations on the market. Even when only looking at the observable and legal bases under which credit is extended, the instances already cited ought to be sufficient to demonstrate that the importance of the central bank rate is different in each country.

Of much greater importance, however, is the Banks' policy for determining the actual amount of credit extended. Whether a bank extends a loan to a certain person and in what amount is mostly delegated to the complete and free discretion of its functionaries. Sometimes a line is indirectly drawn by the decision of a bank's governing body that it is obligated to select its officers from certain circles; however, even this limitation is basically irrelevant. More often the benchmark for creditworthiness is determined by the general guidelines of that bank, and the particular principles for making such decisions that have developed over time at each individual institution and from which great care is taken not to depart. Yet under these general principles the officials in charge have a completely free hand. Thus, even at the various branches of the *same* bank, the same practice will not be completely followed, let alone at the central banks of different countries. In these circumstances, any conclusions would be incorrect that are based on a comparison of the absolute levels of central bank discount rates. Only from their trends, either rising or falling, can conclusions be drawn about changes that are occurring on the currency markets.

The same is true for the private discount rate. Its importance also differs from country to country, and even from place to place within the same country. In addition, it is also subject to temporal and also secular and periodic changes. Even in the same location, the individual financiers in the brokering of private bills cultivate their own particular views about what constitutes first-class bills and refuse to accept other investments into their portfolios that they consider questionable. The number of firms whose credit is universally recognized as "excellent" is infinitesimally small. The decisive factor in determining the membership in this small circle is based on established business practices and the judgments of the participants in the credit transactions. Following these top, private discounts, there is also at some stock exchanges another level of "second-class" bills, which are locally awarded the characteristics of trustworthiness and reliability in private brokering. In addition, there are also investments that are indeed traded at the private discount rate; however, they are not considered fungible, and at the close of the business day on the stock exchange a specification of its status is required. All of these delineations are fluid and often are only discernible with difficulty owing to the intermingling of the normal brokering of bills with private brokering of bills at the bourse.[41] Only

41. See Prion, *Das deutsche Wechseldiskontgeschäft* (Leipzig, 1907), pp. 62ff.

the choicest, first-class bills of exchange can be spoken of in terms of absolute liquidity in international transactions, and only the signatures of a few large banks and large bankers—"international houses" in the literal sense—are considered to be in this category. The majority of the other, private discounts are dependent upon local circumstances linked to their particular market, so that even within the same country differences in the private discount rate can appear; and in periods of crisis, when the needs for currency are more pressing and general confidence has been shaken, considerable differences can appear in these rates without actually bringing about currency flows.[42] More understandable are similar events in relation to the stock markets of different countries. It would therefore be premature for one to assume from the mere existence of differences in the private discount rates between two countries that compensating flows of the precious metal are called for, or that the absence of such flows suggests obstacles have been placed in the way of the mobility of gold.

The private discount rates on individual bourses differ in their importance because they generally have completely different institutional arrangements. An equilibrium in the flow of currencies can be established not only through a formal equality between the discount rates; there can also be an inequality between discount rates on different bourses that corresponds to an internal balancing within a bourse in which capitalists are too timid to deposit money abroad because of their limited knowledge about foreign markets or other various legal and political circumstances; only an especially strong incentive for undertaking foreign investments may overcome this.

In this way, different discount rates existing at the same moment in different countries can be explained regardless of differences, also at the same time, in the foreign exchange rate between areas having the same precious metal as their currency. This is because the harmonization of currency markets is not shown by a tendency for equalization between central bank discount rates or between private sector discount rates within the same country. Instead, harmonization is seen when there emerges an international abundance or scarcity of money, and movements in the discount rates move along parallel curves in the various currency markets. Gold flows do not result in creating a mathematical equilibrium between discount rates; rather they result in the

42. See Weill, *Die Solidarität der Geldmärkte* (Frankfurt, 1903), pp. 26ff.

establishment of a certain equilibrium relationship between interest rates in the individual countries; in their absolute level, however, the discount rates are influenced far more by national determinants than by international ones.

It is clear that the discount rate within the monarchy is dependent upon events on the international currency market. The private discount rate in Vienna rises and falls in parallel to the markets in Berlin and London; and whenever exceptions appear, these can always be traced back to particular events on the national currency market, regardless of whether there is an especially large excess supply of or demand for currency. The types of domestic events that can counteract international tendencies occur just as frequently on the currency markets of the Western countries.

It would be misleading in such a discussion to ignore the monarchy's large foreign indebtedness. These debts are owed on the capital markets, and not on the currency markets where foreign–owned assets in Austria occasionally confront the much smaller counterclaims of Austrian-owned assets abroad. This strongly contrasts with the situation in Imperial Germany, where German-owned foreign investments are estimated to be 16 billion marks; yet Germany is continually borrowing large amounts from abroad on the currency market.

Foreign countries can acquire bonds in Vienna by returning Austrian and Hungarian investments they hold; but due to the high ratings of these securities, such operations are not easily accomplished. The lack of short-term debt abroad strengthens the position of the Austrian currency market to an extraordinary degree during times when discount rates are high. Foreign countries are not able to withdraw assets from the monarchy at these times, because they do not have debts at their disposal that are coming due; instead, they have to shift to borrowing on the Austrian money market. In Austria, such foreign applications for loans have to compete with the opportunity offered to Austrian capitalists for lending their money in Hungary instead. The official Bank rate provides only a very unsatisfactory indication about the interest rate prevailing in Hungary, parts of Galicia, and in Bukovina. The Austro-Hungarian Bank is considered of limited use for lines of credit in these areas. The need for credit by producers and traders in these parts of the empire are primarily provided by private banks, provincial banks (called "Sparkassen" in Hungary), and trade associations, whose intermediation enormously increases the cost of credit. Only indirectly does the central bank influence the terms for credit through these other institutions.

In Hungary, mortgage rates of 6 to 8 percent are not unusual, and for personal or corporate debt it can be as high as 10 to 12 percent. Those provincial financiers are in a position, even at the high interest rates they pay, to assure themselves of 2 percent or more above the Bank rate. Austrian lenders enjoy a monopoly over these financial assets, because they are the only ones in a position to judge the creditworthiness of these individuals and institutions. Their incentive to loan funds abroad is always very low, because they can enjoy a rate of interest in their Hungarian transactions that widely exceeds the highest rate they can earn at any time on the international currency market.

If foreign claims on the currency market of the monarchy are thus relatively low, then so too are the domestic claims. No complaint is repeated more often in the Austro-Hungarian Bank's annual reports than the lament that a more intensive use of the Bank's capital is not possible. If the smooth development of the German economy suffers from the fact that the demand for new capital exceeds available savings, the opposite is true for Austria, though less so in Hungary. Investment activity is low and the unfortunate political situation has paralyzed the enterprising spirit in Austria. The previous Austrian minister of commerce correctly pointed out that in Austria monetary liquidity is not a sign of economic prosperity, but instead a sign of stagnation and the languishing of entrepreneurial activity.

Even if it were assumed that legal resumption of specie payments would change this unfavorable economic situation and bring about a rise in the rate of interest, there still would be no reason to resist its implementation. The goal of a sound economic policy is not maintenance of a low market rate regardless of the circumstances. Rather, its goal is to unleash the use of the country's productive resources. Between the two evils of an economic depression or high interest rates, the latter is certainly the lesser of the two evils.

VI
The Costs of the Foreign Exchange Policy

Professor Georg Freidrich Knapp is the author of the pathbreaking work *Staatliche Theorie des Geldes* [The State Theory of Money]. He has received credit for being the first to attempt a unified, comprehensive view of modern currency policy. He is also generally known for diametrically opposing the Austro-Hungarian Bank's foreign exchange policy of coordinating its discount policy with that of other central banks. Both are acts of exodromic management.[43] Exodromic interventions are necessary in order to establish intercurrency exchange rate stability, Knapp argues, because the exchange rate does not, as commonly believed, automatically adjust even when there are full-fledged specie payments. Every exodromic action requires sacrifices, Knapp says. Those businessmen who discount bonds and who receive loans at the Bank on the basis of collateral make these sacrifices in the form of reduced profits as the price for the Bank's following its discount policy.

The Bank also makes sacrifices due to its foreign exchange policy, Knapp states. However, at the end of the day the Bank does not really make this sacrifice, because it expects to be compensated for it by the state. The Bank employs a portion of its capital to purchase a large quantity of bills of exchange on the English market and continually replenishes it as soon as any particular bills reach maturity. It occasionally purchases these bills with the intent of making a profit whenever the exchange rate should prove favorable; but more often than not, the Bank acquires the bills at unfavorable rates regardless of what they may cost. In addition, the Bank releases these bills at parity as soon as the exchange rate becomes unfavorable. In this way, the Bank indeed suffers losses, except in the unusual case when the bills that it is holding were purchased at a favorable time in terms of their price. The parity rate is reestablished through these interventions, which otherwise would be left to the anarchic forces resulting from the blind gambles of individual interests; thus an important goal of public policy is achieved that is well worth the sacrifice, Knapp concludes. And the Bank can expect that the state will compensate it for the losses that it may suffer from this process.[44]

It is not our purpose here to examine to what extent Professor Knapp's theory is correct concerning the pantopolic character of the intercurrency exchange rate.[45] It can only be judged and accepted in the context of the logical structure of his overall theory of money. However, a debate cannot be avoided over his view of the foreign ex-

43. ["Exodromic" refers to policies meant to stabilize movements in exchange or exchange rates.—Ed.]
44. See Knapp, *Staatliche Theorie des Geldes*, pp. 247ff.
45. ["Pantopolic" refers to all market activities relating to the balance of payments.—Ed.]

change policy followed by the Austro-Hungarian Bank. Above all, it must be stated that the Bank's foreign exchange policy required no sacrifices on its part; on the contrary, as was previously mentioned, it led to considerable profits. The investment of a portion of the Bank's assets in foreign exchange and in interest-bearing gold investments abroad yields significant profits; even the quite negligible fluctuations in the exchange rate that are kept within narrow bounds through the Bank's actions favorably influence its income. The Bank does not buy foreign exchange when it is up in price, but rather when it is down, and then releases that foreign exchange at rising prices for a profit.

It is also incorrect to say that the Bank releases bills and checks abroad at parity; more often it demands the price corresponding to the prevailing market rate. In order to prevent an increase in the exchange rate above the theoretical upper gold point, the Bank always acts to prevent its holdings of foreign exchange on the market from running out. In no way does it achieve this by presenting itself as a buyer on the market; indeed, there would be no more blundering method than that. The appearance of a new buyer on the market can only function to drive the prices even higher. As we have shown, when the price of exchange is moving in an unfavorable direction, the Bank more often seeks to increase its assets through gold exports. It increases the available supply of foreign exchange and creates the possibility for satisfying all subsequent claims that may be presented to the Bank.[46]

Because the demand for foreign exchange normally occurs most intensely on particular days and during particular months of the year, the Bank's purchases of foreign exchange when its price is low and its sales of foreign exchange when its price is high serve to reduce the fluctuations in the price for foreign exchange. Thus, the divergence of the price for foreign exchange from parity seems less apparent in Austria than in London and Berlin. Looking over longer periods, however, the average height of the prices for foreign exchange is dependent upon supply and demand over the entire period under consideration and not upon these short-term influences.[47]

The supposed opposition between discount and foreign exchange policies should be considered just as incorrect. The Austro-Hungarian Bank is not relieved of the need to counteract temporarily unfavorable

46. See Müller, op. cit., pp. 14ff.
47. See Heyn, "Kritische Erörterung des Projekts der Beseitigung des Goldagios in Spanien," *Jahrbücher für Nationalökonomie und Statistik*, 3rd ser., vol. 25, pp. 756ff.

patterns in the balance of international payments by implementing interest rate increases, as well as through an intelligent use of its large foreign exchange holdings. In the case of defending the currency, the foreign exchange reserve is really best suited for increasing the precious metal holdings (indeed, it is the cheapest and easiest way). If the Bank wanted to yield up its entire inventory of foreign exchange holdings to foreign demands and use the resulting revenues to increase its gold reserves, the Bank could render the same services to the economy in the future as surely as it does less conveniently and more expensively at present. This is because the Austro-Hungarian Bank's management of reserves is no different from the specie payment system used in England and Germany, only more refined and flexible. It is a specie payment system resulting from the centralization (one is tempted to say, the nationalization) of gold exports.

An otherwise sharp-eyed judge of foreign exchange policy emphasized that the Bank undertakes operations that appear to contradict all the rules of arbitrage with regard to approaching payment dates. For example, it acquires German bills at a 4 percent Reichsbank discount, even though its own discount rate is higher; or it sends gold abroad, even though the foreign exchange rate is still quite far from the gold exporting point.[48] Upon closer examination, however, these operations lose their unusual appearance and can be easily explained. That is to say, the Bank's assets in the form of foreign bills represent an advantageous capital appropriation whenever its own discount rate is higher than foreign rates. In the Bank's portfolio, an entirely different importance is accorded to foreign bills in comparison to domestic bills. From the perspective of Bank policy as well as partly from a legal standpoint, foreign bills primarily serve as reserves just like the precious metal holdings which they partly replace. In comparison with the non-interest-bearing precious metal holdings any interest income, however small it may be, appears in a favorable light. Critics of the Bank's foreign exchange policy start with the assumption that the monies invested in foreign assets are drawn away from funds otherwise available for domestic discounting of bills. If the critics were correct, then the Bank's foreign exchange policy would have exactly the opposite effect ascribed to it (which would be incorrect, as we have demon-

48. See "Die Devisenpolitik der österreichisch-ungarischen Bank," *Frankfurter Zeitung*, May 17, 1908.

strated). It would drive up the domestic discount rate instead of pushing it down.

In truth, however, the monies employed in foreign exchange dealings are withdrawn from the stockpile of the precious metal and not from the Bank's domestic bond portfolio. Undoubtedly, it is within the Bank's power to apply these monies to the domestic currency market as well; this would have to be accompanied by a reduction in the coverage of notes and giro assets[49] with the reserve of precious metals and foreign gold-backed assets. The Bank's liquidity might be negatively affected and would be dangerous for maintaining the equilibrium in the balance of payments. Moreover, the resulting reduction in interest rates would promote the development of unhealthy speculation. These are reasons enough for viewing an expansion of domestic discount activities at the cost of the precious metal reserves to be highly undesirable.

That the export of gold is always lucrative for the Bank, even when the foreign exchange rate has not yet reached the gold export point, emerges from the most recent literature as well as from earlier statements.

It is inappropriate to speak, therefore, about costs that are imposed by the Bank's foreign exchange policy, or about sacrifices caused from that policy in the name of maintaining the currency. The Bank's policy is to the greatest advantage of the entire economy; that the policy yields tidy profits, as well, for the Bank's shareholders and the two governments that receive a high proportion of the proceeds cannot be denied. It has been repeatedly explained by the Bank's leading personages that the Bank ultimately has profits in mind in its currency and foreign exchange dealings. It is only necessary to look at the numbers in the Bank's business reports to see that the proceeds have been increasing, year by year, from this branch of its business.

VII
The Form of the Bank Constitution

All fears expressed about the legal resumption of specie payments are unfounded. The legal resumption of specie payments will not require

---

49. ["Giro" refers to a form of bank transfer by a payer from his account to the person or business entity to which a sum of money is owed.—Ed.]

the slightest change in the current policies of the Bank. That which the Bank currently does voluntarily will be obligatory in the future, but there is no reason to believe that legal specie payments will cause any more difficulties than de facto redemption does now. However, should maintaining the gold-backed currency ever become impossible for the Austro-Hungarian economy in a time of crisis, the Bank's legal obligation to redeem notes will prove neither an aid nor an obstacle. In any case, it is an illusion to think that halting foreign exchange transactions by the Bank, that is, halting de facto specie payments to maintain the currency's exchange rate, would generate results any less serious than would be the halting of legal specie payments.

It must, in any case, be admitted that the existing rules under which the Bank currently operates might be impaired by the implementation of a law requiring specie payments. An entire series of changes in the present statutes of the Bank can be recommended to facilitate a continuation of the Bank's current policy.

In this regard, an initial increase in the amount of foreign exchange that can make up a part of the precious metal reserve could be proposed. It would be advantageous to replace the rule that fixes the quantity of foreign exchange that can constitute a part of the Bank's specie reserves with a variable amount, perhaps along the lines of saying that the Bank is granted the authority to invest a certain proportion of its precious metal holdings, for example, up to 10 to 15 percent, in foreign exchange. By this method, the costs of increasing the precious metal holdings would be at least partially reduced.

An increase in the amount of tax-free notes that may be issued by the Bank, which has been limited to 400 million crowns for more than two decades, could also be considered. A reduction in the 5 percent tax on banknotes issued in excess of those 400 million crowns could be especially advantageous under some circumstances. In order to remove every difficulty in the way of the Bank's investing gold abroad, the banknote tax could be fixed at a level of half of a percent below the existing bank discount rate. The government's revenue shortfall from reducing the tax on the banknotes that would occur from time to time when the interest rate was lower than 5.5 percent need not be worried about; it could be recouped by the higher income earned by the state due to the Bank's increased revenues. The Bank would have a free hand to exchange gold for foreign exchange without fearing that it would suffer losses due to more frequent transgression of the tax-free limit on the issue of notes, which might then result in the Bank having to raise the discount rate. On the other hand, at interest rates of 6 percent and above, an increase in the revenue from the tax on banknotes would occur, which certainly no one would oppose. Any conflict between public and private interests that might exist, because the higher discount rate might be perceived as an undue pressure on the entire economy from which the central bank gained an advantage, would thus be essentially eased.[50]

It already appears to be a forgone conclusion that the smaller note denominations of 10 and 20 crowns will have to be retained, that the stamping of silver token coins will have to be augmented due to increasing demand, and that the silver florin, which will eventually be replaced by a two-crown piece, will be removed from circulation. Then the Bank and the exchequer can stop imposing gold coins on commerce, which has accepted them only grudgingly.

As it is assumed that the public's habit of preferring paper to gold will not change in the foreseeable future, it may well be that in the future only banknotes and token coins will circulate domestically, while the essential role of note coverage and guardianship of commercial payments would devolve upon gold. It cannot be ignored that such a "constitution" for management of the currency would be in significant ways very far from the ideal of a gold-backed currency, which was envisioned by the champions of gold monometallism in the second half of the nineteenth century. It would not be correct, however, to describe such a monetary system as a paper currency with gold reserves for foreign commercial transactions. Even under such a system, gold would remain the standard of value in Austria-Hungary, while notes redeemable in gold would circulate at all times.

The single advantage of "saturating" domestic commerce with gold is the creation of a reserve upon which one can draw at times of war. A war chest can also be constructed in other, more efficient ways by increasing the country's primary central reserve. This would not be allowed to lie fallow; rather, in the form of assets held in foreign exchange and investments abroad, it would be generating income. The Bank could take over its management.

Based on these assumptions, nothing speaks against the resumption of legal specie payments, while, on the other hand, much speaks for it. It would above all strengthen the international credit of the monar-

---

50. See Schumacher, "Die deutsche Geldverfassung und ihre Reform," *Jahrbuch für Gesetzgebung, Verwaltung und Volkswirtschaft (Schmollers Jahrbuch)* 32 (1908): 1344ff.

chy, which is urgently needed given the monarchy's enormous foreign debts. The transition to a legally binding gold currency would offer the nation's creditors no more of a guarantee for compliance with payment obligations than is already assumed under the current system of de facto specie payments. However, the great moral consequence of implementing this measure is not to be doubted. It would quite conspicuously bring to the consciousness of a wider domestic and foreign audience the reality of the currency reform's success.

VIII

The Bank Feud Between Austria and Hungary over the Legal Resumption of Specie Payments

The problem of the legal resumption of specie payments raises a particular complication due to its relationship to Hungary's efforts to dissolve the bank association between the two halves of the Dual Monarchy.

Since the conclusion of the Déak Compromise in 1867,[51] Hungarian politics have ceaselessly endeavored to loosen the common bonds that connect that country to Austria. The achievement of economic autonomy from Austria has appeared as an especially important goal for Hungarian policy as a preliminary step leading to political independence. The national rebirth of the non-Magyar peoples of Hungary—Germans, Serbo-Croatians, Romanians, Ruthenians, and Slovaks—will, however, pull the rug out from under these endeavors and contribute to the strengthening of the national ideal of a Greater Austria.[52] At the moment, however, Hungarian policy is still determined by the views of the Magyar nobility, and the power of the government rests in the hands of the intransigent Independence Party.

51. [The "Déak Compromise of 1867" refers to Ferenc Déak (1803–76), a leading Hungarian political figure of the nineteenth century, who proposed the establishment of a "Dual Monarchy" of Austria-Hungary to replace the former Austrian Empire. He argued, in opposition to those Hungarian nationalists who wanted to establish a completely independent Hungary, that the Magyar nation would financially and economically gain by maintaining a political union with Austria under the rule of the Habsburg Monarchy.—Ed.]

52. [The "national ideal of a Greater Austria" refers to what in the nineteenth and early twentieth centuries was sometimes called the "Austrian idea." The vision was for a multinational empire under Habsburg rule in which each of the nine major linguistic and ethnic national groups who populated the Austro-Hungarian Empire would have equal rights, civil liberties, and local governing autonomy through which all of the member groups would gain by sharing a common political and economic "space" in Central Europe. Many Austrian classical liberals advocated it as the alternative to the growing nationalist antagonism and disunity within the Habsburg domain.—Ed.]

For this party, however, the Bank question has great political significance. Over the course of not quite three years of rule, the Independence Party has had to abandon one point after another in its program. If it were to concede on the Bank question as well, it must justifiably fear that in a short period of time a more radical group will displace it. Thus, political motives primarily influence the party's opinion concerning the Bank question.

The Austro-Hungarian Bank appears advantageous for Hungary only when viewed from a purely economic standpoint. It generously makes available to the Hungarian economy the rich funds of the Austrian money market. Hungary's portion of the Bank's discount portfolio is much greater than Austria's. Calculating to which part of the Dual Monarchy go bond payments, Hungary's portion amounts to 60 to 65 percent, while Austria's hovers between 35 and 40 percent. And this does not exhaust the advantages for Hungary. The negotiability of Hungarian bonds in Austria enables their issuance to Austrian capitalists and private banks, because it can always count on the central bank rediscounting them in emergencies. The competition for Austrian capital on the Hungarian currency market doubtless depressed the interest rate in Hungary, which still remained abnormally high.

Hungary is a country with an unfavorable balance of payments. According to Fellner, who certainly had no intention of painting a bleak picture, the annual deficit of the Hungarian balance of payments to all foreign creditors amounted to 176 million crowns. However, it should be noted that out of the total assets of 277 million, not less than 145 million, or far more than half, rest upon cash remittances from emigrants that are subject to fluctuations based on the circumstances in the countries to which Hungarians have immigrated. In addition, on the asset side are the notable postings of an export surplus of 96 million and transactions for finished products of 24 million crowns. On the debit side, there appear interest, dividend, and bond transactions worth 352 million crowns.[53] Much more hazardous for Hungary is its exceedingly high rate of debt to Austria. The unity of the currency market has reached the point where the Austrians have deposited incredibly large amounts in short-term investments in Hungary. As long as the Dual Monarchy lasts, these obligations pose no threat to the Hungarian currency. This would be different following a political separation.

53. According to Fellner, op. cit., pp. 151ff. For similarly unfavorable results arrived at by a different set of calculations, see Gärtner, "Der österreichisch-ungarische Ausgleich," *Archiv für Sozialwissenschaft und Sozialpolitik*, vol. 25, pp. 391ff.

Hungary would be able to prevent the withdrawal of these monies only through large sacrifices in the form of higher interest rates.

On the other hand, Austria has little to fear from dissolution of the Austro-Hungarian Bank. Austria has, in contrast to Hungary and other foreign countries, a favorable balance of payments even without including investment exports. Assuming that Austria wanted to withdraw monies with short maturities that are deposited in the land of St. Stephen's crown,[54] it would create a currency surplus on its own money market, which should in part enable industry to find new markets to replace the ones lost in Hungary. Only a devaluation of the Hungarian currency, which could easily occur as a result of dissolution of the Austro-Hungarian Bank, would be hazardous for Austria. Initially this would be because of Austria's large holdings in Hungarian investments; later, for as long as the customs union persists, that is, until 1917, the agio resulting from a Hungarian currency devaluation would reduce the competition of Austrian producers facing the Hungarians. However, there can be no doubt that the banking and currency policies implemented by an independent Hungary would attempt everything possible to prevent a devaluation of its monies.[55]

Nevertheless, at the conclusion of the last compromise in the fall of 1907, Austria knowingly inserted a series of stipulations to be prepared in case of a possible appearance of a gold premium in Hungary. A special ordinance in the final protocol of the compromise, which has the power of law, determines that if the bank and currency union is terminated the method for calculating all payments should be in gold. This would not only apply for reciprocal state financial benefits, that is, the benefits from country to country, but also for all other benefits to the nation, in regard to which there exists a contractual obligation between the two countries. This also applies to benefits concerning all parties in the country insofar as they are subject to contractual obligations. This pertains not only to sales taxes, in particular the beer, brandy, sugar, and mineral oil taxes, but also freight payments by the railways, because parity in the railway tariffs was agreed upon in the compromise.[56]

54. [The "land of St. Stephen's crown" refers to the historical territory ruled according to "divine right" by the kings of Hungary. Tradition says that St. Stephen I held up the crown during his coronation in the year A.D. 1000 as an offering to the Virgin Mary to symbolize a "contract" between her and the holder of that royal office.—Ed.]
55. See Spitzmüller, "Die staatsfinanzielle Vereinbarungen im österreichisch-ungarischen Ausgleich," *Zeitschrift für Volkswirtschaft, Sozialpolitik und Verwaltung*, vol. 17, p. 391.
56. Ibid., pp. 392f.

Terms accepted in the initial protocol (dubbed in honor of their initiator the "Benedikt formula") relating to the Bank go even further in their regulations, which, while not having the force of law, possess, however, the character of a binding contract. Accordingly, the two governments are obligated to reach agreements, prior to the reorganization of an autonomous Hungarian note-issuing bank, to assure the execution of the ordinances under the treaty concerning the regulation of trade and commercial relations between the two nations. In particular, the agreements prevent any impediments or interference with the goal of free trade between the two nations that might arise from any eventual differences in the value of separate Austrian and Hungarian currencies.[57]

It appears ever more likely that Hungary would be prepared to give in on the Bank question for setting the conditions under which the Austro-Hungarian Bank will be legally obligated to pay in specie. Hungary's interest in the "crowning" of the currency reform is a purely political one. If the Bank's privilege has to be renewed once more, the monetary constitution should contain this type of redemption rule, so that the construction of an autonomous bank will at least be possible later. For that reason above all else, Hungary wants to be financially independent from Vienna, to at least partially pay off its debts to Austria, and to receive new support in Western Europe for this. The possibility, in the first instance, of having investments in Hungarian crowns in France remains very limited, however, as long as a gold-backed currency does not exist in Hungary.

As was shown, Austria has at the moment no reason to refrain from giving legal sanction to the current currency situation; from the standpoint of enhancing Austria's international credit standing, there is much that speaks for it. Even the financial emancipation of Hungary cannot appear undesirable. Austria's large holdings of Hungarian bonds make it much too dependent on the changing fate of the Hungarian economy; the sale of a part of these investments, which at present is difficult to accomplish, could only improve Austria's position. Currently, Austria possesses, not including domestic bonds, a barely appreciable amount in investments that have an international market: in times of

---

57. See Bunzel, "Die Bankformel," *Neue Freie Presse*, November 28, 1907; November 27, 1907; December 19, 1907. The fact that the bank formula is not able to insure Austria completely from the results of a devaluation of the future autonomous currency is emphasized in particular by Reitler, "Die Bankfrage in Österreich-Hungarn," *Der Tag*, October 15, 1908. See also "Die Bankfrage," *Das Vaterland*, December 13, 1908.

war, this could hinder fund raising far more than is desirable. After creating a large market for Hungarian bonds in Paris, those Hungarian investments remaining in Austrian possession would become a valuable asset. The Hungarian market would receive a further powerful boost, in that the domestic demand for investments would turn more than previously toward bonds on the international market.

Austria's opposition to the legal resumption of specie payments rests solely on fears concerning what its impact will be on the structure of the discount rates. We believe we have demonstrated the erroneous nature of these fears. To fight against an institution that would be beneficial for Austria merely on the basis of a traditional mistrust that says that anything that Hungary actively desires must be disadvantageous for Austria is not an intelligent policy. Just because Hungary could also profit from the change, and even if the general bitterness of the Austrians toward the dodges of the Magyar politicians is justified, it is wrongheaded on that basis to oppose legal specie resumption.[58]

Neither in Austria nor in Hungary can substantive arguments be made for the continuation of the current currency situation of de facto specie payments. Nothing speaks against the legal requirement that would be the fait accompli of the transition to the gold-backed currency.

58. See the speech by the director of the Viennese Giro und Kassenvereins, Dr. Hammerschlag, in the meeting of the Viennese Chamber of Commerce on May 12, 1903 (minutes, ibid., p. 217).

CHAPTER 3

The Foreign Exchange Policy of the Austro-Hungarian Bank[1]

The monetary system of the Austro-Hungarian monarchy has, during the last few years, aroused general interest in economic circles both at home and abroad. Theorists were first attracted to this question by Prof. G. F. Knapp's excellent work,[2] which found as many ardent admirers as opponents. In the recent bank *enquête* [inquiry] instituted by the German Government this subject was exhaustively treated. Under such circumstances, it may not be out of place to devote a little attention to this question, removing the numerous misconceptions both in the monarchy and abroad.

I

According to the law paper currency is still the standard currency, for the legal tender of the Austro-Hungarian Bank is inconvertible. In 1892, it is true, a number of legislative measures were taken in order to pave the way for a gold currency. One such measure obliges the said Bank to buy any quantity of gold offered to it at the rate of 3,280 kronen per 1 kilo pure gold (less 2 kronen for coining), thus hindering once and

1. [This article originally appeared in English in the *Economic Journal* (June 1909). See Ludwig von Mises, *Notes and Recollections* (South Holland, Ill.: Libertarian Press, [1940] 1978), pp. 43–44: "In the fall of 1908 Professor [Francis] Edgeworth asked Professor [Eugen von] Philippovich to contribute an article to the *Economic Journal*. Such an essay, to be no longer than ten pages, was to analyze for the English-speaking world the foreign exchange policy of the Austro-Hungarian Bank. Philippovich declined and recommended me to [Edgeworth]. I accepted." The reader will see that part of the argument in this article is an abridged version of the longer analysis that Mises provided in his German-language article "The Problem of Legal Resumption of Specie Payments in Austria-Hungary," Chapter 2 in the present volume.—Ed.]
2. *Staatliche Theorie des Geldes* [The State Theory of Money] (Leipzig, 1905), pp. 249–52, 377–94.

for all any increase in the value of the Austro-Hungarian standard with respect to gold.

Since that time pure gold cannot be valued at less than k. 3,278 per kilo in Austria-Hungary, for should it decline the Bank must continue purchasing until the price rises again to par. A further measure, which was actually carried out, was the coining of gold, silver, nickel, and bronze coins. The old silver coins were withdrawn from the market, only the silver gulden remains, and even today it has unlimited legal tender quality. Since 1879 the silver gulden has been coined for account of the State only; in 1892 the coining was stopped, and at the moment (November, 1908) there are about 300 million kronen of such gulden in the Monarchy. This stock will very shortly be reduced by 28 million kronen, which will be recoined into 5-kronen pieces to meet the increasing demand for these coins. The 5-kronen pieces are, however, tokens; their coinage is limited, and no private person can be compelled to accept more than k. 250 in such coins as payment. Since the beginning of 1908 the Bank has been withdrawing the silver guldens and storing them in its cellars. These silver guldens will be gradually recoined into small coins, for, since wages have continually risen, the demand for fractional coins is especially great. Considering the unlimited legal tender quality of the silver gulden, the currency of Austria-Hungary must still be taken as a "limping standard," even were the banknotes redeemable, just as the French currency must be described owing to the unlimited legal tender quality of the 5-franc piece.

In 1892 another very important measure was taken, viz., the redemption of the Government paper currency, i.e., legal tender notes issued by the Government. The Government raised a great loan and handed over the proceeds in gold to the Bank to enable it to redeem the Government paper currency for account of the State. This has actually been done, and today Government paper currency is a thing of the past.

The Bank, however, did not give gold for this Government paper currency, but banknotes, and in part silver guldens and silver fractional coins; the gold was retained as cover for the banknotes. In place of the not redeemable legal tender Government notes, not redeemable bank notes have been substituted. Whereas the old Government paper currency was not covered, the banknotes are partly covered by metal, bills, and loans, as in other Continental states.

To perfect the transition to a gold currency and thus finish the projected reform instituted in 1892, the Austro-Hungarian Bank ought to have been obliged to redeem its notes in gold when required. The law, however, has not yet prescribed such a procedure. Nevertheless, both the Government and the Bank have not lost sight of this point. The latter, especially, has done its utmost to augment continually its gold reserves. Besides the gold it possessed previous to 1892, and that already mentioned, which the Governments of both Austria and Hungary transferred for the redemption of the paper currency, it has also been able to purchase larger quantities of gold favored by the extremely good rates of exchange existing for a number of years. On the 7th of December 1908, the gold reserve of the Bank amounted to 1,135 million kronen, being only surpassed by the Bank of France and the Russian States Bank. But the Bank did not stop at the mere accumulation of gold, but endeavored to acquire a great number of bills payable in gold.

The Bank is obliged to cover its notes in circulation by at least 40 percent metal. As metallic cover the law recognizes gold coins, coined in Austria or Hungary, gold bullion and foreign gold coins, further Austrian and Hungarian silver guldens and fractional coins. For the so-called metallic cover of the notes in circulation are also recognized bills on foreign places, payable in gold within three months, and provided by at least two signatures of well-known endorsers, further foreign banknotes payable on demand in gold, the two together in the aggregate 60 million kronen. The other part of the cover has to be discounted bills and warrants, and loans against security. The Bank is permitted to include also in this part of the cover foreign gold bills and gold notes. As soon as the notes in circulation exceed the metal reserves, prescribed by law, by more than 400 million kronen, the Bank is obliged to pay a tax of 5 percent of the surplus. This latter clause is analogous to the German bank law.

Since 1899 the Bank is also entitled to have assets abroad and to draw checks, etc., on them.

Under such legal circumstances the Bank could very easily acquire great amounts of foreign bills and assets abroad. The gold lying in the Bank's cellars does not bear any interest, but as soon as a part of it is exchanged for bills on Berlin or London—the Bank is allowed to do so to the extent mentioned above—it yields interest.

II

The Bank having in this manner increased its gold reserves and accumulated a great stock of foreign bills payable in gold, it took a further important step in 1896 to stabilize the foreign exchanges; it began to sell bills on foreign markets without reserve at a price which would be lower than the above gold point after the introduction of the gold currency. The sole aim of the Bank since then has always been to maintain a large stock of foreign assets payable at demand to enable it to satisfy any demand whatever that may be made, and in this respect has been very successful. It could sell bills on London or Berlin under such conditions that the exchange never rose above the par higher than it rises in countries with a perfect gold currency, and in which the banknotes are redeemable at demand.

In August 1901, the Bank went still further, and began to issue gold coins of k. 20 and k. 10, and discounted bills and granted loans partly in gold instead of notes, and transferred gold to the Treasury for the salaries of their officials and other Government payments.

This change found but little sympathy among the public. For more than half a century only paper money circulated in both halves of the realm, and everybody got so accustomed to it that they were but little at home with the gold coins. Even today the public prefers banknotes to gold, and those gold coins issued soon find their way back into the Bank. The Bank, however, constantly sets them in circulation again, only to have them returned shortly afterwards. From August 1901 to the end of 1907 the bank gave out 1,616.4 million kronen, 1,381.7 of which returned by the 31st of December 1907, only 234.7 million kronen remaining out of the Bank. Of this latter amount only a part is in actual circulation, the rest being either in the State pay offices, at the private banks, or at the railway offices.

The state of things today is about as follows:

The Bank, it is true, is not compelled by the law to redeem its notes, but in fact it is always ready to do so. For home purposes gold is seldom, if ever, withdrawn, for—as mentioned—the public cannot break themselves of the use of banknotes and silver coins for small and moderate payments, and then, again, checks of the joint stock banks and the postal check service, as well as the clearing service of the Austro-Hungarian Bank, are all becoming more in vogue from year to year. As a rule the Bank is not called upon either to issue gold for payments abroad; this is merely because it always sells foreign bills at such a price that it is cheaper to purchase and forward checks or bills than gold. The monarchy enjoys in this way every advantage of a gold currency, while it is able to carry on the circulation with a medium the least expensive.

It is clear to everybody that the Austrian monetary system is thus almost that ideal which David Ricardo once upheld.[3] The Austrian system differs but in two points from that of the great master of political economy. One is of small importance. Ricardo wished to avoid the use of gold coinage as a medium of circulation, and, as he presumed that if everybody had the choice of using £1, £2, or £5 notes or gold, they would naturally prefer the latter, he saw no other way of preventing this than by subjecting the Bank to the delivery of uncoined gold or silver, at the Mint standard and price, in exchange for their notes instead of the delivery of guineas. With the above-described habits of the public here such a restriction is superfluous; even were the Bank compelled to exchange the notes for gold, people would prefer to use paper to gold, as is the case nowadays where the Bank willingly pays notes in gold.

The second difference is of more importance, still not one of principle. It is that the Bank keeps a great part of the cover for its notes not in actual gold but in foreign gold bills, and besides, to meet its other daily obligations, holds a further stock of foreign bills and other foreign assets at short notice; further, that the Bank sells such foreign bills to those wishing to make payments abroad, and consequently the bankers and merchants do not want gold, but bills and checks, to pay debts or to loan money abroad. Should the foreign bills or other assets abroad in possession of Austrians and Hungarians prove insufficient to cover the bills drawn on inland places and the checks in foreign hands, then the Bank exports gold on its own account. The gold is exported betimes, and bills acquired for it that the Bank then gives in exchange for its notes.

This policy of the Bank has been the cause that the rate of exchange in Austria-Hungary does not fluctuate as in other countries. This seems only natural, for today Austria-Hungary actually has a gold currency, although not *de jure*, because for more than twelve years the bank has voluntarily paid in gold or gold bills.

3. [David Ricardo, "Proposals for an Economical and Secure Currency," [1816] reprinted in Piero Sraffa, ed., *The Works and Correspondence of David Ricardo*, vol. 4, *Pamphlets and Papers, 1815–1823* (Cambridge: Cambridge University Press, 1951), pp. 41–141.—Ed.]

The Bank having succeeded for so many years always to keep a sufficient stock of gold and foreign assets to meet any possible calls made on it, it must be concluded that the Bank will also be able to pay its notes in gold on demand should the law prescribe it. Such a prescription would only alter the face of things in one respect, viz., that, whereas the Bank redeems its notes nowadays voluntarily, it would in future merely follow the demands of the law. But even then gold would not be taken by the public for home payments, though the Bank is empowered to issue small notes.[4] Should the law prescribe payment in specie, the Bank can still buy foreign bills for its portfolio, and offer them at prices below the export prices, so that bills are used for sending money abroad instead of bullion or gold coin.

III

Nevertheless, numerous protests are made in Austria against the legal payment in gold for the following reasons, which must be considered. It is asserted that the discount rate of the Austro-Hungarian Bank has been lower and changed less than the foreign note banks. This is doubtless correct. The rate of discount of the Austro-Hungarian Bank was, as the following table shows, always lower during the last few years than that of the German Reichsbank, and often lower than that of the Bank of England, whereby we must not overlook the fact that the Bank of England also discounts below its official rate; the Austro-Hungarian and the German Reichsbank never do so.

The yearly average of the bank discount rates was:

Year	Bank of England	German Reichsbank	Austro-Hungarian Bank
1903	3.75	3.84	3.50
1904	3.64	4.84	3.50
1905	3.01	3.82	3.70
1906	4.27	5.15	4.33
1907	4.93	6.03	4.89

The great stability of the discount rate of the Austro-Hungarian Bank is especially remarkable. It never rises as high as the German or

4. Nowadays kronen 20 notes may be given out at any time under the same conditions as k. 50, k. 100, and k. 1,000 notes; on the other hand, k. 10 notes may only be issued in the aggregate of 160 million kronen, and then if specially covered in full by gold.

English, nor falls so low. Even in the critical November days of 1907, when the Bank of England increased its rate to 7 percent, the German Reichsbank to 7.5 percent, the Austro-Hungarian Bank did not exceed 6 percent. On the other hand, its rate of interest has never fallen below 3.5 percent. From 1892 till 1907 included, the Bank of England altered its discount seventy-four times, the German Reichsbank fifty-seven, and the Austro-Hungarian Bank only twenty-one times.

The private discount rate, too, is not always higher than Berlin and London, often even lower. This was distinctly perceptible during the crises in the last quarter of 1907, when in November the private rate for three months' bills, on an average, was Vienna 5.28 percent, Berlin 6.62 percent, and London 6.54 percent.

If the Austro-Hungarian Bank were legally constrained to redeem in gold, the opponents of such a measure maintain that the discount rate in Austria would always have to be higher than abroad, for the monarchy has foreign obligations, and must necessarily entice her foreign creditors by a higher rate to leave their money in Austria-Hungary. The suspension of the gold payments had the advantage of the Bank being empowered to pay in cash if it wishes, or, in other words, redeem its notes in gold or gold bills, but by no means compelled to do so. Importers wishing to pay for goods bought abroad, and those[5] who have to pay the interest and amortization quota on foreign loans could always get the desired amounts from the Bank at any time in gold bills or checks. On the other hand, by refusing to sell bills when wanted merely for the purpose of sending capital abroad to profit by the higher rate of discount, the Bank would be protected against losing large sums of gold, and can easily maintain a lower rate than the foreign banks. Presuming the legal prescription of gold payments the Bank would be forced to participate in the international fight for gold like other banks, and as an only protection against attacks on its gold reserves raise the discount rate. In favor of industry and agriculture an increase of the interest on the home market must, however, be avoided at all costs.

This theory, which is supported by nearly every political party in Austria, is, however, entirely false.

First of all, it is not at all true that the Bank refuses to deliver bills and gold if it thinks they are for investments abroad. Far from upholding such a policy the Bank itself sends money abroad when the market

---

5. As such are considered first of all the State, the Crownlands, Corporations, then the large railway companies and mortgage banks.

appears to be favorable. If the momentary home demand is small and the gold reserves in the Bank fairly large, the Bank exchanges a part of its reserves for foreign bills in order to procure, in this way, interest on its capital, which otherwise would lie idle in its cellars. The moment greater demands are made on the Bank for bills for profiting by the difference in the discounts abroad, a corresponding rise in the rates of discount immediately takes place.[6]

Did the Bank act otherwise, i.e., refuse to sell the bills and gold, as it is wrongly accused of sometimes doing, the exchange would immediately rise considerably. This is best seen if the present state of affairs is compared with those existing prior to the actual introduction of the gold payments in 1896. In 1893 a great tightness existed on the international money market owing to the Australian and North American crises. As at this period the Austro-Hungarian Bank declined to raise its rate of discount, the foreign holders of Austrian bills returned them to Vienna and demanded payment. Neither gold nor gold bills were to be had on the Austrian market and the Bank would not dispose of them either; the London bills on the Vienna Exchange rose to 127.65 guldens. This rate meant an agio of 6.3 percent, as compared to the par of 120.09 guldens fixed in 1892.

Later it also repeatedly happened that difficulties on the London and Berlin money markets caused an external drain in Austria. The Bank then immediately raised its rate of interest, and sold bills below the imaginary export point, as it would be after the redemption of gold payments. The same as note banks of other countries, it was able, in this way, to secure the stability of the Austro-Hungarian standard. Professor Knapp, therefore, is greatly mistaken in assuming an essential difference between the policy of the Austro-Hungarian Bank and that of other central note banks. In such cases the Bank of England redeems its notes in gold, the Austro-Hungarian Bank in gold bills, viz., gold in foreign hands. Yet the public who present their notes to the Bank are quite satisfied with this procedure, because they get bills at a price apparently so advantageous that they prefer to buy and forward *Devisen* (foreign bills) abroad instead of bullion or gold coins. To have the requisite stock of *Devisen* and able to meet any demand, the Bank sends gold abroad and procures bills in exchange. The whole difference, as compared to England and Germany, is that gold is not exported by

6. Bilinski, *Über internationale Zahlungen*, 1906, p. 3.

private businessmen but the Austro-Hungarian Bank itself. True, it cannot be denied that the large Austrian private banks sometimes do not export gold for the mere reason of fearing to offend the Bank who, otherwise, could possibly place difficulties in the rediscounting of their bills. In Germany, affairs are very similar but much more severe, and have absolutely no relation with the suspension of gold payments and the *Devisen* policy.

The cause of the comparatively low discount in Austria-Hungary must be sought in the bad state of business in Austria. The speculative spirit of the populace is almost entirely wanting, and the unfortunate state of politics is a stumbling block to active production. The former Minister of Trade, Dr. Baernreither, rightly declares that cheap money in Austria is by no means a sign of economic soundness, but, on the contrary, of stagnation and want of speculative spirit.

Another misleading assertion is that Austria-Hungary is burdened with obligations abroad, and consequently compelled to maintain a higher discount rate than other countries. For these obligations are only on the capital market, i.e., on the long loan market, and consequently the interest for rents and mortgages is higher than in Germany, not to speak of England. On the other hand, there are times on the money market, i.e., market for short loans, when the greatest Austrian foreign assets are met with but a trifling set-off on the part of the foreigners. This contrasts vividly with the state of affairs in Germany, whose holding of foreign stock may be estimated at 16 milliards of marks, even after deducting German stock in foreign hands, and nevertheless is regularly indebted abroad on the money market for big amounts. True, the foreign markets can get bills on Vienna by returning Austro-Hungarian stock, but the high classification of this paper hinders such an operation. The want of short foreign loans remarkably strengthens the Austrian money market in times of high discounts, for then the foreign markets are not able to withdraw money from it, but in the absence of claims due must accommodate themselves with loans on the Austrian money market.

IV

Professor Knapp regards the foreign exchange policy of the Austro-Hungarian Bank as diametrically opposite to the discount policy of other central note banks. He is of opinion that it is not right for two

States having the same metallic currency automatically to reestablish the par of the standard by the use of metal. The authorities ought to make it their special duty to maintain the standard value in international exchange. The English and German discount policy and the Austro-Hungarian *"Devisen"* policy could be taken as examples. In both cases some sacrifice has to be made. With the discount policy the sacrifice falls upon the business people, who are accustomed to discount bills and take Lombard loans[7] from the Bank. The *"Devisen"* policy also demands some sacrifice; the Bank, it is true, bears it in this case, but only because it expects some compensation from the State.

The Bank employs a great part of its capital to purchase a number of bills on England, and regularly replaces them as they fall due. The Bank buys these bills at any price, and sometimes in the hopes of making a profit should the rate be favorable, but more often than not without any such prospects whatever, especially when the rate is unfavorable. Further, the Bank has decided to sell these bills at par as soon as the rate becomes unfavorable. With very rare exceptions, it loses on the bills. The exception is with bills bought at propitious times. By this intervention in the rates which otherwise are determined to suit personal interests, the par of exchange is reestablished, and a weighty administrative task performed that is well worth the sacrifice. The Bank may, therefore, justly expect the Treasury to recompense its losses.[8]

It does not lie within our sphere to inquire how far Professor Knapp's view that "an automatic reestablishment of foreign exchanges does not take place" is correct or not. Because this theory is closely connected with his general conception of money, it consequently can only be judged in connection with it. Such a task would surpass the limits of this article, which is devoted exclusively to the "Devisen" policy of the Austro-Hungarian Bank. But Knapp's opinion of this policy must receive a little more attention.

First of all it must be shown that the "Devisen" policy claims no sacrifice from the Bank; on the contrary, it gives it enormous profits. The investment of a part of its assets in foreign bills and current accounts with foreign banks throws off a considerable profit in interests; also the fluctuations of the foreign exchanges, however small they may be, have a favorable influence on the Bank's balance. For the Bank does not

---

7. "Lombard loans" are loans with securities pledged as collateral.
8. Knapp, pp. 247–52.

buy bills when they are high, but when low, and sells them with rising rates at a profit.[9] It is not true either that the Bank's foreign bills and checks are sold at par, but at the corresponding market price of the day. To prevent the rates rising above the ideal gold export point, the Bank endeavors to keep a plentiful stock of foreign bills at the disposal of the market. As soon as this stock gets low it is replenished. But the Bank never appears on the market as buyer when the price of foreign bills is high; this would be the worst step it possibly could take. The appearance of a new buyer would be more likely to drive prices up still higher. As already mentioned, the Bank—when the price of foreign bills is high—strengthens its stock by exporting gold, and thus places itself in a position to meet all and any demand that may be made.

The Bank is also able to drive the rates up if it buys foreign bills at low prices; but then its economic importance is entirely different. The demand for foreign bills being better distributed over the single days and weeks of the year, the fluctuations in the rates are more equalized; the average level can naturally not be affected in this manner.

The contrast drawn by Knapp between "foreign bill policy" and "discount policy" must also be described as equally incorrect. By its great stock of foreign bills and the clever use it makes of them, the Bank is not freed of its duty to prevent any temporary unfavorable situation of the balance of payments by raising the discount rate. To maintain the gold standard the stock of foreign bills merely acts as a strengthener of the metal reserves—an augmentation both the cheapest and the best. Were the Bank to realize the whole stock of foreign bills and augment the gold reserves with the proceeds, it could do the same economic service in future, true, less to the purpose and dearer, but with just as much security as nowadays. For the system of the Austro-Hungarian Bank is nothing else than a system of gold payments like England and Germany, yet better and more appropriate. The sole difference is the monopolization of the gold export by the Bank.

V

Consequently, it is utterly wrong to believe that the discount rate of the Bank and the market would be higher than at present after any legal prescription of gold payments. For more than twelve years the Bank

9. In 1907 the Bank's profits of the foreign moneys and foreign bills was k. 5,732,672.

has upheld the policy of a gold-paying bank, and, therefore, any legal prescription can affect it but little. Even such law could not prevent it from always keeping in future a large stock of gold bills and gold assets abroad, and in this manner maintain a cheaper reserve than would be the case with the whole reserves lying idle in its cellars.

On the other hand, the monarchy will profit immensely by a legally prescribed gold payment, for its international credit, which it urgently needs for its enormous foreign debts, would considerably improve. For only the *de jure* gold payments would clearly convince everyone abroad that Austria-Hungary enjoys nowadays a perfectly regulated currency.

CHAPTER 4

On the Problem of Legal Resumption of Specie Payments in Austria-Hungary

A *Reply to Walther Federn*[1]

The remarks that I published in this journal last year about the problem of legal resumption of specie payments in Austro-Hungary[2] have received a response by Walther Federn[3] in this journal's first issue for this year. The author says that my claim that the Austro-Hungarian Bank made foreign exchange available at all times at a rate that was lower than the upper gold point does not correspond to the facts, and, therefore, my conclusions are incorrect. In his article Mr. Federn develops his own theory (with which I disagree) more substantially and in far greater detail than in his previous, shorter newspaper articles. He is, without a doubt, one of the few representatives speaking in favor of the advantages from the current currency arrangement in Austria-Hungary who should be taken seriously. Thus, it seems appropriate that his remarks should not be left without a response.[4]

There is a great theoretical importance to the problems discussed here. On the one hand, there is a close relationship between this problem and the questions that Knapp's *State Theory of Money* has placed at the center of modern theoretical economics. No less important, however, is the practical importance of this issue for the Austro-

---

1. [This article originally appeared in German in the *Jahrbuch für Gesetzgebung, Verwaltung und Volkswirtschaft (Schmollers Jahrbuch)*, vol. 34, no. 3–4 (1910).—Ed.]

2. ["The Problem of Legal Resumption of Specie Payments in Austria-Hungary," Chapter 2 in the present volume.—Ed.]

3. [Walther Federn (1869–1949) was a prominent economic and financial commentator in Vienna before and after the First World War. In 1908 he founded *The Austrian Economist* magazine (modeled after *The Economist* in Great Britain), which he edited until 1934. He first immigrated to Sweden and finally came to the United States, where he lived until his death.—Ed.]

4. I will not say anything further here about Mr. Federn's remarks directed against my essay in the newspaper he publishes, *Der österreichische Volkswirt* (July 31, 1909), because he does not raise them again in the essay in this journal.

Hungarian Monarchy, where the question about the legal resumption of specie payments has not disappeared from the agenda. It is also of importance in Imperial Germany, where the Reichsbank is attempting to establish a position of power on the foreign exchange market similar to that already held by its Viennese sister institution.

I

The Development of Erroneous Views about Foreign Exchange Policy

I believe I have already said everything essential in connection with the question about the legal resumption of specie payments in my earlier essay, and Mr. Federn's new remarks do not induce me to recant a single word of it. It should be emphasized, again, that the claim that the Austro-Hungarian Bank sometimes denied the release of foreign exchange to interest rate arbitrageurs is absolutely inconsistent with the facts.

If one asks how such an incorrect claim could be made at all, one comes upon the following:

Several banks and private bankers have complained that the Bank sometimes capitalizes on its preeminent position on the foreign exchange market to demand high prices for the foreign exchange that they request; however, it should be pointed out that the prices are always still below the upper gold point. Similarly, here and there laments are made that the Bank occasionally does not release any foreign exchange. Concerning this latter grievance, it turns out that whenever the foreign exchange rate is a considerable distance from the upper gold point the Bank sometimes shows no interest in supplying some of its foreign exchange, that is, it instructs its representatives on the foreign exchange market to reply negatively to every request for surrendering foreign exchange. Whenever the demand for foreign exchange is not insignificant, the Bank's restrictive policy results in a rise in the foreign exchange rates. Then, when the foreign exchange rates have reached a certain level, the Bank again releases foreign exchange onto the market and brings any further increase in the exchange rates to a halt.

However, the importance of the Bank's intervention is that it constantly occurs before the foreign exchange rate has reached the upper gold point. It is this last point that is of importance for monetary policy. How high may be the price that the Bank demands for its foreign exchange is a matter of complete indifference, so long as it demands less than would justify the costs of actually exporting gold. That the Bank, *ex facto*, pays specie for foreign exchange is unaffected by this. Whether it is to settle debts coming due abroad or merely to invest money abroad, anyone wanting to purchase foreign exchange or checks should certainly be pleased that it is supplied to them as inexpensively as possible. It is, of course, understandable that as long as it does not interfere with its monetary policy goal of keeping the foreign exchange rate below the upper gold point, the Bank manages its foreign exchange portfolio to earn the highest proceeds possible by charging the best price it can get for its foreign exchange.

When absolutely no gold was obtainable on the unofficial foreign exchange market of the Austro-Hungarian Empire,[5] the Bank lacked any precise way of determining whether or not the upper gold point had been reached or even surpassed. In those early years of its new policy (1896–1900), the Bank sometimes released German foreign exchange at a rate of 0.75 percent, or sometimes even at one percent, above parity; indeed, once it did so at an even higher rate on March 23, 1900. However, even this represented significant progress in comparison with the older situation; indeed, in 1893, an agio emerged of up to 6.5 percent. The desired stability of the foreign exchange rate had not yet been completely achieved.

Beginning in the second half of 1901, when the Bank began to supply gold on the unofficial market, it had a reliable indicator of whether or not the upper gold point had already been reached. Whenever this point was reached, gold in circulation began to be exported and the Bank received inquiries whether it would be willing to release gold as well as surrendering foreign exchange.

To counteract such inroads into the monarchy's gold reserves, the Bank needs no other method than to increase its discount rate. As far as banks in Vienna are concerned, the most important foreign exchange market outside Austria-Hungary is the banking centers in Germany. In comparison, the foreign exchange markets in London and Paris are only of secondary importance. The great importance of the German foreign exchange market dates from the time of close political ties be-

---

5. [The "unofficial market" was the private market on which gold was bought and sold; it was also the name for the Austro-Hungarian Bank policy after 1896 of de facto redemption of its banknotes for foreign exchange and then after 1901 for gold, though the Bank was still not legally required to do so.—Ed.]

tween Austria and the countries of the German Confederation, and it is the many economic connections between Austria and Germany that explain the persistence of this preferential treatment.[6]

In 1908, trade with Imperial Germany amounted to 42 percent of Austria-Hungary's total foreign trade. According to estimates by the Austrian Ministry of Finance, foreign investment in Austria and Hungary at the end of 1901 came to 9,353 million crowns, of which 4,568 million crowns were held by citizens of Germany, or almost 49 percent of the total. Besides this, it should also be pointed out that a large portion of the monarchy's trade with other foreign countries takes place through German intermediation.

Therefore, the Austro-Hungarian Bank turns its attention first and foremost to the foreign exchange market in German banking centers. Since the end of 1900, the Bank has intentionally maintained the purchase price for its foreign exchange and, as a rule, it has never risen more than one-quarter of a percent above the specie parity rate of 117.563. Only on a few days in the second half of March 1907, and then in November and December of 1909, did it rise above this to a maximum of 117.925 (0.31 percent above parity); and only once, on March 26, 1907, did it reach a rate of 118.05 (0.41 percent above parity).

II

The Bank's Policy in Light of the Statements by the Bank's Governor and the Viennese Stock Exchange

Federn's claim, that the Bank occasionally denies the release of foreign exchange, however, can only be demonstrated through counterevidence. It should be noted that Federn stands out in making this case, because other supporters of the same viewpoint have little knowledge of the detailed facts and simply assert their claims about the supposed benefits for interest rate policy from a suspension of specie payments. Their claims about the advantage from an "isolated" currency not embroiled in the international fight for gold have been repeatedly refuted.[7]

---

6. [This refers to the period before the Austro-Prussian War of 1866, when Austria was expelled from the German Confederation as a result of Prussia's victory in the conflict.—Ed.]

7. Thus Kuranda, a Member of Parliament, explained just recently in a speech given for the Lower Austrian Trade Union, "For myself—and I know myself to be one of many—I firmly hold the conviction that the 'splendid isolation' of Austria's interest rate policy must and will

If, as Federn claims, the Bank actually did occasionally deny the release of foreign exchange to interest rate arbitrageurs, then financial circles in Vienna would have some knowledge of its actions. This is, however, not the case. Whenever increases in the prime rate were being considered in Vienna due to increases in foreign exchange rates and rising interest rates on foreign markets, a refusal by the Bank to release foreign exchange has never appeared in the statements made by experts and is never mentioned in the newspapers. Rather, everyone completely understands that the Bank releases foreign exchange at a higher price and must unconditionally supply it, if it does not want to trigger a panic increase in the foreign exchange rate.

Completely opposite to what Federn alleges are the remarks made by the Austrian finance minister, Leon Ritter von Bilinski, who was governor of the Austro-Hungarian Bank at that time.[8] Bilinski explained that opponents of mandatory specie payments incorrectly assumed that variability in the interest rate would arise only in the case of legal resumption of specie payments, since the Bank was already required at that time to coordinate its interest rate policy with other foreign central banks. The Austro-Hungarian Bank, he said, did not consider every export of gold to be a catastrophe. The gold did not absolutely remain in the vaults of the Bank simply to cover its banknotes; rather, it was used to cover international payments as well, insofar as they resulted from the legitimate requirements of trade and commerce.

This last statement appears to give support to Federn's theory that the Bank satisfies only the "legitimate" requests for foreign exchanges, and sometimes refuses to release foreign exchange to the interest rate arbi-

---

come to an end with the resumption of specie payments. At that moment when the Austro-Hungarian Bank will be obligated to unconditionally hand over for every note presented at its doors the equivalent in legal, metal money, the Bank's treasury will become a capillary vessel into the system of international flow of money and gold. At a minimum, it will have to set its interest rate at the same level of that country which is momentarily most in need of the precious metals. The waves of the international economic situation will then pull our monetary and credit services into their maelstrom, regardless from whichever and however far away the center of the agitation may be from which it arises." (See *Fremdenblatt*, November 6, 1909.) This argument was already refuted years ago in the writings from which I quoted in my original essay.

8. [Leon Ritter von Bilinski (1846–1923) was a leading Polish political figure and economist in the Austro-Hungarian Empire, who served at various times as general director of the Imperial Railway and Austrian finance minister, as well as governor of the Austro-Hungarian Bank. He also was a governor of Bosnia-Herzegovina. After the First World War, he briefly served as minister of finance in 1919 in the newly independent Poland.—Ed.]

trageurs. However, Bilinski's next statements show that the Bank knew of no deterrent other than an increase in the discount rate to counter illegitimate requests for international means of payment. Namely, Bilinski then continued, "Thus, we vigorously resist every unjustified export of gold; for example, in October 1905, we already increased the interest rate as soon as gold exports exceeded two million crowns; conversely, we also often send gold to foreign markets whenever we have the expectation that this method will prevent a further increase in the foreign discount rate. By this means we stem any future export of gold from the monarchy that would require us to increase the Bank's discount rate."[9]

That is exactly the opposite of what Federn has alleged to be the policy of the Bank.

Concerning the events in 1907, about which Federn has claimed that the Bank denied the release of foreign exchange, it is stated in a report to the Viennese stock market that at the end of June, "multiple requests were sent to the Austro-Hungarian Bank, as well as other domestic institutions, whether gold bullion or gold coins could be released for export (namely to Germany and the Netherlands). Since the Bank *wished to maintain its voluntary adoption and up to then impeccable record of acting as an institution that paid in specie*, it was compelled to increase the discount rate from 4.5 percent to 5 percent on the 27th of June because of the small amount of gold available on the unofficial markets of the monarchy." This increase in the rate of interest achieved the desired goal of stemming the outflow of gold.[10] That it was not necessary for the Bank to increase its interest rate beyond 6 percent in the autumn of that same year can be traced back primarily to its policy earlier in the year, as can be inferred from the same report to the stock exchange: money was readily available in Vienna in November due to the precautionary action exercised by the Bank.[11]

Incidentally, there is nothing peculiar in the large difference in the private discount rates and the central bank rates during times of crisis. Precisely in such times, financiers become more anxious over risks that

9. See von Bilinski, "Über Internationale Zahlungen" [On International Payments], lecture in the special session of the Fourth Polish Judicial and Political Economy Conference in Krakow on October 2, 1906.
10. See *Jahresbericht der Wiener Börsenkammer. Der Verkehr an der Wiener Börse und der Geldmarkt in Jahre 1907* [Annual Report of the Viennese Stock Market: Transactions on the Viennese Bourse and the Currency Market in 1907] (Vienna, 1908), p. 193.
11. See ibid., pp. 200f.

are always connected with foreign investments during a crisis; they prefer lending their money at lower interest rates closer to home to bearing the increased risk of a better rate of return abroad. In turbulent times, noticeable differences appear even between currency markets within the same country, such as between Berlin and Frankfurt.

However, even if it can be ascertained that the Bank does not proceed as Federn has depicted, a moment should still be spent to consider whether such a policy would even be possible, and in what manner an increase in the foreign exchange rate could be prevented in spite of the Bank's refusal to release foreign exchange. There are two instances that Federn cites here. Initially, he refers to the fact that an increase in the foreign exchange rate decreases the gains from interest rate arbitrage. That this is true has never been denied. The entire objection appears invalid, however, if it is taken into consideration that since 1900 this increase in the foreign exchange rate has extended only to the upper gold point for foreign exchange at German banking centers. Thus, a limit to foreign exchange speculation receives little support on this count.

III
Transactions During the Bosnian Crisis

Additionally, Federn states that during the Bosnian Crisis[12] the Bank took particular advantage of the fact that it was not obligated to release actual gold upon demand in support of its interest rate policy. If it had been obligated, in fact, to unrestrictedly release gold, the banking sector would have prudently withdrawn gold from the Bank and sent it abroad, Federn says. However, because the Bank did not have to actually release gold, the demand would have been concentrated on foreign exchange.

But the Bank only reluctantly satisfied this speculative demand for foreign exchange, Federn argues. It allowed the rate of foreign exchange to rise above the redemption rate, indeed somewhat above the upper gold point, and successfully countered the speculation. Who-

12. [In 1878, Austria-Hungary occupied and obtained international recognition to administer the province of Bosnia-Herzegovina, which up until that time was under the control of the Ottoman (Turkish) Empire. On October 6, 1908, the Austro-Hungarian government announced the formal annexation of Bosnia-Herzegovina and precipitated an international crisis that threatened war between several of the leading European powers. In April 1909, an agreement was signed among the Great Powers recognizing Austria-Hungary's annexation of the province.—Ed.]

ever wanted to buy foreign exchange had to purchase it above the price for gold: consequently, he would have to bear an exchange risk and therefore decided to delay making the purchase thinking that there would always be time to acquire foreign exchange the next day in case the situation deteriorated. There would have been no need for such patience if the Bank had been obligated to release gold at its going rate, because then this risk would have disappeared. The Bank's precious metal holdings would have been prematurely weakened, with all of the disadvantages that go hand in hand with this, Federn concludes.

In response to this argument it may be pointed out that during the entire period of the Bosnian Crisis (from October 1908 to the end of March 1909), the rates for foreign exchange at the German banking centers, without exception, ranged *below* the mint parity; the rate of foreign exchange in London ranged *below* mint parity during most of this period, with the maximum never exceeding 0.08 percent above mint parity during those six months.[13]

If Federn's allegation about foreign exchange is thus completely unsubstantiated, the same goes for the claim that the Austro-Hungarian Bank did not release gold during the Bosnian Crisis. It was precisely during the Bosnian Crisis in March 1909 that an admittedly unimportant, domestic demand for actual gold occurred for the first time in Austria; when the reservists rallied to the banners and the active-duty officers and reserve troops departed for the borders, they required certain sums of money. This increased demand resulted from runs on a few provincial savings banks, and was satisfied without exception by the Bank. To have done anything else would have shaken the solid trust among the people that the Bank's wise policies had built up over a long period of time.

Federn claims that banks carry a risk connected with the purchase of foreign exchange, while the acquisition of actual gold bears no such risk for them. It should be pointed out that the purchase of actual gold at the current parity rate for gold appears more expensive than the purchase

13. See *"Der Compaß" Finanzielles Jahrbuch für Österreich-Ungarn* ["The Compass" Financial Annual Journal for Austro-Hungary], vol. 43, no. 1 (Vienna, 1909), p. 92. For foreign exchange on the Paris market, the maximum rate amounted to 0.288 percent above parity during that six-month period: in the most critical month, March 1909, it was 0.078 percent above parity. On average, for the month of March 1909, foreign exchange in the German banking centers was posted at 0.436 percent above parity, foreign exchange in London at 0.119 percent above parity, and foreign exchange in Paris at .0137 percent *below* parity.

of foreign exchange, since the latter is purchased at a rate that is already close to the gold point.

Federn makes a similar error when he claims at another point in his argument that the Bank hampers interest rate arbitrage when it releases foreign exchange under fixed-term contracts while denying foreign exchange for cash. A capitalist who desires to take advantage of a higher interest rate abroad can most easily achieve his goals by purchasing long-dated foreign exchange at foreign banking centers. If the Bank were to actually pursue the policy alleged by Federn, this could in no way counter interest rate arbitrage. Only those individuals would seemingly be damaged who had to make foreign payments coming due in the short run, since in order to settle such payments, short-term foreign exchange is needed.

The Bank has no other means to limit a rise in the foreign exchange rate above a certain level than by satisfying the demand for foreign exchange at a lower rate, regardless of the reason behind that demand. This is the policy that the Austro-Hungarian Bank has followed for more than a decade.

CHAPTER 5

The Fourth Issuing Right of the Austro-Hungarian Bank[1]

The Austrian law of August 8, 1911 (*Imperial Law Gazette* no. 157), and the Hungarian Article of Law no. XVIII of 1911 (which are substantially the same) brought to a provisional close a disagreement that has continued for several years.[2] They extended the note-issuing right [*Privilegium*] of the Austro-Hungarian Bank that had already expired on December 31, 1910, and which had remained in force after that date only through temporary arrangements made between the governments of both halves of the country and the Bank. Also simultaneously extended until December 31, 1917, was the coinage and currency treaty that had existed between the two countries since 1892, and which was supposed to expire at the end of 1910. The banking and monetary union, whose continued existence appeared to be in danger due to the fierce hostility of the Hungarian Independence Party, was assured at least for the short term. The status quo was also maintained in the areas of monetary and banking policy until 1917, the next crucial year when the *Ausgleich*[3]

1. [This article originally was published in German in the *Zeitschrift für Volkswirtschaft, Sozialpolitik und Verwaltung*, vol. 21 (1912).—Ed.]
2. In addition to the numerous articles in the daily and professional press, see especially the parliamentary materials relating to the government bill, including a report on the reasons for the fourth privilege (No. 1043 of the supplements to the stenographic protocols of the House of Deputies, Session XX, 1910). A representative overview of the reform and a rich bibliographic list are contained in Zuckerkandl's appendix to "Österreichisch-Ungarische Bank" in the *Handwörterbuch der Staatswissenschaften*, vol. 8, pp. 1186–91. [Robert Zuckerkandl, "The Austro-Hungarian Bank," in *Banking in Russia, Austria-Hungary, the Netherlands, and Japan* (Washington, D.C.: Government Printing Office, 1911), pp. 55–118, but without the accompanying bibliography in the original German.—Ed.]
3. [The *Ausgleich*, or "Compromise," of 1867 refers to the agreement under which the Austrian Empire was transformed into the Austro-Hungarian Empire. Hungary was recognized as a self-governing nation within the empire, with the two halves sharing a common defense, and a customs and monetary union under the authority of the Habsburg emperor, Francis Joseph. The "Compromise" was to be renewed every ten years.– Ed.]

will come up for renewal. This end to almost five years of conflict over the Bank was predictable, as there was never any doubt that an independent Hungarian central bank would not be founded on January 1, 1911. Such a solution to the Bank question would have been severely harmful for Hungarian interests, and would have been mourned from the Austrian side, as well. It was hardly likely that the governments and parliaments of both nations would have chosen such a course since it would have benefited no one and, indeed, would have resulted in severe disadvantages for the general economic development of the monarchy.

The Hungarian opposition to continuing the banking union was based solely and exclusively on political, and not economic, grounds. Hungary (or, more specifically, an influential group of Magyar politicians) demanded the establishment of an independent Hungarian bank, claiming that the mere existence of a common central bank was inconsistent with the status of the Kingdom of Hungary. Aside from vague national sentiments, even the most fervent advocates for a separate Hungarian Bank could not seriously assert that the banking union impaired Hungary's economic interests.

The advantages that accrue to Hungary through the banking and monetary union with Austria were too obvious to allow for any differences of opinion on this matter. Hungary owes its unhampered access to the Austrian money and capital markets to the Bank, as well as the fact that Austrian resources are widely available to Hungary's industries and its agricultural sector throughout its provinces. Austrian money supports Hungarian credit banks, and the sums that have flowed from Austria into the Hungarian mortgage market are astronomically high. The common central bank also serves as a primary source to satisfy Hungarian credit demands.

Beginning in 1906, the Austro-Hungarian Bank began publishing information about the territorial use of bank credit based on the location of the discount payments on the bills of exchange. Thus, the total of each region in the Bank's bills of exchange portfolio were:

Year	Austria	Hungary	Bosnia and Herzegovina
1906	44.1%	55.9%	—
1907	41%	59%	—
1908	38.7%	61.3%	—
1909	36.9%	63.1%	—
1910	38.1%	61.2%	0.7%
1911	38.8%	60.3%	0.9%

The drawdown from the Bank's discount credit, therefore, is much larger in the Hungarian part of the empire than in the Austrian part. Without a common central bank, the interest rate in Hungary would undoubtedly be higher than is currently the case; the implications of this for the development of Hungarian industry are clear.

On the other hand, Cisleithania [Austria] had the greatest interest in the continuation of the banking union. The unity of the money and capital market assures Austrian industrial dominance over the Hungarian markets. Additionally, as long as there continues to be a common tariff area, an independent Hungarian monetary system could, under the current circumstances, bear serious consequences for Austria. However unlikely, it is possible that a separate Hungarian currency could be devalued; a falling exchange rate would hinder Austrian exports to Hungary and facilitate the importing of Hungarian goods into Austria.

Thus, the battle that was fought against the continuation of a joint central bank had to end with a complete success for the Bank's defenders. The issuing right of the joint central bank was extended to 1917. The decision about its further continuation will be made simultaneously with the decision about the future form of the political and economic relationships between the two halves of the monarchy.

Along with the question about maintaining a joint central bank, the other question that has been at the center of banking discussions for several years has been the problem of legal resumption of specie payments. As is widely known, the currency reform initiated in 1892 has not yet come to a statutory conclusion. The "crowning" of the reform effort through the legal resumption of specie payments has yet to be fulfilled, and according to the letter of the law, the monarchy's medium of exchange still remains a paper currency. This is because the Austro-Hungarian Bank is not obligated to redeem its notes for gold.

The actual situation is admittedly very different. For fifteen years now, the Austro-Hungarian Bank has surrendered any amount of gold and gold-backed foreign exchange demanded for commercial purposes at a price that lies below a level which would be equal to the upper gold point for specie payments, as similarly practiced in the English banking system. In fact, the Austro-Hungarian Bank is a specie-redeeming institution; the monarchy, therefore, already has enjoyed all the advantages of a regulated currency for several years.[4]

4. See my remarks in the *Schmollerschen Jahrbuch*, vols. 33 and 34. [See "The Problem of Legal Resumption of Specie Payments in Austria-Hungary" and "On the Problem of Legal Resumption of Specie Payments in Austria-Hungary," Chapters 2 and 4 in the present volume.—Ed.]

Thus, nothing stands in the way of the legal resumption of specie payments. It would simply represent a legal sanctioning of a long-standing practice. Economically, it would be irrelevant. However, it would have all the more meaning for the international prestige of both parts of the monarchy. The legal culmination of the transition to a gold-backed currency would give visible expression that Austria-Hungary had overcome the period of its fragmented financial management. With one blow, the value of the crown traded on the financial markets would become the value of gold. The psychological importance of that moment should not by any means be underestimated. The stimulus this would create would certainly do much to improve the monarchy's reputation, which has been severely shaken by the domestic political events of the last several years.

Nevertheless, the suggestion that the Austro-Hungarian Bank be legally obligated to redeem its notes with specie is met with strong opposition in Austria (though not in Hungary). This antagonism is a consequence of the inflationary tendencies that have repeatedly played a large role in the history of the Austrian currency. The "theory" about the alleged advantages of an "isolated" monetary system for the setting of the rate of interest is as popular in Austria today as it was three or four decades ago. A bank that is not obligated to redeem its notes in specie, one hears, can emancipate itself from any need to consider the international monetary situation when setting its own official rate of discount. According to this theory, it can allow any degree of "tension" to exist between its central bank rate and that of foreign central bank institutions without any concern, because no gold could be withdrawn from its bank. As early as a generation ago, Wilhelm von Lucam, who served as secretary general of the Austro-Hungarian Bank for many years, laid this error completely to rest; since that time, distinguished authors have repeated his rebuttal. However, serious scientific works are unable to convince those who refuse to come face-to-face with their arguments.

Seven years ago the publication of Knapp's *The State Theory of Money* offered renewed confidence to the opponents of a gold-backed currency. In Austria, a small literature appeared in brochures, the daily newspapers, and in popular reviews that fought with zeal and passion against the legal resumption of specie payments. Knapp, and his followers to a greater extent than himself, misconceived the essence of the often-referred-to foreign exchange policy of the Austro-Hungarian Bank. They have neither acknowledged nor refuted the criticisms leveled against their views.[5] Regardless of this, however, essays constantly fill the columns of the daily newspapers and economic weeklies promoting Austria-Hungary's "modern" monetary system and reproaching the monetary institutions of all other countries in the world as being backward. It is characteristic of many authors from this group that the monetary history of the last twenty years, in terms of the developments in America, Asia, and India, has completely escaped them. It is self-evident that they are conversant neither with the literature on monetary theory nor the most recent works about the gold exchange standard. They hardly know anything about Carl Menger,[6] William Stanley Jevons,[7] Leon Walras,[8] Friedrich von Wieser,[9] J. Laurence Laughlin,[10] or David Kinley.[11]

5. See my remarks in the *Schmollerschen Jahrbuch*, vol. 33, pp. 1027–30. [See pp. 31–82, in this volume.—Ed.]

6. [Carl Menger (1840–1921) was the founder of the Austrian School of economics. After working as a journalist and civil servant in the Austrian Ministry of Prices, he was appointed a professor of political economy at the University of Vienna in 1873, a position that he held until his retirement in 1903. In 1876, he was tutor for Crown Prince Rudolph, the heir to the Austrian throne who later committed suicide. He also served on the Imperial Commission on Currency Reform in 1892, which resulted in Austro-Hungary's moving toward establishment of a gold standard.—Ed.]

7. [William Stanley Jevons (1835–83) was one of the developers of the theory of marginal utility, which he formulated in his 1871 book *The Theory of Political Economy*. He also wrote extensively on monetary theory and reform, and a sunspot theory of business cycles. He was appointed to a chair in political economy at University College, London, in 1876. He died in a drowning accident.—Ed.]

8. [Leon Walras (1834–1910) formulated a version of the theory of marginal utility in his 1874 book *Elements of Pure Economics*. Walras is also recognized as one of the early developers of mathematical general equilibrium theory. Walras also was a prominent monetary theorist who developed a "cash balance" approach for the demand for money. He was appointed to a chair in political economy at the University of Lausanne in 1870, and stepped down from his position in 1892 following a nervous breakdown.—Ed.]

9. [Friedrich von Wieser (1851–1926) was one of the leading members of the Austrian School of economics in the period before and immediately after the First World War. His major contributions were to the theory of marginal utility, the concept of opportunity cost, and the theory of the determination of the value of the factors of production. After serving in the Austrian civil service from 1872 to 1883, he was appointed professor of political economy at the University of Prague in the Austrian province of Bohemia. He was appointed professor of political economy at the University of Vienna in 1903, following Carl Menger's retirement. Wieser served as minister of commerce from 1917 to 1918 in the last government of the Austro-Hungarian Empire.—Ed.]

10. [James Laurence Laughlin (1850–1933) was appointed in 1892 to establish an economics department at the University of Chicago. He was well known as a monetary theorist and historian who wrote widely on the gold standard. He was also an outspoken advocate of laissez-faire at a time of growing interventionist sentiments in the United States.—Ed.]

11. [David Kinley (1861–1944) founded the economics department at the University of Illinois at Champaign-Urbana in 1895. He was the author of *Money: A Study of the Theory of the Medium of Exchange* (1904). He also wrote extensively on government regulation of business in American society.—Ed.]

Among the opponents of the legal resumption of specie payments, Walther Federn, in a certain sense, temporarily held a special position. Federn held the view that the current legal situation offered the Austro-Hungarian Bank the opportunity to leave unsatisfied any demand for foreign exchange for so-called interest rate arbitrage, and to limit the release of foreign exchange solely for the "legitimate" needs of importers and those persons and corporations owing debt payments abroad.

According to Federn, the Bank also availed itself of the following possibility. The foreign exchange rate cannot increase beyond a desired level when foreign exchange is not supplied for short-term investment abroad, because when the foreign exchange rate is above a certain level, the demand for foreign exchange for this purpose decreases of its own accord. This was an argument against the legal resumption of specie payments that would have carried considerable authority if it had been valid. I believe that I have produced the proof for the incorrectness of this and similar claims in the above-cited articles, and more recently in another publication.[12] The Austro-Hungarian Bank has not (at least prior to the autumn of 1911, during which its policy suffered a fiasco) attempted to deny issuing foreign exchange for use in interest rate arbitrage.

In addition, Federn has surrendered his original viewpoint on the question of the Bank's policy. In an essay[13] that appeared last year there was missing his claim that an increase in the foreign exchange rate does not occur in spite of the Bank's refusing to issue foreign exchange. Instead, Federn tried to demonstrate that, in fact, the foreign exchange rate on the Vienna bourse often increased above the upper gold point, and that, as a consequence, the Austrian currency did not have a stable value. It is quite difficult to debate with an author who constantly changes his views. Perhaps in another setting I will return to Federn's statements and reveal their deficiencies to those people for whom they may not have been obvious up to now.

As could be expected under the circumstances, the Austrian government has had to deal with the opposition to the legal resumption of specie payments. Quite unlike in the Upper House of the Austrian Parliament, it would have been completely futile to attempt to gain agreement on a new issuing right for the Bank in the Austrian House

12. Ludwig von Mises, *The Theory of Money and Credit* (Indianapolis: Liberty Fund, 3rd rev. ed., [1924; 1951] 1981), pp. 384–86.

13. *Schmollerschen Jahrbuch*, vol. 25, pp. 1379ff.

of Deputies [the Lower House] that would have included the legal resumption of specie payments.[14]

On the other hand, the Hungarian government had to insist (likewise due to parliamentary considerations) that the status quo be moved at least slightly in the direction of a legal resumption of cash payments, because in Hungary there was a general desire for the legal completion of the task for currency reform. The Hungarian politicians are more closely linked to business life and banking transactions than their Austrian counterparts; they do not underestimate the significance of the legal resumption of specie payments for easing Hungary's access into the money markets of the West.

The two conflicting tendencies are reconciled by a compromise in the new Bank Law. The suspension of the Bank's obligation to redeem its notes for specie under Article 83 remains in effect until further notice. Abrogation of the suspension may occur only in accordance with the usual procedures of an act passed by both the Austrian and Hungarian legislatures. However, the third paragraph of Article 111 of the statutes grants the Austro-Hungarian Bank the right to petition both legislatures for ending the specie suspension under Article 83 at a point in time when the Bank considers that the international financial situation is favorable for a resumption of specie payments.

In the event that the Bank makes this proposal, the Austrian government is obligated under Article V of the Bank Law to immediately enter into negotiations with the Hungarian government, to conduct these negotiations with all expediency, and in accordance with established procedures of the Hungarian government. Identical drafts are to be submitted in both houses of the Parliament, on the appointed day, for approval of the Austro-Hungarian Bank's petition for ending specie

14. [In the Austrian part of the Dual Monarchy, the parliament was composed of an Upper House (*Herrenhause*) that included all of the archdukes in Austria; seventy nobles selected by the emperor; seventeen archbishops and bishops of princely rank; and 140 life members appointed by the emperor in recognition of their service to the state or the church. In the early years of the twentieth century, the Lower House (*Abgeordnetenhause*) consisted of 425 members serving for a six-year term, who represented five "classes of electors" in each province. Eighty-five were chosen by the large landowners; twenty-five were selected by the chambers of commerce and certain industrial corporations; 118 were elected by residents in urban districts who paid over fifty florins in direct taxation; 129 were elected by inhabitants of rural areas who also paid in direct taxes at least fifty florins; and 72 were chosen by all electors who did not belong to any of the other groups, but who had residency qualification for at least six months.—Ed.]

suspension under Article 83. The approval of this petition is granted by affirmative decisions in both houses of Parliament. A negative decision by just one of the two houses results in the denial of the approval of this petition. If within a period of four weeks from the time the draft has been submitted during the parliamentary session no decision is reached by one of the two houses, then the petition is considered approved by that respective house or both houses of the Parliament.

These provisions, which are analogously covered by Hungarian law (with one inconsequential difference), are extremely idiosyncratic in the context of the constitutional relationship between the two halves of the monarchy. The underlying motive is clear, considering the obstructionist elements that currently influence both the Austrian and Hungarian parliamentary systems.

The constitutional objections to this procedure should be partially eliminated in Austria by the provisions of the special law of August 8, 1911 (*Imperial Law Gazette [Reichsgesetzblatt]* no. 158), that was announced on the same day as the Bank Law. This law instituted a series of special provisions to assure the government's businesslike handling of the draft submitted to the House of Deputies, based on the Austro-Hungarian Bank's petition for abolishing specie suspension under Article 83 of the Bank Statutes. The president of the House has to immediately assign the draft (without a first reading) to the committee appointed for the preliminary discussion. The committee has to submit a written report about the draft to the full House within a period of no more than one week. The president must, without objections, place the committee's report as the first item on the agenda of the session immediately following the dissemination of the report; and it must be the first item on the agenda for every subsequent session of the House until a decision has been reached.

If the committee has not submitted a report within the one-week period, then the president must, likewise without objections, present the government draft for a final resolution as the first item on the agenda of the session occurring immediately after the expiration of the deadline set for the committee; and it must be the first item on the agenda for every subsequent session of the House. If debate over the draft extends up to the third day prior to the expiration of the four-week period set by Article V of the Bank Law, then the president must declare the debate closed, whether or not the delegate who has the floor has finished his remarks and whether or not there are still delegates registered to speak on the issue. The president must, at the latest, call the vote the next day after debate has been closed.

It is not our task to address the constitutional aspects of these provisions. From a purely economic point of view, the new Bank issuing right offers plenty that is of interest.

Article 1 of the Bank Statutes obligates the Bank to ensure, with all means at its disposal, that the price of foreign exchange reflects the value of its banknotes, and that this remains stable over time. The value of the Bank's notes shall also correspond to the legal mint parity price of the crown currency. In the case that the Bank does not meet this obligation (i.e., for as long as suspension of specie payments continues), its noncompliance will result in the Bank losing its issuing privilege in accordance with paragraph 2 of Article 111, insofar as this is not superseded by a "higher power" recognized by both governments. An exception is made for a temporary suspension of the Bank's obligation if there has occurred a lawful decree simultaneously approved in both nations of the monarchy.

The Gordian thought processes that led to this provision in the Bank Statutes can be understood only in the context of the polarized views that exist in the two parts of the monarchy over legal resumption of specie payments. Indeed, it was aimed at somehow legally sanctioning the status quo of de facto specie payments without employing the (in Austria) unpopular idea of specie redemption of notes. Each of the two governments could return home as victor rather than vanquished from the debate over the Bank Act.

Obviously, that was not completely achieved, because what in the plain language of the law would have constituted a decision equivalent to the Bank being given the obligation to institute specie payments was not achieved in this provision. Foreign countries will continue to consider the value of the crown as not being equal to its gold par value, and will view Austrian and Hungarian credit as being substandard.

From a technical legal viewpoint, the frequently discussed item in the Bank Statutes concerning the parity value of the currency can hardly be described as successful. Even the style in which it is expressed is quite awkward. As is highlighted in the report about the reasons for the law, it is not meant to force the Bank to guarantee that the foreign exchange rate constantly coincides with the mint parity of the currency. Instead, henceforth, the Bank's legal obligation would be to maintain its current practice, which it has followed for years without legal compulsion, of not allowing the foreign exchange rate to rise above the upper gold point. Thus, the Bank must continue to pursue the same policies that it has followed up to the present; in the future (as has currently been the case), it must simply ensure that the upper gold point is not exceeded. In other words, it must guarantee that there occur no significant fluctuations in the foreign exchange rate above the currency's mint parity. A shrewd loophole was left open, wherein the range in which the foreign exchange rate might vary above the mint parity was not defined in this law or elsewhere.

It is superfluous and contradictory to all legal terminology if, as it is expressly noted in Article 111, the Bank does not lose its issuing rights when it fails to comply with the obligation to uphold the exchange rate parity, other than in situations in which a temporary suspension has been decreed in a lawful manner in both nations of the monarchy. It appears that during the compilation of the Bank Statutes, the legal rule *"lex posterior derogat priori"*[15] was completely forgotten.

According to Article 83, paragraph 2 of the Bank Statutes, there does not occur a loss of issuing rights due to failure to comply with this obligation after the resumption of specie payments, if it is prevented from doing so by a higher power recognized as such by both governments. The official report points out that there could be cases in which the Bank might be prevented by insurmountable external circumstances from meeting its obligations to redeem its notes, and a temporary cessation of note redemption could not be immediately decreed in a lawful fashion. The official report also indicates that there also could be similarly valid reasons in regard to the Bank's failure to meet its obligation to maintain the exchange rate parity. In practice, this gives both governments the authority to relieve the Bank at any time of its obligation to maintain the foreign exchange parity, and its obligation to make specie payments. Due to the vagueness of the term "higher power" applied within the area of finance, it may well be possible for the governments to find any pretext for such a suspension of the Bank Act. Any deterioration in the balance of payments can be viewed, with a stretch of the imagination, as being an act by a higher power. It is, however, hardly to be feared that the governments will misuse the authority that has been placed in their hands.

15. ["More recent law abrogates an inconsistent earlier law."—Ed.]

By far the most important innovation in the Bank Law is the expansion of the tax-free quota for the issuance of banknotes. In 1887, the Austro-Hungarian Bank's second issuing right broke with the system of strictly limiting the number of banknotes in circulation; this system had been introduced by Plener's Bank Act of December 27, 1862, in the manner set by Peel's Bank Act.[16] The second issuing right declared that any issuance of banknotes not backed by precious metals in excess of the 200 million florins (Austrian currency) quota was subject to a tax of 5 percent on any notes in circulation exceeding that maximum.

Since that time the quota of 400 million crown notes has not been increased, and has remained at that level for almost five decades.[17] In recent years, the issuance of notes in excess of 400 million crowns has occurred primarily in the autumn months. In 1907, there were no fewer than 21 times when the total number of notes in circulation was in excess of that maximum amount. The new Bank Statute expands the tax-free note quota from 400 million crowns up to 600 million crowns. Whatever significance this expansion of the tax-free quota of notes will have on the financial markets cannot be discussed here in any detail. Doubtless the effect will not be as harmless as is asserted in the official report, which leaves quite a bit to be desired on these points.

In any case, it is deplorable that the Bank Statute did not establish, as the German model does, that the quota of notes be determined at a higher level for the end of the quarters as opposed to the average level during the year. The official report cited the German provision and included as a quasi explanation that the quarterly deadlines (at the end of March, July, September, and December) regularly bring certain tensions on the German financial markets. The report remains silent as to the question (which surely would have merited a detailed explanation) about whether it has been ascertained that the same deadlines cause tension on the Austrian markets.

Indicating yet another tendency, an amendment has been made to the regulations concerning the backing of notes in circulation. In the agreements made incidental to the conferral of the third issuing right

16. See Chapter 2, "The Problem of Legal Resumption of Specie Payments in Austria-Hungary," footnote 18.
17. [The 1892 Austrian Currency Reform Act converted the old florin into a new crown at the ratio of two new crowns for one old florin. Hence the 200-million-florin quota on notes issued by the Austro-Hungarian Bank that were tax-exempt became 400 million of the new crowns.—Ed.]

in 1899 between the two governments and the Bank, the Bank was allowed to employ an amount of 401,305 million crowns in national gold coins (that has originally been supplied by the two governments) to cover the ten- and twenty-crown notes that had been issued in place of an equivalent amount of state notes. The Bank was not allowed to include this amount, which formed 40 percent of the precious metal backing of its notes, in the summary of its specie reserves.

Article VI of the Bank Law Amendment abrogates this limitation. At the same time, the previous limitations on the issuing of ten- and twenty-crown notes are dropped. In their place appeared a provision (Article 82 of the Bank Statutes) that to cover transactions of less than fifty crowns, twenty- and ten-crown banknotes can be issued in any amount mutually agreed to by the two finance ministers. Due to this, banknotes in denominations of twenty and ten crowns will become a permanent institution. This corresponds to the principles first promulgated in the specie payment guidelines of 1903, and which stand in contradiction to straightforwardly adopting the English and German institutions, which were envisioned by the legislators of 1892 and 1899.

Also taken from the 1903 guidelines was authorization for the Bank to include in its calculation of specie reserves an amount up to 60 million crowns in holdings of foreign exchange and foreign banknotes that are payable in gold or an equivalent precious-metal-backed currency.

From a financial perspective, the expansion of the tax-free note quota was partly a compensation for the increased share of the Bank's net profits taken by both governments in the monarchy. In general, the provisions concerning the division of the Bank's net profit remained unchanged, though with a modification. Previously, the two governments received two-thirds of the net profits whenever common stockholdings exceeded 7 percent of the equity capital; in the future, the two governments under those circumstances will receive three-quarters of the net profits. In addition, the Bank is obligated to establish twenty new subsidiaries, ten in Austria and ten in Hungary, at locations determined by the ministers of finance.

In general, nothing was changed in the Bank's time-tested organization: it remains as it had been until 1917, and hopefully will remain so long into the future. And there are a few provisions about the handling of the gold reserves at the expiration of the issuing right in 1917, as a reminder that that possibility must be kept in mind in all calculations about the future.

Foreign judgments of the situation following the passage of the new note issue right will likely conclude that little success has been made in solving the Bank question. Fault will be found with the complicated parliamentary procedures preceding the future resumption of specie payments, and with many other details and aspects of the new issuing right. This is completely aside from the fact that foreign opinion will hardly be able to comprehend why the new issuing right fails to validate the de facto situation of specie payments by sanctioning the legal resumption of specie payments.

Anyone who completely understands the situation in the monarchy will in no way agree with such a disparaging judgment. For it is indeed the truth that the Bank's issuing right, in spite of all its defects, unquestionably demonstrates a full and complete success for the Austrian ideal of the nation-state. An important part of imperial unity was secured for the coming years. What that will mean, and how the diplomatic and political success of the two governments is to be estimated, can only be answered by those worthy to judge, those who truly understand the parties in Cisleithania and Transleithania [Austria and Hungary], ruled as they are by rallying cries and only seldom guided by dispassionate logic.

CHAPTER 6

Financial Reform in Austria[1]

After more than a century of chronic budget deficits, about twenty years ago Austria succeeded in reestablishing a balance in its public finances. From 1889 to 1909 the national accounts generally showed a surplus. The situation changed again in 1908, and the estimate for 1909 predicted a deficit, which could be converted into an apparent surplus of 60,000 crowns only by the introduction of a fictitious entry of 29 million crowns. The budget for 1910 already openly admits to a deficit.

It cannot be determined exactly how much the deficit amounts to in the ordinary budget, and which has to be covered by new increases in taxes. On this point differences of opinion will always exist, ideas being divided on the question of what should be understood by investment and what must be considered as current expenditures. One fact is certain: this deficit is very large. The minister of finance evaluates at about 17 million crowns the increase of revenue that the state will have to obtain annually from a tax increase or by the creation of new taxes. To this must be added a deficit of about 40 million crowns, which has come about in the budgets of the various Austrian provinces. Since the provinces are not able to cover it with their own resources, it too must be made up for by the state. Thus there is, at this moment, an assured budget deficit of 110 million crowns; and this figure will increase significantly in future years if new resources are not found in time.

In fact, enormous expenses will have to be met soon. The army and the fleet have been completely neglected for many years. Their allocation has not been raised for twenty years, while at the same time all the other European states have considerably increased their defense forces. Moreover, the weaponry of the army leaves much to be desired, and

1. [This article originally appeared in French in the *Revue Économique Internationale*, vol. 7, no. 4 (October 1910).—Ed.]

the reduction of service time from three years to two, which cannot be postponed much longer, will entail enormous costs. The navy, too, will be the object of more serious attention in the future. In the presence of the enormous naval armaments of Italy, aimed directly against Austria, our navy too will be forced to construct some "dreadnoughts."

The obligations of social insurance will likewise impose heavy expenses on the state. According to the calculations in the government's plan, the contribution of the state to social insurance will in the end amount to 100 million crowns per year. How are the needed resources to be obtained? Neither the government nor Parliament has so far said a word about it. One can already perceive here an essential difference between the causes for the financial embarrassment of Austria and those of the other states (Germany, France, and England) that are presently struggling with financial difficulties. In these latter countries, it is mainly military and social burdens that have swollen the budget; in Austria, on the other hand, the deficit already exists even though the state has up to now only insufficiently fulfilled its military and social obligations.

Nevertheless, for the last ten years governmental expenditures in Austria have gone from 1.5 billion to 2.3 billion crowns. If we investigate the causes of this huge increase, we shall immediately discover that during the same period interest and amortization payments on the national debt rose from 345 million to 411 million crowns (of which 356 million were for the payment of interest and only 55 million for amortization). Direct taxes and the excise on beer together produced just enough to provide this amount.

Excluding the increase of payments related to the national debt and national defense, the increase in expenditures comes mainly from the rise of those relating to domestic administration. These expenditures have increased considerably in the last few years: for the Finance Ministry they have gone from 61.2 million to 105.9 million crowns; for postal employees, from 48.9 million to 92.1 million; for the Ministry of Justice, from 58.4 million to 92.5 million; for pensions, from 48.6 million to 91.6 million crowns. Up to 1908 the state has paid out for the acquisition of the railway network about 4 billion crowns, which it obtained on the basis of credit. The interest on the capital invested in the railroads amounted to 173 million crowns.

By contrast, in 1908 the surplus from the operation of the state railroads was only 95 million crowns. Thus the state had to cope with an operating deficit of 78 million crowns. To remedy this state of affairs the fares of the state railroads were raised after January 1, 1910, by such a proportion that a profit of 47 million crowns can be counted on for annual receipts. In spite of this, the management of the railroads will always be in serious deficit and will constitute a burden for the budget. In Austria the administration of the state's railroads is excessively expensive; moreover, in the unanimous opinion of all the interested parties it operates exceptionally badly. This deficit must be attributed only secondarily to the fact that the state also operates—for strategic and political-economy reasons in general—certain lines that scarcely yield anything; it is due just as little to the circumstance that the creation of the Austrian state's railroads is very burdensome, given the difficulties of construction in a mountainous country; the principal cause is, instead, the incompetence of an administration that does not have a commercial and economic character, an administration in which everything depends upon political and personal points of view, while the economic point of view matters least. A reform of the administration of the railroads is desirable not only in the interest of shippers and travelers but also in the interest of the public treasury.

The organization of the Ministry of the Interior is just as irresponsible. If this fact generally attracts less attention, it is only because one cannot be given an account of the results of the Interior Ministry in the same way as the results of a state-run firm like the railroads. Some years ago Minister Koerber,[2] who was then in power, had prepared and published a memorandum concerning the reform of the interior ministry, which constituted the most acerbic criticism of his own activity that was ever made by the government of a country; in it the Austrian government is the object of a merciless criticism.

One of the most important measures recommended by Minister Koerber was to intensify the productivity of state agencies. This idea sank along with Minister Koerber himself, as did other impressive plans of that statesman. One of the chief ills, which the Austrian government suffers from and which considerably increases its expenses, is the coexistence and cofunctioning of a dual administrative apparatus. Along-

2. [Ernest von Koerber (1850–1919), a liberal Austrian statesman and prime minister of Austria in 1900–1904. A popular figure, he engaged in an ambitious economic expansion program for the Habsburg Monarchy, encouraged industry and commerce, and introduced laws guaranteeing individual rights. Nationality crises in Bohemia and Hungary caused his fall in 1904. During World War I he served as the joint Austro-Hungarian minister of finance.—Ed.]

side the national administration and the national authorities there exist, absolutely independent of them, the autonomous authorities of the provinces and of the municipalities. The administrative organs of the state are appointed by the government and depend upon it. On the other hand, the autonomous administrative organs depend solely on the Diets (Landtag)[3] and the municipal administrations, both of which are the result of elections. Far from trying to support each other mutually, these two organs often have a tendency to oppose their reciprocal endeavors. This is especially the case in those districts where a powerful and energetic party is in power in the Diet and in the municipalities. In these conditions, and aside from the fact that it entails excessive expenses, this administrative dualism does not in any way appear to be an advantage to the population. Nevertheless, a reform in this area is difficult to carry out since the Diets and the municipalities do not want to give up any of their prerogatives. And yet such a reform would be the first step toward a reduction of the bluntly excessive cost of the administration.

In Austria, the problem of reestablishing equilibrium in the management of public affairs is particularly complicated by the fact that it is a question of reforming not only the management of the state but also that of the provinces, and that in this activity one must take a whole series of difficulties into account. The constitution grants to the provinces the right to collect taxes, in addition to the direct taxes of the state to cover their expenses. If these supplementary taxes do not exceed 10 percent of the national taxes, they do not have to be authorized by the government or by the emperor; however, if they exceed 10 percent, a special approbation by the emperor is needed. Moreover, the provinces are free to introduce their own indirect taxes, with imperial authorization.

Twelve years ago, at the time of the creation of the new income tax, it was feared that the provinces and municipalities might use the right to collect supplements to the new income tax too liberally and might raise the level of taxation to such a point that the temptation to make false declarations would become very great. The Parliament of the empire did not have the right to forbid the municipalities and provinces to

---

3. [A Landtag (Diet) is a representative assembly or parliament in German-speaking countries with some legislative authority.—Ed.]

collect such supplements to the income tax; that is why it had to act in another way to keep the above-mentioned tax free of supplements. Until the end of 1909 the Reichsrat[4] allotted a certain portion of the yield of the income tax to those provinces that committed themselves not to impose supplements to the income tax for purposes related to provincial and municipal administration. That is what happened in all the provinces. Meanwhile, different individual provinces began to create their own indirect taxes, which previously had not been done. Later, when in 1901 the excise tax on alcohol was raised, a part of the yield of the excise was again assigned by the state to the provinces on the condition that they, on their part, would renounce any provincial excise on alcohol. From then on the provinces and municipalities fell back upon the taxation of beers and imposed special taxes on them. Thus three independent excises on beer coexisted in Austria: that of the state, that of the provinces, and that of the municipalities.

In spring 1909 Finance Minister Bilinski[5] presented a plan based on the following principles: The state would raise the excise tax on alcohol from 90 crowns or from 110 crowns, respectively, to 140 crowns or 164 crowns per hectoliter[6] of pure alcohol and the tax on beer from 34 hellers[7] per hectoliter to 70 hellers. The total yield from these two tariff increases was estimated by the government to be 95.5 million crowns. Of this total the government intended to assign 32.2 million crowns to the provinces on the condition that they would renounce their individual taxes on beer, and in addition it allocated to them 40 million crowns on the condition that they should give up the special tax on alcohol and continue to leave the income tax free of supplements. Thus there would have been left to the state a gain in revenue of only 22 million crowns.

Among the public this financial plan was first blamed for focusing

4. [The Austrian Parliament.—Ed.]
5. [Leon Ritter von Bilinski (1846–1923), a conservative Polish-Austrian statesman, who was highly favored by Emperor Francis Joseph. In 1912–15, he occupied dual posts of imperial finance minister and Bosnian governor.—Ed.]
6. [1 hectoliter (hl) = 100 liters = 26.42 gallons.—Ed.]
7. [The Heller or Häller was a German coin valued at half a pfennig (a penny) named after the city of Hall (today Schwäbisch Hall). The coin was produced beginning in the 13th century as a silver pfennig (Häller pfennig). Heller was also the term used in the Austrian half of the empire for 1/100 of the Austro-Hungarian crown (the other being fillér in the Hungarian half), the currency of Austria-Hungary from 1892 until after the demise of the empire.—Ed.]

on only indirect taxes and for putting the entire burden of expenses required by the new needs of the state on the least fortunate classes. In spite of the government's promise to introduce a provision that would increase the yield of the inheritance tax by more than 10 million crowns, this fiscal reform could not be justified in the eyes of the parliamentary parties. The government was therefore obliged to have recourse to other means. It presented a plan that would also raise direct taxes.

Meanwhile Parliament was adjourned, and in the autumn the minister of finance presented a new fiscal proposal to Parliament. This time the minister had completely discarded increasing the excise tax on beer, leaving the provinces with the problem of obtaining (by raising of their own taxes on beer) the part that they would otherwise have received as an indemnity for giving up the right to levy an individual tax on beer.

Here are the tax proposals on which the new financial plan is based: increasing inheritance taxes and gift taxes. The present Austrian inheritance tax is graduated only according to the connection linking the successor to the decedent. It amounts to 1.25 percent in the case of the transmission of the estate or of various objects to spouses, ascendants, or descendents [i.e., parents/grandparents or children/grandchildren] and to 5 percent in the case of the transmission to other relatives, including nephews and nieces. In all other cases it is 10 percent; nevertheless, if the heir is employed or salaried by the decedent and if the inheritance or legacy does not exceed either 100 crowns of annual income—for the duration of his life or for a specific number of years—or 1,000 crowns in capital, the tax is only 1.25 percent. If the total assets without the deduction of debts do not exceed 100 crowns, the inheritance is tax-exempt provided that it passes to spouses, ascendants, and descendents.

Now, it is also desired to apply the principle of progressivity to the inheritance tax. In the future, it will be differentiated in two ways: first, according to the personal situation of the heir with regard to the decedent, then according to the amount of the inheritance. On the one hand, five groups of heirs have been distinguished. The first group includes, as before, spouses, ascendants, and descendents; the second group includes, unlike the provisions in force up till now, collateral relatives up to the third degree, except for nephews and nieces. All the other physical persons except those who were employed or salaried by the decedent are relegated to the third group.

In each one of these three groups the inheritances are treated according to their size. In the first group, inheritances that do not exceed 500 crowns are exempt; those above 500 crowns but not exceeding 10,000 crowns pay 1.25 percent, the rate rising then, little by little and by degrees, up to 4 percent, which is applied to inheritances of the seventh and last category, that is, those above 2 million crowns. Each of the second and third groups has nine steps. For inheritances up to 1,000 crowns the rate is 5 percent in the second group and 10 percent in the third, and it rises then little by little to 13 percent and 18 percent respectively for legacies above 2,000 crowns. The inheritances falling to persons who were employed or salaried by the testator are included in the fourth group. They pay no tax up to 500 crowns; from 500 to 1,000 crowns they pay 1.25 percent. Above that amount the inheritances going to such persons are taxed according to their personal situation with relation to the decedent. Those left to indigenous charitable teaching institutions or humanitarian work are included in the fifth group; they are taxed at the rate of 5 percent no matter what their value.

Besides the inheritance tax, the beneficiaries of the real estate inheritances are presently charged with additional estate taxes according to their gross value. This tax amounts to 1 percent in case of transmission to spouses, ascendants, and descendents if the value of the estate does not exceed 30,000 crowns, and goes up to 1.5 percent for a value above the latter. In case of transmission to other beneficiaries, the tax is 1.5 percent up to a value of 20,000 crowns, and 2 percent for a value above 20,000 crowns. The real estate taxes, which are imposed in virtue of the law of June 18, 1901, are continued for the future along with the inheritance tax.

The yield of the present inheritance and gift taxes annually amounts to an average of 19 million crowns without counting the income from real estate taxes. The government expects an annual gain of 10.3 million crowns from the increase of the inheritance tax. The gain from the increase of the gift tax cannot be estimated at present. In addition to the national inheritance tax, an equivalent tax exists in all provinces of the Crown and in many municipalities. In 1905 the yield of the national inheritance tax amounted to 19.2 million crowns and the provincial and municipal taxes to 8.7 million crowns, which added up to approximately 45 percent of the yield of the national inheritance tax.

Although the taxation on inheritances will therefore reach a very high level in Austria in the future, the proposals to increase inheritance taxes arouse almost no opposition. The attacks are generally directed only against such applications, the adoption of which would create an inequality in the fiscal taxation of different classes of the population.

In the matter of indirect taxes, the minister proposes, a series of increases and the introduction of new taxes. The increase of taxes on alcohol should bring the state an increase in receipts of about 35 million crowns. This increase, likewise, has met only weak opposition.

In addition, the creation of a match monopoly has been proposed. The yield from this monopoly has been estimated at 15 million crowns. The idea of the match monopoly is generally supported for both social and financial reasons.

On the other hand, two additional taxes proposed by the minister are encountering a vigorous opposition, namely, the tax on natural mineral waters and the tax on soda. Soda will be subject to a tax of 6 hellers per liter. The profit from this tax is estimated at about 1.8 million crowns. The fierce opposition to the tax is based on the fact that the cost of collecting it will be very high since many small establishments produce soda.

Natural mineral waters will pay 10 hellers per liter. All mineral waters that are not suitable for use as refreshments and table drinks but only for medical use will be tax-exempt. However, it has been pointed out that many natural mineral waters are used both for medical use and as refreshments and table drinks. A peculiar fact is that the government also wants to tax mineral waters intended for export. The yield from the taxation of natural mineral water is evaluated at 2.25 million crowns.

An objection to the taxation of soda as well as of natural mineral water is that in many localities water supplies are of such bad quality that the residents are forced to buy soda or mineral water; it is not desirable to create a tax that would, to a certain extent, contribute to the spread of typhus. It is not very likely that the government will succeed in getting these two taxes passed by the Parliament.

It is also doubtful that another project of the finance minister will be accepted that would do away with the tax-exempt status for automobile gasoline. It is pointed out that automobiles are still not widely used in Austria, and it is more important to remove the obstacles that stand in the way of automobile utilization than to create new ones. Besides, the proposed gasoline tax would bring no more than a million crowns.

Finally, the minister has proposed to increase the tax on wine. The existing tax presently brings in 6 million crowns, but in the future it should yield 12 million crowns. Moreover, a special tax on sparkling wines is to be introduced, which should produce 1.5 million crowns, as well as a separate tax on bottled wines, which will yield another 1.5 million crowns. In this case the total yield from the tax on wines will amount to about 16 million crowns.

The government is also proposing to increase the income tax, which is provoking much greater attention and opposition. First, the plan projects an increase of the rate of income tax for those whose income is above 20,000 crowns. Today the highest income tax rate is just below 5 percent; in the future it will reach 6.5 percent. This increase will yield 6 million crowns annually. Second, the rate of income tax will be increased by 15 percent for the taxpayers who do not live together with at least one other member of the family (spouse or child) and by 10 percent for taxpayers who do not live with at least two other members of the family. The yield from this increase is estimated at 5.2 million crowns.

In Austria, the profits of stock corporations are taxed at the enormous base rate of 10 percent. To this tax the state adds supplements for the benefit of the provinces and municipalities, so that it often reaches the rate of 20 percent to 30 percent. It must be also mentioned that what the law views as the next taxable profit of the corporation by far exceeds the real net profit as the businessman normally determines it.

In addition to the general tax on corporations, companies that distribute dividends above 10 percent of the invested capital are subject to a special supplementary tax on the amount used to pay this excess of dividends. This supplementary tax is presently 2 percent of the amount necessary to distribute the 11th to the 15th percent of the dividend and increases to 4 percent for the amount distributed beyond that figure. According to the government's proposal, the supplementary tax on dividends will not come into play when the dividends exceed 10 percent with regard to the capital stock invested, but only when they reach this level in proportion to the capital stock invested and the reserve. On the other hand, the rate of the supplementary tax will be considerably raised. The amount necessary to form the 11th and 12th percent will be taxed at the rate of 2 percent, the 13th and 14th percent at the rate of 4 percent, and the 16th percent at the rate of 6 percent. The yield from this tax increase would be about 700,000 to 800,000 crowns.

The tax on directors' profit shares would constitute an innovation. The Austrian tax on dividends is obviously modeled on that of the German Empire, which was introduced in 1906. But while the German tax affected only the supervisory boards of stock corporations, the Austrian tax also applies to the director, board of directors, management, and members of the corporation. The rate of this tax is progressive and goes from 2 percent to 8 percent. Its yield is estimated at 1 million crowns.

Finally, one last provision of the new plan must be pointed out, which is stirring up vigorous opposition in commercial and industrial circles: in the future, according to the plan, fiscal authorities will have the right to inspect the books of businesses and industries. Austrian entrepreneurs rightly see in this arrangement an intensification of the harassment that the authorities display toward them.

In Austrian governmental circles, people like to compare the Austrian finance minister's plan with that of Lloyd-George. Just like the English budget, they say, the Austrian plan focuses on the wealthy classes and tends to grant relief to the less well-to-do. The Austrian minister of finance, Mr. Bilinski, attempts to parry the attacks directed against his fiscal plans by businessmen and industrialists by making tirades against them; his assault on business considerably exceeds in harshness and hostility anything that has ever been said by the Austrian government against any other group whatsoever. One is reluctantly tempted to make a comparison between these almost-personal attacks of the Austrian ministers, and the oratorical procedures that English ministers use in the electoral battle against the peers.

In the end, all of that may cause public opinion to lose sight of the essential differences between the Austrian scheme and the British budget. The English fiscal reform as a whole constitutes a surtax on the real estate owner: it is directed above all against the land-owning lords, whether they own property in the city or in the country. The targeted social class is the conservative aristocracy and the circles immediately associated with it. The English project carries no trace of hostility toward big industry and commerce. It is precisely the opposite of what characterizes the Austrian project.

Austria today is a country which by necessity has become a large importer of cereal grains. It imports these grains partly from Hungary (which, though in a customs union with Austria, should be considered as a foreign territory in all respects) and partly from other foreign countries. Austria then must be regarded as an industrial country since its economy is based on industrial production. The political strength and importance of the urban industrial population, however, does not correspond to the existing state of affairs. In the Reichsrat the representatives of the agrarian interests have the majority. Large and small real property owners join together to fight the urban and industrial interests. Moreover, the representatives of the cities and the industrial localities are not in agreement. Only a rare few deputies who represent large industries and the socialist deputies are resolute partisans of modern economic evolution and modern industry. The other elected officials from urban electoral districts represent primarily the interests of the petite bourgeoisie and do not understand anything about the general interest in the development of industry. They are always ready to form alliances with the agrarians against industry. Even in questions of commercial policy they often march in step—though not overtly—with the agrarian deputies.

Thus the agrarian deputies have succeeded in gaining great advantages in the fiscal arena. It can be seen most clearly in the taxation of profits, the income tax, and among indirect taxes where the excise tax on alcohol is concerned.

While all other direct taxes continually increase, real estate tax is the only Austrian tax that has gone down during the last decade, and not only in relation to the other receipts of the state but also in absolute terms. The real estate tax is an assessment tax, and from 1881 to 1896 the yield of this tax for the whole empire was evaluated at 75 million crowns. Since then, it has fallen to 59.5 million crowns. The real yield of the property tax, however, remains well below that figure. Every year, large reductions are granted for damages caused by the weather. Thus, in 1907, the real estate tax actually brought in only 54.5 million crowns.

The privileges of rural real estate owners are no less in the area of income tax. Here, however, the farmers are favored not by the law but by certain provisions concerning the instructions for its execution, and especially by practices which are completely different in the country and in the cities. That is why the yield from the tax in the countryside is so small from the fiscal point of view. In 1908, on a total gross income of 4.268 billion crowns that were subject to tax, only 308 million or 7.2 percent was associated with income from rural property. It is a distressing result considering the importance of agricultural production in Austria.

The advantages that agriculturists draw from the legislation on alcohol excise are much greater. Just as in the German Empire, the excise tax on alcohol is presently set up on a dual basis: 1,017,000 hectoliters of alcohol are taxed at the lower rate of 90 crowns; the rest at the higher rate of 101 crowns. The distilleries among which these 1,017,000 hectoliters are distributed therefore enjoy an expense differential of 20 crowns per hectoliter sold. Thus the system of taxation on alcohol brings them an annual benefit of 20 million crowns.

Of the total of 1,017,000 hectoliters—called the "Alcohol contingent" [or quota]—only 155,000 hectoliters have to do with distilleries belonging to industrialists, all the rest being allotted to distilleries owned by rural proprietors. The new government plan lowers the contingent attributed to the professional distilleries by a further 40,000 hectoliters in order to raise the contingent of the agricultural distilleries. In addition, the difference between the higher rate and the lower rate has grown from 20 to 24 crowns, so that the value of the contingent tax will be even greater. For each hectoliter in the future, the distiller will gain not 20 but 24 crowns, and the profit that the distilleries will obtain at the expense of the community will rise from 20 million to 24 million crowns.

As if that is not enough, the agricultural distilleries will continue to enjoy a production subsidy, which in 1908 totaled 7,000,317 crowns. However, the new law is meant to slightly reduce this subsidy.

Since he is eager to increase the resources of the state, the finance minister should, without any doubt, start with removing the advantages granted to the land-owning distillers by fiscal legislation. A gradual diminution of the difference by raising the rate of tax for contingent alcohol would assure the state's gain of about 20 million crowns without the slightest surcharge for the population.

This should be the direction of a financial policy that aims at an equable distribution of the tax and not at a differential increase of burdens on the urban population. Political conditions and the party division in the House of Representatives, however, are not favorable to such a policy. Far from following the path indicated above, the government constantly seeks to reduce the taxes of the agrarian population. For years the tax on urban buildings has been considered crushing. The government is moving toward reform very slowly and timidly, but at the same time it is lowering the tax on buildings in the countryside by 6.3 million crowns, where it is already not excessive.

While in full financial distress, the government has just voted in a law opening up an annual credit of 6 million crowns on the funds of the state in favor of Austrian agriculturists in hope of advancing certain particular branches of agricultural production. If we consider how reluctantly the government grants even the most insignificant credit for any other purposes of recognized necessity, we can understand the censure that this financial policy generates in urban areas.

None of the new taxes proposed by the finance minister move in the direction of leveling the fiscal inequalities that exist between the city and the country.

The increases in income tax affect the urban and industrial population most severely, for it is they who, in the main, pay the income tax. The rate of income tax in the country is unchanged; the increase proposed by the government targets exclusively commercial and industrial urban populations. Likewise, the introduction of the tax on mineral water and soda as well as the elimination of the tax exemption for automobile gasoline will affect the rural population only minimally. As far as the new proposal for an excise tax on wine is concerned, the wine consumed by wine producers, members of their families, and their employees will remain tax-exempt, as it is at present: the increase of the tax on wine will then affect only the wine consumers, who almost exclusively reside in the cities and industrial areas.

The essential feature of the current Austrian economic policy is the fight against the capitalist mode of production. In the matter of industrial policy there is an attempt to support the artisan class and to save it from its inevitable demise. In the matter of tariff policy, the raising of import taxes on grains and meat raises the cost of living for the working classes, thus diminishing their ability to consume industrial products, and thereby exerts an unfavorable influence on the development of large industry.

In Austria, public opinion is hostile to the capitalist system of production, in contrast to the dominant opinion of all the Western countries. This tendency in Austria should not be compared to what is called anticapitalism in England, the United States, and other Western countries. The large profits of capitalist enterprises are not, of course, looked upon favorably in Western Europe and America, but nobody there would like to bring about a reversal of industrial evolution. In Austria, the most influential political parties are firm adversaries of the entire modern economic system. The agrarian parties dislike industry because it raises wages. Big industry and big commerce irritate the petite-bourgeoisie parties (to which the small artisans and small businessmen belong) because they have the upper hand in commerce. But these two parties, the petite bourgeoisie and the agrarians, have a huge majority in the Austrian Parliament: on the one side, hundreds of representatives of agriculture and small business, and on the other side, some twenty representatives of big industry. This state of affairs is aggravated by the fact that the bureaucracy exercises an excessive influence in the administration, and that the free initiative of the individual is constantly frustrated. The same tendencies dominate financial policy. Large industry and big business, the prospering of which is hampered in all possible ways by legislation and by the administration, must bear the greater part of public expenses.

In the long run, such policy cannot be continued. Even in Austria we will have to resolve to remove the obstacles that stand in the way of industrial evolution and thus favor the flourishing of industry, for which all the required natural conditions exist. Fiscal policy, too, must be modified: the agricultural producers, who today are practically free of tax burdens, will have to be taxed more heavily, and the privileges of large property will have to disappear. A radical reform of the Ministry of the Interior is also absolutely necessary.

CHAPTER 7

The General Rise in Prices in the Light of Economic Theory[1]

The problem of rising prices, which has for many years occupied the attention of our best minds, cannot be dealt with in the usual statistical-empirical manner. The collection and comparison of price data is not a substitute for the intellectual work of theoretical economists; nor can it lead to clear thinking and a correct understanding of the interrelationships involved. The multivolume publications of the statistical bureaus, with a wealth of figures and tables, have not brought the problem one step closer to a solution. What we know about the origin, nature, and significance of fluctuations in prices has not resulted from the processing of statistical materials. On the whole, statistical material is valuable only insofar as it can be used in conjunction with the findings of economic theory. Those who seek to find their way through the darkness of statistical figures will succeed only where economic theory lights the way.

Once the work of gathering the numbers is completed, the statistician has finished his job. The conclusions drawn from the assembled material are determined by economic theory. The conclusions are not strengthened by being linked to a statistical apparatus. They do not follow with the force of logical deduction from the study of the statistical material. Contradictory conclusions can easily be drawn from the profusion of complementary and opposing economic factors, the relative significance of which the observer must determine by means of abstract reasoning for the purposes of his investigation. Apart from a few trivial matters of detail, it is impossible to ascribe to price statistics any role other than that of illustrating the sound results of price theory. If we

1. [This article originally appeared in German in *Archiv für Sozialwissenschaft und Sozialpolitik*, vol. 37 (1913).—Ed.]

look more closely we can easily see that every writer who did not limit himself to the assembling of data but also tried to study causal relationships started out from certain theoretical conceptions that guided his thinking. The literature on inflation is completely dominated by the premises of price theory, and these form the basis of the various articles on the subject.

Nowadays, these articles are not always of the highest caliber. Very often—insofar as we are speaking about German writings, it would unfortunately be more correct to say nearly always—we find lines of reasoning that have long since been surpassed by more recent scholarly developments. The basic theory of supply and demand and the quantity theory of money are referred to and challenged in these articles in a manner similar to what one would expect to find one or two hundred years ago. But this is only a minor problem. The cost of production theory is presented in a naïve manner as well; and frequently we even run into the layman's favorite theories presented with ethical and political commentaries that seek to make commodity speculation and usury responsible for all our economic ills. The forty-year-long development of the theory of subjective value has made hardly any impact at all in Germany.[2]

In addition to these "internal" difficulties, there are equally great "external" ones that confront the scholarly treatment of the problem of inflation. Rising prices are now one of our most important political problems. Every political party is committed to a specific theory about the causes of inflation, and each has a specific prescription for combating it. Whoever tries to examine the problem runs the risk of falling out with all the parties at the same time. Such a person would be getting off lightly if either the "political pragmatists" merely ignored his explanation as the work of a "theoretician alienated from the real

2. [This refers to the development of the theory of marginal utility, or subjective value, especially as formulated by the "Austrian economists." See Carl Menger, *Principles of Economics* (New York: New York University Press, [1871] 1981); Eugen von Böhm-Bawerk, *Capital and Interest*, vol. 2, *The Positive Theory of Capital* (South Holland, Ill.: Libertarian Press, [1914] 1959), pp. 121–256. On the resistance of the German Historical School to the ideas and methods of the Austrian School, see Eugen von Böhm-Bawerk, "The Historical versus the Deductive Method in Political Economy," (1891) reprinted in Israel M. Kirzner, ed., *Classics in Austrian Economics: A Sampling in the History of a Tradition* (London: William Pickering, 1994), pp. 109–29; and Ludwig von Mises, "The Historical Setting of the Austrian School of Economics," [1969] reprinted in Bettina Bien Greaves, ed., *Austrian Economics: An Anthology* (Irvington-on-Hudson, N.Y.: Foundation for Economic Education, 1996), pp. 53–76.

world" or if the attacks directed against his scholarly efforts remained within the bounds of civil decency. Anyone daring to question the popular dogmas on the causes of and the cures for inflation must be prepared for rough treatment.[3]

General Price Increases and Particular Price Increases

When a general rise in prices, or simply higher prices, is referred to, this means a decline in the purchasing power (or the objective exchange value) of money. In an economy in which a general medium of exchange is not used, if the exchange relationship between one economic good and another changes, this refers to a rise in the price of one good relative to another. In this case, a higher or lower price cannot be discussed without more detail. If we set aside the use of money, it is clear that one good cannot become more expensive without all other goods becoming less expensive.

The problem that exclusively concerns us is a general rise in prices. We certainly do not claim that this is the only problem that is of interest in terms of increases in prices. Besides those changes in the exchange relationship between money and all other economic goods that originate from the side of money, there is also the issue of changes in the relative price relationships among different economic goods. It has to be recognized that a general increase in the level of prices does not affect the prices of all goods proportionally. The prices of some goods may rise more than others, and the prices of some goods may, on the contrary, actually decline.

This phenomenon is by no means attributable solely to the fact that the changes in the value of money always bring with them changes in the distribution of wealth and income, and therefore lead to changes in consumption, which then influence supply and demand and through them the prices of consumer goods. A number of independent causes lead to this phenomenon, and in the majority of cases it is not difficult to discover them. If it is in reference to the prices of meat, of milk, or of housing, the causes are seldom hard to find. Even the efforts of interested parties cannot succeed for very long in misleading the public about it. It is abundantly clear that the problem of general inflation (the

3. [On Mises's recollections of his own confrontations with members of the German Historical School during the years before the First World War, see "Remarks Concerning the Ideological Roots of the Monetary Catastrophe of 1923," Chapter 29 in the present volume.—Ed.]

general rise in the prices of goods) and the increase in the price of a
particular good (the rise in the prices of individual goods or services)
must be strictly separated. There is much confusion in journalistic discussions due to the failure to distinguish between the two.

The prices of individual commodities can rise or fall at the international level, though it is not always the case. It can happen that
such changes are limited to the local level. If, for example, the price
of brandy rises in Austria because the tax on brandy is increased, or if
the price of meat goes up because the importation of cattle and meat
is prohibited, this has no direct effect on the prices of brandy and meat
in other countries. Foreign prices are not directly changed due to these
taxes or regulations; if there is any indirect influence that takes place,
it tends to work in the opposite direction. For example, it can lower
the price of meat in Romania because exports to Austria have been
banned, and therefore Austrian demand for Romanian meat has been
stopped. To the extent that there is a general rise in prices, it is international in character. This results from the fact that at the present time
gold is the international money. Gold is the world's money, nowadays,
and not only the money of a particular region or nation; therefore a
lowering in its value always occurs at the international level.

The Quantity of Money and the Value of Money

The exchange relationship that exists between money and other economic goods must experience a change if individuals in the economy
have a change in their demand for or supply of money. Ceteris paribus,
the purchasing power of the monetary unit must decline if the quantity of money is increased and, conversely, the purchasing power of the
monetary unit must rise if the quantity of money is decreased. This is
the essence of the quantity theory, the oldest and most unchallenge-
able conclusion in the theory of money.[4]

The demands for money by individuals are not only satisfied by
money alone. The same service can be provided by money substitutes,
that is, generally recognized and secure claims to money that are payable on demand (e.g., banknotes, cashier's checks, small coins, and the
like). Money substitutes may or may not be "covered" by money. When

4. Cf. my *Theory of Money and Credit* (Indianapolis: Liberty Fund, 3rd rev. ed., [1924; 1951]
1981), pp. 146–77.

they are covered by money, we call them "money certificates," and when they are not covered they are called "fiduciary media."[5] It is clear that an increase or decrease in the quantity of fiduciary media must result in the same effect on the value of the monetary unit that is caused by an increase or decrease in the quantity of money.

If the supply of money (in the wider sense, including the supply of fiduciary media) is increased while the demand for money (in the wider sense, including the demand for fiduciary media) remains unchanged, then the objective exchange value of money will decline. This decline is, however, by no means inversely proportional to the increase in the supply of money; in addition, the change in the value of money does not occur simultaneously in the entire economy to the same extent with respect to all goods. It is not necessary to justify and explain this further, since I have done this elsewhere.

All attempts to use the quantity theory of money for statistical investigations into the causes and degree of change in the objective exchange value of money must always remain a failure. Of the two factors whose interactions determine changes in the value of money, only one, the supply of money, can be determined. The other one, demand for money, is one whose size is dependent upon subjective factors that in the best of cases only can be approximately estimated.[6]

But even were it possible to quantitatively determine the changes in both the supply of and demand for money, this would still be very far from being able to reach any quantitative conclusions about changes

5. Ibid., p. 154. [In *The Theory of Money and Credit*, pp. 63–67, 155–56, 393–404, and in *Human Action: A Treatise on Economics* (Indianapolis: Liberty Fund, [1949; 4th rev. ed. 1996] 2007), pp. 432–44, and his other writings on monetary theory and policy, Mises defined "money substitutes" as claims to a commodity money such as gold in the form of banknotes or checks that are readily and generally accepted in transactions and that are believed to be fully redeemable on demand at the banking institution that has issued them. Mises distinguished between money substitutes that are backed 100 percent by commodity money reserves at the issuing institution ("money certificates") and those money substitutes issued by a bank that are less than fully backed ("fiduciary media"). Loans extended on the basis of 100 percent reserve backing were referred to as "commodity credit" and those loans extended on the basis of less than 100 percent reserve backing were called "circulation credit." Mises argued that it was the extension of fiduciary media not covered by 100 percent reserves that was the source of business cycles, in that it created the illusion of more savings available in society (in the form of money loans extended through the banking system) to support and sustain investment and capital formation than really existed.—Ed.]

6. [See Ludwig von Mises, "The Position of Money Among Economic Goods," (1932) in Richard M. Ebeling, ed., *Money, Method, and the Market Process: Essays by Ludwig von Mises* (Norwell, Mass.: Kluwer Academic Press, 1990), pp. 55–69, especially 59–62.—Ed.]

in the value of money. As was already pointed out, movements in the objective exchange value of money are not inversely proportional to those that take place in the relationship between the supply of and the demand for money. Furthermore, we lack the ability to precisely measure changes in the objective exchange value of money.

All index number methods, even the most ingenious and complete, can make no claim to such precision.[7] Usually, statistical investigations into the value of money ignore all of this. They quietly assume that the changes in the quantity of money (in the narrower sense, not including fiduciary media) indirectly cause proportional changes in the purchasing power of the monetary unit—and that such changes simultaneously affect the prices of all goods throughout the entire economy.

While index numbers are considered a method for precisely measuring changes in the purchasing power of money, this view is no more justifiable even when they are constructed by combining several different principles and procedures. These procedures turn an allegedly scientific work into a meaningless juggling of numbers and words. The errors in this approach end up damaging the reputation of economics as a science, since the general public always tends to blame economic theory for the "failures" of those providing economic information through the collecting and manipulating of the statistical data.

In general, economic theory is not likely to lead to blunders in economic policy. In only one area is there an incomplete theoretical understanding which can lead to questionable conclusions for purposes of policy. It is customary to ignore the fact that fiduciary media have the same effect on determining the objective exchange value of money as money itself. Ceteris paribus, an increase in the quantity of fiduciary media will lead to the same decline in the purchasing power of the monetary unit as will an increase in the quantity of money proper.

In a complete reversal of all that economic theory demonstrated five generations ago, it is now again believed that it is possible to reduce the rate of interest by increasing the quantity of fiduciary media in circulation. This has generated very strange results. On the one hand, a battle

7. [See Mises, *The Theory of Money and Credit*, pp. 215–23; also, Ludwig von Mises, "Monetary Stabilization and Cyclical Policy," (1928) in Mises, *The Causes of the Economic Crisis, and Other Essays Before and After the Great Depression* (Auburn, Ala.: Ludwig von Mises Institute, 2006), pp. 73–79; Mises, "The Suitability of Methods of Ascertaining Changes in Purchasing Power for the Guidance of International Currency and Banking Policy," (1930) in Ebeling, ed., *Money, Method, and the Market Process*, pp. 78–95, and especially 86–90, and *Human Action*, pp. 219–23.—Ed.]

is undertaken against inflation, though certainly with more pretension than with any serious intention behind it. On the other hand, there is an attempt to increase the number of unbacked banknotes in circulation, including efforts to artificially expand the supply of fiduciary media through the use of checks. This generates a tendency for a decline in the purchasing power of money.[8]

Recently an argument has been made that opposes what has been said above about the influence of changes in the relationship between the demand for and the supply of money on the purchasing power of money. Othmar Spann[9] considers as more or less useless a theory that explains inflation as being due to the increase in gold production, as an attempt to employ one underlying concept for explaining the phenomena of rising prices.

Therefore, "everyone who has a good instinct for inductive analysis of economic relationships becomes distrustful of a theory which tries to explain increases in prices and finally the whole history of prices, with its great rising and falling price curves, according to a surplus or a shortage in the media of exchange, rather than by the 'inner progress' of the economy, itself." The older Physiocratic[10] attempt to understand economic processes by basically assuming the absence of money should be reintroduced and viewed with greater respect than it has enjoyed up until now. For analyzing general movements in prices, this method allegedly would be especially useful in order to be able to precisely separate the effects caused by money in circulation from those effects that are inherent in the underlying economic processes.[11]

One of Spann's claims does entirely agree with our own view: an ex-

8. [Mises, *The Theory of Money and Credit*, pp. 377–404.—Ed.]

9. [Othmar Spann (1878–1950) was a prominent and highly popular professor at the University of Vienna during the period between the two world wars. He was an opponent of individualism, political and economic liberalism, Marxism, and materialism. He referred to individualism in all its forms as "the dragon-seed of evil." Instead, he advocated what he called "universalism," a conception of society as an organic whole or totality greater than the individuals of which it was composed. He proposed a corporativist structure to society, in which each sector of the economy would be organized in a hierarchy of guilds. He was greatly admired by many Austrian fascists, but was prevented from teaching by the new Nazi regime after the German annexation of Austria in 1938.—Ed.]

10. [The Physiocrats were a group of eighteenth-century French Enlightenment thinkers who often referred to themselves as "the Economists." Opponents of mercantilism, they developed a theory of society's "natural order" that emphasized the self-regulating patterns of the market.—Ed.]

11. Cf. Spann, *Theorie der Preisverschiebung als Grundlage zur Erklärung der Teuerungen* [Theory of Price Change as Foundation for the Explanation of Inflations] (Vienna, 1913), pp. 3–5.

planation of inflation not by one principle but—as the next section will show—by two different principles which interact in their effect. For the rest, however, Spann's remarks must be rejected as being wrong.

For a long time, it has been customary in economics to first discuss the problem of the formation of prices (the prices of goods, wages, real estate rents, interest on capital, etc.) under the assumption that it was as if there was direct exchange. Not only did the Physiocrats assume this, as Spann mentions, but so did all economic theorists; a glance at the works of the classical or modern writers on economics will easily convince anyone of this. The knowledge that can be gained by this method, and by this method alone, then needs to be completed by a study into how the result is affected by the use of money and fiduciary media.

In addition to the theory of direct exchange, there is the theory of indirect exchange—the theory of money and of fiduciary media (that is, money and banking theory). If a criticism were to be raised against economic theory during the last several decades, it would certainly not be that this distinction between direct and indirect exchange has been neglected. Quite to the contrary! Though the study of direct exchange logically must precede the study of indirect exchange, the problems of the former have so thoroughly claimed the attention of economists that the problems of the latter have been passed over. Among those that have suffered severe neglect, for example, is the problem of economic crises, the complete understanding of which can be provided only by the theory of indirect exchange.[12]

Among the economic processes that can and should be studied under the assumption of direct exchange, the problem of a general rise in prices is not one. A general rise in prices means a change in the existing exchange relationship between money and other economic goods. In an economy in which money is not used, a general inflation of prices is not possible.

How can money be excluded from the investigation? Spann, of course, attempts this obviously hopeless task. If he presumes to explain "a higher price level" on the basis of natural [barter] exchange, he demonstrates a misunderstanding of what in everyday speech is called, for the sake of brevity and convenience, "price," but what more fully and correctly should be called the "exchange relationship between money

12. [See Mises, *Human Action*, pp. 201–03.—Ed.]

and goods." If the following exchange relationship prevails today: 5 kilos of A = 7 kilos of B = 9 kilos of C = 16 crowns; and tomorrow 5 kilos of A = 7 kilos of B = 9 kilos of C = 18 crowns, then the change that has occurred overnight can never be explained from causes which lie in the relationship between A, B, and C.

Devaluation as a Consequence of Certain Characteristics of Indirect Exchange

A change in the objective exchange value of money does not occur only due to a change in the relationship between the demand for and the supply of money. There is another reason for such changes, and it is to be found in certain characteristics of indirect exchange. There is a fundamental distinction between the exchange relationships existing between money and the other economic goods and the structure of exchange relationships among the other economic goods themselves.

In direct (or barter) exchange, an exchange can be carried out only if each of the two parties in the transaction values less highly the quantity of goods that he is to give up than the goods he is to receive in exchange. If this assumption does not hold, there will be no exchange. This holds for indirect exchange facilitated by money only with an important modification. The willing buyer can decide to pay the price demanded by the seller on the presumption that, even if the price is beyond his appraisement of the value of the goods, he hopes that he will be able to obtain a higher price for the goods and services he brings to market because he has paid higher prices for the goods and services that he purchased.

The higher money price does not at all have to mean also a higher "own price"; it can very well be the case that in terms of barter relationships the exchange relationships among goods themselves (with the exception of money) has remained unchanged. The only change that has occurred is in the exchange relationship between money and all other goods.

If workers demand higher money wages and the entrepreneurs give in to their demand, this does not by any means signify that there has been an increase in real wages. It can happen that the entrepreneurs succeed in passing the wage increase on to the consumers, so that the prices of goods also rise, with the result that real wages remain the same or do not rise to the same extent as money wages have gone up.

If the producers of a certain product push through an increase in its price, this also does not have to mean an increase in the "own price"; in this case, too, the price increase may be only a nominal one.

This can also sometimes happen due to the type of information possessed by the producer and the consumer when they are in a face-to-face relationship with each other. This is, however, by no means necessarily the case. Market conditions are more clearly and easily understood and compared when consumption and production are more directly connected.

The situation is different in the more developed stages of a national and, especially, the global economy. The lay of the land in the market is not as easily surveyed as it was when the market was smaller and exchange relationships were more direct. The producer no longer comes into direct contact with the consumer. The product is "taken up by the market," which means that the evaluation of the good by consumers may not be the same as the one upon which the producer based his calculations.

Producers and traders face an unknown factor; they can anticipate the future decisions of consumers with only a greater or lesser degree of skill; but, of course, they cannot talk about it with any degree of certainty. For the majority of ready-made consumer goods, dealing with individual consumers is impossible. The producer and the trader must set "fixed" prices, which the consumer either accepts by paying the money prices asked or refrains from buying and not paying the money prices being asked. This either maintains or alters the purchasing power of money.

In order for there to be a tendency for a decline in the objective exchange value of money that encompasses the entire economy due to an exchange process mediated by money, significant disturbances must occur in the relationships between production and consumption. In a static, or more or less static economy, reciprocal exchange relationships between economic goods (excluding money) experience no or only minor changes. Under such conditions businessmen and workers do not have an incentive to push for increases in their prices and wages.

It is otherwise during times of significant change in production and consumption, if there are also significant changes in the reciprocal exchange relationships. Then sellers (including the sellers of labor services) are groping and feeling their way, trying to establish new prices for the goods and services that they are bringing to market. They set prices that, according to their perspective, are prices at which their goods and services can be sold; but they can easily aim too high. If they have aimed too low, that is, asked for too low a price, they will quickly become aware of their mistake as soon as the demand exceeds the supply.

In the opposite case the error is not so quickly recognized. If the sellers demand too high a price, then, as the law of price teaches us, quantity demanded will be less than quantity supplied. The unwillingness of buyers to purchase the good will finally force the sellers to reduce the price they are asking. But here the special characteristics of indirect exchange come into play. The willing buyer does not hold back from buying the product even if the price asked exceeds his valuation of the good by only a small amount because he, on his part, also hopes to get more money from the sale of the goods and services that he brings to market. The seller has raised his price and he sees that the buyers accept it; and for the same reason that the buyers paid higher prices for his product, he, in turn, also pays them. Everyone expects that their higher monetary costs will be balanced by their earning higher money incomes; they expect a decline in the purchasing power of money which their own behavior in fact brings about.

Because of the particular ways in which markets are organized, upon which money facilitates transactions, major changes in the reciprocal exchange relationships among economic goods create a tendency for declines in the purchasing power of the monetary unit.[13]

The Social Effects from General Inflation

Before we use an important example to explain what we have said, it seems appropriate to add a few words about the social significance resulting from a general rise in prices. If changes in the objective exchange value of money were to appear simultaneously and to the same degree in the entire global economy, if the prices of all goods and services were to rise or fall simultaneously and proportionally, the social effects on the structure of contractual obligations fulfilled through the use of money would be very limited. All deferred payments are affected if money rises or falls in value. If the purchasing power of money declines, debtors gain while creditors lose. The assumption here, of

13. [See Mises, *The Theory of Money and Credit*, pp. 185–89.—Ed.]

course, is that when debtors and creditors entered into their contracts they did not anticipate and incorporate into the contract future changes in the objective exchange value of money. This is a reasonable assumption, since for various reasons it is impossible to foresee the extent to which there may be changes in the purchasing power of money.

If changes in the purchasing power of money really occurred simultaneously and proportionally throughout the entire economy, then complaints about inflation nowadays would not be so loud and would hardly result in governments undertaking anti-inflationary policy measures. Creditors who have binding contracts specifying particular sums of money to be paid would most probably not calmly accept the damages they would suffer. No doubt they would attempt to bring about changes in prices more favorable to their situation. However, it is highly unlikely that they would succeed in this attempt. Their complaints would hardly be likely to bring any positive response from the majority of the population. The numbers of people whose incomes are mainly or exclusively derived from invested capital is much too small in most countries for their desires and interests to significantly influence the direction of economic policy.

The detrimental effect that is experienced by most people from a monetary devaluation is not due to the fact that it hurts the interests of creditors; rather it is due to the fact that it only appears gradually throughout the economy. The prices of various goods do not rise proportionally all at once. Inflation first appears in some particular part of the economy, affecting only some goods, and then gradually spreads out from there. Let us first consider the case of a monetary devaluation that comes about due to an increase in the quantity of money or fiduciary media, while the demand for money remains the same, or does not rise at the same rate in the broader sense as the money supply has increased.[14]

Let us suppose, for example, that a new gold mine has been opened. The new gold first pours into the hands of the gold producers; it in-

14. [The idea of the "unevenness" or "nonneutral" effects on prices following an increase (or decrease) in the quantity of money has been a central theme in the Austrian School theory of money, especially in the writings of Ludwig von Mises. See Mises, *The Theory of Money and Credit*, pp. 160–68, 225–46; "Monetary Stabilization and Cyclical Policy," pp. 80–88; Mises, "The Non-Neutrality of Money," (1938) in Ebeling, ed., *Money, Method, and the Market Process*, pp. 68–77; and *Human Action*, pp. 398–432; also, Friedrich A. Hayek, *Prices and Production* (New York: Augustus M. Kelley, [1935] 1967), pp. 1–31, 129–31.—Ed.]

creases their income, reduces their subjective valuation of the monetary unit, and so intensifies their desire to purchase goods on the market. They now express on the market their demand for those goods that they now more intensely desire than before; they can offer more money for the goods they wish to acquire. These are the goods that first rise in price, and the objective exchange value of money declines first in terms of these goods. This is the point at which the monetary devaluation begins. The next step in this process is that those who sold the goods that were purchased by the first possessors of the new money now, in turn, have an increased buying power and are able to express a greater demand for the goods that they desire to buy, so the prices of these goods rise, as well. The rise in prices continues until, to one degree or another, the prices of all goods are included in the process.

This gradual progression of rising prices causes its associated effects. The particular social groups who first receive the new quantity of money benefit from the process, while those are harmed who receive the money only later in the process. So long as the monetary depreciation has not yet worked its way through the entire economy, those who already receive a higher money income reflecting the eventual decline in the value of money are able to purchase all or some of the goods they desire at prices that do not yet fully incorporate the devaluation of the monetary unit. On the other hand, those whose money incomes do not yet reflect the new situation pay for the goods they demand at prices that have already adjusted to the higher price level.

The exact same process is at work, of course, with those changes in the value of money that, as was described earlier, arise from sellers raising their prices. Here again, the increase in prices starts at some point in the economy and gradually spreads out from there. That group of sellers who begin the process of raising prices also benefit even if, over time, the prices of the goods they buy increase in proportion to the prices of the goods they sell. For while the process is continuing that leads to a general devaluation throughout the entire economy, they enjoy an advantage they will no longer have when prices will have fully adjusted to the new situation.

It is precisely this circumstance that provides an explanation of the practices followed by the groups that initiate the rise in prices. This applies to actions of cartels and trusts—insofar as they are not monopolistic practices—and also the methods employed by trade unions. The latter now require some further comments.

Increasing Wages and Inflation

It can hardly be denied that reciprocal effects exist between the movements of money wages and movements in the money prices of finished goods. Modern economic theory is distinct from the widely popular older theory of value that tried to explain a rise in prices of finished goods in terms of a rise in the cost of the factors of production. It is an anachronism to explain those movements in the objective exchange value of money that are caused by changes in the relationship between the supply of and the demand for money, by referring to the labor time in production and the influence of the money prices of the factors of production as the basis for the prices of consumer goods.

This customary way of analyzing the problem is seen to be untenable without much difficulty. Any useful result will require a different chain of reasoning. One thing that is common in all economic theories of wages is that they consider the determination of the level of wages to be a part of the theory of value. The different answers that were given over time to the problem of explaining the value of goods also led to different attempted answers to the problem of explaining wages. The objective theories of value followed paths different from those of the modern theory of value.

The modern theory of value was the first one to fully appreciate the significance of the problem. The theory of imputation developed by Böhm-Bawerk,[15] Clark,[16] and Wieser[17] demonstrates how the individual complementary factors of production factors are evaluated; it forms the

---

15. [Eugen von Böhm-Bawerk (1851–1914) was one of the leading members of the Austrian School of economics in the years before the First World War. His major contributions were to the theory of capital and interest, as well as the general theory of value and price. He was a professor of political economy at the University of Innsbruck from 1880 to 1889. He worked in the Austrian Ministry of Finance throughout the 1890s and served three times as minister of finance, the longest and last time from 1900 to 1904. Böhm-Bawerk returned to teaching as a full-time professor of political economy at the University of Vienna in 1905, a position that he held until his death.—Ed.]

16. [John Bates Clark (1847–1938) was a leading proponent of the marginalist approach in the United States. His 1899 volume, *The Distribution of Wealth*, developed the theory of marginal productivity to explain the allocation of income among the factors of production. He was professor of economics at Columbia University from 1895 to 1923.—Ed.]

17. See Chapter 5, "The Fourth Issuing Right of the Austro-Hungarian Bank," footnote 9.

indispensable logical link between any theory of the formation of the prices of the factors of production and the distribution of the product among the factors of production.

The only interventions that can influence the level of market-determined wages are those that work within the laws of the market. Any wage policy that wishes to change the level of wages from the one that tends to form on the unhampered market, and which we can call the "natural wage," must modify the factors whose interactions jointly determine the actual level of wages prevailing on the market. For example, it is possible to lower wages if one encourages the immigration of foreign workers, and one can push wages up if one restricts the influx of workers. The market price for labor is indirectly influenced by the use of these methods; the market wage that is formed under the influence of these changed conditions is the "natural wage" in this new state of affairs.[18]

Any direct influence on wages is as unworkable as with any other price on the market. It necessarily leads to a reaction that reestablishes the "natural" market situation. This is equally true for tax rates as it is for the wage policy of organized labor through trade unions. The older Classical School already understood this, even though it was based on an untenable theory of value.

We set aside for any further consideration the role organized labor may play for economic life, in politics, for law and social customs, or for national identity. We have only one question before us: whether or not organized labor can raise wages above their natural level. This question is immediately answered in the affirmative for all those cases in which labor unions can succeed in influencing the conditions of the labor market. As for influencing the demand side, in general the answer is no. More often the unions can succeed in influencing supply according to their wishes. If this influence is limited to individual industries, it always comes down to a question of advantages for the workers in one branch of production at the expense of all other workers. Artificially reducing the supply of labor in one or more branches of production results in an increased supply of labor in all other branches of industry; if the wages are pushed up in the former, then they must fall in the latter.

18. [See Eugen von Böhm-Bawerk, "Control or Economic Law," (1914) in *Shorter Classics of Böhm-Bawerk* (South Holland, Ill.: Libertarian Press, 1962), pp. 139–99, for a detailed analysis of this argument by a leading member of the early Austrian School.—Ed.]

This by no means exhausts the consequences from such monopolies of the labor force in particular branches of industry; their effects go further than this. They also prevent the optimal combination of the factors of production, and as a result reduce the value of the total product. This second effect shows itself most clearly when the supply of labor is restricted not in one but in all branches of production. Two cases are conceivable: a decrease in the availability of new workers through a reduction in the total population (a reduction in fertility, for example), or a decrease in the supply of labor with no change in the total number of workers by shortening the number of work hours. The latter can be brought about either through legislation (a limit on the workday), or through the actions of labor unions, or due to a restriction in the output of the workers (passive workers' resistance, or a "ca' canny" policy).[19] If, however, the factors underlying the formation of wages are left unchanged, then a permanent deviation of the level of wages from its natural level cannot be achieved. That is generally true for almost all labor unions. Labor unions cannot permanently raise the level of wages because they cannot also change the underlying conditions of the overall labor market.

The last several decades seem to contradict this conclusion. We see organized labor move forward from one success to another; wages keep rising higher and higher. No doubt part of this increase in wages is merely a consequence of the increase of the supply of money (gold production and an increase in fiduciary media), which has brought about a fall in the objective exchange value of money. Yet another part is to be attributed to the increase in profits resulting from improvements in productivity; a part of the reward for this productivity goes to the workers in line with their direct contribution to the production process. This gain would have gone to the workers even without labor unions and wage conflicts. But is that all that labor unions have achieved?

Very many are of the opinion that the workers have achieved far more by uniting their forces than what would have fallen into their laps anyway. One can read today in all sociopolitical writings that the labor unions have raised the level of wages; people want to believe that this provides an inductive proof against the conclusions of those theories that declared the impossibility of increasing wages through this

---

19. [A ca' canny policy is a deliberate reduction in the working speed and production by workers to demonstrate their discontent with working conditions.—Ed.]

method. This is taken to be so obvious that no one has taken the trouble of designing a theory of wages to justify it.

One has difficulty figuring out what is the theory of wages in the approach of the German Historical School. One of its leading representatives tells us that, in the face of the limitless difficulties involved in finding a universally applicable explanation, the School has given up on developing a theory of wages.[20] But these writers must have had something in mind if they spoke about wages and a wage policy. We do not think that we are far wrong if we assume that they vaguely had in mind a naïve "exploitation" theory of wages. Today it is the folk theory of wages. It can look back upon a famous literary past in the form of Marx's theory of surplus value, an honorable but fruitless attempt by an ingenious spirit.

But Marx did not create the exploitation theory. He merely picked it up off the street and tried to formulate and establish it scientifically, an undertaking that by no means seemed pointless given the state of political economy at that time. It had already become widely known, however, long before Marx. The fact that Marx adopted it and the activities of the Social Democrats carried it out into the world may have multiplied its inherent attractiveness by a hundredfold. However, its strength and popularity are not rooted in the Marxian theory of value; thus it was able to survive the collapse of Marxism without being harmed.[21]

Many have read *Das Kapital*, but only a few have understood it. Even among the leaders of the Social Democratic Party one can find only a small group who are connoisseurs of the Marxian theory of value. Today, the basic conception of the theory of value in the Social Democratic movement is a naïve idea of exploitation, which is more closely related to that of Chartism[22] than to the objective theory of value in the dialectical system of Karl Marx. This traditional exploitation theory, which, to vary a Marxist expression, one could also call people's

20. Thus Bernhard, "Lohn und Löhnungsmethoden" [Wage and Payment Methods], in *Handwörterbuch der Staatswissenschaften*, vol. VI, p. 513.

21. [Here Mises is alluding to Böhm-Bawerk's famous critique of Marx's theory of surplus value and exploitation of workers under capitalism; see Böhm-Bawerk, *Capital and Interest*, vol. 1, *History and Critique of Interest Theories* (South Holland, Ill.: Libertarian Press, [1884] 1959), pp. 281–321; and Böhm-Bawerk, "The Unresolved Contradiction in the Marxian Economic System," (1896) in *Shorter Classics of Böhm-Bawerk*, pp. 201–302.—Ed.]

22. ["Chartism" was a social and political reform movement in Great Britain in the middle of the nineteenth century dedicated to extending voting rights to the working class as a means of acquiring the power to influence social and economic policy in a more socialist direction. Chartists were willing to use physical violence in the form of strikes and political demonstrations to advance their goals.—Ed.]

socialism,[23] is, of course, never offered in a scientifically precise, mature, and conclusive manner. Nevertheless, at least in Germany today, one must designate it as the *communis opinio*. For outside the narrow circle of the friends of economic theory, it almost reigns unchallenged. It is the basis of what is taught everywhere nowadays about the nature of wages, whether in the textbooks, from the podium, in parliaments and in the press, in the churches, or in the National Assembly.

It influences legislation, and it serves as a guiding principle for the policies of the labor unions. Even the entrepreneurs have not been able to completely avoid its influence.[24] The folk theory of exploitation seems to divide society into two mutually hostile classes: on the one side are the workers, whose industry creates all value and to whom by right the full product of labor ought to go. On the other side stand all those who live off unearned income; they live exactly on what they withhold from the workers. Wage determination is the outcome of a battle between entrepreneurs and workers; the more successful the workers are in this battle, the higher their wages rise and the greater their share of the national product. Labor unions strengthen the power of the workers and thus help them to achieve results.

If one disregards this naïve theory of exploitation, whose indefensibility probably does not need to be more carefully explained, there is not much to be found in the sociopolitical literature that can be used to support the supposed correctness of the doctrine that labor unions can succeed in raising wages. Nevertheless, it is striking that all those writers who start off with no comprehensive economic theory of value and price have no hesitation in asserting that it has been the unions who have had the power to raise the real wages of the workers.

So, on the one hand, it is said that the scientific theory of wages provides us with no basis upon which to decide whether the unionized organization of the workers can raise wages; on the other hand, we have the undisputed assertion that the organization of the workers increases the labor force's share of the social product at the expense of the other classes in society. Or can we assume that all those millions of workers who see their salvation in union organization, and that all those thousands of entrepreneurs who oppose them, deceive themselves in their judgments about the effects of labor organization?

23. I find this expression in Vogelstein, "Das Ertragsgesetz der Industrie" [The Law of Profit of Industry], *Archiv für Sozialwissenschaft und Sozialpolitik*, vol. 34, p. 775.
24. Cf. Eugen von Böhm-Bawerk, *Einige strittige Fragen der Kapitalstheorie* (Vienna, 1900), pp. 110ff.

This seemingly insoluble contradiction with which we are confronted is easy to explain with the help of the theory that we developed earlier. It is true that no effort by labor unions can permanently succeed in pushing wages above their natural level. In the best of cases, all that they can achieve is to raise wages, but they cannot prevent the necessary adjustment of wages back to their natural level. The adjustment, however, does not come about by nominal wages coming down again to their old level. The money wage remains unchanged. The rise in the prices of goods has the effect of bringing real wages back to the "natural" wage that corresponds to the given conditions of the market.

Employers can raise wages above the natural level only in the expectation that they will be able to retain their entrepreneurs' normal profit by passing the wage increase along in the form of higher prices for their products. What the consumers can do, however, to pay or not pay the higher prices can be seen from what has been said above. Hence the success of the organization of labor lies in the advantages that come to the workers during the transition period, before the higher money wages have been adjusted back to the natural level of wages through the rise in the prices of finished goods. If this adjustment is completed, then any success that the working class has achieved by raising the money wage is completely gone. The labor unions can make permanent this advantage offered to the workers only by attempting over and over again to raise the money wage above its natural level. They repeatedly create, however, a new tendency for a change in the objective exchange value of money.

In a static economy there would be no place for such an influence by the labor unions. In such a static economy, the law of wages would have to rule with its full force. Only in a dynamic economy does there come into effect that which has just been explained. Under dynamic conditions the labor unions can also do something more; for example, they can reduce the number of unemployed during the transition periods.[25]

A Shortage of Raw Materials as a Cause of Rising Prices

People are used to often asserting that a rise in the costs of production is a particular reason behind a general inflation. This view cannot be reconciled with the theory of subjective value. The modern school of

---

25. In the static state there are no unemployed.

economics points out that the prices of the goods of higher order are dependent upon the prices of goods of the first order. Thus, the popular explanation must be rejected in advance. Moreover, it does not solve the problem; it only postpones it. Instead of the question of what causes a rise in the prices of consumer goods, it shifts the question to what causes a rise in the prices of the means of production.

Behind this concept stands the idea that the supply of goods becomes smaller and that as a consequence there is a tendency for the prices of these goods to rise. The economic interest in the availability of consumer goods always eventually leads back to the availability of higher goods that are provided by nature. All of man's production activities amount to nothing more than combining the original forces of nature in such a way that a particular desired result will be forthcoming. The materials and forces existing in nature constitute the only fund that we have at our disposal. The progress in developing the methods of production certainly makes it possible for us to enlarge the quantities of goods available by employing higher and higher orders of goods and following longer and technically more fruitful roundabout paths of production.

Yet the assumption is still taken for granted that technological progress lags behind the consumption of the existing supply of resources. From time to time we hear geologists and engineers express the fear that we are more and more rapidly approaching a point in time when the exhaustion of the mineral wealth of the Earth will bring about a severe crisis for us or our posterity. How far these assertions are justified, economic theory cannot say. But we shall assume that they fully agree with the facts. Thus, a general rise of the money prices of goods would result from this if money, alone among all economic goods, were not subject to this same tendency. While in the case of all other economic goods the relationship between supply and demand would change unfavorably for supply, it would have to be otherwise for money.

However, if the same change were to happen with money, too, then the supply of money available to individuals would decrease and the change in the exchange value between money and other economic goods would not occur. If a change occurred in the exchange relationship existing between money and other goods, then its explanation would have to lie among those provided by the quantity theory. Either the supply of and the demand for money had changed in a different direction than that between the supply of or demand for goods, or the latter has remained unchanged while the former has changed. We obtain no new knowledge either for economic theory or for a new approach to economic policy.[26] It is completely reasonable, on the other hand, to bring up the progressive depletion of the natural resources available for mankind to explain the rise in prices for specific groups of goods. The rise in the prices of furs or of caviar is, of course, not that significant, but they are the most obvious examples.

The Recognition of the Reasons for Inflation and Inflationary Policy

Public opinion sees in inflation one of the most disturbing aspects of economic life. The struggle against inflation is proclaimed by governments and by political parties today with the same determination as was the battle against the decline in the prices of goods during the time between 1873 and about 1895.

He who wants to fight against an evil must first recognize what it is. One cannot get rid of inflation as long as one does not understand its causes and its nature. What the mass of consumers are most directly critical of, in the first place, is the rise in the prices of particular individual goods, and most especially the price of food. The protective tariff policy that all countries, with the exception of England, have been following for years has raised the prices of specific groups of goods in every country. In this instance, the fight against inflation coincides with that against high protective tariffs. General inflation is only an incidental consideration. Generally only those producers who are disadvantaged by the protective tariff refer to it in order to direct the attention of consumers to the obvious and easily correctible reasons for the rise in particular prices.

One speaks of the "international character" of rising prices in order to disguise the national policies behind the inflation; and one refers to the "generality" of rising prices in order to obscure the fact that, in addition to the rise in prices in general, a rise in the prices of a number of particular goods has been observed. In all of this there is no honest desire to debate the problem of inflation in general, so as to gain a clear sense about the significance and role that economic policy should take with regard to it.

26. Cf. John A. Hobson, *Gold, Prices, and Wages: With an Examination of the Quantity Theory* (London: Meuthen & Co., 1913), pp. 94ff.

The general hand-wringing about inflation, with which the general public is more or less in agreement, leaves little doubt that the general depreciation of money is widely unpopular. But the views of those who oppose inflation are by no means clear, and even less so in the case of the millions who agree with their opinions. It is known that in Europe and in America during the last quarter of the nineteenth century inflationism has had more advocates than opponents. The inflationist projects, especially the plan for an international bimetallic currency, have not been realized; but that is only because in the leading countries of the world there have been small but strong supporters of sound money, led by gifted leaders who have triumphed over the fiat-money people. Who knows whether the outcome would not have finally gone against the gold standard if the struggle had lasted a few years longer?

The "friends" of rising prices turned their attention in other directions; they became advocates of tariff protection because they saw in protective tariffs an appropriate tool for achieving their ends. In addition, the general decline in the objective exchange value of money that began in the second half of the 1890s, and which is still continuing, made the case for bimetallism irrelevant. The economic policy goal of most countries between 1873 and 1895 was attained.[27] If today a violent reaction is taking place [in response to the general decline in the value of money], this can be explained by the great social changes that have taken place in the meantime.

The interests of producers, which until recently were still a determining factor in politics, are being partly superseded by the interests of consumers. If previously the slogan "good prices" was popular, today the slogan is "cheap prices." It seems quite certain that the attractiveness of this slogan will continue to grow in the coming years. Nevertheless, it remains doubtful whether this will last, and whether it will succeed in destroying the old deeply rooted notion that high prices mean national economic prosperity.

If we look at the social consequences of the changes—it is the consequences from the devaluation that alone concern us here—from the objective exchange value of money, we find that their meaning is different depending on the underlying cause. A general decline of the purchasing power of money always brings with it changes in the dis-

27. [An end to the general decline in prices and the rise in the general purchasing power of money.—Ed.]

tribution of wealth and income, from whatever cause it springs. But in every case, some groups of society benefit from it and other groups are harmed by it. If the objective exchange value of money decreases because the relationship between the supply of and the demand for money has undergone a change due to a disproportionate increase of the quantity of money in circulation, then those parts of the population to whom the additional money flows first achieve the greatest benefit, while those to whom it goes last are most severely harmed. Generally, no matter whether the increase in the quantity of money (in the broader sense) is caused by the production of money [an increase in the mining and minting of gold] or by expanding the quantity of fiduciary media, on the whole the entrepreneurs will have an advantage relative to the workers and clerical employees. It is certainly conceivable that in such circumstances clerical employees and workers, in general, easily could be won over to the side of those who oppose monetary devaluation.

But at the present, changes in the relationship between supply of and demand for money are not the sole and probably also not the most important cause behind the general rise in prices. We have succeeded in showing that, as a result of certain technical features of how markets are organized, forces are set in motion where money is the intermediary in exchanges that necessarily lead to a constant decrease in the objective exchange value of money. Those people are at an advantage who better understand than others how to anticipate the rise in the prices of the goods and services they sell. These are not always the entrepreneurs. Alongside the best-organized cartels are the best-organized labor unions. The big cartels of so-called heavy industry and the unions of the most easily organized clerical employees and working class members are the beneficiaries of the rise in prices so far as it is rooted in these causes.

At a disadvantage, however, are the groups that are difficult or impossible to organize. They can raise the prices of the goods and services they sell on the market only if the goods and services they buy have already risen in price; because of this lag between the rise in the prices of the goods they buy and the prices of the goods they sell, the harm which they always suffer in the meantime cannot be made up for. Only creditors who have monetary claims to specific amounts of money under contract obligations are in both cases harmed relative to their debtors.

Aside from this, however, since the social effects from a rise in prices are different depending upon their cause, there can be no single policy prescription.

In the first case is a relatively narrow circle of groups who are the beneficiaries of such changes in the objective exchange value of money; it does not include the broad stratum of wage earners whose burdens and demands are nowadays the decisive factor in politics. These groups, therefore, would prefer a monetary system in which the relationship between the supply of and the demand for money remains constant: that is, a situation in which there are no factors tending to bring about a change in the objective exchange value of money. Since this ideal is unachievable, then from the perspective of the wage earner (and also from the viewpoint of the many entrepreneurs who on this issue have the same interest as the workers, as well as from the standpoint of all creditors), those measures are condemned that aim at a reduction in interest rates brought about by an artificial increase in the quantity of fiduciary media. As was already explained, a permanent reduction in the rate of interest can never be brought about by an increase in unbacked banknotes and by an extension of the use of checks; the end result of such measures can only be an increase in the price of goods.

Judged quite differently are those changes in the objective exchange value of money that arise from those previously described particular properties of prices formed on the market through the intermediation of money. They benefit not only the most easily organized groups of businessmen, but also the best-organized strata of labor, which is to say, all those who better anticipate the rise in the prices of the goods they buy on the market relative to increases in prices of the goods and services they sell on the market. Insofar as the rise in prices has its root cause in this process, there is nothing that can be done to stop it. The only conceivable method would be government price controls; however, that would be in insoluble contradiction with the individualistic principles of organizing the economy.

It may appear to many that the struggle against the progressive rise in the prices of goods and services has only a small chance of success. There seem to exist few effective methods to slow down this process even a little bit, unless there again comes a time in which—as in between 1873 and 1895—there is a decline in gold production and a strong tendency for a progressive change in the economy that brings about a decline in money prices. It would be a gross exaggeration to think, however, that people would want to see this happen again.

As I have explained elsewhere,[28] there is a serious danger for the future of the individualistic organization of the economy in the development of fiduciary media; if the legislature does not put some obstacle in the way of its expansion, an unrestrained inflation could easily come about, the destructive effects of which cannot really be imagined. Even if we ignore this, as yet, not immediate threat, there is sufficient risk from the very nature of the system of fiduciary media. We have already mentioned that it would be desirable to put an end to the artificial expansion of fiduciary media. It would not only slow down the rate of devaluation, but it would also be the best way of preventing economic crises.

If one pays no attention to this, then there is no reason why a progressive rise in prices should be seen as a disruptive influence. Only the completely uninformed can, perhaps, imagine that a rise in prices is a symptom of a deteriorating provision of goods that is leading to a progressive impoverishment of the population.

In reality, the disadvantages that it brings to some and the advantages that it brings to others are only transitory in nature. The fact that price increases keep going on results in its being appealed to over and over again, but then it arises again and again with its impact being reinforced by the fact that inflation and effects of inflation have occurred before.

As far as price increases have their cause in an increase in gold production, one must accept it as an unavoidable ill. It still can be hoped that the growth in gold production will once again experience an interruption. Insofar as inflation is a result of the method by which market prices are formed through indirect exchange, one must see it as a sign of the lively activity in the economic process coming from constant changes in the relationship between production and consumption. Only one who prefers the peace of the cemetery to the bustling whirl of life can be sorry that the purely static condition of an economy is only a conceptual device of theory; reality always means dynamism, change, and development.

28. Cf. *The Theory of Money and Credit*, pp. 368–90.

CHAPTER 8

On Rising Prices and Purchasing Power Policies[1]

In the middle of the nineteenth century, prices increased dramatically all over Europe and reached their peak in 1874. At that point, prices began to decline and continued their downward movement until the mid-nineties. Since about 1896 a new upward movement in prices has set in, and its end point is nowhere in sight. This decline in the purchasing power of money has given new impetus to the old demand for a type of money that would not be susceptible to fluctuations in its objective exchange value. Ideally, with this type of money, the exchange relationship between money and all other economic goods would be stable from the money side. Similarly, there could be no general increase or decline in prices. The only disturbance in these stable market relationships would be a decline or rise in individual commodity prices with respect to each other, something that would be acceptable from the standpoint of both economic theory and political reality.

Money with an invariant objective exchange value, however, is an unattainable ideal.

It was commonly believed that the quantity theory of money provided the means to attain this goal. According to this theory, a change in the relationship between the supply of and the demand for money implied a change in the objective exchange value of money. All other

---

1. [This essay was originally delivered in German as Ludwig von Mises's inaugural lecture at the University of Vienna in February 1913, on the basis of which he received the status of *Privatdozent* [unsalaried lecturer]. It has not been previously published. From 1913 until the spring of 1934, Mises regularly taught a seminar almost every semester (except during the war years of 1914–1918, when he served in the Austrian Army) at the University of Vienna on a wide variety of topics in general economic theory, monetary and business cycle theory, economic policy and comparative economic systems, and methodology of the social sciences.—Ed.]

things equal, an increase in the supply of money had to lead to a decline in the purchasing power of the monetary unit. This is one of the oldest and most firmly established doctrines of monetary theory.

Two factors, however, impede the practical application of this insight for stabilizing the value of money. The first is the inability to precisely predict how great will be the effect from a given change in the quantity of money in circulation. For even though it is certain that a decline or a rise in money's purchasing power will result from an increase or reduction in the quantity of money, the extent of the changes in the objective exchange value of money brought about by specific changes in the quantity of money can never be predicted in advance. Changes in the quantity of money do not directly affect prices. Contrary to the notions of the older mechanistic price theory of supply and demand, changes in the quantity of money affect prices not directly but indirectly, by influencing the subjective valuations made by individuals.

Given this insurmountable problem, some proposals were made that accepted the intrinsic impossibility of creating money with a stable exchange value and settled for a more limited goal. For the bulk of transactions, money as we know it today would continue to be used despite all its imperfections. For credit transactions, however—whether by legislation or by voluntary agreement between the parties concerned—the means of exchange would not be money but a uniform composite of the majority of commodities. The debtor would agree to fulfill his obligations by repaying not a nominal sum of money but a sum of money representing the same purchasing power for a fixed number of commodities. The idea was to supplement a currency based on precious metals with a currency based on commodities.

These more modest reform proposals limit themselves to keeping the value of money stable only for long-term credit transactions and possibly for salaries of persons with a guaranteed position. But even the implementation of these proposals would not preclude a general rise in prices and the adverse consequences that would result from this in transactions between individuals.

Even within this self-imposed limitation, the compensatory commodity currency project has another deficiency. While it has managed to circumvent one of the problems faced by all proposals for stabilizing the value of money, it founders on the second flaw, which makes all these proposals unrealizable. Its mistake lies in its assumption that the fluctuations in the objective exchange value of money can be accurately measured. The various index number systems seem to be precise, but in reality they are not.[2]

To obtain useful results, index numbers must differentiate the effects between individual commodity prices. Changes in the price of wheat will not have the same impact as changes in the price of poppy seeds. Commodities must be treated according to the role they play in consumption. To take this into account, a weighted average is used, that is, changes in one commodity are counted more heavily than those in another according to a predetermined relationship. Changes in the price of wheat, for example, are given a hundred times greater weight in the determination of the index numbers than changes in the price of poppy seeds.

Obviously, the most important thing is the assignment of the proper weights to each commodity. The relatively best method of weighting is provided by the American budget method. Individual commodities are weighted according to the frequency with which they appear in individual households budgets. This method would be unobjectionable if consumption patterns did not tend to change over time; it is flawed because in the real world the relative amounts of these commodities keep shifting, reflecting the way human beings change their subjective valuations concerning those commodities. Just think how different is the pattern of consumption in a household in 1913 from a household in 1863, let alone 1813.

Even if we make the dubious assumption that we are merely comparing a contemporary social group with a social group in the past of comparable standing and income, many problems are left unsolved. Even a city dweller of modest means has different needs from those of his forebears fifty or a hundred years ago. And even with the same needs, we now have different ways and means of satisfying them than in days of old.

This lack of an objectively valid method for establishing a weighted average fully explains why all proposals that have been made in the course of the last three generations for stabilizing the objective value of money have fallen by the wayside.[3]

2. [See Chapter 7, "The General Rise in Prices in the Light of Economic Theory," footnote 7.—Ed.]

3. [Also see Basset Jones, *Horses and Apples: A Study in Index Numbers* (New York: John Day, 1934), and Michael A. Heilperin, *International Monetary Economics* (London: Longmans,

More recently, the American economist Irving Fisher proposed ending the free coinage of gold as a way to create money with a stable objective exchange value.[4]

Fisher takes the currency situation in India, the Philippines, and Austria-Hungary as his model. He maintains that these countries maintain currency parity with countries using a gold-backed currency by increasing or decreasing the quantity of money in circulation according to the state of the foreign exchange rate. Fisher has no support for this—erroneous—view of the gold exchange standard. The parity value of the Austro-Hungarian currency is not maintained by increasing or decreasing the amount of currency in circulation. Parity is not exceeded because the notes of the Austro-Hungarian Bank are in fact convertible into foreign exchange at a fixed exchange rate. It is the legal right to freely coin gold that preserves the currency's parity.

The same can be said of all other countries with a similar arrangement, except for their having legally established the convertibility of notes into gold. People have sometimes claimed that the Austro-Hungarian Bank occasionally refuses to issue foreign currency and that the exchange rate might then exceed the gold point.[5] Whether or not this claim is correct, all it would prove is that in the eyes of its advocates prompt convertibility of notes into foreign currencies is a prerequisite for parity of the coinage.

Starting from this erroneous assumption, Fisher proposes that banknotes should be convertible not into a given amount of gold agreed to in advance, but to an amount of money that corresponds to a given purchasing power. He suggests that the quantity of gold against which notes are converted should increase when the purchasing power of the gold unit goes down and it should decrease when it rises. It is apparent that Fisher's proposal is merely an expansion of the idea of a

---

Green, 1939), the appendix "Note on the Use of Statistical Constructions," pp. 259–70; also, Gottfried Haberler, *The Different Meanings Attached to the Term "Fluctuations in the Purchasing Power of Gold" and the Best Instrument or Instruments for Measuring Such Fluctuations,* Official No. F/Gold.74 (Geneva: League of Nations, 1931).—Ed.]

4. [Irving Fisher (1867–1947) was one of the most prominent American economists in the first half of the twentieth century. He formulated a widely used version of the quantity theory of money, utilizing the equation of exchange in *The Purchasing Power of Money* (1911). He advocated using a system of index numbers to vary the gold content of the dollar to maintain a stable purchasing power of the monetary unit.—Ed.]

5. [See "On the Problem of Legal Resumption of Specie Payments in Austria-Hungary," Chapter 4 in the present volume.—Ed.]

complementary commodity currency. It contains nothing that would help overcome the above-mentioned difficulty, that is, the impossibility of accurately measuring the fluctuations in the objective exchange value of the monetary unit. Neither does it offer anything to overcome the difficulties inherent in using monetary policy to manage changes in the quantity of money in circulation. Fisher's proposals thus can be easily rebutted by the very same persuasive arguments that Karl Helfferich[6] recently presented against similar projects.

Given that a monetary system with a fixed domestic exchange value is not attainable, Helfferich concludes that no government policy seeking to regulate the value of money can serve a useful purpose. Much as he may regret the subservience of our modern monetary system to the vicissitudes of gold production, he nevertheless considers it preferable to a dependence on human failings and errors and to policies catering to unbridled special interests. Even if one concurs with Helfferich's views on this point, one might still favor government intervention against a decline in the purchasing power of money in some cases.

Notwithstanding complaints about increasing prices and despite all efforts to increase the purchasing power of money, the quantity of money in circulation, that is, notes and bank credit not covered by commodity money, is steadily expanding. In Austria-Hungary and especially in Germany there is a steady pressure to enlarge the circulation of uncovered notes. Both in the German Reich and in Austria-Hungary the quantity of tax-exempt notes has risen markedly in the last few years; Austria has seen a 50 percent increase, from 400 to 600 million crowns.[7]

Attempts are being made in Germany to extend the use of checks for smaller and medium-sized payments; the German *Reichspost* [post office] has added increasingly popular checking transactions to its services. The Austrian and Hungarian postal savings banks offer postal money orders that are exemplary. Yet these measures go counter to all the teachings of economic theory.

Since the time of Adam Smith, economic studies have confirmed that when businessmen complain about lack of money, they are re-

6. [Karl Helfferich (1872–1924) was a German economist, politician, and financier. His most important book on monetary themes was *Money* (New York: Augustus M. Kelley, [1903] 1969). —Ed.]

7. [See J. van Walre de Bordies, *The Austrian Crown: Its Depreciation and Stabilization* (London: P.S. King & Son, 1924), p. 37, for the amounts by which Austrian banknotes in circulation increased between 1909 and 1914.—Ed.]

ally referring to a lack of capital; yet this lack of capital cannot be remedied by an expansion of the money supply. There is no dispute today about the basic correctness of this insight. Nevertheless, the attempt persists to relieve the lack of capital and to lower the interest rate by increasing the money in circulation. In truth, all these efforts in trying to lower the interest rate are of no avail. The only effect is to increase prices.

What should be done, therefore, is to give up all attempts to artificially expand the quantity of money in circulation. Presumably the flaws in the current policy will soon be recognized. It is already generally admitted that the sharp increase in the quantity of money and fiduciary media is one of the most important causes of the currently high level of prices. There is no need to decrease the quantity of fiduciary media, nor must their future expansion even be impeded. To moderate price rises, one must merely avoid artificially expanding them.

All this assumes, of course, that a policy to prevent increases in prices is inherently reasonable, as one might well imagine from the general clamor in support of this idea. In theoretically examining this problem, one must first clarify why a decline in the purchasing power of money is considered to be deleterious. One must also investigate whether all groups in society suffer from it equally, and whether certain groups might not actually benefit from a rise in prices. Only then can a purchasing power policy be integrated harmoniously into the whole system of social policies.

If changes in the purchasing power of money occurred simultaneously and affected all goods and services proportionally, their only effect would be to favor debtors over creditors. All those engaged in credit transactions who have claims on money would feel the effect of a reduced purchasing power, unless they had foreseen the impending change in the value of money at the time that they extended credit, and accordingly included this expectation when they drew up the loan contract. If it were possible to predict exactly the direction and extent of future changes in the objective value of money, appropriate provisions by one side or the other concerning monetary repayments could be included in long-term contracts. As no perfect prediction of this kind is possible, creditors are the ones who suffer from a decline in the value of money. The clamor against higher prices has such unanimous support, however, that it cannot be out of concern for those persons who derive their income from interest on their capital. The true reason for the unpopularity of rising prices lies elsewhere.

The fact is that rising prices will never affect all goods simultaneously and to the same extent, as was assumed above. Changes in the quantity of money in circulation spread out from a specific point, showing themselves wherever additional amounts of money flow into the economy. If the change is triggered by increased gold production, gold producers will be the first to experience the increase. The first possessors of the additional quantities of money will first express their changed evaluation of the value of money to those persons with whom they exchange. The decline in the value of money is then spread progressively from one class to another, from one economic group to the next, until it finally affects all commodities.

It should be noted, incidentally—though we will not go into any details—that not all commodities are equally affected by the change in the purchasing power of money even at the end of the process. Certain differences may well persist because changes in the value of money have a differential impact on various individuals and will therefore cause a shift in the underlying supply and demand relationships.

Furthermore, the fact that changes in the value of money do not affect all commodities simultaneously has a decisive influence on the way they are interpreted in society. The hardest hit are those persons who offer goods and services on the market whose prices have not yet been increased by the decline in the purchasing power of money, but who must already pay higher prices for commodities and services that they buy. They must pay more for what they buy, although they still sell only at the older prices.

Public servants with fixed incomes are especially victimized by rising prices because, generally speaking, their income lags behind changes in the price of goods. Public servants already must pay higher prices, although their salary has not yet gone up. When, finally, their remuneration commensurately goes up, the increase fails to compensate them for the loss they have incurred in the meantime. In Austria, for example, the salaries of senior public servants have not been raised in the last forty years. The same applies for certain incomes that tradition and customs have set at a fixed level, and where changes are exceedingly slow. Typical examples are physicians' fees, fees for certain services, examination fees, and so on.

The situation is different with most wage earners, particularly workers and employees in private enterprises. We shall examine, next, how wages are formed and therefore identify a second cause for the changes in the purchasing power of money.

Wage earnings have been steadily rising for several decades. This undoubtedly depends in part on the unionization of workers and lower-level employees. One of the most controversial issues with respect to the problem of increasing prices, and in the theory of wages as well, is whether and to what extent this rise in real or "nominal" wages has any bearing on rising commodity prices. One side maintains there is no cause and effect between these two events. According to the other side, wage increases are the most important cause behind the rise in commodity prices, while a third group attributes the increase in wages to higher commodity prices.

There is no doubt that the working class has improved its economic position in the last several decades. All observers agree on that point, and even the most fanatical adherents to Marx's theory of pauperization cannot fail to acknowledge this fact in the long run. The upward social mobility of the working class has generally been ascribed to the activities of the trade unions, for instance in Lujo Brentano's[8] and Sidney Webb's writings.[9]

When it is asserted that trade union organizations are enabling workers to obtain a higher wage level, a serious difficulty arises from the fact that all scientifically developed wage theories deny the possibility that workers can permanently secure higher wages through trade union contracts. All wage theories share the view that the determination of wage rates is connected with the theory of value. The various solutions to this problem have led to numerous attempts to solve the problem of the theory of wages. The labor theory of value naturally pursued a different path from modern subjective value theory, the latter being the first approach to adequately deal with this problem.

Imputation theory provides a way to determine the value of the indi-

8. [Lujo Brentano (1844–1931) was a German economist and social reformer. He was a founding member of the Verein für Sozialpolitik (Society for Social Policy) and a supporter of the social market economy, which rejected both socialism and laissez-faire capitalism, combining private enterprise with heavy government regulation and social welfare. In 1914, he signed the "Manifesto of the Ninety-Three," which galvanized support for the war throughout German schools and universities. After the revolution of November 1918, he for a very short period served as people's commissar (minister) of trade.—Ed.]

9. [Sidney Webb (1859–1947) was an early member of the British Fabian Society, which called for the achievement of socialism through incremental legislation. He was also a prominent intellectual force in the British Labor Party, having written in 1918 the famous "Clause Four" in the Labor Party program that called for the nationalization of the means of production. In 1935, he coauthored with his wife, Beatrice, Soviet Communism: A New Civilization? in which he predicted that the Soviet system of central economic planning would eventually spread around the rest of the world. In 1929, he was granted the title Lord Passfield.—Ed.]

vidual complementary factors of production. It thus supplies the indispensable logical link for any theory about the formation of the prices of factors of production, and thus to any theory of the distribution of the final product.[10]

The level of wages is a market phenomenon and can never be influenced by interventions outside the marketplace. A wage policy, that is, a policy that shifts the level of wages away from the level it tends to reach in an unhampered market (the "natural wage level," in Clark's terminology), can operate in only one way. It must act by influencing those factors whose joint action on the market determines the specific level of wages. One can lower wages, for instance, by facilitating the immigration of foreign workers and raise wages by impeding this immigration. These methods exert an indirect influence on the market determination of wages. Whenever wages are formed in the marketplace under the influence of such changed conditions, the "natural" level of wage will reflect this new state of affairs.

It is just as impossible to directly influence wages as it is to directly influence other market prices, because a reaction will inevitably set in to restore the natural level. Officially set wage rates are no more effective than any wage policy imposed by trade unions.

Since trade unions are generally incapable of changing market conditions, they can have only a limited impact on wages. Clark[11] gives a detailed discussion of the cases where trade unions can bring about a real improvement in workers' income. These are exceptional cases in which the actual wage level would have stayed below the natural wage level if not for trade union intervention.

Clark is convinced, however, that trade unions cannot permanently push wages above their natural level, and in this respect Clark actually

10. [The theory of imputation attempts to demonstrate the process by which the value of the finished product on the market is reflected back into the relative values of the factors of production utilized in its manufacture, thus determining the distribution of income among those factors. The theory was most systematically developed among the early Austrian economists by Friedrich von Wieser, *Natural Value* (New York: Augustus M. Kelley, [1889] 1971). See also F. A. Hayek, "Some Remarks on the Problem of Imputation," (1926) in *Money, Capital and Fluctuations: Early Essays* (Chicago: University of Chicago Press, 1984), pp. 33–54; and Hans Mayer, "Imputation," (1928) in Israel M. Kirzner, ed., *Classics in Austrian Economics: A Sampling in the History of a Tradition* (London: William Pickering, 1994), pp. 19–53. The more generally accepted answer to this problem is derived from the theory of marginal productivity developed by John Bates Clark, *The Distribution of Wealth* (New York: Augustus M. Kelley, [1899] 1965).—Ed.]

11. See Chapter 7, "The General Rise in Prices in the Light of Economic Theory," footnote 16.

agrees with Marx, or at least Marx in his early writings. It is a well-known fact that Marx took the iron law of wages as his starting point and proclaimed this openly in *The Communist Manifesto*. The iron law of wages essentially contests the possibility that the wages of workers can be permanently raised above their natural level.

It is usually asserted that Marx subsequently abandoned the iron law of wages. What is overlooked is that the theory of surplus value rests on this law. For surplus value is defined as the difference between the value of the product produced by labor and the amount of that value received as wages. The product of the labor force is the amount of work required to produce and maintain the labor force. That is another way of saying that it is the wage corresponding to the iron law of wages. In the recently published text of a lecture given by Marx in 1865, we read that Marx, like Clark, believed that trade unions could make only a marginal contribution to the betterment of workers' wages.[12]

The actual wages in the last few decades are difficult to reconcile with these scientific wage theories. This fact has encouraged the Historical School of economics to give up on wage theories altogether. But there is one scientific theory of wages developed by the modern school that can actually be brought to bear on the facts of the case.

While it is true that trade unions are incapable of raising wages permanently above their natural level, they nevertheless can affect the point in time when wages change in response to changes in the purchasing power of money. It is of course of vital importance whether increases in wages, which are bound to occur sooner or later in conjunction with changes in the purchasing power of money, occur sooner rather than later; any negative effect resulting from the delay, discussed earlier, will thereby be avoided.

There is a further point: the working class may overshoot the mark in its struggle, and may at this time force wages up to a level that will prove to be unsustainably too high. Let us assume that wages increased 10 percent above the natural wage level. Though a reaction is unavoidable, this reaction may not take the form of a reduction in money wages but of a corresponding increase in the prices of all products. The increased money wage is sustained, but the real wage is eventually forced back to the natural level of wages.

---

12. [See Karl Marx, *Value, Price and Profit* (Chicago: Charles H. Kerr & Co., [1865] 1910).—Ed.]

Price theory teaches us that potential buyers resist any excessive price demands by potential sellers. This indisputable proposition applies in this manner only to direct exchanges; in indirect exchanges mediated by money, which is the only significant form of exchange at the present stage of economic development, a modification in the theory must be introduced. The potential buyer may decide to pay a money price that exceeds his evaluation of the commodity's worth in the hope that when he himself acts as a seller, he will in turn receive a higher money price when he sells the product. The employer may give in to wage demands of unionized workers that he considers to be excessive on the assumption that he will be able to sell his product at a higher price. The consumer pays the higher price asked by the producers because he is not only a consumer and buyer but also a producer and seller; and he, in turn, expects to obtain higher prices in his capacity as a producer and seller. This is what is likely to happen under conditions of indirect exchange.

In fact, the more that improvements in communication permit a globalized expansion of markets, the more predominant will be these processes of indirect exchange. Only where all parties are fully represented in the marketplace, that is, only at daily, weekly, or annual markets in isolated areas or when certain branches of business assemble at the bourse, can face-to-face bargaining be effective.

In all other situations where two traders meet face-to-face, they represent only very small cross-sections of the global market for a particular commodity. Under these circumstances, bargaining is pointless, since what matters is not the respective strength of the two particular traders confronting each other on the market but the relative strength of all buyers and sellers of that particular good. We can thus see why a seemingly "fixed" price is being substituted in more and more places for a price set by bargaining. When prices are "fixed," there are only two options: forgoing the purchase, something that may not always be feasible when an essential want is involved, or paying the higher price in anticipation of obtaining an equally higher price oneself on another segment of the market. This is a correct way to visualize how business and labor unions influence price formation under current conditions.

As long as increases in the prices of goods stem from these features of indirect exchange, they do not warrant the concern they often arouse. On the contrary, they should be viewed as symptoms of buoyant activity, burgeoning development, and unceasing transformation in the nature of production and consumption. The mutual exchange relations for economic goods are constantly in flux because every day sees the emergence of new consumption demands and of new ways to satisfy them. And from a sociopolitical point of view, price increases have even fewer adverse consequences—to the extent that they are attributable to this cause.

We have already referred to the fact that rising prices benefit organized labor and improve its position at a slight expense to those who live off their capital, a consequence that can hardly be given much weight.

In light of this, a comprehensive policy to deal with rising prices that pays no attention to the basic cause for the decline in the purchasing power of money is not worth implementing. Once we have broken down into their various component parts the forces that drive up commodity prices, we can restrict our countermeasures to those components that warrant an intervention.

CHAPTER 9

Disturbances in the Economic Life of the Austro-Hungarian Monarchy During the Years 1912–1913[1]

In 1912–13 Austria and Hungary weathered a severe economic crisis, the effects of which are yet to be surmounted.[2]

The economic upturn on the world market, which had surpassed its three predecessors in almost all sectors of manufacturing, reached its zenith in 1912; however, 1913 brought a market reversal and the

1. [This article originally appeared in German in the *Archiv für Sozialwissenschaft und Sozialpolitik*, vol. 39 (1914/1915).—Ed.]

2. Two official publications contain information about the crisis of 1912/13:

    1. *Bericht über die wirtschaftliche Lage Oesterreichs in den Jahren 1912/13* [Report on the Economic State of Austria in 1912/13], 4th ed. Communications by the Commercial Center of the United Chambers of Commerce and Manufacturing, and the Central Organization of Industry in Austria, no. 127 (Vienna, 1914). 104 pages.

    2. *Wirtschaftsstatistische Chronik. Rückblick auf das Jahr 1913* [Statistical Economic Chronicle. A Look Back at 1913], 8th ed. Special Publication of the Statistical Journal in 1914 (Brünn, 1914). 41 pages.

    Both publications owe their creation to the present crisis; neither the Commercial Center nor the Statistical Central Commission had previously published economic reports of this type.

    The "statistical economic chronicle" was supposed to be continued as a monthly report by the Bureau of the Statistical Central Commission. The overview of the months of January and February 1914 did indeed appear in the "Statistical Communications" (Year 8, no. 9). Karl Pribram and Karl Forchheimer supplied the compilation.

    The article "Die Arbeitslosigkeit in Wien bei den der Gewerkschaftskommission Oesterreichs angegliederten Verbänden in den Jahren 1910–1913" [Unemployment in Vienna in the Member Associations of the Austrian Manufacturing Commission], *Soziale Rundschau*, April 1914, III, pp. 169–79, based on inquiries by the social-democratic workers organizations, can be viewed in a certain sense as a supplement to the previously mentioned publications.

    See also Dub, "Die Geldkrise in Oesterreich-Ungarn" [The Monetary Crisis in Austro-Hungary], *Jahrbücher für Nationalöekonomie und Statistik*, series III, vol. 47, pp. 643–57; Broch, *Die wirtschaftliche Krise, ihre Ursachen und Rückwirkungen* [The Economic Crisis, Its Causes and Repercussions], *Beilage zur Kaufmännischen Rundschau*, 1913.

weakening of the business cycle.[3] Though this general recession probably intensified the Austro-Hungarian crisis, it was not the cause. Austro-Hungary was already experiencing a severe downturn in 1912, but as long as the economic boom continued abroad, the effects of this domestic crisis could not have caused a breakdown in all branches of the economy. Thus, when, in 1913, the weakening of the world market occurred, the crisis in the monarchy became a general one. One must, however, keep the following in mind: the Austro-Hungarian crisis was an incident that occurred independently of the events on the global market, and the causes and development of the crisis can be explained only by the particular circumstances of the monarchy.

The hardening of the international monetary market in the last weeks of 1912 and in the first months of 1913 is viewed partly as a direct result of the bellicose developments in the Balkans and the fears associated with them. The Austro-Hungarian Monarchy was affected by these events more than any other country partly due to its geographic closeness to and strong economic ties with the Balkans, but primarily because the troubles in the region increased the monarchy's domestic political difficulties and made a war with Russia a very serious concern. However, the economic crisis that Austria-Hungary weathered in 1912–13 was not caused by the war in the Balkans, though the war did contribute significantly to its intensification. The Balkan states ordered a general mobilization only in the last days of September 1912, and that war actually broke out only in October.[4] Until then no one in Austria-Hungary had even considered the possibility of a war on the empire's borders. The crisis, however, was already extant in the first months of 1912: in mid-February the secretary general of the Austro-Hungarian Bank advised against any additional extensions of credit

3. See Feiler, *Die Konjunkturperiode 1907–1913 in Deutschland* [The Economic Cycle 1907–1913 in Germany] (Jena, 1914), pp. 129ff.

4. [The Balkan conflict was the cause of two wars in Southeastern Europe in 1912–13 in the course of which the Balkan League (Bulgaria, Montenegro, Greece, and Serbia) first conquered Ottoman-held Macedonia, Albania, and most of Thrace and then fell out over the division of the spoils. As the result of the First Balkan War (October 1912–May 1913), almost all remaining European territories of the Ottoman Empire were captured and partitioned among the members of the Balkan League, and an independent Albanian state set up. Despite their success, the Balkan states were unsatisfied with the peace settlement, which brought about the Second Balkan War (1913) between Bulgaria and its former allies Serbia, Greece, and Montenegro, with Romania and the Ottoman Empire also intervening against Bulgaria. The outcome turned Serbia, an ally of the Russian Empire, into an important regional power, alarming Austria-Hungary and thereby indirectly providing an important cause for World War I.—Ed.]

and announced a stricter credit policy on the part of the Bank for the near future. The outbreak of the economic crisis can be dated from this point.

Those who seek instruction about the evolution and the proportions of the crisis can find abundant opportunity in the publications cited, though much of the data still requires modification, and the presented material is sketchy in more than one area. There is no doubt that in one or two years we will be able to survey the effects of the crisis much better. Yet the swift publication of the data, though suffering from unavoidable deficiencies, deserves special acknowledgment.

Understandably, both official publications say very little about the *causes* of the great economic crisis, and whatever is offered relates primarily to the general crisis on the world market and to the military crisis. We learn relatively little about the particular circumstances in the monarchy which led to the Austro-Hungarian crisis both prior to and after the weakening of the global business cycle. It is exclusively this issue that concerns us in the following presentation.

In one of the articles published as a series in the *New Free Press* [*Neue Freie Presse*], Böhm-Bawerk recently attempted to explain the increased deficit in the monarchy's balance of trade.[5] He points out that "it is said, and it may very well be correct, that many private persons in our country live beyond their means. However, it is certain that for some time many of our public bodies have lived beyond their means. The nation, the Crownlands, and the municipalities rival one another in the growth of their expenditures. The increase in revenues has not kept up with the increase in expenditures, and the difference must be compensated for by the assumption of debts. As the domestic capital market is not in the position to satisfy the large demands made upon it by the government's budgetary requirements, the state had to turn abroad for funding. The increase in foreign debt is thus expressed as liabilities in the balance of trade. One must view these circumstances

---

5. For three decades, from 1875 to 1906, the Austro-Hungarian Monarchy's balance of trade had been uninterruptedly positive. In 1907, the balance of trade became negative again for the first time, and indeed to the amount of 45 million crowns; in the following years, the liabilities in the balance of trade increased (by millions of crowns) to 427, 434, 787, and 823 million crowns. In 1913, it sank to 631 million crowns. It has increased again since that time. In the first quarter of 1914, liabilities amounted to 230 million crowns, in contrast to 169 million crowns in the first quarter of 1913, 268 million crowns in the first quarter of 1912, and 184 million crowns in the first quarter of 1911.

as the ultimate cause of the deficit in the balance of trade: we have become large and freewheeling in our economic expenditures."[6]

These remarks by Böhm-Bawerk indicate the direction for an explanation of the most recent Austrian economic crisis. However, they are not completely satisfactory in their interpretation of the causes of the liabilities in the balance of trade.

In Austria and in Hungary, too much is consumed, or, in other words, too little is produced. The country, the provinces, and the municipalities have been led astray by the ease with which the modern banking system readily supplies loans. In the decade from 1902 to 1912, the country's debt (for the Crownlands and provinces represented in the Parliament) increased from 3,640 million to 7,240 million crowns. The continual issue of new debt has unfavorably affected the price levels of pensions and the rate at which new loans have been extended. In 1903, the small sum of 6 million crowns, which would require a standardized 4.2 percent annuity for repayment on the occasion of its conversion, could be offered at par. Subsequent loans were issued at continually worsening terms. The crown annuity, offered in January 1912 at the nominal value of 200 million crowns, was issued to the consortium at a market rate of 89.50. Since that time, it has been absolutely impossible to issue crown annuities at 4 percent. The exchange rate for gold has had to replace the exchange rate for crowns, and an interest rate of 4.5 percent has replaced the 4 percent annuity rate, while treasury notes and bonds have replaced the annuities. The 4.5 percent treasury bonds that were issued in March 1914 at a face value of 396.6 million crowns, and which were repayable within 15 years through an installment lottery, were assumed by the consortium at a market rate of 94.5 percent. The actual burden, which accrued to the national treasury due to this assumption of debt, is estimated at 5.3 percent. The demand price for the Austrian 4 percent crown annuities on the Vienna bourse was 100.34 on average in 1905; it was 83.07 on average in 1913. The provinces and municipalities were doing no better, with a similar situation in Hungary.

In Austria, it is primarily the imperial administration that functions poorly and is too expensive. More than one hundred years ago,

---

6. See Böhm-Bawerk, "Unsere passive Handelsbilanz" [Our Negative Balance of Trade], *Neue Freie Presse*, January 6, 8, and 9, 1914.

Stein wrote about the bureaucracy in the Austrian government, that they "concern themselves solely with the employment of a system of clumsy and labyrinthine formalities that halts the free activity of human beings at every instant, in order to substitute in their place masses of paper, and the civil servants' negligible idiocy or laziness."[7] Stein would probably find this scathing judgment appropriate for the current Austrian administration; indeed, even official publications arrive at the conclusion "that throughout the entire organization of the domestic administration, beginning with the lowest body and continuing up to the highest judicial courts, substantial problems exist that prevent an adequate deployment of actions in the government's areas of responsibility."[8] The excessive expenditures of the provincial governments, even more than the imperial government, explain why sufficient funds cannot be found, in spite of the fact that the tax revenues are more oppressive than in most other countries. As a result, new bonds must be constantly issued to keep up with expenditures.

A substantial portion of the public debt can be ascribed to the growing trends in a socialist direction of the last few decades at both the national and municipal levels that has resulted in the government taking over existing enterprises and building new factories with public funds. Nowhere has this trend been as strong as in Austria.

These large state companies are the greatest hemorrhage point in the national Austrian budget. They are poorly managed; they yield no income, and instead require subsidies every year to cover their deficits. These have been met from additional tax revenues or by issuing new

7. See Pertz, *Das Leben des Ministers Freiherrn von Stein* [The Life of the Minister Freiherr von Stein] (Berlin, 1850), vol. II, pp. 433f. [Heinrich Friedrich Karl Freiherr von Stein (1757–1831) was a Prussian officer, statesman, and reformer who served as Prussian minister of economics and finance during the Napoleonic period.—Ed.]

8. See *Studien über die Reform der inneren Verwaltung* [Studies on the Reformation of the Domestic Administration], p. 21. This exposé published by the Körber administration in 1904 renders a scathing verdict on the abilities of the Austrian government. See also *Enquete der Kommission zur Förderung der Verwaltungsreform. Veranstaltet in der Zeit vom 21. Oktober bis 9. November 1912 zur Feststellung der Wünsche der beteiligten Kreise der Bevölkerung in bezug auf die Reform der inneren und Finanz-Verwaltung* [Inquiry of the Commission for the Promotion of Administrative Reform] (Vienna, 1913). Additionally, *Bericht des Mitgliedes der Kommission zur Förderung der Verwaltungsreform Professor Dr. Josef Redlich über die Entwicklung und den gegenwärtigen Stand der österreichischen Finanzverwaltung sowie Vorschläge der Kommission zur Reform dieser Verwaltung* [Report by the Member of the Commission for the Promotion of Administrative Reform, Prof. Dr. Josef Redlich, About the Development and Present State of the Austrian Financial Administration and also Proposals by the Commission for Reforming This Administration] (Vienna, 1913).

bonds. The negative financial effect of these state enterprises has been most obvious in the largest of them, the National Railway Company. The failures of the Austrian state railway system, even in comparison with the performance of the Prussian-Hessian state-owned railroad, are commonly explained by the assertion that the conditions in Austria are essentially different from those in Prussia, and that the Austrian state railway labors under a series of circumstances that hamper its proper operational management.

Yet quite recently, one of the most successful Austrian industrialists, Georg Günther, the general director of the Austrian Berg- und Hütten-werks-Gesellschaft [Mining and Steel Company], in a speech based on comprehensive quantitative data (including an exact comparison of the individual entries in the income statements of the Austrian and Prussian state railways), attempted to provide evidence that these difficulties could justify only a portion of the adverse performance of the Austrian state railroad. Even with a generous allowance for all of those circumstances that could unfavorably influence the Austrian state railroad, Günther arrived at the conclusion that the expenditures of the Austrian state railway were approximately 80 million crowns too high, and that this could be traced back primarily to the large number of employees, or, in other words, to the low work expectations for individual employees. Namely, if the disparities of the operational conditions were factored in, the results showed that the Austrian state railway employed approximately 50,000 more employees than would be employed by the Prussian state railroad in the same circumstances.

While each employee of the Prussian state railway is responsible for the service of 42,500 axle-kilometers, the corresponding service responsibility in Austria amounts to only 32,900 axle-kilometers. Most notable is the disparity for employees at the central service; in Austria job performance per worker is 571,400 axle-kilometers, whereas in Prussia each individual's performance is 1,115,000 axle-kilometers. Within the central service in Austria alone, there are approximately 5,400 employees too many, requiring an annual expenditure of 23 million crowns. This explains quite sufficiently why the Austrian state railroad is incapable of delivering an income that corresponds to its investment capital despite higher tariffs.[9]

9. See Günther, *Die Gebarung der österreichischen Staatsbahnen* [The Financial Policy of the Austrian State Railroad] (Vienna, 1914). Günther's remarks were subjected to a very sharp criticism by one of the top officials of the Austrian Railway Ministry in a public speech. See Burger,

It also explains the poor state of public finances and the growth of the public debt, the enormous increase in tax burdens, and the difficulties hampering production and trade due to the defective functioning of the national transportation system.

However much the causes of the crisis may be found in the government's overspending, a more fundamental reason is budgetary mismanagement in the private sector. Austria-Hungary proportionally produces less than Western Europe. Even the number of people actively employed in production is relatively lower than elsewhere, since the public sector draws too many people away from productive labor. That which was said above about the national railway administration is equally true about all branches of the national government: it employs far too many people everywhere.

However, even the producers' economic labor is less profitable than in other countries. The high protective tariffs on grains and the prohibition against meat importation preserve a farming culture functioning in a long-outdated manner, which, located far distant from Western European agricultural activity, expects all salvation to come from established subsidies and so on, which the state (and the agricultural majority selected for the committees in the parliament) unsparingly guarantees from the tax monies levied on the urban, manufacturing population. The owners of large latifundia seldom care personally for the administration of their estates; this is more often left to an officialdom that uses the government's leisurely and unimaginative business administration as a model. The property's fideicommissary dependence prevents the transfer of the land to better landlords. In the largest of the Austrian Crownlands, Galicia, agriculture appears as large-scale landholdings, on the one hand, whose prosperity is hindered by a lack of capital, scarcities of agricultural labor, and the owners' lack of ability; and smallholdings (more than 800,000 properties, ca. 80 percent of that entire number amounting to less than 5 hectares),[10] which can offer only meager nourishment to a family; the category of the mid-sized agricultural holding is almost completely absent from this province. In a special report about the ratio of agricultural output to general price in-

---

Die Gebahnung [sic] *der österreichischen Staatsbahnen und andere Bahnverwaltungen* [The Financial Management of the Austrian State Railroad and Other Rail Managements] (Vienna, 1914).

10. [A hectare is a metric unit commonly used for measuring land area. It is equal to 10,000 square meters, about 107,639.1 square feet, 2.47 acres, and 0.00386 square miles.—Ed.]

creases, which Graf Hardegg reported to the Herrenhausen [the upper house, or House of Lords, of the Parliament] in 1912, the backwardness of Austrian agriculture was characterized in the following manner: "In broad areas, we remain closely tied to the old three-field system, which is inadequate for the agricultural resources and has long outlived its usefulness, where the land appropriate to the highest yield is barely worked, let alone cultivated, and where conventions and customs still hold sway that can no longer be considered up-to-date. We have, in fact, predestined entire landed areas to animal husbandry, where the number of animals has constantly decreased instead of increasing, where the production of provender for the animals is low, where the cultivation of the alps, feedlots, and meadows appears to have hardly moved past the initial stages, and where animal husbandry, directed in a completely irrational manner, bears tragic fruit."[11]

A few numbers illustrate most clearly the backwardness of agriculture in Austro-Hungary. In 1912, the crop yield per hectare (in hundredweights per meter) amounted to:[12]

In	Rye	Wheat	Barley	Oats	Potatoes
Germany	18.5	22.6	21.9	19.4	150.3
Austria	14.6	15.0	16.0	13.0	100.2
Hungary	11.9	13.1	14.1	10.1	72.3

In the German Reich, 58.9 cows are supported by one square kilometer of productive agricultural land, whereas in Austria, the same area supports only 32.5 cows.

The situation in industry is no better. The Austrian worker (and the same is true for the Hungarians to an even greater extent) labors less intensively than, for example, the Germans or even the Americans. Entrepreneurial activity, for which only the slightest tendency exists, is impeded at every turn by a legislature that has set itself a goal of inhibiting the development of large firms to the best of its ability. The above-mentioned exposé of the Koerber administration includes the remarks: "The protection of the small firm, which is suppressed by the new form of economic life; the impediment of speculation in the exploitation of advantageous business activities in all directions; these

11. See no. 113 of the supplements to the stenographic protocols of the House of Lords, 21, session 1912, p. 17.
12. In 1911.

and other attempts, whose partial validity should not be denied from an ethical point of view, have impaired the prosperity of our economic life in many cases, without bringing about any of the specified, desired results."[13] In 1912, a report by the economic commission for the Austrian House of Lords [Upper House, *Reichsrat*] concluded "that the improvement in the entrepreneurial spirit and, with this, the expansion of our industry outward, leaves so much to be desired that an 'anticapitalist' spirit, having encountered no resistance, has propagated itself with stultifying effect."[14]

The farmer, the tradesman, the worker, and above all the civil servant work and earn little; however, they still desire to live comfortably, and thus they spend more than their circumstances would allow. The frivolity of the Austrians and Hungarians sets them sharply apart from the sober thriftiness of the Western Europeans. There appears little concern for the future, and new debts are added to old, as long as willing lenders can be found.

As long as the lenders are willing. Thus we arrive at the crux of the matter.

If cash payments were generally common in business dealings in Austro-Hungary, then this living beyond one's means could never have achieved the broad extent that it has acquired in the last decades. Consumer credit could only have been obtained as a bank loan. The amounts which might have been supplied to consumers by this means would have remained far below the enormous sums that have been accessed with commercial credit. Additionally, one should certainly not underestimate the scope of consumer credit. A not insubstantial amount of credit available for agriculture, urban real estate, and small trade has found use, not for productive, but for consumptive goals. Included in the total, however, should be those large sums of consumer credit that the credit requirements of the civil servants have drawn down. Loans have been guaranteed to the state, provincial, county, and local public officials, who cannot be fired while they live; to officials of the public funds, the court, the railway companies and suchlike, the security of which loans are based solely on the references of the borrowers. As a rule, the pay office disbursing the salary assumes the loan, and this office extracts the monthly interest, expenses, and amor-

13. See *Studien über die Reform der inneren Verwaltung* [Studies About the Reform of the Domestic Administration], cited above, p. 7.

14. See no. 113 of the documents cited above, p. 3.

tization quotas from the debtors' emoluments, and pays them over to the lenders. In this manner, many thousands of public officials receive only a portion of their income paid in cash, often only the minimum required for existence remaining free of garnishment. The lenders are safeguarded quite well by this system. The risk that the debtor could die prior to repaying the debt is allowed for by insurance; these premiums increase the already quite substantial costs of these credit transactions, which are conducted not only by private moneylenders, but also by specific credit institutions that are generally organized based on confraternal links.[15]

If monetary loans were the only form by which consumer credit were guaranteed, then those circumstances that led to this crisis could never have developed. Whoever takes out a loan also has to pay it back eventually; the assumption of debt does not expand his consumer power, it merely relocates it temporally. The matter is different for the system of long-term commercial loans, as they are currently common in Austria and Hungary. The consumer does not pay for his purchases in cash; he remains in debt. This is true for both the exclusive customers of the glittering luxury boutiques in the center of Vienna and also for the miserable poor, who satisfy their needs in squalid country stores in Galicia or Slavonia. The major gentlemen's tailors in Vienna owe hundreds of thousands of crowns, many of them even more; however, the business requirements of even the smallest "general stores" reach quite sizable numbers. If a customer makes a one-time partial payment on his debt, then this is often only the lead-in to a greater exploitation of commercial credit.

The retail dealer, who has direct commercial dealings with the end user, typically has insufficient capital; indeed, he often lacks his own operating capital. He could not extend long-term credit to his clients,

15. Among the institutions that guarantee consumer credit to civil servants, the *Erste österreichische Beamten-Kreditanstalt* [First Austrian Civil Servants' Credit Institution] in Vienna, founded in 1908 with a fully paid capital stock of 1,500,000 crowns, appears of particular interest. This institution extended loans to employees with fixed annual salaries, and also to retired public officials having fixed annual pensions, and other state civil servants (either from one of the kingdoms or provinces represented in the *Reichsrat*, or local officials), against cession of their official emoluments for the collection of payments authorized to this public corporation. The performance of these loans, including interest and ancillary charges, was secured by nationally or provincially guaranteed insurance on the borrowers against their demise, as well as against their inability to repay while still alive. The province of Lower Austria assumed subsidiary liability. The bank bonds based on these lending activities, offered at 4.5 percent and amounting to a face value of 30 million crowns, were declared to be *gilt-edged securities*.

if he were not also in a position to receive long-term credit for his own purchases; he remains indebted to the wholesaler in the same way that the consumer is indebted to him. The Austrian industrialist has to guarantee long-term credit, because otherwise he would not be able to market his wares domestically. In trade rivalry, neither the product's excellence nor the lower price tip the scales; whosoever would drive the competition from the field has to guarantee more auspicious payment conditions, must seek to accommodate the purchaser through increasing deferrals of the payment dates. Under such circumstances, the bill of exchange has practically vanished from many commercial sectors. Even where it still appears, it does not ensure the punctual observation of the agreed-upon payment dates. If the debtor will not pay on the date of maturity, then the exchange is prolonged. Decades ago, one of the greatest initiates of the monarchy's credit system had already made the statement that the exchange formula "in three months to the day, I will pay," should correctly read, in Austria, "in three months to the day, I will extend." Since that time, the conditions have only become generally worse; only where powerful cartels rule the market (iron, sugar, hemp) is it otherwise. In all those sectors, however, in which the formation of market-determining consortia was unsuccessful, the producers, for whom higher domestic production costs have barred the path to exports, must accommodate themselves to inauspicious payment customs. It has gone so far that today "cash payment" is, according to customary usage, understood to mean several months of credit.

A reform of these conditions would have to begin with the end user. The consumer would have to become accustomed to paying in cash, or at least punctually on the agreed-upon, not-too-distant, payment date. The large department stores, store chains, and cooperatives have completed this educational process abroad, as such stores must insist upon cash payment by virtue of their organization. In Austria, the middle-class policy of commercial development places insurmountable difficulties in the path of this form of retail trade; the policy supports the small shop owner and the handcrafter.

It is true that the small merchants are not pleased by their customers' poor habits of payment. Even they would prefer to be paid in cash. However, a keen rivalry also reigns among them: the number of small commercial enterprises is far too high; the possibilities for earning a living in Austria are low. The required certificate of qualification generally impedes the path to an independent business, and, in addition to this, a number of industries are further hampered by the concession system. For many, therefore, no option is left except to establish small trading operations. Capital is either not necessary, or only a little is required. Anyone about whom nothing prejudicial is publicly known can easily gain access to credit from the manufacturers and wholesalers. This explains the superabundance of small trading operations, which often guarantee their owners a meager income despite considerable industriousness.

If the small trader wants to do any business at all, then he has to extend credit. And he may neither hand-select his customers, reject doubtful people, nor deny credit to those whose debts have grown too large. The village shopkeeper must view it as a special honor whenever the beadle or even the community recorder offers him their custom. Woe be unto him if he dares to demand from them (regardless of whether it is only after several months or even years) a settlement of accounts. Indeed, he is dependent upon the representatives of national and autonomous local administrations for every aspect of his business. They manipulate those hundreds and thousands of laws, ordinances, edicts (*ukases*), which are partly an inheritance of the *vormärz* absolutism,[16] and partly the creation of the modern currents of the middle class and socialist politics. Whether or not the shopkeeper receives the concessions, permissions, and so on, which he requires to conduct his business, he remains completely dependent upon administration officials; they can make things uncomfortable for him during the assessment of taxes, in the exercise of authority by the commercial and market police, or sanitary inspectors, and in one hundred other ways. He has to play things correctly with them, and with their varied and numerous relations, no matter the cost. In Galicia and in Bukovina, in Hungary and its neighbors, everyone believes that he ought to be entitled to the claim that he, and only he, should receive credit unhesitatingly, and should always receive credit thusly. The merchant sees the sum of his outstanding credits with trepidation, not only as an absolute number, but also as growing in relation to his sales figures from year to year. However, he is powerless against the circumstances.

Someday, sooner or later, the day had to come on which it became clear, that a large portion of these outstanding loans, which were posted

16. [The term Vormärz (pre-March) Years (1815–48) refers to the political situation prior to the 1848 revolution during the rule of the Austrian Chancellor Prince Clemens von Metternich. He strongly believed that maintaining social order within the multiethnic composition of the Austrian Empire required comprehensive suppression of national movements at home and within other nation-states.—Ed.]

in the merchants' account books as assets, were irrecoverable. All these officials, employees, functionaries of the public administration, local home rule, and so on, all these farmers and craftsmen had lived far beyond their means, they had accepted debts that they were neither willing nor capable of repaying. The officials' emoluments were ceded or disdained up to the limit with only the minimum required for existence remaining free of garnishment; the farmers' immobile properties were burdened by mortgages beyond their market value; the monetary creditors, who were able to safeguard themselves at the signing of the contract, regularly preempt the mercantile creditors, who, due to the reasons delineated above, can only approach the debtor energetically after a year and a day. It required only the gentlest external push in order to manifest the irrecoverability of these demands.

The much cited speech of Secretary General Pranger in the *Wiener Saldierungsverein* [Viennese Banking Association] gave this push. As a warning signal, it came years too late; nothing could be changed in that which had already occurred. He exhorted the lenders to caution and restraint, and provoked the inevitable and undelayable liquidation. The scope of the restrictions on and divestments of credit, which resulted in the first months of the crisis, were highly exaggerated; yet they were indeed large enough to be the final straw. The retail merchant, for whom credit was impeded, began to measure his outstanding loans and must have recognized, to his horror, that a portion of them were irrecoverable. In many cases, the retailer saw himself now forced to suspend payments himself; this functioned retroactively from the end consumers step-by-step back to the producers. Credits, which had for years been entered into the account books as "good," were revealed at one stroke as rotten. The businessman recognized too late that he had already lost a majority of that which he thought he had earned through years of hard work.

The insolvencies mounted up. The Wiener Kreditorenverein [Viennese Society of Creditors] for protection from demands in cases of insolvency, to which textile firms primarily belonged, accrued:

In the year	Cases	With liabilities (in millions of crowns)
1909	1001	45.2
1910	935	40.3
1911	904	42.8
1912	1805	112.0
1913	1674	73.2

The 1912/1913 crisis brought about the liquidation of the unsustainable borrowing system of previous years. It is true that not everything was liquidated; more than enough remained reserved for the future. And yet it is the pernicious system of poor payment conditions that remains; from this, the Austrian economy is threatened by ever-new dangers. As long as the overproduction on the domestic market lasts, and the unfavorable production circumstances impede industrial exports, no change, however, can occur.

The monarchy has to export goods in order to maintain equilibrium in the balance of payments without increasing the foreign debt. Today, remittances by emigrants form the most important asset of the monarchy's balance of payments; this is an unhealthy circumstance that cannot be sustained over the long term.

Therefore, a pleasant sign of improvement must be welcomed, this being a recent increase in the export of textile goods. The Austrian cotton industry has suffered for years from a surfeit of new spindles that were established as a result of the 1907 economic boom. For years, attempts have been made in this industry to control overproduction through business restrictions on the one hand, and through forced exports, even at loss-generating prices, on the other. The result has not failed to appear. Exports amount to, in this and a few related articles (in thousands of hundredweights):

	Cotton yarns	Wool yarns	Linen yarns	Hemp yarns	Cotton wares
1908	43.0	10.4	59.0	4.2	67.6
1909	40.8	20.7	78.9	5.7	72.0
1910	52.2	20.3	76.2	8.3	96.1
1911	71.0	22.3	69.3	7.4	120.1
1912	107.4	21.4	84.5	5.6	131.4
1913	247.0	29.4	97.2	8.6	174.8

For 1913, the statistics demonstrate an essential increase in the export of semifinished and finished goods overall. Most notably, the increase in sugar exports is of consequence: from 254 million crowns in 1912 to 295 million crowns in 1913.

Nowhere is there as much discussion about the necessity of improving the balance of payments, of boosting the export of goods (and last but not least foreign commerce), as in Austria. However, the people remain a far cry from pursuing the single path that will lead to the desired goals. Because in this case, all of those small, beloved options, by which people in Austria prefer to solve large problems, fail. Only one possibility could help: the radical elimination of all hindrances that the economic policies have laid in the path of the development of productive forces.

PART 2

Economic Policy Issues in the Midst of the Great War

CHAPTER 10

On the Goals of Trade Policy[1]

I

The elements of a foreign trade policy can be designed based only on an understanding of what emerges from the free play of economic activity: a regional division of labor that results in the greatest supply of goods at the least cost. From this point of view, protectionist policies can never be justified on economic grounds. All theoretical attempts to do so have failed. The arguments of the advocates of free trade, which culminated in Ricardo's formulation, cannot be shaken, let alone refuted.[2] If completely free trade prevails, then each country specializes in that branch of production for which its domestic conditions are relatively most favorable. Every artificial influence that disturbs this arrangement must, in the end, result in a deterioration in the quality and a decline in the quantity of goods.

The free trade argument has not been refuted by Friedrich List's[3] claim that otherwise idle productive resources are employed under a system of protective tariffs. The fact that without the protective tariffs

1. [This article originally appeared in German in the *Archiv für Sozialwissenschaft und Sozialpolitik*, vol. 42, no. 2 (December 1916).—Ed.]

2. [David Ricardo (1772–1823) was one of the leading and most influential "Classical" economists of the nineteenth century. His formulation of the logic of division of labor and comparative advantage in *The Principles of Political Economy and Taxation* (1817) in Piero Sraffa, ed., *The Works and Correspondence of David Ricardo*, vol. 1 (Cambridge: Cambridge University Press, 1951), pp. 128–49, became the foundation and rationale for a system of free trade; see also Ludwig von Mises, *Human Action: A Treatise on Economics* (Irvington-on-Hudson, N.Y.: Foundation for Economic Education, 4th rev. ed., 1996), pp. 159–64; and Gottfried Haberler, *The Theory of International Trade, with Its Applications to Commercial Policy* (London: William Hodge and Co., 1936), pp. 125–208.—Ed.]

3. [Friedrich List (1789–1846) was a German political economist who formulated a five-stage theory of economic development in his 1841 book, *The National System of Political Economy*. He argued that, for an industrializing nation like Germany in the nineteenth century, economic protectionism was essential to national development.—Ed.]

they would not be utilized shows that they are less productive than other resources that can be employed instead.

A tariff to support infant industries also cannot be justified on economic grounds. Older industries have an advantage in many ways over younger ones. The emergence of new industries can be considered economically worthwhile, in general, if their lower productivity in the short run is compensated by their greater productivity in the longer run. If the new enterprises promise to be economically profitable, the private sector will create them without any "aid" from a tariff. With every newly started enterprise it is anticipated that various initial outlays will be recouped later on. It is not a challenge to this argument to point out that almost all countries have supported the development of industries through protective tariffs and other protectionist measures. It remains an open question whether healthy industries would have developed even without such aid. Within a country's borders similar differences in productive conditions are solved without any such "external" support. In areas within a country that previously were not industrially developed, we see industries emerge that not only successfully compete against older industrial areas of that country, but also often drive them completely out of the market.[4]

Schüller argued against the idea that unrestricted freedom of trade was advantageous from the international point of view. Generating the largest possible total production, he said, was not only dependent upon taking advantage of the most productive opportunities, but also exploiting the unutilized productive opportunities as well.[5] The weakness of this argument is already apparent in the fact to which Schüller refers with particular emphasis: that the conditions under which various producers operate are dissimilar, not only in different countries, but also within the individual countries themselves. Less advantageous production opportunities are exploited only insofar as more advantageous ones are no longer available. The only influence from the protective tariff would be in that less advantageous opportunities are exploited while more advantageous ones elsewhere within that same country remain

4. [See Ludwig von Mises, "The Disintegration of the International Division of Labor" (1938) in Richard M. Ebeling, ed., *Money, Method, and the Market Process, Essays by Ludwig von Mises* (Norwell, Mass.: Kluwer Academic Press, 1990), pp. 113–36, especially pp. 114–15 on the infant industry argument.—Ed.]

5. See Schüller, *Schutzzoll und Freihandel* [Protective Tariffs and Free Trade] (Vienna, 1905), p. 228.

unutilized. However, that no increase in total productive output can be achieved by this method requires no further explanation.

II

Ricardo's theory of foreign trade starts with the assumption that the free movement of capital and labor operate solely within a country's boundaries. Domestically, any regional difference in rates of profits and in employment is equalized through movements in capital and labor. This is not true for differences between several countries. If there was free mobility between countries as well, this would lead to the following result: capital and labor would flow out of the country that offered less advantageous production opportunities and into the country with more advantageous opportunities. A series of emotional factors "which I should be sorry to see weakened" (which Ricardo, the patriot and politician, inserts into the theoretician's exposition) are raised in opposition to this. Capital and labor remain, in spite of the fact that they suffer from a lower level of income, in their own countries and turn to those branches of production for which they are, if not absolutely more favorably, then at least relatively more favorably qualified.[6]

The premise for the theory of free trade, therefore, is the fact that capital and labor do not move across national boundaries due to noneconomic reasons, even when this would be advantageous from an economic point of view. This may have applied, in general, during Ricardo's day; however, it has not been true for quite some time now. The obstacles that inhibit the generally free mobility of capital and labor become smaller every day; even the World War will only temporarily hinder this development. When peace returns, those circumstances also will gradually return that, in the decades before the war, cultivated the free mobility of capital and labor between nations. These developments were not random; rather, it was the necessary result of the ever-closer economic ties between the individual countries of the

6. [See Ricardo, *The Principles of Political Economy and Taxation*, p. 136: "Experience, however, shows, that the fancied or real insecurity of capital, when not under the immediate control of its owner, together with the natural disinclination which every man has to quit the country of his birth and connections, and entrust himself with all his habits fixed, to a strange government and new laws, check the emigration of capital. These feelings, which I should be sorry to see weakened, induce most men of property to be satisfied with a low rate of profits in their own country, rather than to seek a more advantageous employment for their wealth in foreign nations."—Ed.]

world, that is, the transition from individual national economies to a global economy.

If, however, the basic assumption of Ricardo's theory disappears due to the effects of free trade, then the theory would disappear with it. There would no longer exist a reason to search out a basic difference between the effects of freedom of trade in domestic trade and foreign trade. If the mobility of capital and labor domestically and their mobility between countries differs only as a matter of the degree, then economic theory cannot make a fundamental distinction between them. The theory must, instead, necessarily arrive at the conclusion that the inherent tendency under free trade is to draw labor and capital into the locations having the most favorable natural production conditions, regardless of political and national boundaries. In the end, unlimited free trade must therefore lead to a change in the conditions under which the entire world is settled; capital and labor will flow out from the countries with less favorable production conditions into those countries with more favorable production conditions.

Even if a theory of free trade like Ricardo's is modified in this manner, nothing from a purely economic viewpoint would speak against free trade, and everything would warn against protectionism. However, because the theory leads to completely different results in terms of the effect of free trade on the regional distribution of capital and labor, it offers a completely different starting point for examining the economic case for and against a tariff system.

III

The natural conditions for production are unequally distributed among individual countries: there are countries with more favorable and others with less favorable production conditions. This relationship is immutable. Over the course of history, the importance of this fact has often been reduced due to intense metamorphoses resulting from the exhaustion of the soil, through the clearing and utilization of new fertile areas, by changes in the climate, and so on. Of greater importance are those changes that have their origin in advances in production technology, which enable the use of previously worthless or less utilizable natural resources.

If one adheres to Ricardo's assumption that capital and labor are not disposed to emigration abroad, even when more favorable production conditions are present elsewhere, then the result is that the same expenditures of capital and labor lead to different results within individual countries. There are wealthier and poorer nations. Commercial policy interventions cannot alter this circumstance. Such interventions cannot make the poor nations any wealthier. On the other hand, protectionism in the wealthy nations appears completely preposterous.

If one drops Ricardo's assumption, however, then a tendency toward an equalization of profits and wage rates would prevail across the globe. Thus there are, in the end, not poorer and wealthier nations, but rather more and less densely populated countries.

This is the developmental tendency that the world today is facing. From a purely economic point of view, this outcome cannot be described as harmful. However, this tendency does come into conflict with the principle that reigns over modern politics, that is, the nationalist principle. The nation-state would correspond with the nationalist ideal only if it has an area under its control in which the quantity and quality of the natural conditions for production are such that it can offer its people space for the natural increase in population within its national boundaries without the danger of overpopulation.

A growing population must be able to find employment within the national boundaries without becoming more densely settled than corresponds with its natural production capabilities. The nation ought to be able to develop unimpeded within its national territory; however, the population should not increase within the nation's borders beyond that level that would be achieved by the complete and free international mobility of capital and labor.

This stipulation, which is derived with obligatory logic from the nationalist principles of the nineteenth century, is contrary to neither the primarily or purely industrial state, nor the primarily or purely agricultural state, nor even the monocultural state. If a country's economic potential is determined by its natural production possibilities, then in this country the most favorable exploitation of the land and, ceteris paribus, its greatest possibility for supplying goods for the population, will result from the free play of economic forces. A country's economic potential is negatively affected only if labor increases beyond the level indicated by its natural production possibilities. However, until a country reaches such a situation, its economic possibilities remain "positive," whether viewed from a global or a national economic point of view.[7] If the pro-

---

7. [See also Ludwig von Mises, *Nation, State, and Economy: Contributions to the Politics and History of Our Time* (Indianapolis: Liberty Fund, [1919] 2006), pp. 46–63; also Lionel Robbins, "The Optimum Theory of Population," in T. E. Gregory and Hugh Dalton, eds., *London Es-*

duction conditions were not exceedingly different within individual national economies,[8] then these extremely differentiated types would be the norm.

In its commercial application, the nationalist principle does not demand self-sufficiency in the sense of complete isolation from foreign trade. It is in no way intrinsically opposed to an increase in the general welfare by means of an international division of labor. The nationalist principle has nothing in common with the demand, which is increasing due to certain ethical and political outlooks, for maintaining the current status quo in the division of labor, the intensity of international trade, and impediments to the broader expansion of the global economy.

A country's national character is not endangered by the use of products made by foreign labor. That the German wears American cotton and Australian wool in his clothing, that he drinks Brazilian coffee and eats Italian lemons, remains of no concern to the nation insofar as there exist German products which serve as the means by which such imports may be paid.

The point of conflict must be found elsewhere.

The surface of the globe is divided among the nations. This division is the result of historical processes in the past and does not correspond to the production possibilities and population patterns of the present. Therefore, there are nations whose area would be more densely populated and others that would be less densely populated, if unfettered movement of people and goods were a reality. The problem of relatively over- and underpopulated areas has to be solved by migration, the movement of people.

These migrations have resulted in the citizens of various nations moving from countries where less favorable production conditions prevail to those countries where there are currently more favorable conditions, with population densities adapting to the more or less attractive natural production possibilities around the globe. In a similar manner, capital goods move to where more favorable returns can be earned. The country from which they move loses both capital and labor. The exported capital assists the importing country in exploiting its productive capabilities. The emigrated labor assimilates itself to its new home.

---

says in Economics: In Honor of Edwin Cannan (London: George Routledge & Sons, 1927), pp. 103–34.—Ed.]

8. See Schüller, op. cit., pp. 9ff.

Emigrants who settle in previously uninhabited areas can retain and foster their culture in their new home. They are not lost to their nation, even if they politically separate themselves from their native country. The Canadians, Australians, and the residents of Cape Province in South Africa are not the only members of the English national culture, which spans the globe, but so are the Yankees.

Circumstances unfold differently when the emigration is directed toward an already populated country and the colonists, due to their numbers or their military inferiority, are not successful in driving out the previous inhabitants, such as successfully happened in North America with the European colonists. These numerically inferior emigrants must then, sooner or later, lose their mother tongue, national culture, customs, and manners. They learn the language of their new country, and they soon adapt to it in all other characteristics. Whether the assimilation is completed quickly or slowly depends upon a series of particular circumstances; however, it remains unavoidable. We are not interested here in the origins of this occurrence; the fact that it occurs is sufficient for us.

We now perceive the meaning and the goal of trade policies. Insofar as they do not unnecessarily encourage an already existing developmental tendency, such as industrialization, or are not solely directed against the trade policies of foreign countries, a country's trade policies are to be guided by the idea of increasing or retaining its territory in defiance of the relative unfavorability of the production possibilities within its national borders.

This goal cannot be achieved, however, at least not in a manner beneficial to that nation. The country with the relatively less favorable production conditions must, as one says, export either citizens or goods. This is true. However, one ignores the fact that the export of goods is possible only if that country enters into competition with nations that have more advantageous production conditions, that is, if, in spite of higher production costs, that country can sell goods just as inexpensively as countries that produce at lower costs of production. This, however, must depress wages and profits on capital within that country. Unless the emigration of capital and labor is legally impeded or forbidden, this will actually boost emigration; this also completely ignores the fact that the cultural level of the citizens is also depressed by such competitive actions.

Over the long term, an overpopulated country (in the sense

characterized above) does not have the means to impede the emigration of the superfluous citizenry. Ultimately, the population must decrease to whatever level corresponds to the utilization of that country's domestic production conditions. As long as the emigrant can find work in the exploitation of possible production that is more advantageous than the least advantageous utilization at home, and insofar as his emigration has not been impeded, the emigrant will improve his economic life through leaving his country. The fact that agricultural tariffs and also industrial protective duties (which offer industry the possibility of retaining high domestic prices through cartels and trusts while marketing underpriced goods abroad) increase the costs of living, requires no more detailed explanation here.

The fact that these developmental tendencies could be misunderstood, not only by the political leaders but also by parts of the media, can be traced back to the circumstance that it was previously possible to compensate for market losses in one area that was progressively industrializing, by developing new markets in other areas. By this method, English industry was able to stay ahead of the Germans, as could the French and the Belgians. Soon, however, the time will come when this ability to get ahead of others in a new market will fail. If all of the agricultural countries (insofar as it is possible for them to do so in accordance with their natural production conditions) were to develop industries, then the primarily industrial country would be capable of exporting its goods only insofar as its natural production conditions were superior to these others.

A number of writers have constantly stressed with the greatest emphasis[9] the grave peril to the economic future of the "primarily industrialized countries" that will emerge with "industrialization" in agricultural countries. Yet the correctness of our conclusions cannot be questioned by anything that has been offered in opposition to them.

The scientific treatment of the subject has suffered from the fact that it has been merged with the political-economic battle over protective tariffs versus free trade. In fact, the use of protective tariffs has suggested itself to those who have perceived a future danger facing the industrialized countries from the progressive industrialization of agri-

9. From the comprehensive literature, see especially Wagner, *Agrar- und Industriestaat* [Agricultural and Industrial States], 2nd ed. (Jena, 1903); Hildebrand, *Die Erschütterung der Industrieherrschaft und des Industriesozialismus* [The Shattering of the Rule of Industrialism and Industrial Socialism] (Jena, 1910).

culture nations. However, as we have seen above, this possibility is not available.

The industrialized countries are not in a position to prevent the agricultural countries from transitioning into being industrial nations, which would have been an effective means of retaining the status quo in the international economy, if it had only been possible to do so. From the national point of view, another method is available: the annexation of colonies that have a primarily agricultural character to the extent that the home country and the colonies together form an area that appears to be, in relation to the quality of its natural production conditions, no more densely populated than the territory of other nations. This is the path that England has followed and which Germany ought to have followed, had it not degenerated into the misery of provincial factionalism while the Russians and the Anglo-Saxons conquered the world.

What can a protective tariff achieve here? It cannot prevent the agricultural countries from closing their own borders through protective tariffs and other administrative measures. Quite the contrary, it actually incites them to do so, because it hampers the marketing of their own agricultural products and challenges them to protect themselves with tariffs against the "dumping" of industrial goods by the already industrially developed country. The industrial exporting country ought to function as a free trading partner in order to convert the agricultural countries to free trade by setting a good example; however, England's situation demonstrates how little can be achieved by this method.

Thus, the proponents of protective tariffs must ultimately arrive at the conclusion that salvation lies in the limitation of the population. What, then, is the need for a protective tariff? No type of political intervention, however well developed, is necessary in order for German lands to nurture as many citizens as would correspond to the conditions compatible with their natural production possibilities. That is, indeed, the goal of trade policies: to ensure the existence of a larger population within a limited area. To relinquish the achievement of *this* goal is to absolutely reject the justification for trade policies. Trade policies are, then, left with only small tasks of transient importance; they are no longer ranked among the important tasks in a nation's global-historical battle for existence.

Ever since humans have lived upon the earth, there has been only *one* effective and enduring means to battle overpopulation: emigration. Séfur's statement, that the history of humankind reflects the people's efforts to continually move from poorer living conditions to better ones, is also true for the present.

IV

The supporters of protectionist policies have not failed to understand that their goals cannot be achieved through this method.[10] And, yet, they still do not admit defeat. Indeed, they cry out ever more loudly for the protection of national labor. The history of recent decades demonstrates that they have been quite successful in this: almost all countries in the world currently practice protectionism.

To make an appraisal of modern tariff policies, a distinction has to be made between the policies of overpopulated countries and those of underpopulated countries. In the underpopulated countries (those that are less densely populated than favorably corresponds to their production possibilities), agricultural production almost always outweighs manufacturing in terms of the number of those employed in the farming sector, and more or less in terms of the value of the products produced. These countries are usually characterized as agricultural countries because they are primarily considered to be exporters of agricultural products and consumers of industrial goods. There are two separate types of agricultural countries in which modern protectionism has developed in terms of motives behind the policy.

The first type includes the long-established cultural areas. Even if these countries are primarily agricultural, this does not mean that they are lacking in manufacturing production. Prior to the development of modern, global economic relationships, they already had a manufacturing base that supplied the needs of that country's domestic market. Now that the country is being gradually drawn into the global market, the old autarky is disappearing. Agricultural products are exported and industrial goods enter the country from abroad. In this way, the larger, foreign industries on the global market meet local autochthonic manufacturing, which mostly operates in the form of less efficient handcrafting and cottage industries, or at most in medium-sized enterprises.

The foreigner, with his economic and technical superiority in manufacturing, initially is "victorious" in this battle. As a result, small

10. See especially Wagner, op. cit., pp. 81ff.

manufacturers and workers in the vanquished industries become unemployed. When looked at from a purely economic perspective, there
appear to be two options for the workers who have been let go: either
to emigrate to more industrially advanced countries and find employment in their larger industries, or to remain in their home country and
return to working in agriculture or in one of the other older forms of
domestic production.

The second option seems to be almost impossible, because of the
practical difficulty for manufacturing workers to transition back into
agricultural labor. The first option is a viable one, though it involves
certain disadvantages for the first generation of such workers as they
transition from small-scale to large-scale factory employment. However, those workers are, then, "lost" by their native country due to their
emigration. Rather than patiently wait until increasing economic difficulties force handicraftsmen and journeymen to make this final step,
national protectionist policies intervene to limit the "losses" that would
result from emigration.

Protectionism fights against this undesired trend before this happens
by trying to prevent the misery of the workers. A nation's protective
tariffs accelerate domestic industrial development to hinder the immi-
nent emigration of some of its citizens. Again, this policy cannot be
defended from a purely economic perspective, though it is understandable from the point of view of national policy.

The second group of agricultural countries was created out of areas
that were more recently colonized. The colonists were primarily farmers, and their demands for manufactured goods were satisfied through
imports from their native country. Originally, import tariffs in these
colonial areas were introduced for budgetary reasons and evolved into
extremely significant sources of revenue. It is also the case that these
tariffs encouraged the emergence of colonial industries. Eliminating
these tariffs would have negatively affected the citizens of these colonies, the more so because one of the effects was to stimulate immigration for employment in the industries created under the protection of
the tariffs. A point was reached when a decision was made to reform
the import tariffs into protective tariffs. This occurred, for instance,
during the development of the United States and Australia.

The industrial protective tariff is popular in agricultural countries,
in spite of the fact that from a purely economic perspective it cannot
be justified in terms of the interests of the citizens of those countries.

Even the farmers, who are primarily harmed by these tariffs, came to consider them to be beneficial. National and political interests increasingly prevailed over purely economic interests.

The industrial protectionist policies in these agricultural countries were justified through the use of an "exploitation theory" in contrast to the teachings of those who spoke of a "harmony of interests" among nations, similar to the way labor unions in the industrialized countries attempted to use a vulgar, socialist theory of exploitation to give an ethical justification to their fight against the individualistic social order.

The patriot of the agricultural country sees the industrial exporter as the exploiter who unfairly enriches himself through his trading with the agricultural country. He casts a disdainful eye on the wealth of the industrial countries and compares it with the simpler and poorer circumstances of his homeland. The animosity that he bears toward the citizens of the industrial world is the same that the nobles felt toward the burghers and that the squires held for the barons of industry, only aggravated and embittered, now, by national antagonism.

Friedrich List, a German, contributed the most in creating this "neomercantilist" ideology, which has ended up being turned against the German people. The Russian sees an enemy in the German, who upsets the productive development of the Slavic peoples with his superior industry. The name of the originating country, the "made in Germany" stamped on German export goods, has a provocative effect on those who are critical of these imports.

A completely different orientation is found in the protective policies of the overpopulated countries, that is, those that would become the targets of emigrants if there existed full freedom of movement. These are generally industrialized countries. Protectionism does not emerge from one single source in these countries: it does not view development as something undesirable, nor does it wish to either halt or delay the tendency toward development. Two types of protectionism are to be found in these countries. The first type of tariff is meant to foster development in less favorable areas of production, or to maintain production in areas of the economy that have become less favorable due to changes in trading patterns or technology. This type of tariff may be characterized as primarily an agricultural tariff that is justified due to differences in costs of production in the home country compared to abroad. Tariffs of the second type are imposed to support the exporting sectors of the economy. They are supposed to foster the formation of cartels that raise domestic prices so goods may be exported at lower prices. They are cartel tariffs.[11]

Whether they are "production cost" tariffs or cartel tariffs, their ultimate effects are absolutely identical to all protective tariffs: they reduce national income. They reduce the availability of economic resources in relation to consumption demands, and thus completely fail in terms of the goal they were meant to attain. They can only bring about transitory effects.

The superficial view that sees nothing in the system of protective tariffs other than one-sided class politics advantageous to commercial producers goes far astray in its criticisms of the motives for and effects from protectionism. This much may be conceded: that it is fruitless in the attempt to delay the development of the global economy.

V

In recent years, there have been changes in the lives of people that cannot leave unaffected the assumptions underlying trade policies.

The development of and price reductions in the methods for transportation have offered an unforeseen expansion in the seasonal movement of labor. It is not impossible that emigration will lag behind the international *Sachsengängerei*[12] in extent and importance,[13] at which point the businessmen and the laborers will oppose each other. With this alteration in the character of labor migrations, the disadvantages resulting from people being limited to areas with less favorable production conditions will be more strongly felt than they are today. Countries that occupy land less well endowed by nature will not have to fear falling behind other, happier countries in terms of numbers of citizens; however, they will continue to be handicapped in terms of affluence and culture. The nationalist incentives trying to eliminate these factors, however, will not become weaker, but grow in intensity.

Continuing emigration to foreign countries will, predictably, encounter ever more difficulties in the future. Previously and still today,

11. For this article, which limits itself to the basics, there is no purpose in discussing the other means of protective policy (e.g., export premiums, railway duties), because these are similar in their effects to either the cartel tariffs or the tariffs on production costs.

12. ["Going to Saxony," where the sugar beet harvest marked the annual beginning of the seasonal migration of agricultural workers.—Ed.]

13. See Moritz J. Bonn, *Die Idee der Selbstgenügsamkeit* [The Idea of Self-Sufficiency], Festschrift für Lujo Brentano (Munich and Leipzig, 1916), p. 68.

emigrants generally remain at a lower rung of the cultural ladder. They brought little or nothing of their national culture with them on their trip abroad; social climbing in the new country brought them closer to the national culture of the host country. As a consequence, there are no great barriers to assimilation. Schools, libraries, and newspapers, which are founded by well-intentioned groups and supported by the émigrés' home government, can do nothing to change this. However, it can be altered by an improvement in the education of the emigrants and through increased participation of the lower classes in the national culture. The European emigrant today already takes with him something more than memories of misery and subjugation. Still, this cultural dowry is not enough to prevent assimilation; however, even today it already impedes and retards it.

The problem of immigration, therefore, takes on a new quality. The special interests of industrial workers who are threatened by immigration, and who previously had to acquiesce in the face of the greater national interest of the benefits from immigration, now are able to raise the threat to "national unity" whenever they wish to hold back the arrival of more immigrants. No one can have any doubts that all countries whose national composition is threatened by immigration will effectively close their borders, just as the countries settled by Caucasians have for a long time now closed their borders to Asian immigrants.[14]

The drop in the birth rate ultimately must also influence the problems that constitute the starting point for economic policies. Indeed, the causes behind migrations cannot be mitigated by a gradual increase, cessation, or decrease in the birth rate, if this were to happen uniformly across the entire globe. If, over a certain period of time, there would occur a similar reduction in the population of every individual country, this by itself would not alleviate the overpopulation of one country relative to the underpopulation of another. Just as previously, there would still be areas too densely populated relative to the favorableness of the conditions of production, and other areas would remain too sparsely populated. The tendency would remain unchanged to bring about an equivalent distribution of people across the surface of the world.

14. [See Ludwig von Mises, "The Freedom to Move as an International Problem," (1935) in Richard M. Ebeling and Jacob G. Hornberger, eds., *The Case for Free Trade and Open Immigration* (Fairfax, Va.: Future of Freedom Foundation, 1995), pp. 127–30.—Ed.]

Assuming that the decrease in population does not exceed a certain rate, the total amount produced by a smaller number of workers need not be equal to the decline in the number of workers; rather, due to the law of diminishing returns, the average amount of per capita income might increase with a declining national income. It is abundantly clear that trade policies are able to exercise a greater effect on this type of income pattern than with the case of an increasing population and, ceteris paribus, a declining per capita income.

VI

The experiences of the World War allow arguments in favor of economic self-sufficiency to appear particularly relevant. Only those countries would be in a position to victoriously survive a war that are independent of foreign imports for the supply of goods needed to wage war and maintain the existence of their populations during the conflict. Where issues of national defense are concerned, all other considerations fall by the wayside. The trade policies of the future, therefore, would aim at bringing about an equivalent distribution of labor between all branches of domestic agriculture and industry.

The advocates of extreme collectivism will not be persuaded in any way concerning the unattainability of these goals of trade policy. They will argue that emigration can be forbidden in order to impede the drop in the number of citizens. They will claim that emigration has nothing to do with the fact that a nation to whom history has granted a narrow, limited area upon the earth (an area poorly endowed by Nature) will have to live more humbly than other, happier nations. They will say that moral and bellicose virtues flourish more widely in poverty than in affluence. The new, national ideal is created, under which all things are judged in terms of making of primary economic importance the possibility of waging a war of starvation.

Yet there is a substantial error in this line of reasoning. It overlooks the fact that in war it is not the mere existence of equipment and weapons that is important, but also their quality. The nation that has to produce the material means for waging war under less favorable conditions of production will be more poorly equipped and armed than its opponents in the field. Up to a certain point, personal bravery can compensate for these material inferiorities; however, there is a limit beyond which all the valor and self-sacrifice in the world can no longer suffice.[15]

VII

A country can gaze tranquilly upon its future that controls settled areas of such a size and quality of natural conditions of production that any increase in population need not cause a danger of overpopulation. We consider a country to be overpopulated whenever it is more densely populated than would be the case if there were freedom of movement around the entire world. This is true in the same way for both large and small countries. For larger nations, however, the political implications of this situation are admittedly different than they are for smaller nations. If a larger nation's future is secure, then its position as a world power is also secured.

At the beginning of the twentieth century, we see three large, global empires that have risen far beyond other nations in the size of their territories and the numbers of their citizens: England, the United States, and Russia. In each of these empires, the attempt has been made to employ trade policy in order to influence the regional divisions of labor in favor of their own countries. In each, the concept of national economic self-sufficiency as a national ideal is growing, and events from distant history (the division of the world's surface as completed during the seventeenth and eighteenth centuries) offer the possibility of their realizations.

The problem appears simplest in Russia. A generation ago, Russia was an enormous agricultural country with almost no industry and few industrial characteristics, although there was a strongly increasing demand for industrial goods. High protective tariffs enabled the creation of industry in many sectors, and in others it merely accelerated this process. The Russian people are in the fortunate position of controlling a large expanse of the world's surface that is provided with favorable production conditions. The Russians need not fear being removed from the list of great nations within the foreseeable future. Their sons can remain in the country, which offers room for an increasing population due to a multiple of factors.

---

15. [See Mises, *Human Action*, pp. 828–30, on "War and Autarky."—Ed.]

The situation is similarly favorable for the English people. Great Britain became an industrialized nation one hundred years ago: the world became its sales market and granary. When, at the end of the nineteenth century, the increasing industrialization of these overseas markets appeared to place the future of British manufactured exports in doubt, the British politicians turned their attention to their large colonial settlements. Thus, there is room for an increasing population within the English empire. Not only India, but also Canada, Australia, and South Africa appear as the foundation for the global position of the English people.

The United States is also large enough and wealthy enough in natural resources to be able to feed its current population several times over.

It is possible that others will join these three great global empires of the present. The external indicators appear favorable for China and India. In any case, the following nations have developed into global powers of the second rank: Japan; Spain, in connection with formerly Spanish South America; and perhaps Portugal in connection with Brazil; and Italy due to its expansion in North Africa. For the French nation as well, the political and economic prerequisites are favorable for an expansion along the northern coast of Africa if a different birth rate resulted in an increase in their population.

The foundations of a global empire are its population, which must increase at approximately the same rate as in other global empires, along with the territory under its control so it can offer the room for its expanding population. Trade policies can add nothing to the foundation of a nation as a global empire if these conditions are lacking.

The German people currently lack these foundations. Germany can only provide for the population within its territory by manufacturing goods made with foreign-supplied raw materials that are then sold to foreign buyers, in order to acquire those raw materials required for its own consumption, and to pay wages and other industrial incomes. This situation cannot be sustained over the long term. For this reason, the German people need colonies for settlement if they do not wish to lose their global ranking.[16]

---

16. See Jentsch, *Der Weltkrieg und die Zukunft* [The World War and the Future] (Berlin, 1915), pp. 96ff.

There are other nations that find themselves in a similar position. However, by far the largest and most powerful of the "unsatisfied" nations is Germany. When German men and women leave their homeland, they cannot find another country in which they can maintain their nationality. This is because all of the lands in which Caucasian people could prosper as farmers and laborers are in the hands of foreign countries, with the exception of a negligibly small amount of land offered in southwestern Africa.[17] Everywhere in the world, wherever there is free space for white men, there Germans have settled over the last 150 years. Five million Germans (not including Austrians) immigrated to the United States alone during the years 1820 to 1906.[18] They and all of their descendents are lost to the German people.[19]

Even though German foreign policy has hardly attempted, up to now, to acquire foreign areas for settlement, the fact is that all other peoples who control more land than they will need for their own future development consider Germany their natural opponent in this endeavor. Of all the reasons for the unfriendly attitude toward Germany (which the neutral foreign countries adopted during the World War), this one is more understandable due to the solidarity of interests of those people who, at the time when the world was politically divided up, did not arrive too late, unlike the poet who did.[20]

17. [From 1884 to 1915, the present African nation of Namibia was a colony of Imperial Germany, under the name of German Southwest Africa. In the first decade of the twentieth century, several rebellions by the native African population led to a brutal German military response. By the time of the First World War, about 10,000 Germans had settled in the colony, in comparison to about 200,000 native African inhabitants. The German military forces surrendered to an invading British army from neighboring South Africa in 1915, which permanently ended German control.—Ed.]

18. [Between 1820 and 1914, an estimated 3.7 million people immigrated to the United States from Austria-Hungary.—Ed.]

19. The German emigration statistics indicated a large decrease in the number of emigrants over the last two decades. This does not contradict that which appears above in the text. On the one hand, this decrease coincided with the complete development of German industrialism and with the fortification of the defense system, according to the efforts of the era of Chancellor Count Georg Leo von Caprivi, which had to lead to a temporary containment of emigration. However, it should be observed that for Germany, a particular characteristic is the emigration of highly skilled workers (technicians, commercial associates, etc.), which is not highlighted in the statistics.

20. [This refers to Johann Wolfgang von Goethe (1749–1832) and his presence at the Battle of Valmy when the Revolutionary Army of France defeated an invading German army under Duke Carl August of Saxe-Weimar on September 19, 1792, as recounted in Goethe's *Kampagne in Frankreich* [Campaign in France]. See G. P. Gooch, "Goethe's Political Background," in *Studies in German History* (London: Longmans, Green, 1948), pp. 166–89, especially 172–74.—Ed.]

VIII

A widely held view argues that national antagonisms would eventually be removed by the economic solidarity of interests. Insofar as this idea claims to be an expression of the fact that the purely economic point of view speaks for free trade and against national isolation through protective policies, it may possibly be true.[21] As was demonstrated earlier, protective policies can only find their justification in non-economic arguments. At least for the next few years, any expectation that purely economic considerations about the handling of trade policy problems could triumph over national-political ones must be rejected as unfounded. In contrast, the principle of nationality is politically gaining ever more momentum at present.[22]

In terms of the national problem in Austria-Hungary, this idea tends to be expressed in a particular sense. The economy is the unifying tie that holds together all of the people of the Austro-Hungarian Empire, who for nationalist reasons are otherwise striving to be free. This is primarily Karl Renner's point of view.[23]

Renner views the modern state as an "economic community," that is, as an "organized economic area." Countries, nowadays, are "political units, because they are externally enclosed by the tariffs walls of other nations, and are internally connected by the blood, veins, and nerves of their transportation system that surrounds the fixed and powerful centers of their capital cities." With the second statement, Renner actually indicates the geographic basis of state unity; we will not busy ourselves with that any further.

We are interested in the concept of the state as a tariff community. Renner reverses the situation: it is not the political unit, but instead the tariff community that appears as the constitutive characteristic of the state. "One can, for example," Renner continues, "hardly conceive

---

21. [See Mises, "The Clash of Group Interests," (1945) in Ebeling, ed., *Money, Method, and the Market Process*, pp. 202–14.—Ed.]

22. [See Mises, "Economic Nationalism and Peaceful Economic Cooperation," (1943) in Ebeling, ed., *Money, Method, and the Market Process*, pp. 155–65.—Ed.]

23. See esp. Renner, *Oesterreichs Erneuerung* [Austria's Renewal], 2nd ed. (Vienna, 1916), pp. 30–35. [Karl Renner (1870–1950) was a leading Austrian socialist who headed two coalition governments of the new Austrian Republic between November 1918 and the summer of 1920. In April 1945, at the end of the Second World War, he formed a provisional government under the supervision of the Soviet Union that proclaimed the reestablishment of Austria as a democratic republic; in November of that year, he was elected president of Austria, a position that he held until his death.—Ed.]

of an odder acquisition of hitherto existing statehood, than Austria's acquisition of Galicia.[24] The association, which lasted more than one hundred years, made this area organically part of the political body of the monarchy: its wood and grains, its petroleum, gasoline, and ethyl alcohol would be immediately lacking in every household, in every factory, if the territory were occupied by the enemy. Reciprocally, the entire paper, textile, and iron industries would feel the abrupt loss of the market area."

Is it any less true, however, that wool, cotton, rubber, coffee, tea, hides, and so on are just as important for supplying the western Austrian markets, and would not the sugar industry feel the loss of its usual market territory no less heavily than any other sector of the economy? Would one not have to come to the conclusion that the United States, England and its colonies, and Brazil, in short, that the entire world is just as organically connected to western Austria as is Galicia? Had the Détente Powers[25] succeeded in dividing Germany and Austria in the usual manner, then a proponent of Renner's doctrine might have found, after around one hundred years of association, that Brandenburg was "organically" connected to Russia, Westphalia to France, Tyrol to Italy.

It is true that a long-term tariff association forges strong economic relationships. An alteration in these circumstances, whether it is due to the erection of new tariff boundaries, the removal of existing tariffs, or an increase or reduction in the tariff rates, brings with it, as a result of the new circumstances, a great rearrangement in production and sales relationships. However, similar rearrangements occur as a result of every other change in the conditions of production: every new invention, every discovery of new sources of raw materials may bring this about.

Renner finds the separation of a primarily agricultural country from an industrial economic area to be particularly ruinous, because it low-

24. [Galicia was the easternmost area of the imperial Austrian domains under the Austro-Hungarian Empire, containing the city of Lemberg (now Lvov), the birthplace of Ludwig von Mises. It was annexed by Austria in 1772 as a result of the first partition of Poland. It was incorporated into the re-created state of Poland at the end of the First World War. Most of Galicia, including Lemberg, was annexed by the Soviet Union in September 1939 as a result of the military conquest and division of Poland between Nazi Germany and the U.S.S.R. Since 1991, it has been part of the Republic of Ukraine.—Ed.]

25. [The "Détente Powers" refers to the victorious nations in the war against Napoleon, who following the defeat of France reorganized the borders of the countries of Europe at the Congress of Vienna in 1815.—Ed.]

ers the value of the land. However, the same effect would have been generated by the removal or lowering of agricultural tariffs; would Renner dispute this, as well? It is true that, from a purely economic point of view, the primary goal is to expand the economic community into a free trade area to the greatest extent possible, and the entire populated surface of the earth is the largest of these possible areas. However, as we have already seen, special interest groups in individual nations currently demand the establishment of economic autarky. On the other hand, the free trade idea makes the case for tariff reductions and always throws into question the rationale for protectionism; the undeniable power of the argument for free trade, sooner or later, will triumph over every tariff that is not justified by the principle of nationalism.

Naumann's *Mitteleuropa* [Central Europe] also suffers from the complete misunderstanding of these facts.[26] According to Naumann, it is particularly difficult for the smaller nations to maintain their independence next door to the larger nations of the world, that is, next to the Anglo-Saxons, the Russians, and the Asians. In Naumann's words, nothing binds these smaller peoples more closely together than that they find in unity the power to resist; and nothing appears more natural than that the German people, as the greatest and most well endowed among the weaker peoples, should assume the leadership of this federation. However compelling this may seem in the name of national self-preservation, two circumstances currently hinder the path to this conclusion.

On the one hand, there is the authoritarian and authoritative state of mind and constitution of the Germans, which has surpassed for quite some time that of other peoples around the world.[27] The fact that the future German federation is primarily planned as an economic federation is no less important. The Magyars, Romanians, Serbians, Bulgarians, and all of the other peoples between Berlin and Baghdad can and will not forgo creating their national industry. They do not want to remain merely agricultural countries, sales territories, and suppliers

---

26. [Friedrich Naumann (1860–1919) was a social liberal reformer who attempted to organize programs to improve the conditions of the German working class as a counterbalance to the Marxian and Social Democratic appeal for more radical social change. He was also strongly nationalistic. His book *Central Europe* (New York: Alfred A. Knopf, 1917) made the case for unifying the small states of central and southeastern Europe under German leadership to form an "economic and protectionist community."—Ed.]

27. See Preuß, *Das deutsche Volk und die Politik* [The German People and Politics] (Jena, 1915).

of raw materials to German industry. They will not passively observe as their surplus population eventually immigrates to Germany, and becomes Germanized as laborers in German factories. They may perhaps agree to a political federation with the German Reich, as a defensive and offensive alliance to guarantee their own national independence; however, they will never agree to an economic and tariff alliance. They would happily observe the market possibilities for their agricultural products expanded into Germany and Austria; however, they will not forgo the creation of their national industry and the gradual replacement of German imports.

The tariff and economic associations are claimed to be the ties that bind the individual members of a nation-state to an empire.

Let us first examine the relationship between Austria and Hungary. The two countries form a unified tariff area, though they are legally completely independent, with each entitled to direct its commercial relations with foreign countries without consideration of the other. This unity is advantageous to both countries. It offers the Austrian industry a profitable sales territory in which it does not have to fear competition from superior industrial countries; Hungarian agriculture can sell its products in Austria at a price that exceeds the global market price by the amount of the tariff. However, on the other hand, the tariff association does inhibit the development of a Magyar national industry. This makes the tariff association unbearable to Magyar nationalist feelings; it would have gone to pieces long ago if the Hungarian legislature and administration had not understood how to wage a decisive campaign against Austrian exports to Hungary, even without tariffs. Austria and Hungary are indeed part of a tariff and currency union; however, they do not associate in an economic relationship; rather, they exist in a state of permanent economic warfare. Thus, they have succeeded in starting up and protecting industry in Hungary without creating an intratariff zone. However, this was possible only through constant frictions, expansions, and controversies between the two halves of the monarchy, which have generated much bad blood. The coexistence of the two countries in this association was conceivably the worst possible situation, not in spite of, if not primarily because of, the tariff association.[28]

---

28. [See Eugen von Philippovich, "Austrian-Hungarian Trade Policy and the New German Tariff," *Economic Journal* (June 1902), pp. 177–81.—Ed.]

Let us now leave the Austrian situation. Germans and Czechs, the two strongest nations according to the number of their peoples, have the same interests in regard to Cisleithania [Austria and Crownlands] as do the Hungarians and other countries. Indeed, industry in the German-speaking area of the Sudetenland is more highly developed than in the Czech-speaking areas.[29] Yet even the industrial development in the Czech lands (in comparison to what is common in Austria) is quite extraordinary. A large portion of the industry in the Czech-speaking lands still remains in the hands of German industrialists; however, even these facilities contribute to increasing and strengthening the Czech nation, and the Czechs additionally hope that sooner or later the leadership of these industries will become Slavified. Both nationalities making up the population of the Sudetenland have the same *national* interests regarding the parts of the monarchy that are still primarily agricultural. Both feel threatened by the increasing closeness of the Austro-Hungarian Monarchy's common tariff area; both fear the industrialization of Hungary or Galicia. In comparison with these internal and powerful external common interests, the superficial observer overlooks the bitter economic battle that is constantly being waged domestically. There, every subsidiary, every business, every individual facility becomes a battleground. There is, admittedly, no conflict on the basis of purely economic reasons, nor is it led by the manufacturers, who are only concerned about the profitability of their operations. It is a national fight. Its proponents are primarily the politicians and literati, those whom Renner derisively calls the *Wirtschaftlosen*, those without access to capital.

However, behind these leaders stand not only all of those who might hope to gain an advantage from the expected changes; the entire nation stands solidly behind them, because the country strives for national greatness and national prosperity through industrialization. The autonomous administrations in the countryside, regions, and communities participate in this battle, as do also the powerful national banking institutions, savings banks, and confraternities, who also think

29. [The Sudetenland was the westernmost area of Bohemia bordering on Germany. It was incorporated into the new nation of Czechoslovakia at the end of the First World War, even though the vast majority of its population was German-speaking. In September 1938 the area was annexed by Nazi Germany as a result of the Munich agreement between Germany, Great Britain, France, and Italy. It was returned to Czechoslovakian control at the end of the Second World War, and the approximately 3.5 million German-speaking residents were expelled from the country as part of an Allied Powers agreement.—Ed.]

about the "national advantage" along with profit opportunities in all their dealings.

It is not only Austria's German manufacturers, against whom the Czechs have initiated economic warfare, who lament these circumstances; all do who feel themselves to be and call themselves Austrians. These are the circumstances that force Austria into the background in the competition with the Great Powers. Because, when the not very large and poorly endowed economic area of Austria is reduced in this fashion into a number of tiny economic regions, then any possibility is lost for developing specialized industries. One can lament these circumstances (and I will not line up to declare that I also lament them), but there would be no purpose in denying them.

Of the other nationalities that are included in the Austro-Hungarian tariff area, the Ruthenians, Romanians, and Slovenians still stand at such a low level of economic and political development that they cannot yet consider an industrial protective policy. Within their economic areas, their national political efforts are devoted to intensifying their agricultural operations. In this, they are supported by the monarchy's agricultural trade policy. There can remain no doubt that in the foreseeable future even these nations will attempt to create a national industry, the rudiments of which are already present today.

CHAPTER 11

Inflation[1]

Inflation and Devaluation

There are two options for the government to meet its enormously in-creased financial demands to cover the costs of the war.

The first one is for the government to issue *war bonds*. Subscribers pay the specific amount for the bonds by drawing upon their own capi-tal or borrowing the money from third parties who have the liquid as-sets to lend. A practical and important example of this is the major banks that use their customers' deposits and savings to finance the war loan.

The second option is for the Treasury to issue debt to the Austro-Hungarian Bank. Since the Bank has no assets of its own to lend to the state, the only method at its disposal to meet the government's request is by *issuing banknotes*. The Austro-Hungarian Bank is currently little more than a purely formal intermediary between the Treasury and the public. In practice, it would make little difference if this intermediary were to be removed and the two Treasury departments [of Austria and Hungary] were to directly put paper money into circulation.

Ample use has been made of this method for financing the war. The amount of currency issued by the Austro-Hungarian Bank has become something of an avalanche.

The figures are as follows:[2]

1. [This article was delivered as a lecture in German in Vienna in late summer 1918. It has not been previously published.—Ed.]

2. [After the war, the Austro-Hungarian Bank publicly released more complete data on the growth of the money supply during the war. In July 1914, before the start of the war, the quan-tity of money in circulation was 3.4 million crowns. By the end of 1916 it had increased to over 11 billion crowns. And at the end of October 1918, shortly before the conclusion of the war in No-vember 1918, the currency had expanded to 33.5 billion crowns. From the beginning to the end of the war the Austro-Hungarian money supply in circulation had expanded by 977 percent. A cost-of-living index that stood at 100 in July 1914 had risen to 1,640 by November 1918.—Ed.]

Before the outbreak of the War	2.1 million
End of 1914	5.1 million
End of 1915	7.2 million
End of 1916	10.9 million
End of 1917	18.4 million
Mid-1918 (approx.)	22.5 million

The increase in the quantity of paper money in circulation has resulted in a *loss of purchasing power of the monetary unit,* that is, *the crown.* This was neither a coincidence nor an unexpected and surprising consequence. The fact that an increase in the supply of money (also known as *inflation*) must necessarily lead to a decline in the value of the currency has long been taught by economic theory, and also has been confirmed over and over again by historical experience.

The devaluation that results from an increase in the supply of money manifests itself, on the one hand, in a general increase in the price of all goods and services, and, on the other, in the increased cost of foreign currency, that is, a rise in the exchange rate.[3] Both of these phenomena, the increased cost of goods and the rise in the exchange rate, are inextricably linked to each other. One is inconceivable without the other; they are two aspects of one and the same phenomenon, and all economic policy tools are powerless to combat them as long as the inflation continues.

Imposing price controls or taxes on prices, or imposing penalties on profiteering and the like, have proven to be ineffective and unsuccessful measures, just as have the various attempts to reduce the exchange rate through the imposition of currency controls.[4] This, too, does not come as any kind of surprise as a result of the war. It was already well known to those who have made a study of economic policy, and historical experience has taught us that there is no other remedy than to restore order to the nation's finances. All attempts by the authorities to

3. [As an indication of the depreciated value of the Austro-Hungarian crown on the foreign exchange market during the First World War, in August 1914, 100 crowns traded for 97.5 Swiss francs. But in June 1918, shortly before Mises delivered this lecture, 100 crowns exchanged for only 43.01 Swiss francs, reflecting a 45 percent decline over this four-year period.—Ed.]

4. [On the extensive system of price and wage controls and production regulations and planning methods imposed on the Austrian economy during the First World War, and their many negative consequences on the functioning of the market, see Joseph Redlich, *Austrian War Government* (New Haven: Yale University Press, 1929), pp. 107–35.—Ed.]

combat rising prices with the full force of the law have come to naught, from the "edictum de pretiis rerum venalium" issued by the Roman emperor, Diocletian,[5] through the "Maximum" that was decreed during the French Revolution,[6] down to the price controls imposed by the belligerent powers today.

The massive increase in the price of goods that we have witnessed cannot, however, be entirely attributed to the money side, as the supply of goods also plays a role. Goods of all kinds have become scarcer as a practical consequence of the war, with imports cut off from abroad and production crippled at home. But this explains only one part of the rise in the price of goods. The increased amount of paper money would necessarily have led to a rise in the prices of goods, even if there had been no inflationary factors on the supply side of goods.

A general increase in the prices of all goods can only arise as a result of an increase in the money supply. This is the situation in which we currently find ourselves. The reduction in the availability of goods has gone hand in hand with the enormous increase in the supply of money. We can trace the disruption in relative price relationships to the reduction in the availability of various individual goods; and we can trace the increase in the overall level of prices to the increased quantity of money. The former is the cause of the shortages from which we are suffering and will continue to endure as long as the current war situation persists, whereas the latter is the cause of the rise in the general price level.

It is true to say that part of the increased circulation of paper money reflects an increased demand for money. The setting up of military

5. ["Edictum de pretiis rerum venalium," or the "Edict of Maximum Prices," was issued in A.D. 301 by the Roman emperor Diocletian in the face of dramatically rising prices due to the debasement of the currency to finance the huge spending of the Roman government. The price controls failed abysmally, merely succeeding in creating massive shortages of food and an extensive black market. By A.D. 305, around the time of Diocletian's abdication, the edict was virtually ignored throughout the empire because of its distortive effects on economic activity.—Ed.]
6. [Shortly after the start of the French Revolution in 1789, the revolutionary government resorted to the printing of a new paper currency, the assignat, to finance its expenditures, leading to a massive price inflation for the next several years. In 1793, the government began imposing price and wage controls throughout the French economy. The attempt to artificially regulate prices in the face of the monetary inflation merely created shortages of virtually all essentials. In spite of a vast bureaucracy to harshly stamp out violations of the price controls, black markets emerged everywhere in France. Finally, in December 1794, the price controls were lifted and food and other goods once again flowed into the market.—Ed.]

payment facilities for soldiers, the extended circulation of our currency in the occupied territories,[7] the spreading of money at home, and, by no means less important, the hoarding of earnings that some sectors of society have been frightened into—these have all contributed to the increased demand for money; so a moderate increase in the amount of paper money in circulation has taken place without, at the same time, contributing to the rise in prices. However, the increase in the issue of banknotes has far exceeded the amount needed to cover the increased demand for money without causing a rise in prices.

Implications of Changes in the Value of Money for National Finances

For the Treasury, which has primary responsibility for all debts incurred by the state, devaluation offers financial relief. As the value of the currency falls, the burden carried by the debtor decreases; he still has only the same fixed amount of principle and interest to eventually pay back in crowns, regardless of whether or not the purchasing power of the crown has decreased in the meantime. On the other hand, as the currency is devalued, state revenues partly will increase. The revenues from various taxes will increase because real estate, dividends, and income expressed in money terms will also go up. This explains the favorable trends in income taxes, capital gains taxes, stamp duties, death duties, and various other taxes. So while state revenues as expressed nominally in money terms are largely on the increase, the greater part of the state's debts, also expressed in money terms, remain unchanged.

However, it should not be overlooked that these favorable effects for the Treasury from devaluation apply to only a part, albeit the major part, of the national budget; but looked at from a different perspective, they are accompanied by unfavorable consequences for the exchequer. To the extent that the state has incurred debts expressed not only in crowns but also in a foreign currency or in gold, a devaluation of the crown means that, expressed nominally in money terms, the debt be-

---

7. [In March 1918, the new Bolshevik government in Russia signed a separate peace with Imperial Germany and Austria-Hungary, taking Russia out of the First World War. A large area of western Russia at that time, which included what is today Estonia, Latvia, Lithuania, Belarus, Moldova, and Ukraine, came under German and Austro-Hungarian occupation as a result of the peace settlement. Most of southern and part of central Ukraine fell under Austrian occupation, with the Austrian crown widely used in this occupied territory.—Ed.]

comes more of a burden. The higher the foreign exchange rate and the more the price of gold rises against the currency, the greater the required expenditure in crowns in order to obtain the same amount of marks or gold coin to pay the interest on the foreign loan.

On the other hand, not all state revenues rise as a result of the devaluation. Some taxes, such as property taxes and some business taxes, and fixed duties, remain unchanged, as they have been set at certain amounts. Devaluation thus results in relief for these taxpayers, expressed in real terms. If they are to be brought into line with current conditions, these taxes and duties in particular need to be increased. Tax increases such as these, however, only can be gradually introduced and involve great political difficulties because the population, having been hit hard by the rise in prices, will regard any such increase in taxation as an additional and unbearable imposition, rather than as an attempt to adjust the tax burden to the changed circumstances.

The extent of the Treasury's financial relief from devaluation is, therefore, undoubtedly far less than is often claimed. But even this presumed benefit is, to a great extent, offset by the disadvantages arising from the decrease in the value of the currency, including the threat to the creditworthiness of the state. It is fear of a further decline in the value of the currency, more than any other consideration, which deters potential creditors from investing in war bonds. This is why, in spite of the central bank's interventions, there has been such an unfavorable trend in the interest rates paid by the state on war bonds and its debt in general, and why subscriptions to the war bonds have been so disappointing. Certainly there would be no greater incentive for subscription to these bonds than an end to any further borrowing from the Austro-Hungarian Bank and an end to any further inflation.

Side Effects from Devaluation and Their Social Consequences

As the currency is devalued, all pension payments are reduced in real terms. There has been a decrease in the number of those holding government bonds, as well as in the number of creditors and mortgagers, together with holders of railway bonds and creditors of any other kind who may only claim interest on and final repayment of principle in terms of the original nominal amount lent, regardless of whether or not the purchasing power of this sum of money has diminished in the meantime. They continue to earn only the same nominal payment, even though they can now only purchase and consume less with this amount than they were previously able to.

In general, a debtor's loss is a creditor's gain. Seen against this background, a superficial view might suggest that a shift in the relationship between creditor and debtor in favor of the latter is always a positive development. It is a popularly held belief that the debtor is always the poor, needy person while the creditor is the rich capitalist. This view is very wide of the mark. The vast majority of debt is not owed by poor individuals; it has not accumulated from consumer credit being extended to the poor, but, instead, consists of loans extended to industrialists to finance production. It is a credit supplied for capital investment and to cover operating costs that have been taken out by landowners, entrepreneurs, and the public sector. The creditors are by no means always "rich" and the debtors by no means always "poor." The major part of all outstanding debt is owed by the richer portions of society to the poorer ones. The less well-off classes of society are disproportionately represented among the creditors. They make up the majority among savings bank members and savings account holders at banks and with cooperatives. Therefore, anyone who regards as an unquestionable "social good" the disadvantage for the creditor and the accompanying advantage for the debtor from devaluation is deluding himself. The greatest amount of wealth rarely exists in monetary form, but, instead, exists in land and property values, in industrial enterprises and in shares, all of which remain immune from inflation; the money value of these assets tends to rise in proportion to the rate of inflation.

It is the middle classes, above all others, who have their assets invested in receiving interest payments from the public purse. Civil servants, army officers, and other professions rely on salaries from the public purse. As a result of the general liquidation of commercial enterprises caused by the war, we can now add to the list of state dependents practically all members of the middle class previously engaged in commerce and retail business. During the course of the war, these shopkeepers and tradesmen have had to sell their stocks and inventories; the sums of money that they received in exchange for them, together with the sums that would have been earmarked for maintenance and repair of their business enterprises, have long since been invested in loans, primarily into war bonds.

Thus the lost purchasing power of the currency has deprived the middle classes of their standards of living and the means of earning a living, as well as depriving the thrifty factory worker or farmhand of the fruits of his labor. The bourgeois is dragged down into the proletariat and the aspiring proletariat is dragged down to the level of the "Lumpenproletariat"[8] subclass. These classes seethe with rage, even though their adherence to social norms previously would have withstood all temptation or sedition.

Nothing contributes more to political upheaval than the economic destruction of those strata of society that are most responsible for its maintenance.

8. ["Lumpenproletariat" often is used to refer to the lower and ignorant segment of the working class. The term seemingly was first used by Karl Marx in his 1845 work *German Ideology*, designating a portion of the working class lacking in proper "class consciousness" of their "true" class interests.—Ed.]

CHAPTER 12

On Paying for the Costs of War and War Loans[1]

The favorable outcome of a war is not solely dependent on the number of soldiers, or the valor and brilliance of their military commanders. An equally important factor is the capacity to provide the army with supporting material, arms, and military equipment of every kind. Military commanders are thus faced with additional tasks besides recruiting, training, and deploying troops. They must prepare the supporting material needed for the actual fighting, as has become particularly obvious during the present conflict, which our enemies have turned into a war of attrition. They have accomplished this by cutting off our and our allies' economies from access to foreign raw materials and industrial products, thus forcing us in wartime to rely on our own resources for all military materiel and civilian food requirements without any help from outside the country.[2]

Up until now we have withstood the test. We have succeeded in supplying whatever is needed to wage war—weapons and ammunition, soldiers' clothing and equipment, food for the army and the entire do-

---

1. [This article was originally delivered as a lecture in German in Vienna in summer 1918 and was then published as a pamphlet.—Ed.]

2. [Shortly after the outbreak of the First World War in summer 1914, Great Britain undertook a naval blockade of the North Sea ports of Imperial Germany in an attempt to prevent the importation of war-related material and food supplies for the military and civilian populations of Germany and its allies, including the Austro-Hungarians. The blockade was extended to preventing Austria-Hungary from importing supplies from neutral nations through its ports on the Adriatic coastline, especially after Italy entered the war in 1915 on the British and French side. Because of the blockades, shortages of food and other necessities greatly affected the civilian German and Austro-Hungarian populations as the war progressed, contributing to the growing problem of famine and malnutrition at the end of the war. The blockade finally ended in summer 1919, more than half a year after the armistice of November 11, 1918, when Germany signed the Treaty of Versailles in June 1919.—Ed.]

mestic population. Our economy has demonstrated that it can bear the burdens of four years of war on land, at sea, and in the air in Europe and Asia. Our people have provided not only the manpower and their blood for fighting the war, but also all the required military supplies.

It has been observed that three things are needed to wage war: money, money, and more money. However paradoxical and exaggerated this remark may sound, it contains a kernel of truth. And the truth is that the supporting material for waging war decisively influences the outcome of a military conflict. However, from an economic perspective, what counts is not money but necessary material, because money is everywhere in the economy merely a medium for obtaining commodities. What matters in war, therefore, is not whether a people has more or less money but whether it has more or less commodities available for waging war. Had the Austro-Hungarian economy spent several billions more in money than it actually possessed, it would hardly have made any difference, since these billions could not have been used to procure goods from other countries.

For four years we have been able to stand up against the enemy and have not only liberated our country's territory from hostile invasion but have also penetrated deep into enemy territory with our arms.[3] This outcome must be credited as much to the efforts of our entrepreneurs, workers, and farmers as to our brave soldiers.

The war has imposed very substantial material sacrifices on our economy. Many formerly flourishing areas are devastated, long stretches of railroad tracks have been destroyed, the stock of cattle has been decimated, and agricultural productivity has been reduced by inadequate replacement of worn-out equipment. The whole economy has been depleted by the exhaustion of preexisting supplies. The enterprising among us will be doubly spurred to work hard when peace returns, while weaker natures will view the future of the economy with alarm. Personality traits alone decide into which of these two categories one belongs. But no one needs to worry about our capacity to pay for what the war has already consumed.

It is our economy that supplied the material means to wage war. It is

---

3. [Mises is referring to the Austrian occupation of a large part of Ukraine as a result of the Treaty of Brest-Litovsk in March 1918, which ended the war between Bolshevik Russia and the Central Powers, including Austria-Hungary. On the Austrian occupation of Ukraine, see Gustav Gratz and Richard Schüller, *The Economic Policy of Austria-Hungary During the War in Its External Relations* (New Haven: Yale University Press, 1928), pp. 91–136.—Ed.]

the hard work of our people that created these means and put them at the disposal of the combatants. Our economy, which has been almost completely cut off from other countries, has supplied our armies with what they needed and all by itself bore the costs of war—a proof of its strength and capacity.

That is what really counts. How to distribute among the individual members of the population the war burdens and losses that the economy as a whole has had to endure is a different matter. It is this aspect that people have in mind when they talk about "paying" for the cost of war.

It is misleading to speak of the national economy. What we really mean is not the unified management of the economy as a whole, but the sum of all the individual economic activities of each citizen. In this light, the state treasury is only one among many economic entities, albeit the largest and most important of such entities. The treasury engages in economic exchanges with individual citizens. When it needs work to be done, it pays employees and workers; when it needs commodities, it buys them from their owners. The means for these transactions are acquired by taxation, if we disregard the state's relatively insignificant amount of productive wealth. The treasury bears the greatest part, by far, of the economic costs of war. The state is responsible not only for the entire cost of armaments, equipment, and the provisioning of our troops, but also for the cost of compensating individuals for wartime losses. It is critical for the outcome of the conflict that commodities be available for waging war. The question of how the treasury transfers these items from the possession of its citizens to itself, that is, the fiscal aspect of waging war, is simply a matter of the state's internal organization. Important as it is, it is a secondary matter. When there is a fire, it is paramount to utilize firemen, hoses, and water; how to pay the fire brigade is a secondary consideration at that point.

If we leave aside the payment of war damages by the defeated enemy, there are three options for the treasury in acquiring the means to pay for the war. The first option is to take possession of the required goods without compensation. This would seem to be the simplest approach. From the point of view of equity one could justify it by saying that taking commodities away from their owners, while a serious encroachment on the personal rights of individuals, is far less serious and onerous than universal conscription. The readiness to give one's life for one's country calls for a far greater sacrifice than to give up a large part of one's property.

There are strong reasons, however, why states avoid this option in wartime and generally pay compensation for property that is taken. States were unwilling and unable not to take advantage of that strongest of incentives for maximizing economic activity, namely self-interest. If goods that were available at the beginning of the conflict had been sufficient for the pursuit of the war, it would have been a different matter. These goods could then have been confiscated and used for the war. But a sufficient quantity of such goods was in fact non-existent or inadequate at the beginning of the war. Production had to be converted to meet military demands. Factories making sewing machines and typewriters had to be converted to the production of machine guns, factories making agricultural implements had to be converted to ammunition production, and so on. Maximizing the production of military goods was the ultimate objective, which could be achieved only by giving entrepreneurs a free hand and letting their material interests serve as their incentive. If factories had been taken over by the state, individual initiative would have been stymied.

The system that we deployed unquestionably proved its effectiveness. It allowed us not only to maximize the production of manufactured goods already produced in peacetime, without a marked reduction in their quality, but also to start the production of entirely new goods. We not only replaced the weapons and equipment used up during the war, but also put into use new weapons and new equipment. Our artillery now has far better guns than at the beginning of the war, the ammunition has become much more effective, our infantry now disposes of weapons for hand-to-hand fighting that were unknown at the beginning of the war. Airplanes and submarines, which were not far along four years ago, have attained increasing importance in the course of the war. Our industry has met all these demands.[4]

4. [On the importance of relying upon the incentives of the price system even in wartime to effectively supply the material needed to win a war, see Ludwig von Mises, *Nation, State, and Economy: Contributions to the Politics and History of Our Time* (Indianapolis: Liberty Fund, [1919] 2006), pp. 117–21; and *Human Action, A Treatise on Economics* (Irvington-on-Hudson, N.Y.: Foundation for Economic Education, 4th rev. ed., 1996), pp. 825–28; also see F.A. Hayek, "Pricing and Rationing" (1939) and "The Economy of Capital," (1939) in Bruce Caldwell, ed., *The Collected Works of F. A. Hayek*, vol. 10, *Socialism and War: Essays, Documents, Reviews* (Chicago: University of Chicago Press, 1997), pp. 151–56 and pp. 157–60, for Hayek's discussion

To realize the importance of this achievement, one need only look at Russia. The Russian army entered the war with fine weapons, good and abundant ammunition, and durable, ready-to-use clothing and equipment. Yet Russia was incapable of replacing the items that were used up or lost in the course of the war, since Russia received inadequate supplies from its allies, whose first priority it was to equip their own armies. The Russian army was so poorly supplied with weapons and equipment in the spring and summer of 1915 that this circumstance alone would have prevented its ability to resist our offensive. In the first months of the war, the Russian artillery units had more guns and more pieces of ammunition per gun than ours; by 1915 we surpassed them in the number of guns and the amount of ammunition.[5] The same holds true for infantry weapons as well. The state was therefore in no position to expropriate what it needed without compensation. It could resort to this procedure only for supplies of goods not produced at home.

Another option for the state treasury in securing the means needed for waging war is to impose new taxes and increase existing taxes, an option it has pursued to the fullest extent possible during the war. Some people took the view that the entire costs of war should be paid for by taxes while the war was in progress; they cited the fact that England had followed this policy in previous wars. It is certainly true that England largely covered the cost of its smaller wars by collecting taxes during these conflicts, but for such a wealthy country these costs were insignificant from a financial standpoint. When England was engaged in large-scale wars, however, this was not the case. It did not follow this path during the Napoleonic wars, nor is it doing so in the present war, the biggest the world has yet seen.

If the huge sums required for this war were to be collected entirely

---

of the superiority of the market price system over government planning and rationing during time of war.—Ed.]

5. [During the first year of World War I, from August 1914 to May 1915, after an initial advance into Russian Poland, the Austro-Hungarian Army was forced back by Imperial Russian forces that occupied most of the Austrian province of Galicia. In the second year of the war, from May to September 1915, the Austrian Army in a coordinated attack with German forces successfully recaptured Galicia and advanced into Russian Ukraine. The battle line remained relatively static until December 1917 when, shortly after the Bolshevik seizure of power in Russia, an armistice was signed with Germany and Austria-Hungary. The Soviet government formally withdrew Russia from the Allied side in the First World War when it signed the Treaty of Brest-Litovsk on March 3, 1918, with Imperial Germany and Austria-Hungary. German and Austro-Hungarian military forces occupied Russian Poland, the Baltic provinces (Estonia, Latvia, and Lithuania), and Ukraine.—Ed.]

from taxation and therefore without incurring government debts, taxes would have to be imposed and collected without any regard for the fairness and uniformity of the distribution of the tax burden. One would have to take what one could at that moment. Owners of liquid capital (not only those with large amounts of capital but also owners of small amounts of capital, notably owners of postal saving books) would have to give up all they had, while owners of real property would be asked to contribute little or nothing.

That is, of course, unthinkable. If these high wartime taxes (and they inevitably would be very high to cover fully the annual cost for military expenditures) were to be levied equitably, those without cash on hand to pay taxes would have to go into debt to procure the means needed to pay them. Landowners and owners of business enterprises would then be forced to go heavily into debt or even to sell part of their property. In this case private individuals rather than the state would be forced into debt and would have to pay interest to the owners of capital. Private credit is generally more expensive to obtain than public credit. Landowners and property owners would have been forced to pay more interest on their private debts than they would have paid indirectly for interest on the state debt. If they were forced to sell a smaller or larger part of their property to pay their taxes, that sudden sale would have depressed most real estate prices. As a result, the owners would have suffered large losses and the capitalists with cash on hand at the moment would have made big gains by buying the property cheaply.

It is true that the state did not cover its entire war costs by means of taxes but largely relied on government bonds, on which interest has been paid from tax revenues. It is a mistake to believe, however, that the owners of capital are the beneficiaries from this situation. On the contrary, it is the interests of landowners and business owners that are safeguarded.

Some people claim that financing the war by state loans is tantamount to passing on the costs of war from the present generation to future generations. It is sometimes said that this transfer is fair because war is waged not only in the interest of the present generation, but also for that of our children and grandchildren. Nothing could be further from the truth. War can be waged only out of currently available goods. One can fight only with the weapons on hand; all military needs must be met out of existing wealth. It is the present generation that is waging war from an economic point of view, and it is this generation that must bear all the material costs of the war. Future generations are affected only insofar as they are our heirs. We will be leaving less behind for them than if war had not happened. This is an unavoidable fact, whether the state finances the war by indebtedness or by any other means.

The fact that the bulk of the war costs have been financed by state loans is not in the least an indication that the burdens of the war have been passed on to future generations. All it means, as explained above, is that war costs have been distributed according to certain principles. Let us assume that the state is obliged to extract half of each citizen's wealth in order to finance the war. It would make no difference whether the state asked each citizen to pay half his wealth in taxes immediately or whether the state collected annually by way of taxes the amount corresponding to an interest payment on half his wealth. It makes no difference to citizens whether they pay 50,000 crowns all at once or whether they pay interest on these 50,000 crowns year after year.[6]

It does become a significant issue for those citizens who would be unable to raise these 50,000 crowns without going into debt and who would have to borrow to pay their taxes. For they would have to pay more interest on this loan as private persons than the government, which can borrow at the lowest rate from its creditors. Let us assume that this difference between the more expensive private credit and the cheaper government credit is only one percent. Taxpayers would then save 500 crowns a year in our example. They would save 500 crowns annually compared to what they would have to pay annually in interest for a private loan that would enable them to pay the high war taxes prevailing over a few years.

The term "war loan" is subject to a multitude of misinterpretations. The legal structure of the loan is in no way affected by the fact that the

6. [This proposition is sometimes called the Ricardian equivalence theorem after British economist David Ricardo; see "Funding System," (1820) in Piero Sraffa, ed., *The Works and Correspondence of David Ricardo*, vol. 4, *Pamphlets and Papers, 1815–1823* (Cambridge: Cambridge University Press, 1951), pp. 149–200, especially pp. 186–87. Ricardo argued that all that the borrowing option entailed was a decision whether to be taxed more in the present or more in the future, since all that was borrowed now would have to be paid back plus interest at a later date through future taxes; therefore in terms of their financial burden the two funding methods can be shown to be equivalent, under specified conditions. However, Ricardo also pointed out that due to people's perceptions and evaluations of costs in the present versus the future, they were rarely equivalent in their minds. On Ricardo's analysis of war financing and the issue of taxation versus debt, see also Carl S. Shoup, *Ricardo on Taxation* (New York: Columbia University Press, 1960), pp. 143–67.—Ed.]

loan was assumed by the state to procure the means to wage war. War loans are loans of the Austro-Hungarian State. They do not differ from older loans assumed by the two states prior to the war. The layman's view that these loans are less secure than other state loans because they are "war loans" is thus completely erroneous. All state loans taken together constitute the state debt. The only differences between the individual issuances of state indebtedness are those stipulated when they were issued, which anyone can read in the text of the loan document. The differences lie in the interest rate, conditions for redemption, and bundling. There is no difference in the legal status of the debtor. The owners of older state loans, for instance, the owners of a crown annuity emitted before the beginning of the war, have no greater legal guarantee that their interest payments and capital repayment will be met than the owners of war bonds. War bonds do not constitute a lien on the state, where creditors are ranked differently.

Some people who are not knowledgeable about economic affairs voice the fear that the state might refuse to redeem coupons and repay capital after the war, in the light of Russian experiences. They fail to note a highly significant difference between conditions in our country and in Russia. The Russian loans were foreign loans; that is, the owners of Russian obligations were largely non-Russians, for example, the English and the French. When the present Russian rulers declared the loans null and void and stopped interest payments, foreigners who were of no concern to them were victimized.[7] At this juncture England and France are in no position to exert military pressure to make Russia fulfill its obligations toward its creditors. In their actions, Russia's present rulers have disregarded later, more distant consequences.

There is no doubt that state bankruptcy will eventually weigh heavily upon the Russian state. It is obvious that Russia from here on out will either be unable to obtain foreign loans at all or able to only under very unfavorable terms. One of the terms will surely be prior payment to their creditors. Foreign loans are indispensable if Russia wishes to restore its economy to its former level. It will therefore have to agree to all the terms that its creditors will impose. But, as stated above, Russia's present rulers have been oblivious to any of these considerations.

7. [On February 10, 1918, the new Bolshevik government officially repudiated all foreign debts accumulated by both the former Imperial Russian government and the short-lived Provisional Government that came to power following the abdication of Czar Nicholas II in February 1917, and which was overthrown in the communist coup led by Lenin in November 1917.—Ed.]

Their only concern has been to extricate themselves in the short run from their financial difficulties, and at the same time to display their ideological hostility to private property.

Things are quite different in Austria-Hungary, which has no obligations abroad. The war loans are in the hands of domestic creditors, and so are most of the older Austrian and Hungarian government loans. It is erroneous to assume that only rich capitalists own state obligations. Our government securities were not issued solely to the rich and wealthy segments of the population. Directly or indirectly, their owners are largely the poor and poorest. The assets of savings banks and cooperatives are mainly invested in government securities, so that even the smallest savers have a stake, via the savings banks, in the continued servicing of the government's debts. State bankruptcy would affect not wealthy foreign capitalists but small and very small domestic savers. Citizens, not foreigners, would be victimized. Any government, no matter what its political orientation or party affiliation, will have to bear this fact in mind. State bankruptcy might well have adverse political consequences. Interest payments would have to be maintained in order to avoid alienating all those for whom the stopping of interest payments would involve a substantial loss.

The Russian situation obviously doesn't apply to us. Differences do not end there. The Russian armies have been defeated; the Russian state has collapsed. Our armies, on the contrary, have been victorious; they have chased the enemy from our country's territory and have made deep incursions into enemy territory.

Although state loans are not threatened by cessation of interest payments, a more serious threat to them may be the debasement of the currency. All belligerent countries have been forced to cover at least part of their military expenditures by loans provided by their note-issuing central banks. Such loans are a highly questionable instrument of credit policy. The note-issuing bank can provide the requisite sums only by issuing notes. This increase in the number of banknotes in circulation reduces the purchasing power of the monetary unit. Prices rise. The depreciation of money induces significant shifts in income and wealth. It is not our object here to deal with this question. We will limit ourselves to exploring the consequences of the decline in the value of money on public loans. Anyone taking out a 100-ruble loan in 1913 with a promise to repay the final amount in 1918 fulfils his obligation by repaying 100 rubles in 1918, even if the purchasing power of the ruble has vastly declined in the meanwhile. Changes in the value of money must inevitably benefit the debtor and injure the creditor, whether private or public debts are involved. When the purchasing power of money declines, the debt-burden of the state is reduced. In view of this threat, misgivings about investing in public loans are not altogether unreasonable.

At the same time it should not be overlooked that the same risk applies to all capital investments. Anyone with monetary claims of any kind—lien holders and mortgage holders, for instance—will be at the same disadvantage as holders of public loans. They too have monetary claims and suffer equally from the decline in the value of money. It is an illusion to think that investment in liens and mortgages is a protection against the dangers of a decline in the value of money. The net outcome will be a lower interest rate than that offered for war loans without a commensurate increase in security.

It is true that assets invested in real estate and businesses will not face this threat. The price of land, buildings, and factories will rise at the same rate as the prices of other goods. As the value of money declines, the market value of these assets will increase in money terms. The owners of these items will therefore see a rise in the money value of their property. In the event, they will be neither richer nor poorer, as their property has remained the same; all that will have changed is its money value, because money now has a lower purchasing power. They will, however, not suffer from the devaluation of money. Real estate owners who acquired their land before the depreciation of money set in are thus at an advantage. For those who acquired their land later, the situation is different. Anyone who now wants to acquire a piece of land must pay a price that corresponds to the current lower purchasing power of money, and he has to pay an additional premium for the chance of avoiding further losses from his assets if the monetary depreciation progresses. These circumstances account for the exorbitant prices at which real estate now changes hands.

At these inflated prices, the return on invested capital is very low. No form of investment can save individuals from a catastrophe that engulfs the whole economy. Individuals are as powerless to protect themselves from the political consequences of their country's defeat as they are to escape the economic consequences of this defeat.

So everyone has a great deal at stake in a favorable outcome for war loans. Anyone who invests in a war loan comes out ahead by securing a higher interest rate for his assets. He also enhances his economic interests indirectly by preventing a further decline in the purchasing power of money and a further rise in all commodity prices. Investing in war loans is not only a patriotic duty but also a prescription for economic survival.

Nobody would deny that the war has imposed heavy economic sacrifices on us and that we will be suffering from the consequences of the war for many years. We must take these sacrifices in our stride; war has taken an even heavier toll by taking the lives of thousands of the best among us. And yet we must not lose courage. The economic strength of our country has brilliantly withstood the test of war. Cut off as we were from all links to the outside world, we had to rely on our own resources to wage war. Though less prosperous than our enemies, we have outperformed them economically.

Our achievements have been unmatched with respect to fiscal policies. We outdid our enemies to the east [Russia] as well as to the west [Great Britain, France, Italy] in financing war costs through taxes and war loans.

While we have had to resort to the printing press at times to meet war needs, we did so in moderation. Today our monetary system is more intact and sounder than that of our former enemies to the east, and we can look forward to strengthening our situation, whereas our western enemies must anticipate a further deterioration in theirs.

We owe this success to our soldiers on the battlefront and to our businessmen, farmers, and workers on the home front.[8] And everyone who signs up for the war loan will thereby be doing his share.

---

8. [Austria-Hungary, of course, lost the war. The Austro-Hungarian Empire formally disappeared from the map of Europe as a result of the Treaty of Saint-Germain signed in September 1919, which officially ended the war between the Allied Powers and Austria. For Mises's discussion of some of the financial and monetary difficulties facing the new Austrian Republic in the period immediately after the war, see Richard M. Ebeling, ed., *Selected Writings of Ludwig von Mises*, vol. 2, *Between the Two World Wars: Monetary Disorder, Interventionism, Socialism, and the Great Depression* (Indianapolis: Liberty Fund, 2002), especially "The Austrian Currency Problem Prior to the Peace Conference," pp. 30–46, and "On the Actions to Be Taken in the Face of Progressive Currency Depreciation," pp. 47–64. Also see Richard M. Ebeling, "The Great Austrian Inflation," *The Freeman: Ideas on Liberty* (April 2006), pp. 2–3, and "The Lasting Legacies of World War I: Big Government, Paper Money, and Inflation," *Economic Education Bulletin*, vol. 48, no. 11.—Ed.]

CHAPTER 13

Remarks Concerning the Problem of Emigration[1]

Harmful Effects of Emigration

Aside from its general political and economic harmful effects, emigration also involves military disadvantages as well. In the decade before the war the monarchy permanently lost at least 250,000 conscripts in this way.

Emigrants abroad give up the use of their mother tongue; they gradually forget their homeland; and little by little they become citizens of the country to which they emigrate. In the second or, at the latest, in the third generation they become completely assimilated and are no longer distinguishable from the other citizens of the country to which they have migrated.

Causes of Emigration

Emigration from Austria and Hungary is based exclusively on economic motives. The emigrants go forth because they can make their way in the world better in the country to which they immigrated rather than at home.

There has been no emigration from the monarchy due to political dissatisfaction or persecution of political opinions, or because of a person's nationality or their religious beliefs.

Combating Emigration

Emigration can be effectively combated only by successfully eliminating its causes. Economic conditions need to be improved so the in-

---

1. [Mises prepared this memorandum while serving as an economic consultant with the Austrian General Staff in late summer 1918. It has not been previously published.—Ed.]

ducement to emigration disappears. Among the ways this can be done, the following might be considered:

1. Many of the emigrants are agricultural workers or small landholders who emigrate because of no prospects at home of acquiring the ownership of land or enlarging their holdings to the extent they would desire; any land they may have is insufficient to support a family. These emigrants are precisely the most valuable from the economic as well as from the military point of view. Broad areas in Canada have been splendidly settled and cultivated by Ruthenian and Slovakian farmers.[2]

To eliminate these causes for emigration it must be decided to repeal all those legal impediments that up to now have stood in the way of splitting up large estates. Entails[3] must be abolished; de facto or juridical tax favoritism for large estates (e.g., special land taxes or brandy allotment taxes) must be done away with; the exercise of hunting rights must be unconditionally granted to the landowner; furthermore, the so-called peasant fiefdom, or the buying-up of farm properties for the purpose of converting them into hunting reserves, must be prohibited. Through such measures the historical position of the large landowners will not be damaged, yet they will bring about a number of positive changes that will result in some people remaining in the country who otherwise would have emigrated.

2. Our occupational legislation, which is unequaled in the entire world, with its certificates of competency and system of occupational licensing, makes it difficult for those attempting to better themselves to achieve economic independence. Here, too, a complete change must be brought about. If all other nations in the world can make do without the certificate of competency, then surely this would be possible in Austria also.[4]

3. Immigration to overseas colonies also exercised, in part, a certain attraction before the war, because there was no obligatory military service in those countries. A shortening of the term of military service will undoubtedly contribute to reducing the desire to emigrate.

2. [See P. V. Rovnianek, "The Slovaks in America" and Ivan Ardan, "The Ruthenians in America," *Charities: A Review of Local and General Philanthropy*, vol. XIII, no. 10 (December 3, 1904), pp. 239–52.—Ed.]

3. [Limitations on the inheritance of property due to a particular binding succession of heirs.—Ed.]

4. [On the occupational licensing and certificates of competency systems in Austria-Hungary as a carryover of the guild system of the Middle Ages, see Francis H. E. Palmer, *Austro-Hungarian Life in Town and Country* (New York: G. P. Putnam's Sons, 1903), pp. 251–56.—Ed.]

Reduction of the Harmful Effects from Emigration

Introduction of these changes, in the best of cases, will slow down emigration, but it will not completely stop it. It is necessary, therefore, to take measures that reduce to a minimum the harmful effects from emigration. In this political, economic, and military interests all coincide.

However, it is necessary to distinguish between seasonal migration, on the one hand, and permanent emigration, on the other.

Measures relative to seasonal migration

From every possible point of view, seasonal migration is less of an evil than permanent emigration. Seasonal migrants always come back to their native land, and, in general, they return richer; and in many cases also return more professionally proficient and skilled than before they left. They learn a great deal while abroad that they can turn to good advantage when they return home, and they are not lost to the fatherland and the army.

The only disadvantage caused by seasonal migration from the military point of view is the danger that if a war breaks out a part of the seasonal migrants will not be able to return. This danger, however, is not very great in regard to European seasonal migration, since this [Austrian] migration is mostly to Germany and to countries that in the present war and presumably also in future wars will remain neutral (Scandinavian nations, Netherlands, Switzerland).

Again from the military point of view, it should be noted that fulfillment of mandatory military service, and in particular the completion of actual military training, could be regulated to minimize the economic sacrifice imposed on those required to serve; thus, as far as possible, military training should be in a part of the year during which these men cannot find employment abroad. Then they will come back willingly to fulfill their military service. However, if their training falls during the time when they are employed abroad, it can easily happen that they will neglect reporting for duty. (This is more of a temptation when the individual is abroad than when he is at home.) If an individual breaks the law by not reporting for duty and can count on being punished on his return home, the danger exists that he will simply remain abroad.

The state has a responsibility to look out for seasonal migrants.

Consulates must see to the following: seasonal migrants are protected from exploitation; they get medical treatment in case of sickness, and financial support and transportation to get home; the consulates should guide the flow of migrant workers to those regions where the most favorable wage possibilities and working conditions are to be expected. All these governmental measures for the protection of seasonal migrants keep the emigrant conscious of the fact that he is the citizen of a great nation, and that the strong arm of his home country protects him whenever he is abroad. He will, then, be doubly attached to his homeland.

Special arrangements need to be made to keep current the military records of seasonal migrants. It is recommended not to transfer these records abroad, however, to avoid friction in countries where friendly relations are not a certainty; instead, it is better to carry out this supervision as far as possible at border crossings. Military concerns will be fully cared for through the use of records offices in migrants' hometowns, customs stations on the borders, and the consulates and other governmental representatives abroad.

Many improvements can be made for the protection of our seasonal migrants through sympathetic cooperation between the civil authorities and voluntary organizations that often already exist or that can be recruited to start up. For public health and social policy reasons, the countries to which the seasonal migrants travel will support these endeavors since they have a strong interest in foreign workers being properly accounted for and reasonably fed and housed. The problem of seasonal migration can be handled in a satisfactory way with appropriate consideration for all these different factors.

Permanent emigration

No doubt permanent emigration will decline relative to seasonal migration in the first years after the war. Nevertheless, there will still be a very considerable permanent emigration even after the war.

The larger and much more difficult problem to solve will be how the losses suffered by the home country due to permanent migration can be avoided. An effort must be made to get emigrants to go to those regions in which they will have a more assured opportunity to maintain their national identity and preserve their loyalty to the home country.

The best way to achieve this end would be the establishment of an independent Austro-Hungarian colonial possession.

The acquisition of a settlement region

It would be most advantageous if we acquired a colony capable of accommodating a large number of settlers and which also could either partially or completely supply those raw materials not available at home, especially cotton, wool, produce, and certain metals. These two goals for a colonial possession, however, are difficult to achieve in one and the same territory, since these colonial products grow only in tropical or subtropical regions, but are areas not suitable for the settlement of white workers. Therefore, we must try to acquire both types of territories: those in which we can produce desired colonial goods and those in which we can accommodate truly large numbers of settlers.

When the time comes for peace negotiations, the opportunity will arise to deal with the question of acquiring colonial possessions.

PART 3

Austrian Fiscal and Monetary Problems in the Postwar Period

CHAPTER 14

Monetary Devaluation and the National Budget[1]

There exists a close relationship between changes in the quantity of money and changes in the money prices of goods and services. If the quantity of money is increased while other conditions remain the same, then the prices of all goods and services will rise. Of course they will not all rise at the same time nor, as was long assumed, in the same proportion as the increase in the quantity of money; but they will rise, and no measure of economic policy is capable of stopping this from happening.

The rise in the prices of domestic goods and services and the rise of the foreign exchange rate are simply two sides of one and the same phenomenon. The foreign exchange rate is clearly determined by the domestic purchasing power of a country's money. The exchange rate must be established at such a level that the purchasing power is the same regardless of whether I directly buy goods with an Austrian crown or if I first exchange the crown for Swiss francs and then proceed to buy goods with Swiss money.

In the long run, the foreign exchange rate cannot vary from the rate that reflects the relationship between that currency's domestic purchasing power and that of a unit of foreign money. This rate of foreign exchange, therefore, can be designated the natural or static rate. As soon as the market exchange rate departs from it, it becomes profitable to buy up goods with that money which appears undervalued at its rate of exchange relative to its domestic purchasing power and to sell those goods for that money which at its rate of exchange is overvalued

---

1. [This article originally was published in German in the *Neues Wiener Tagblatt* (October 5, 1919).—Ed.]

with respect to its purchasing power. Whenever such profit possibilities present themselves, buyers will appear on the foreign exchange market with a demand for the undervalued currency, and this will drive up its rate of exchange until it has reached its static or equilibrium rate.[2]

However, it should be noted that the changes in the purchasing power of a nation's currency do not take place immediately and do not occur at the same time in regard to all goods. The rise in prices resulting from the increase in the money supply does not happen overnight; a certain time passes before they appear. The additional quantity of money appears somewhere in the economy, and then spreads out gradually. At first, it flows only into certain businesses and certain branches of production, raising the demand for only certain goods and services, and not all of them; later, the prices for other goods and services also start to rise.

The foreign exchange rate is, however, a speculative rate; that is, it arises from the transactions of businessmen who not only consider the current situation but also take into consideration possible future developments. As a result, the devaluation of the currency in the foreign exchange market occurs at a relatively early stage, or at least long before the prices for all goods and services have been fully affected by the inflation in the domestic economy. The market rate of foreign exchange races ahead of expected future price movements, just like every market rate.

The popular view, however, is mistaken that sees the cause for the unfavorable condition of the foreign exchange rate in the actions of speculators. It is true that both at home and abroad those with unclean hands are often the ones dealing in foreign currency and foreign exchange. But to no small degree this is due to government measures that are implemented to obstruct foreign exchange dealings.[3]

---

2. [Mises was one of the formulators of the modern purchasing power parity theory of foreign exchange rates; see Ludwig von Mises, *The Theory of Money and Credit* (Indianapolis: Liberty Fund, 3rd rev. ed., [1924; 1952] 1981), pp. 205–24; and *Human Action, A Treatise on Economics* (Irvington-on-Hudson, N.Y.: Foundation for Economic Education, 4th rev. ed., 1996), pp. 452–58. Also see Joseph T. Salerno, "International Monetary Theory," in Peter J. Boettke, ed., *The Elgar Companion to Austrian Economics* (Brookfield, Vt.: Edward Elgar, 1994), pp. 249–57, for an exposition of the "Austrian" theory of foreign exchange rates along the lines developed by Mises.—Ed.]

3. [Mises is referring to the development of a large black market trade in foreign exchange as a result of the Austrian government's imposition of foreign exchange controls on all foreign currency dealings.—Ed.]

But one thing cannot be denied in regard to these speculators, namely, that they carry out their business in order to earn profits, and not to suffer losses. They can profit only if they have correctly foreseen the future value of a currency. If they have deluded themselves about the future state of the market, they will pay dearly for their mistake. The "bears" lose if they have underestimated the demand for a currency on the foreign exchange market, and the rate of exchange for that currency instead goes up. As was explained above, such an increase in demand must occur if there exists a divergence between the purchasing power of the crown with respect to goods in Austria and its value relative to a foreign currency.

It is also incorrect to try to explain the foreign exchange rate on the basis of the balance of payments rather than on the currency's purchasing power. This view distinguishes between the devaluation of money on the foreign exchange and its declining value in terms of its domestic purchasing power. Between the two phenomena there supposedly exists only a distant or—as many maintain—no connection at all.

It is argued that a currency's foreign exchange rate is a result of the current state of a country's balance of payments. If the amount of payments to be made abroad rises without a corresponding increase in payments to be received from abroad, or if the level of payments from abroad decreases without an accompanying reduction in the payments to be made abroad, then the rates of exchange for foreign currency must rise.

The fundamental error with this theory is that it completely forgets that the amount of imports and exports depends, first of all, on prices. People do not import or export on the basis of a whim or from any "pleasure" just from doing business. They do so in order to make money from differences between prices, and that importing or exporting will continue until those price differentials have disappeared.

This theory overlooks the significance of prices in the international movement of goods. It incorrectly looks at the act of paying for goods rather than seeing the reason for the act of exchange. This is the consequence of that pseudocurrency doctrine which insists on looking at money only as a means of payment, and not as a general medium of exchange, a doctrine that has borne the most disastrous fruits for economic science, as well as for economic policy.

The buyer does not start worrying about how he will obtain the foreign currency to cover the cost of his transactions only when the payment comes due. A buyer who acts in this way will not be able to continue in business for very long. In his calculations, the buyer gives very careful consideration to currency relationships since he must always keep his eye on his selling price; whether he takes advantage of methods for insuring against changes in foreign exchange rates or bears the risk himself, he always keeps in mind expected fluctuations in the foreign exchange rate. The same thing applies also, mutatis mutandis, for those involved in the international travel and freight business.

For five years, government policy with respect to currency devaluation has been constructed on incorrect ideas concerning its cause. It is no wonder that this policy has completely failed. Domestic price controls have had no success. In spite of all the official countermeasures, the prices of all goods and services have been continuously rising. Likewise, the attempts to stabilize the rates of foreign exchange by preventing foreign currency dealings and to improve the balance of payments by limiting imports have led nowhere.

The official foreign currency regulations are not only useless; they are, in fact, directly harmful. For example, exporters are burdened with the obligation to sell their foreign exchange earnings to the central currency office at a price set below the day's actual rate of exchange (for the central currency office's rates of exchange always lag behind the actual rate). The currency office then sells that foreign currency to importers, again below the day's actual exchange rate, so they can pay for those imports that the government wishes to promote.

The obligation imposed upon the exporters [to sell export earnings to the central currency office] hinders the exporting of goods; it works exactly like an export duty. Its effect is to reduce the total amount of exports and thereby to reduce the amount of foreign currency that is available to pay for imports. No other foreign exchange policy is so clearly harmful as this one. This interference with exports also interferes with the importing of the goods that the government wishes to promote. The importer, of course, appears to enjoy an apparent advantage because foreign currency is sold to him more cheaply than at the actual rate of exchange. But the total amount of foreign currency at his disposal to cover all import transactions is less by the corresponding amount by which exports have been reduced, and thus the total value of all imports is less than it might have been.

No less harmful is the requirement to sell exported goods only in exchange for foreign currency. That our exporters are forced to refuse

payment in Austrian crowns from foreign buyers has a severely negative effect on the standing of our currency on the foreign exchange
market. What are foreigners to think about a currency that the citizens
of the country in which that currency circulates are not allowed to accept payment in by order of their own government?

The decline in the value of our currency cannot be stopped by
monetary regulations. When the central currency office was set up,
the Swiss franc in Zurich stood at 152 crowns; today it stands at 1,215
crowns! We must finally realize that the rise in the prices of goods and
in the rate of foreign exchange for the crown will come to a halt only
if the state renounces any further use of the monetary printing press
by reestablishing balance in the national budget. The problem of putting the national budget in order is the most important problem in our
economy. It is high time that it be solved. Otherwise, one day our currency will reach the point that the French assignats came to, namely, a
monetary value of absolute zero.[4] For our urban population that would
be a catastrophe the extent of which one can hardly imagine.

4. [The assignats were the paper money issued by the Revolutionary government in France
between March 1790 and December 1795, during which time they generated an extremely destructive inflation, resulting in the imposition of wage and price controls that disrupted the
French economy even more. See Richard M. Ebeling, "Inflation and Controls in Revolutionary
France: The Political Economy of the French Revolution," in Stephen J. Tonsor, ed., *Reflec-
tions on the French Revolution* (Washington, D.C.: Regnery Gateway, 1990), pp. 138–56; also
Richard M. Ebeling, "The Great French Inflation," *The Freeman: Ideas on Liberty* (July/August
2007), pp. 2–3.—Ed.]

CHAPTER 15

For the Reintroduction of Normal Stock Market Practices in Foreign Exchange Dealings[1]

Increasingly, goods are offered for sale with the stipulation that payments will be accepted only in foreign currency. Already a significant part of wholesale business and real estate transactions are being facilitated through the use of foreign money. The crown is starting to lose its standing even in retail business. It is clear what it would mean if this process were not halted as soon as possible. The decrees that our official economic policy makers love to implement have clearly achieved nothing. They have learned nothing other than to introduce prohibitions and commands.

Anyone nowadays purchasing either finished or unfinished goods from abroad on credit—even short-term credit—in order to sell them on the domestic market, runs a high risk of suffering a loss and a low probability of making a profit due to uncertainties on the foreign exchange market. Since 1914 many companies have sold goods for crowns that they bought with credit from abroad at the rate of foreign exchange that was then prevailing on the market. Great losses have been suffered on these transactions due to the progressive devaluation of our money.[2] Today such experiences have made importers more cautious and no longer willing to engage in similar transactions. Of course, during the war the state persistently speculated in crowns, *à la hausse*,[3] buying on

---

1. [This article originally appeared in German in the *Neue Freie Presse*, no. 19872 (December 23, 1919).—Ed.]

2. [In January 1919, one dollar could purchase 16.1 crowns. In December 1919, when Mises wrote this article, one dollar traded for 31 crowns, for a 48 percent drop in the exchange value of the crown in one year. By May 1923, when the Austrian inflation had finally come to an end, one dollar bought 70,800 crowns on the Vienna foreign exchange market.—Ed.]

3. ["On a rise," i.e., on the expectation of an increase in the price.—Ed.]

credit foodstuffs and other goods from abroad and then selling them at home for crowns. It lost enormous sums at the time, and it still continues with the same policy today.

It is not the case that every merchant and industrialist speculates in attractive but risky foreign currency dealings. The businessman concerned with trade or manufacturing rightly fears that currency fluctuations will result in his losing everything his business brings him, and even more. But if he wishes to eliminate the unfavorable repercussions on his business enterprise due to foreign currency fluctuations, he has no choice other than to sell for foreign currency at home the goods he obtained from abroad, rather than accept payment in the domestic currency. The solution that is available in other countries with fluctuating foreign exchange rates is to "find cover" on the futures market. But this is not possible in Vienna because trading in foreign currency and foreign exchange has been abolished.

The only way to eliminate the dangers from exchange rate fluctuations caused by the existing regulations is to decontrol the trade in foreign exchange. The Foreign Exchange Agency[4] must be suspended, and a real and proper stock market for futures transactions, as well as cash transactions in foreign currency and foreign exchange, must be reintroduced. It has been repeatedly and convincingly demonstrated in the court of public opinion that the foreign-currency policy that we have been following for years is misguided, and that restrictions on foreign-exchange transactions only produce outcomes the opposite of what was intended. If they are, nevertheless, maintained with great stubbornness, this can be solely attributed to the fact that they harmoniously fit into our whole current system of economic policies; it is feared that their elimination would constitute the first step toward dismantling the wartime and transitional economy leading to socialism.[5]

4. [In the face of large outflows of gold and foreign exchange from the Austrian central bank during the First World War, the Austrian government established a Foreign Exchange Agency on February 22, 1916. All foreign exchange received by exporters was to be sold to the central bank at the official rate of exchange. All importers requiring foreign exchange for purchase of goods from abroad were to receive permission and an allotment of foreign currencies from the Foreign Exchange Agency at the fixed rate of exchange. The foreign exchange control remained in place following the end of the war in November 1918, and was not officially lifted until November 1920, about a year after this article by Mises was published.—Ed.]

5. [At the time this article was written, a coalition government made up of the Social Democratic Party and the Christian Social Party governed Austria. They instituted a variety of "social" programs, including a large unemployment and welfare payment system, as well as price controls on food supplies that were supplemented with government rationing and subsidies for

The introduction of a futures market in foreign exchange, however, is also particularly important for a second reason. A country like German-Austria[6] that must import the greater part of its required supply of foodstuffs and raw materials can economically survive only if it exports industrial products. Right now, however, all those countries that can be considered as markets for our exports have currencies that are fluctuating in value. The entrepreneur who buys raw materials and semifabricated products from abroad in order to then sell his finished product abroad must be able to "protect" himself in terms of the foreign exchange in which he makes purchases as well as in the foreign exchange in which he makes sales.

Vienna has become an important trading center since the collapse of the old Austro-Hungarian state. All the governmental chicaneries have not been able to completely prevent this development. The principal competitors of Vienna—Budapest, Trieste, Lemberg, and all the formerly Russian cities—have been paralyzed by present conditions;[7] and, on the other hand, there is a need, more than ever before, for an intermediary in the trade between the newly created national states.[8] Today Vienna is really the place where East and West meet in order to exchange their goods; Vienna's foreign currency and foreign exchange business is one of the most important in Europe.

Vienna suffers, however, under incomprehensible governmental burdens; due to these government restrictions, the business of dealing in foreign currency and foreign exchange has been taken out of the

---

food purchases. These programs were increasingly funded through monetary expansion that was causing the depreciation of the crown and explosion in rising prices.—Ed.]

6. [With the dissolution of the Austro-Hungarian Empire in November 1918, the part that became the new Austrian Republic was often referred to as "German-Austria," in anticipation that the predominantly German-speaking area of the former empire would be politically united with the new German Republic in the aftermath of the First World War.—Ed.]

7. [Political chaos reigned in many parts of Central and Eastern Europe in the years after the First World War. When Mises wrote this article, Hungary was in the grip of a brutal counter-revolutionary "White Terror" in the wake of a "Red Terror" during a short-lived Soviet-type dictatorship in Budapest from March to August 1919. Russia and cities such as Lemberg (in the former Austro-Hungarian province of Galicia) were caught up in the Russian Civil War and later a war between Soviet Russia and Poland. The former Austrian port of Trieste on the Adriatic Sea was the center of a violent dispute between Italy and the newly constituted Yugoslavia.—Ed.]

8. [Following the dissolution of Austria-Hungary, the various parts of the former Habsburg Empire splintered into a much smaller Austrian Republic, an independent Hungary, an enlarged Romania, a new Czechoslovakia, a reconstituted Poland, a Serb-dominated Yugoslavia, and a slightly bigger Italy.—Ed.]

hands of the banks and shifted into those of a more dubious character.[9] If the foreign exchange market were decontrolled it would again be taken up by the banks and on the stock market under the supervision of the public, and it would develop into an important factor for our mercantile and industrial organizations.

It will be argued against this suggestion that some other countries also pursue a policy similar to our own. Hardly anyone will dare to maintain that they have had any greater success with it than have we. The Czechoslovakians, if they continue on this path, will run their currency into the ground just exactly as we have done. Today, however, we are the nearest to the complete devaluation of our money, to the null-point of the currency's value.[10] Hence, we must also be the first to seize measures to avoid the catastrophe.

Of course, it goes without saying that all measures will clearly be of no avail so long as the inflation continues, so long as new notes continue to be pumped into circulation.

9. [Foreign exchange and foreign currency dealings were increasingly being handled by a huge and pervasive black market.—Ed.]

10. [Between March and December 1919, the paper money supply of crowns had increased from 831.6 *million* to 12.1 *billion*. By 1923, it had grown to 7.1 *trillion*. A cost-of-living index, excluding housing (with July 1914 = 1), stood at 28.37 in January 1919, and had risen to 49.22 by January 1920. By January 1923 it had exploded to 11,836.—Ed.]

CHAPTER 16

On Carl Menger's Eightieth Birthday[1]

Scientific development does not take place in a simultaneous and un-interrupted ascent; periods of great achievement are followed by periods of intellectual exhaustion; the masters are followed by the imitators, until men of genius again bring forth a new flowering. Around the middle of the nineteenth century economics had unquestionably reached a point of stagnation. The Classical system was felt to be unsatisfactory, but there was no way to go beyond it. In order to formulate the problems that needed to be solved there was a need for men who were not inferior to David Ricardo.[2] Even John Stuart Mill, the most original of the economists of that time, was not the man for this task.[3]

The Frenchman Jules Dupuit[4] and the Prussian assessor Hermann Gossen[5] tried to follow the path that had to be traveled. Without be-

1. [This article originally appeared in German in the *Neues Wiener Tagblatt*, no. 52 (February 22, 1920).—Ed.]

2. [David Ricardo (1772–1823) was one of the fountainheads of British Classical economics in the first half of the nineteenth century. His *Principles of Political Economy and Taxation* (1817) set the tone and direction for much of Classical economics for the next half century.—Ed.]

3. [John Stuart Mill (1806–73) was one of the leading members among the British Classical economists, with his most important work being *Principles of Political Economy, with Applications to Social Philosophy* (1848). In this work, Mill had argued that there was nothing further to develop in the essentials of the theory of value, based on the idea that some measure of the quantity of labor devoted to the production of goods determined relative prices in the market.—Ed.]

4. [Jules Dupuit (1804–66) first presented an exposition of the concept of diminishing marginal utility in an 1844 article on optimum pricing for a toll bridge. From a curve for the diminishing marginal utility for the consumption of a good, he derived the explanation for a downward-sloping demand curve.—Ed.]

5. [Hermann Heinrich Gossen (1810–58) developed a systematic theory of economic relationships based on the concept of marginal utility in his 1854 work *The Law of Economic Relations, and the Rule of Human Action Derived Therefrom*. The book was totally ignored following its publication until rediscovered by William Stanley Jevons in the 1870s after the publication of his own version of the marginalist concept. Gossen worked in the Prussian civil service but was constantly criticized by superiors for living a life of drinking, gambling, and "bad company."—Ed.]

ing aware of these earlier writings (which had been forgotten), Carl Menger in Austria,[6] Jevons in England,[7] and Leon Walras in Switzerland[8] each independently came forward around 1871. Their works show a remarkable agreement in all of the fundamentals.

Most exciting, however, is the grounding of the general theory of value on the basic idea of the subjective value of goods, as worked out by Menger. Menger's slim volume *Grundsätze der Volkswirtshaftslehre* completely revolutionized economic science.[9] Everything that has been achieved since then is built upon Menger's works. In Austria, marginal utility theory found its most important representatives, besides Menger, in the contributions of Friedrich von Wieser[10] and Eugen von Böhm-Bawerk (who departed from us at much too early an age).[11] It

6. [Carl Menger (1840–1921) was the founder of the Austrian School of economics. In later life he said that he came to the theory of marginal utility (though in his own exposition in 1871 he explained the concept without giving it a name) while he was working for the Austrian Ministry of Prices, and concluded that the labor theory of value could not successfully explain the formation of prices on the market.—Ed.]

7. [William Stanley Jevons (1835–83) developed the theory of marginal utility in his 1871 volume *The Theory of Political Economy*, building on the utilitarian conception that human action is guided by the pursuit of "pleasure" and the avoidance of "pain."—Ed.]

8. See Chapter 5, "The Fourth Issuing Right of the Austro-Hungarian Bank," footnote 8.

9. [Carl Menger, *Principles of Economics* (New York: New York University Press, [1871] 1981). The *Principles* was meant to be the first of four volumes on most of the basic themes in economic theory and policy. In the introduction to the German-language 1923 reprint of his father's *Principles*, Karl Menger Jr. described the unpublished remaining three volumes thus: vol. 2: Interest, Wages, Rent, Income, Credit, and Paper Money; vol. 3: The Theory of Production and Commerce; the Technological Requirements for Production; the Economic Conditions for Production; Commerce: The Theory of the Techniques of Commerce, Speculation, Arbitrage; Retail Trade; and vol. 4: Critique of the Contemporary Economy and Proposals for Social Reform.—Ed.]

10. [Friedrich von Wieser (1851–1926) was one of the leading members of the Austrian School before and immediately after the First World War. His major contributions were to the theory of marginal utility, the concept of opportunity cost, and the theory of imputation, i.e., the determination of the value of the factors of production. His most widely read works on these themes were *Natural Value* (1889) and *Social Economics* (1914), the latter being the only systematic treatise on economic theory by a member of the Austrian School before the First World War.—Ed.]

11. [Eugen von Böhm-Bawerk (1851–1914) was one of the leading members of the Austrian School before the First World War. His major contributions were to the theory of capital and interest, as well as the general theory of value, price, and cost. He developed these themes in *Capital and Interest: A History and Critique of Interest Theories* (1884) and *The Positive Theory of Capital* (1889). He also applied his "Austrian" theory of value and interest to challenge Karl Marx's labor theory of value and theory of exploitation in his famous 1896 monograph *Karl Marx and the Close of His System*. For a short appreciation of Böhm-Bawerk and his contributions to economics, see Ludwig von Mises, "Eugen von Böhm-Bawerk: In Memory of the Tenth Anniversary of His Death," (1924) in *Selected Writings of Ludwig von Mises*, vol. 2 (Indianapolis: Liberty Fund, 2002), pp. 329–32.—Ed.]

is customary to unite these three under the designation "the Austrian School." Under this name they gained a worldwide reputation. In Germany they were able to find some minimal recognition; their success was incomparably greater in England, Italy, the Netherlands, and the Scandinavian countries. Modern American economics is based on the works of the "Austrian School."[12]

In 1883 Menger published his *Untersuchungen über die Methode der Socialwissenschaften und der Politischen Oekonomie insbesondere.*[13] With this book, which was primarily intended as a critique of the relativism and historicism[14] then reigning in Germany, he developed new approaches to the logic and epistemology of the social sciences. At first this, too, was little noticed; more than twenty years passed before its importance was fully recognized. Recent methodological works are definitely under the influence of this book.

Menger was not a prolific writer. In terms of quantity his publications take up only a little space. Moreover, he seldom took up his pen to contribute to the clarification of contemporary economic problems. Of the questions of the day, the currency problem attracted him most.

12. [See Ludwig von Mises, "The Historical Setting of the Austrian School of Economics," (1969) reprinted in Bettina Bien Greaves, ed., *Austrian Economics: An Anthology* (Irvington-on-Hudson, N.Y.: Foundation for Economic Education, 1996), pp. 53–76.—Ed.]

13. [Carl Menger, *Investigations into the Method of the Social Sciences with Special Reference to Economics* (New York: New York University Press, [1883] 1985). This work ignited what became known as the *Methodenstreit*, or "struggle over methods," between members of the Austrian School and the German Historical School. It was rudely reviewed by Gustav von Schmoller, one of the leading figures of the Historical School, to which Menger replied in a short book, *Die Irrthümer des Historismus in der deutschen Nationalökonomie* [The Errors of the German Historical School] (1884), written in the form of sixteen letters to a friend. Menger scathingly criticized Schmoller's antitheoretical approach to economic analysis, saying that it "consists of a primordial ooze of historico-statistical material."—Ed.]

14. [Historicism was a German reaction to the Enlightenment after the French Revolution and the Napoleonic wars, which refused to *wring* general rules from reason and ridiculed the idea of universal theoretical systems. Historicists insisted on observing the "unique" in its endless historical variations, arguing that economic behavior and thus economic laws were completely dependent upon their particular historical, social, and institutional context. Rooted in Hegelian philosophy and the romantic nationalist critiques of abstract theory by Friedrich List and Adam Müller, historicism relied on empirical and inductive reasoning. It offered no principles to guide or restrain political action and was hostile to both the tradition of natural law and utilitarianism. The Younger Historical School under Gustav Schmoller claimed that economics was inherently a normative discipline and thus should be engaged in forging tools for use by policy makers and businessmen. At the end of the nineteenth century historicists, in the form of the German Historical School, had a virtual monopoly over German academia, with very few members of the Austrian School able to obtain academic positions at German universities.—Ed.]

His little treatise about the Austrian currency problem[15] and his exposi-
tions at the Currency Inquiry of 1892 decisively influenced the reform
of the Austrian monetary system. He also repeatedly dealt with the
fundamental aspects of the theory of money, especially in his classic
contribution to the *Handwörterbuch der Staatswissenschaften.*[16]

As already mentioned, Menger's works were not appreciated for a
long time; only later were they fully appreciated, as their reputation
grew from year to year. Without exaggeration, it can be said today that
the Austrian School of economics occupies a permanent place in the
history of the social sciences. Carl Menger can look back on his life's
work with pride and satisfaction.[17] May it yet be granted to him to bring
to completion the great works with which he is still occupied.

15. [Carl Menger, *Beiträge zur Wahrungsfrage* [Contributions to the Currency Question], (1892)
reprinted in *The Collected Works of Carl Menger*, vol. 4 (London: London School of Economics
and Political Science, 1936).—Ed.]
16. [Carl Menger, "Money," (1892) in Michael Latzer and Stefan W. Schmitz, eds., *Carl
Menger and the Evolution of Payments Systems: From Barter to Electronic Money* (Northhamp-
ton, Mass.: Edward Elgar, 2002), pp. 25–107. See also Carl Menger, "On the Origin of Money,"
(1892) reprinted in Richard M. Ebeling, ed., *Austrian Economics: A Reader* (Hillsdale, Mich.:
Hillsdale College Press, 1991), pp. 483–504.—Ed.]
17. [See also F. A. Hayek, "Carl Menger (1840–1921)," in Peter G. Klein, ed., *The Collected
Works of F. A. Hayek*, vol. 4, *The Fortunes of Liberalism: Essays on Austrian Economics and the
Ideal of Freedom* (Chicago: University of Chicago Press, 1992), pp. 61–107.—Ed.]

CHAPTER 17

How Can Austria Be Saved?

An Economic Policy Program for Austria[1]

In spite of the wretched condition in which we find ourselves I consider our situation not to be an unfavorable one. Vienna and Austria would have a positive future ahead of them if we didn't do everything to worsen our own situation. What is occurring is practically the opposite of what needs to be done. It is no wonder, therefore, that things are going badly for us. We are living today, and have been living for years, by devouring what several previous decades of freer economic policy had produced.

What makes me optimistic is the fact that, on the whole, in comparison to the prewar period, the raw materials and foodstuffs that we import from abroad have risen less in world-market price than the manufactured goods that we would be in a position to produce for export, and less than the commercial profits which Viennese business can generate. Indeed, our earnings from the sale of finished goods could be greater than they were in that earlier period.

The objective prerequisites for a flowering of Austria are given; unfortunately the subjective ones are not. Our fellow citizens have not grasped the realities of the moment and instead they chase after illusionary ideas. But, eventually, reasonableness must prevail.

Just a few days ago a politician asked me to draw up an economic policy program in a few short sentences. Here it is:

1. The progressive devaluation of the crown, which manifests itself in a rise in both the foreign exchange rate and in prices and wages, is a consequence of banknote inflation. *It can be brought to a standstill only* if we succeed in eliminating the government's budget deficit.

---

1. [This article originally appeared in German in *Die Börse* (February 17, 1921).—Ed.]

2. The federal, provincial, and municipal budget deficits principally all spring from the same two sources: the inefficient management of public enterprises and of the food subsidy scheme. The goal should be to transfer the public enterprises into the hands of private businessmen and to dismantle the food subsidies. *At the present time the very opposite is happening.* The public enterprises are being expanded through nationalization; and the food subsidy scheme is being expanded, as represented by the fact that the difference between the buying price and the selling price for foodstuffs is being allowed to grow.[2]

3. If things continue to be managed in this way, *then inevitably the time will come when the currency will collapse,* that is, the crown will become completely worthless. Then there will be a frightful catastrophe. Suddenly the country will no longer be in a position to maintain these public enterprises or to sustain the food subsidies. If dismantling both of these occurs in time, then it will be possible to avoid such a collapse, and it will be possible to reduce the difficulties in making the transition to a normal economy.

4. *The attempt must be made to stabilize the value of the currency with the establishment of a fixed rate of exchange between the crown and either gold or the dollar.* The new parity should be set at a level which corresponds to the domestic purchasing power of the crown. To go beyond this parity would be injurious to the economy; any further rise in the foreign exchange value of the currency beyond this point would only hamper exports and stimulate imports, with severely harmful consequences, that is, unemployment. The catchphrase of *a fall in prices* is absurd. Those who are today most loudly demanding a reduction in prices would be hardest hit by such a fall in prices. *We do not need decreasing prices, but incomes that are increasing.* That, however, can only be achieved by a rise in industrial and business activity.

5. The peace treaty requires that *the banknotes in circulation must*

---

2. [In the immediate postwar period, the new Austrian government instituted a huge food subsidy program at artificially low prices and rationing of food through a coupon system to urban, and especially Vienna, residents. When farmers in the rural areas refused to sell their food supplies to the central government in Vienna at those below-market fixed prices, the government attempted to confiscate those supplies. This resulted in the provincial governments in the new, smaller Austria setting up customs barriers and visa requirements to enter or exit their respective jurisdictions to conserve the food supplies in their own districts. The central government then resorted to purchasing foreign food supplies with borrowed money, thereby expanding Austria's foreign debt. By the time that Mises wrote this article in 1921, half the Austrian government's budget deficit was caused by the food subsidies.—Ed.]

be replaced with a new monetary unit within the foreseeable future. It would be unwise to associate this change in media of exchange with any activities associated with the slogans "stamping"[3] and "compulsory loans."[4] The danger exists that the great mass of hoarded banknotes will be shaken loose from people's pockets and will flow into the market for goods, where they would necessarily drive up prices. Banknotes that are hoarded are not harmful to the general public. Hoarded banknotes do not affect prices. He who hoards banknotes grants the state an interest-free loan, so to speak.

6. *Currency trading is to be decontrolled.* Foreign trade has an incomparably greater importance for a small country [like Austria] than for a large one. Businesses should have the chance to free themselves from some of the speculative risks that are connected with foreign trade when there are large fluctuations in the values of currencies. A futures market in currencies and foreign exchange must be permitted on the Viennese stock exchange.

7. *All import prohibitions are to be lifted.* Such prohibitions are worthless for purposes of monetary policy. Moreover, they stimulate retaliatory measures by foreign countries, which only succeed in seriously hampering our exports and as a consequence paralyze our industry.

8. *All impediments to exportation and transit are to be removed.*

9. Austria can cover its need for raw materials and foodstuffs only by importing them. In order to pay for imports it must export finished products, on the basis of which businesses may earn profits. *Austria needs free trade.*

10. Government oversight of industrial production of manufactured goods and the use of raw materials is to be *ended.*

11. *The government management of food supplies is to be abolished.*

---

3. ["Stamping" refers to the fact that with the disintegration of the Austro-Hungarian Empire after November 1918, the "successor states" of Czechoslovakia, Yugoslavia, Hungary, and the new Austria began to "stamp" Austro-Hungarian Bank notes with a national mark, as a prelude to converting those quantities of the old empire currency in their respective territories into new national currencies.—Ed.]

4. ["Compulsory loan" refers to the proposal for a "capital levy," which would be a huge property tax on all real assets and productive enterprises, as a means of transferring a large portion of the private wealth of the society to the government as a method for the government to pay off its accumulated debt. The tax on capital would be set so high that taxpayers would be required either to liquidate their wealth or to borrow against their property to raise the amount owed under the capital levy. See John V. Van Sickle, "The Capital Levy," in *Direct Taxation in Austria* (Cambridge: Harvard University Press, 1931), pp. 136–71.—Ed.]

For the indigent who are incapable of working, government financial support is to be introduced. This would cost incomparably less.

12. *All obstacles to traffic within the Austrian federation are to be removed.* If the provinces should resist, then nothing stands in the way of Vienna going first with lifting all entry and residency restrictions for citizens and foreigners. A city based on commerce and trade should not impede entry and the sojourning of visitors in any way.[5]

13. *The prohibition against the importing and exporting of crowns from the country should be ended.* It is only an illusion that such prohibitions succeed in raising the foreign exchange value of the crown. In reality it has depressed the crown's exchange rate since *foreign speculators no longer want to have anything to do with the crown.* Besides, it does not matter if rather large amounts of crowns are purchased abroad for speculative purposes. Every request for crowns, even one for speculation, drives the exchange rate up.

14. *The Central Foreign Exchange Office*, the Central Office for Import, Export, and Transfers, and all offices that do not appear necessary for the carrying out of the above principles *are to be abolished.* The officials who are relieved of their duties are to be put on leave and, within a foreseeable time, dismissed. They will easily find a job in a thriving market.

15. It is impossible to attract foreign capital into the country as long as the illusionary profits arising from devaluation of the currency are subject to taxation. Stabilizing the value of the currency will provide the necessary remedy. In order not to waste time, tax breaks should be granted for new industrial plants (and for the extension of water power) based on surpluses on the balance sheet and of income as specified in the second and fourth chapters of the personal tax code; these calculations should be made in terms of dollar values.

I scarcely believe that there is a party in the country today that would be inclined to carry out this program. Nevertheless, I hope that that which is sensible and necessary will prevail.

5. [See Ludwig von Mises, "Vienna's Political Relationship with the Provinces in Light of Economics," (1919) in Richard M. Ebeling, ed., *Selected Writings of Ludwig von Mises*, vol. 2, *Between the Two World Wars: Monetary Disorder, Interventionism, Socialism, and the Great Depression* (Indianapolis: Liberty Fund, 2002), pp. 97–118.—Ed.]

CHAPTER 18

The Claims of Note Holders upon Liquidation of the Bank[1]

The notes issued by the Austro-Hungarian Bank from the beginning of the war were only pro forma banknotes; in reality, they were government notes. In order to avoid the unfavorable impression that issuing government notes would have made on the general public, the regime chose not to finance the war with its own notes, as it had done in 1866;[2] instead, it inserted the Austro-Hungarian Bank as an intermediary between the issue of notes and the treasury. The notes made available by the Austro-Hungarian Bank to finance government expenditures were backed by nothing more than the various state securities that were the basis upon which the Bank directly and indirectly issued credit to the state.[3]

The only promise that the holders of these notes had by this procedure was that the state would redeem those securities by withdrawing from circulation a quantity of banknotes representing the equivalent of the value of the loans that had been granted to the state.

That the Bank was inserted as an intermediary into this process more

1. [This article originally appeared in German in two parts in *Neue Freie Presse* (February 25 and 26, 1921).—Ed.]
2. [This refers to the Austro-Prussian War of 1866, also known as the Seven Weeks War, between Prussia on the one side and Austria, Bavaria, Hanover, and a number of other smaller German states on the other. The Prussian victory resulted in Austria being excluded from the German Confederation that was then dominated by Prussia. The Austrian government financed most of its war expenditures through a huge monetary expansion through the issue of government notes. The supply of paper money was increased from 80 million florins in circulation before the war to 300 million at its end.—Ed.]
3. [From July 1914 to October 1918, the Austro-Hungarian money supply increased by 977 percent, from 3.4 billion crowns in circulation at the start of the First World War to 33.5 billion crowns at the end.—Ed.]

for purposes of outward appearances than for any legitimate reasons was shown by the regulations that aimed at restricting the Bank's profits from the issuance of these additional banknotes; instead, the proceeds were funneled back into the government treasury. A special tax was imposed on the Austro-Hungarian Bank on December 30, 1917, on top of those peacetime regulations that assured the state a large share of the proceeds from the Bank's business.

It is clear, therefore, that the holders of the notes issued by the Austro-Hungarian Bank can make no claim against the Bank other than that the legal status of the notes may not be set aside or that the holders of these notes are offered the possibility of converting their notes into a new legal form of payment. To view the holders of the notes as "creditors" of the Bank who can claim a specific amount of metallic money at a fixed rate of exchange would involve a complete misunderstanding of how the current monetary policy developed.

It is true that it is written on the notes of the Austro-Hungarian Bank that the Bank is obliged to pay the bearer in legal metallic money. This wording has been on the notes in use in Austria-Hungary for decades, in spite of the fact that the Bank was exempt from redeeming its notes in metal. It was retained on the new notes issued after August 1, 1914, because of the desire not to change the customary appearance of the bills. Every note holder knew, however, that this promise had no real meaning. It is clear that no one would have thought that any note represented a claim to a specific amount of the gold supply held by the Bank.

If the note holders were to be given something more than what is due them by exchanging their existing notes at their current purchasing power for a new legal means of payment, they would be receiving something that increased the value of those notes above their current purchasing power. For the individual note holder who had acquired them without the expectation of receiving such an extra sum, this would mean nothing less than receiving an unanticipated gift.

There is no doubt, of course, that holders of the notes of the Austro-Hungarian Bank were most severely harmed by the monetary policy of the last few years. With the value of those notes continuously falling during this period, note holders traded them away at a lower purchasing power than when they had acquired them. But this injustice inflicted on note holders over the years cannot be rectified now by giving them an "extra bonus." Those who hold banknotes in their hands today are not the same people who had been harmed over the years by the constant gradual decline in the value of those notes.

On the contrary, today the banknotes are mainly in the hands of those who constantly gained from the process of currency devaluation, and therefore were in a position to increase their wealth (if not absolutely, then at least comparatively) during this time of general economic decline. Moreover, we must not forget that the damage that currency devaluation inflicted on people was not limited to their ownership of banknotes; besides the note holders, also harmed were those who had claims to lawful money and were therefore hurt by the decline in the rate of foreign exchange. These latter damages were far greater in extent than those that arose from the direct possession of banknotes, for these monetary claims play a far greater role in the modern economy than treasury securities.

Those who were harmed in this way by devaluation would not profit at all by any belated indemnification of present-day holders of banknotes.

Just as little could such a measure benefit those whose losses arose from the fact that, during the gradual overall decline in the purchasing power of the currency, the prices of the goods and services that they sold rose more slowly than the market prices of the goods and services that they found it necessary to buy. For these sectors (for example, public employees who have suffered because their income has not risen at the same speed as prices have increased) there would be no compensation if the supply of notes which they have in their hands were to increase right now.

The entire note-issuing activity of the Bank falls completely outside the framework of the other business that it conducted and represents an independent branch, which was only externally connected with its other activities. Those who accepted the notes of the Austro-Hungarian Bank asked only whether the Bank was more or less sound. They were fully aware that the gold supply of the Austro-Hungarian Bank covered only a vanishingly small part of the notes issued; they nevertheless accepted the notes because they regarded them as the currency in circulation, not because they cherished expectations regarding the assets of the Bank.

From the perspective of the preceding remarks, one can, in general, approve of points 1 to 7, 8, and 11 of Article 206 of the International

Treaty of Saint-Germain[4] concerning the liquidation of the Austro-Hungarian Bank. The governments of the successor states are required to convert the notes of the Austro-Hungarian Bank that are circulating in their territories into their own currency. The holders of those banknotes issued after October 27, 1918, are granted no other right than a claim to the debenture bonds on deposit with the Bank for the covering of those notes. This corresponds in its practical effects with the principles that were stated above, even if not the precise wording.

One should now expect that the same principles also apply to those banknotes that were in circulation before October 27, 1918. The holders of these notes received absolutely all to which they could make a claim through their conversion into the money of the country in which their notes were in circulation, in accordance with the regulation under point 4. The next step regarding these notes now must be that they are transferred to the Austro-Hungarian Bank by the successor government that took them out of circulation and replaced them in circulation with its own legal currency. Now, as an equivalent of transfer, the securities of the former Austro-Hungarian government that had been left with the Bank as cover for the banknotes that had been issued should be withdrawn and destroyed or refunded. The peace treaty provides for that too in point 4, even though it gives it a different name.

Even if in this way the debt of the former Austro-Hungarian state that arose from the issuing of notes is cancelled, there would still need to be an internal reckoning up among the successor states. This would involve evening out the difference between the amount of the securities represented by the delivery of the notes and the shares of the national debt of the former Austro-Hungarian state they would have to assume on the basis of agreement among each other.[5]

4. [The Treaty of Saint-Germain (September 10, 1919) formally ended the war between Austria-Hungary and the Allied Powers. It mandated the dismemberment of the Austro-Hungarian Empire into the separate states of the Republic of Austria, Hungary, and Czechoslovakia, with other portions of the empire being integrated into a reborn Poland, an enlarged Romania and Italy, and a newly created Yugoslavia, who were referred to as the "successor states." Article 206, points 1–5 of the Treaty of Saint-Gemain referred to the procedures by which the former banknotes of the Austro-Hungarian Bank would be converted into the banknotes of the respective successor states; points 6–8 and 11 concerned the liquidation of the Austro-Hungarian Bank and the disposition of all claims against the Bank and its assets.—Ed.]

5. [In 1919–21, Ludwig von Mises was in charge of the section of the Austrian Reparations Commission for the League of Nations concerned with the settling of the outstanding prewar debt of the Austro-Hungarian Empire. The commission's task was to agree upon the rules under which each of the successor states would be responsible for a portion of the debt of the former empire.

But no further rights would be granted to the holders of those bank-notes. Their claims against the Bank, as well as against the state that had taken those notes out of their hands and exchanged them for its own new currency, would be completely liquidated.

However, in the peace treaty, Article 206, point 9[6] has a provision that goes beyond this and grants to the note holders a special claim against the total assets of the Bank—"des droits égaux sur tout l'actif de la banque" [equal rights on all the assets of the Bank]; and, even though it is not said, the governments that have taken the notes out of circulation and then present them to the Reparations Commission appear as actual note holders. The character of the rights granted to the note holders in the form of an extra bonus becomes even clearer in that it is declared that the securities presented and deposited by the former and present governments of Austria and Hungary for the covering of various notes issued are not to be looked upon as components of those assets.

It is clear that the same provision that was intended under point 9 also could have been given to the holders of notes issued up to October 27, 1918; that is, an equal right to the entire assets of the Bank, in addition to a right to a part of the corresponding securities deposited for the coverage of the note issue.

How little the right that is granted under point 9 can be reconciled with the nature of the original claims of the note holders is clearly understood from the character of the notes as currency in circulation. It would have been impossible to award ownership to individual note holders. Any attempt to carry this out could only be done by conceding that same right to the successor state that presented the notes to the Bank. In that form, it turns out to be a sort of "war reparation" that is granted to the successor states—at the expense of the other creditors and the stockholders of the Austro-Hungarian Bank.

But even in this form the assertion of this claim by the note holders

---

See Ludwig von Mises, "The Currency Problem Prior to the Peace Conference," (1919) in Richard M. Ebeling, ed., *Selected Writings of Ludwig von Mises*, vol. 2, *Between the Two World Wars: Monetary Disorder, Interventionism, Socialism, and the Great Depression* (Indianapolis: Liberty Fund, 2002), pp. 30–46.—Ed.]

6. [Article 206, point 9 of the Treaty of Saint-Germain says, "The currency notes issued by the bank on or prior to 27 October 1918, in so far as they are entitled to rank at all in conformity with this Article, shall all rank equally as claims against all the assets of the bank, other than the Austrian and Hungarian Government securities deposited as security for the various note issues."—Ed.]

is extraordinarily problematic. For the claim they can make against the Bank arising from possession of the notes is, again, nothing more than payment in the form of legal currency. This demand, however, already has been satisfied by the exchange of those notes for the new notes that circulate only in the country where the old notes were being held.

What more these holders of Austro-Hungarian Bank notes should be able to demand in this situation is therefore not at all clear. The other creditors of the Austro-Hungarian Bank—disregarding here the holders of mortgage bonds, whose position is special—have a claim to a specific amount in legal money. These other creditors fall into two categories: first, those whose claims are for Austro-Hungarian Bank notes, for example, those who have giro credits to claim from the Bank.[7] They are assigned Bank assets equal to the value of the notes to which they have a claim. It is clear to whom their claim goes.

But if possessors of banknotes that were issued before October 27, 1918, and who fulfill the conditions applying for liquidation according to point 9 of the peace treaty, have an equal right to raise claims against the total assets of the Bank, then it is immediately uncertain how these claims can be reconciled with the other claims that can be made against the Bank, as well. If the Austro-Hungarian Bank only had the creditors classified under point 9, and no others, it would be conceivable that (disregarding the rights of the stockholders) the liquidation could be carried out in such a way that the total assets of the Bank could be distributed in equal portions to the note holders designated under point 9. (And let us speak no further about the blatant injustice and violation this would be to the vested rights of the stockholders.)

But since there are still other creditors who have specific amounts to claim against these assets—namely, those who hold foreign exchange or legal currency of a successor state—this method of distribution is utterly unfeasible; for there is no numerical criterion by which to determine the claims of the note holders relative to those who are foreign exchange creditors of the Bank.

Therefore, if we do not wish to declare point 9 meaningless and unworkable, we can only grant it the meaning that is in conformity with the regulations under Article 206: a specific fund becomes available to distribute among the note holders who meet the conditions for

7. [A "bank giro credit" is an arrangement under which a bank customer instructs their bank to transfer funds from their account to a beneficiary designated by the bank customer.—Ed.]

liquidation. In this distribution, the holders of these notes do not compete with any other rightful claims against the Bank. Under the treaty such a fund can refer only to the net assets of the Bank—that is, those assets of the Austro-Hungarian Bank that remain after the settlement of all the other specific quantitative claims have been met.

If point 9 is interpreted in this way, then any difficulty disappears that might result from an alternative interpretation, namely that those who have a quantitatively determinable claim are in equal competition with those who have an aliquot portion to claim.

Regarding the claims that have suddenly been raised by the successor states against the gold stock of the Austro-Hungarian Bank, there is no foundation for it either in the peace treaty or in the older Austrian laws. As defined by the peace treaty, the Republic of Austria alone is entitled to levy any claims against the Bank to which the former Austrian state in association with the Hungarian state were entitled concerning a portion of the Bank's profits and regarding delivery of that amount of the Bank's gold stock that represents gold deposits made by the government.

Of course, the regulations under Article 206 could be understood to mean that after the liquidation had been carried out, governments of the successor states that had notes to present to the liquidation commission would be entitled to make those claims against the Bank in proportion to the quantity of notes which the earlier Austrian and Hungarian governments were entitled to make upon the Bank.

However, no basis can be found for this solution to the problem. It would technically be a possible solution, something that cannot be said about the above interpretation concerning the rights of the note holders in relation to liquidation of the Bank. It also would have the consequence that it would leave undamaged the rights of the stockholders, whom the peace treaty certainly did not intend to harm. But even if one wanted to take this viewpoint, the claims which the successor states are currently making against the gold stock of the Bank are by no means justified.

It is unnecessary to mention that enforcement of the regulations under Article 206 requires certain supplementary arrangements with regard to the difficulties of distinguishing between those banknotes that were issued before or after October 27, 1918, and those that were inside or outside the Austro-Hungarian Monarchy on June 15, 1919. However, this is a difficulty of implementation of Article 206 that is independent of the special difficulties arising from the provisions of point 9.

CHAPTER 19

The Austrian Currency Problem
Thirty Years Ago and Today[1]

From March 8 to March 17, 1892, the government-convened Currency Inquiry Commission met in Vienna. The chairman was Finance Minister [Emil] Steinbach;[2] beside him stood the memorable Eugen von Böhm-Bawerk[3] as section head. Thirty-six experts appeared before the commission to answer five questions that were posed by the government.[4] No Austrian was left off the list of participants at the inquiry who had anything of importance to say on currency matters. Along with Carl Menger, the founder of the Austrian School of economics,[5] there was Wilhelm von Lucam, the highly honored longtime secretary general of the Austro-Hungarian Bank;[6] Moriz Benedikt, the publisher of *Neue Freie Presse* [New Free Press];[7] Theodor Thaussig, the spiritual

1. [This article originally appeared in German in *Neue Freie Presse* (March 17, 1922).—Ed.]
2. See Chapter 1, "The Political-Economic Motives of the Austrian Currency Reform," footnote 5.—Ed.]
3. [See Chapter 16, "On Carl Menger's Eightieth Birthday," footnote 11.—Ed.]
4. [The five questions were (1) whether a gold standard should be adopted as the legal monetary system of the Austro-Hungarian Empire; (2) if so, should it be monometallic or partly bimetallic with silver; (3) what should be the status of government notes in circulation; (4) how should the conversion be undertaken from the existing florin paper money standard to a gold standard; and (5) what should be chosen as the new monetary unit under a reformed monetary system?—Ed.]
5. [See "On Carl Menger's Eightieth Birthday," Chapter 16, in the present volume.—Ed.]
6. [Wilhelm von Lucam (1820–1900) was the secretary general of the Austro-Hungarian Bank in the middle decades of the nineteenth century, and was influential in introducing reforms restricting inflationary policies of the Bank in support of government financing. He worked closely with leading Viennese financiers in an attempt to weather the economic storm that followed the bank crisis of 1873.—Ed.]
7. [Moriz Benedikt (1849–1920) was the publisher and editor of the Vienna *Neue Freie Presse*. Under his leadership the newspaper promulgated liberal and free-market views. He published a series of articles on economic, commercial, and financial subjects, which attracted considerable attention from businessmen and liberal intellectuals.—Ed.]

leader of the Viennese banking world;[8] and Theodor Hertzka, the well-known writer on monetary matters and social policy.[9] The thick quarto volume that makes up the stenographic minutes of the inquiry remains today a source for the best ideas on all matters relating to monetary policy.

The problem that Austrian financial policy had to solve at that time was, of course, different from the one that we face today. At that time it had been more than a quarter of a century since the treasury's last recourse to the note-printing press to cover its budget deficit. It had been decades since government paper notes had been issued and put into circulation, and the banknotes issued by the Austro-Hungarian Bank served strictly commercial purposes. A progressive devaluation of the currency was not the problem giving impetus for a new reform of the currency; instead the problem was a progressive *increase* in the value of the currency. The price for 100 gold guldens (250 gold francs) came to:

Average for the year	Austrian florin notes
1887	125.25
1888	122.87
1889	118.58
1890	115.48
1891	115.83

Reform was being demanded in order to put an end to any further increase in the value of the Austrian currency. That was not difficult. To prevent any further decline in the foreign exchange rate on the Viennese stock market it was sufficient to bring the paper florin into a legally fixed relationship with gold, and to oblige the Austro-Hungarian Bank to exchange its notes for any quantity of gold at this fixed rate. Legislation sanctioned this method. After August 11, 1892, the day when the currency law went into effect, the value of the Austrian florin (2 crowns according to the new denomination) essentially could not rise above the value of 2 francs, 10 centimes or 1 mark, 70.1 pfennig. A limit on any upward movement of the foreign exchange rate was implemented only some years later with the introduction of specie payments as part of the foreign exchange policy of the Austro-Hungarian

8. [Theodor Taussig (1849–1909) was an Austrian entrepreneur, governor of the Boden-Credit-Anstalt, a joint-stock bank that was later merged with the older and stronger Österreichische Credit-Anstalt, with new capital provided by an international banking syndicate including J. P. Morgan and Company.—Ed.]

9. [See Chapter 1, "The Political-Economic Motives of the Austrian Currency Reform," footnote 3.—Ed.]

Bank. From that moment, Austria-Hungary had a gold (or gold-"core") standard—a "gold exchange standard"—similar to the one already in place in British India and many other countries, and one in accordance with the ideas developed by David Ricardo[10] in his work "Proposals for an Economical and Secure Currency."[11]

Today there are a great many difficulties for us to overcome before we can achieve a well-ordered currency situation. First of all, national budget deficits must be eliminated, or at least care must be taken to see to it that budgetary shortfalls are not covered through use of the note-printing press. Only then will it be possible to think about solving the currency problem. Any other procedure would inevitably result in failure. The experiences of the last several years certainly should have convinced even the most zealous policy proponents of artificially stabilized rates of exchange that all such attempts are completely futile.[12]

In 1892, the adherents of the light florin and the proponents of the heavy florin stood in opposition to each other. The former wanted to decrease the value of the currency before exchange rate stabilization, while the latter wanted to raise it. Moriz Benedikt, who, through the accident of the alphabet, was the second speaker to take the floor in the first session of the Inquiry Commission, rejected both proposals. "The best exchange rate after its public announcement will be the one that exerts the smallest influence on the current economic situation. The exchange rate, therefore, should be the one that comes closest to the actual conditions prevailing on the market."

Carl Menger, the most distinguished among the members of the commission, endorsed this opinion. Menger stated that, with some reservations, he was in favor of the exchange rate at the moment of stabilization. Richard Lieben,[13] also, was very decidedly in favor of the

---

10. [See Chapter 10, "On the Goals of Trade Policy," footnote 2.—Ed.]

11. [See "The Gold Exchange Standard," Chapter 22, in the present volume.—Ed.]

12. [See Ludwig von Mises, "Foreign-Exchange Control Must Be Abolished," (1919) in Richard M. Ebeling, ed., *Selected Writings of Ludwig von Mises*, vol. 2: *Between the Two World Wars: Monetary Disorder, Interventionism, Socialism, and the Great Depression* (Indianapolis: Liberty Fund, 2002), pp. 87–90.—Ed.]

13. [Richard Lieben (1842–1919) was a prominent Austrian economist who coauthored with Rudolph Auspitz (1837–1906) *Untersuchungen über die Theorie des Preises* [Investigations on the Theory of Prices] (1889), an early and highly regarded mathematical formulation of the marginalist approach to prices and costs. See Ludwig von Mises, "Richard Lieben as Economist," *Neue Freie Presse*, no. 19835 (November 14, 1919):

Auspitz and Lieben cannot really be considered as part of the Austrian School of economics, though in their ideas and arguments they were closely related to Menger and Böhm-Bawerk. They preferred the mathematical method, which places them closer to the En-

exchange rate existing at the moment of implementation. The arguments upon which these three men gave their viewpoints are today still worth reading and taking into consideration.

Just like today, many raised the question at the time whether there might not be an outflow of gold due to the unfavorable balance of payments. It was thought that Austria, as a country with foreign debts, would not be able to keep its currency system in order for very long. None of the questions that the government put before the commission directly made reference to this question. Yet hardly any expert failed to address it. Of all the issues that were treated in the sessions of the commission, this one has the greatest importance for the present. Even if the concrete situation of today may be quite different from that of that earlier time, the fundamental solution of the problem remains the same under the conditions prevailing in the new Austria. An unfavorable balance of payments does not push up the rate of exchange for foreign money; instead, it is the effect of those interrelationships described by Gresham's well-known law.[14] Nothing other than inflation can endanger the stability of the value of money.

If the world had not departed from the principles followed by Bamberger,[15] Michaelis,[16] and Soetbeer[17] in the creation of the Ger-

---

glishman William Stanley Jevons and the Swiss Leon Walras. Auspitz and Lieben may be placed next to these great names of modern economic theory: they, too, have performed a great service in advancing the theory of price. Their book is one of the richest in modern economics. Besides his [Lieben's] main work, of importance are a number of smaller papers and articles mostly dealing with monetary issues. He was an unquestionable supporter of a "sound money" policy, and never tired of vigorously combating all inflationary ideas. The present generation and posterity will have to admit that he was on the right track. The statements that he made during the currency inquiry of 1892 were among the best said in a brilliant assembly of economists, and they can still be read today by anyone to their benefit. —Ed.]

14. [Gresham's law was named after Sir Thomas Gresham (1517—79), financier and advisor to Queen Elizabeth I. In a proclamation dated September 27, 1560, Gresham warned that since the government had fixed the exchange rate between gold and silver at a level different from the market rate, the more undervalued coins were sure to be exported. In other words, the "bad" (overvalued) money would drive out the "good" (undervalued) money.—Ed.]

15. [See Chapter 1, "The Political-Economic Motives of the Austrian Currency Reform," footnote 51.—Ed.]

16. [Otto Michaelis (1826–90), a German journalist and politician, was a staunch advocate of economic liberalism and free trade and one of the founders of the National Liberal Party. He served as chief editor of the economic section of the Berliner Nationalzeitung and a lecturer in the Federal Chancellery and Ministry of Finance. As a leading member of the National Congress in the Reichstag he led the fight for freedom of movement, abolition of restrictions on interest rates, and ending of compulsory guilds and tests for entry into crafts.—Ed.]

17. [See Chapter 1, "The Political-Economic Motives of the Austrian Currency Reform," footnote 52.—Ed.]

man gold standard, and if it had taken to heart the teachings presented in the arguments of the Austrian Currency Inquiry Commission, the monetary system would look a lot different today. The great monetary chaos through which we are passing confirms anew the correctness of the teachings of the pioneers of "sound currency" and shows where inflationism has to lead.

CHAPTER 20

The Restoration of Austria's Economic Situation[1]

The current economic situation is the most dangerous facing the Austrian state and its people since the crisis began with the overthrow and economic partition of the former Austro-Hungarian Monarchy. The possibility for an immediate catastrophe confronts us. The continued depreciation of the Austrian crown destroys all prospects for reestablishing the state budget until a new bank of issue has been founded. It is not an improbable assumption that the state will be compelled to suspend all payments once it has become impossible to increase the circulation of banknotes—a possibility that entails almost unthinkable social consequences.

In this perilous situation, the Vienna Chamber of Commerce deems it necessary to make an appeal to the lawfully qualified representatives of Austrian economic life—the Chambers of Commerce and the Boards of Workers and Employees—to cooperate in working out, on a purely economic basis and free from all party influences, a program that can tide us over the current situation without a social collapse. We must not allow ourselves to once again design a plan for economic reconstruction that is founded primarily on catchwords and purely party points of view, and which is taken to be "the only one possible" due to a lack of necessary preparation and adequate counter-proposals. To the contrary, the political parties should be compelled to acquire a full mastery of the perspectives of the economically productive classes— both workers and employers, equally.

---

1. [This paper, written in German, was prepared as a position statement for the Austrian Chamber of Commerce and presented on August 28, 1922. It has not been previously published.—Ed.]

In what follows, we propose to outline the foundations for such a program for the transition period. Our sole aim is to point out the essentials for a discussion. We do not wish to assert that our ideas are the only correct or authoritative ones. Indeed, the discovery of the latter will be the purpose of the discussions.

Above all, no further time should be lost in discussing whether or not the Austrian state can have a viable independent existence; all discussion of this subject must remain academic. Only a long period of experience under normal conditions of economic life can provide an answer to this question. Similarly, pointing to the current idleness of our industry proves nothing about the viability of Austria, insomuch as this idleness can be brought to an end through appropriate shifts in production and reallocations of the workforce. A private enterprise may show a deficit for several consecutive years without proving its inability to survive. Only if a cure for the problem is impossible would there be such a proof. For the present, therefore, valuable time should not be wasted on this question.

Our point of view is a purely practical one. The greater part of the state's expenditures automatically increase on the basis of a cost-of-living index number. If the *expenditures* of the state are regulated by an index number, its *receipts* must be similarly regulated. In other words, the state must obtain a large proportion of its receipts in terms of a stable medium of exchange that is independent of the crown. Gold is such a medium. Receipts in gold, therefore, must be obtained in order to cover the given expenditures that are determined by this index number.

The railroads and the postal and telegraph services could be the first to supply receipts in gold. The charges for these state enterprises would be fixed in gold, and the equivalent in paper crowns calculated on the basis of the rate of exchange that is published weekly. It must be pointed out that the present tariffs for these services are far below their prewar level (calculated in gold); therefore, the entire transition to the new postwar level could only be brought about gradually over about a year's time.

Considerable reductions in transport charges would have to be granted for the shipment of foodstuffs, essential raw materials, and coal. Also, efforts should be undertaken to alter those provisions in the peace treaty that require the same rates to be charged for foreign goods in transit as those charged for goods destined for Austria. It is entirely unjust that Austria, as a leading transit country, should have to renounce all profits we might earn from the transport of coal and foodstuffs through our country.

If receipts from the railways and the postal and telegraph services were in gold, then the wages and salaries of the workmen and employees in these enterprises would no longer be paid on the basis of the current index number system; they too would be calculated in amounts of gold. For the present, these wages and salaries could not be as high as in the prewar period; nevertheless, it would guarantee to the employees a more acceptable standard of living than the current paper money payments, which only exercise a corrupting influence and undermine the spirit of sound administration. At the same time, thought must be given to bringing the number of workmen and employees in these enterprises down to their prewar levels, and wherever possible to reduce it even further.

The purpose of these measures is to prevent bankruptcy of the state's essential means of communication, the collapse of which would mean catastrophe. Of course, it would be necessary to bind the state by law to use all such receipts for the maintenance of these transportation and communication enterprises, and for the paying of salaries of all those employed by them.

Furthermore, the prices of all articles sold by state monopolies must be fixed in gold, especially tobacco, which is a nonessential luxury.

On the other hand, all taxes that yield low returns and entail high administrative expenditures should be abolished. The number of taxes must be decreased, the tax collection system simplified, and the yield from individual taxes increased as far as possible.

An important cause behind the idleness of our industry is admittedly the excessive importation of alcoholic beverages; we are powerless to prevent this, since we are forced to import them by neighboring states—especially Hungary and Italy—that otherwise would not have concluded commercial treaties with us. If, then, we cannot significantly reduce their importation by prohibitions or restrictions, we can at least obtain a source of gold for the state by imposing a consumption tax on these luxury items, payable in gold.

In all countries, customs duties constitute an important source of gold receipts for the state. Efforts should be made, therefore, for an early introduction of the new tariff system that has already been drawn up. However, it must be borne in mind from the start that Austria's future depends on free trade, and provision should be made for the gradual abolition of the whole system of import duties.

It must not be forgotten, of course, that the result of such a general increase in government revenues will be to place a horribly heavy cost on all social classes, and inevitably there will occur a very noticeable stagnation. Undoubtedly, many financially insecure enterprises will be ruined by this additional tax burden. It must be kept in mind, however, that any recovery of the Austrian economy cannot be successful without sacrifice; there are many enterprises that came into existence in the last few years that do not possess the necessary capital to survive under normal conditions. Furthermore, there are many recently founded enterprises in Austria whose existence is entirely due to the situation created by the depreciation of the currency and the general economic decline. All these enterprises will have to be sacrificed as part of the recovery process. It is quite impossible to save them. There need be no doubt, however, that the vigorous spirit of enterprise among the people who control such enterprises will find other fields of activity more conducive to the public good.

So far, we have primarily considered the question of getting the revenues of the state on a proper footing. Now we will make a few proposals for fighting the general poverty of the country. The impoverishment of the Austrian economy has been brought about primarily by the delusion that the crown possesses a stable value. This created erroneous ideas about how to evaluate the rise in prices under the current system of price controls. It has resulted in the greater part of Austria's savings and industrial capital being eaten up in the course of the last few years. Price controls are inconsistent with liberal economic principles; however, they are not unbearable under a stable currency.

No respectable businessman desires to earn profits that are "usurious." It would not be necessary to entirely abandon the system of price controls as long as sale prices are calculated in gold. The clearly false assumption that the crown is of stable value must be eliminated in the implementation of the law. It is a mistake to think that the consumption of capital is harmful only for the owners of capital. It constitutes a far greater injury for the society as a whole. The capital within a country, regardless of who the owners are, earns interest, provides work, and enriches industry. A law that necessarily results in the consumption of capital is antisocial to the highest degree and, as present conditions in

Austrian industry show, causes unemployment, indebtedness, and scarcity. It must be strongly demanded, therefore, that the basis for calculating sale prices should be the value of those goods in terms of gold.

But it is not only the price increases permitted under price controls that is the problem; it is also the problem of economic calculation in general with a depreciating paper money. Such calculations make it appear that profits are earned when in fact capital losses are experienced. It exhausts the working capital in the country, and harms our foreign trade. Moreover, due to these false calculations, we suffer from the full force of antidumping regulations. The full extent of the harm done by these false economic calculations may be deduced from the fact that hardly any merchant is in the position to fill warehouses to the usual extent; nearly all warehouses today are but a vestige of their prewar circumstances. Currently, nearly every merchant and every industrial enterprise is obliged to resort to bank loans in order to carry on business. Many industries are forced to limit their output, not owing to lack of orders, but due to a lack of capital.[2]

On the other hand, the loan market represents a continual source of losses to the banks.

Even the highest rate of interest cannot make good the loss incurred through currency depreciation. The banks are certainly heavily hit by the currency depreciation. Their capital resources have in general been overestimated. All large enterprises, therefore, find it difficult to raise sufficient funds to maintain their capital. Loans must be allowed to be calculated in terms of gold, also, so that the real cost of capital may be more correctly estimated. And interest must be calculated in gold as well, to enable banks to earn a sufficient sum to gain back what they have lent and have the incentive to extend and continue lending to profitable enterprises.

A measure that would considerably contribute toward decreasing general social unrest would be to fix wages concluded in collective bargaining contracts in terms of gold; both employer and employee would have a more secure basis for economic calculation. Of course, even under this arrangement, the prewar level of wages will not be possible. For Austria, the wage standard should be that in neighboring competitive countries (the successor states and Germany).

---

2. [See Ludwig von Mises, *Nation, State, and Economy: Contributions to the Politics and History of Our Time* (Indianapolis: Liberty Fund, [1919] 2006), pp. 132–35.—Ed.]

English and American wage standards cannot be used as a basis of comparison. Wages in Austria that are calculated in gold will be lower because her goods are produced from raw materials and coal that are more costly to procure than in other places; moreover, Austria's goods encounter high customs barriers in the areas to which it exports. The conditions of production in the new Austria are not as favorable as in the old state, and even then they were always more unfavorable than in other countries. If Austrian goods are to be able to compete abroad, wages calculated in gold will remain relatively far below their prewar level. Nevertheless, such a system of calculation on the basis of gold will be a considerable advance for both workmen and employers.

In order to prevent the hoarding of foreign securities and bills of exchange, for which there is presently an enormous demand in Austria and which results in a steady increase in their value, it is imperative that the Austrian Bank issue a banknote valued in gold. The bank will have to ensure the uninterrupted maintenance of the gold value of this note, and it must be accepted by the government as well as everyone in the country as being equivalent to gold. A necessary condition for this, of course, is for the state to have no influence whatsoever over the bank of issue.

The foregoing is a brief and of course incomplete outline of a transitional plan. Its main purpose is not to save the crown—that is impossible—but to initiate a new policy on a solid foundation. It has the further advantage of enabling the essential government departments and their staffs to get over this time of crisis, and, in time, of reestablishing the state's budget on a solid gold basis. When this is achieved, it will be seen that Austria's public debt is not so formidable after all. And the administrative machinery of the state, not being encumbered by armament expenditures, perhaps can rest on a more solid foundation than other countries that are considered to be far wealthier.

Compulsory measures, such as government controls on bills of exchange and securities, import and export prohibitions, and so on, have been purposely left out of the plan. Experience shows that all forms of government control are detrimental, and are wholly incapable of preventing unfavorable developments. The first consequence of government compulsory measures is corruption, which is prejudicial to the authority of the state.

It is a fact that the power of our government is but slight, and scarcely makes itself felt outside Vienna. The government only discredits itself by introducing compulsory measures, the enforcement of which requires a powerful government machine. The recent reimplementation of government regulation over bills of exchange has clearly shown how futile such attempts must always remain. The supply of foreign securities and bills of exchange has now entirely ceased. Austrian owners of foreign securities avoid putting them on the market as best they can; and businessmen who can dispose of foreign money keep it out of Austria for as long as possible.

Furthermore, in more remote districts the government's compulsory measures are entirely ignored. Experience amply shows that, for the time being, no positive results can be expected in Austria from compulsory measures. A return to a well-founded administrative policy, capable of inspiring confidence, will do more to improve the situation than any legislation or threats of punishment, however severe they may be. We must make up our minds to return from the extravagant intoxication of spending "billions" to the sober, more modest financial figures of a smaller state. The object of the proposed plan is to avoid a sudden and disastrous collapse.

CHAPTER 21

The Austrian Problem[1]

In his recently published book *The Suicide of a Nation,* Dr. Siegfried Strakosch undertakes a thorough investigation of the problems facing the Austrian economy. Dr. Strakosch, who is active in industry and agriculture, and who, as a writer on agricultural policy, has earned a reputation that extends far beyond the borders of the German-speaking world, is more qualified than almost anyone else to deal with this difficult and complicated question.[2] He untangles the problem as best it is

1. [This article originally appeared in German in *Neue Freie Presse* (February 5, 1923).—Ed.]
2. [Siegfried Strakosch (1867–1933) was a prominent Austrian industrialist and agricultural expert. He was a principled economic liberal who opposed both protectionism and all government subsidies for agriculture. See Ludwig von Mises, "Siegfried von Strakosch (1867–1933)," in *Neue Österreichische Biographie ab 1815,* vol. 15, *Grosse Österreicher* (Vienna: Amalthea-Verlag, 1963), pp. 160–65:

   Strakosch was one of the last representatives of that Austrian upper middle class that, in many ways, provided the character of Viennese life in the era of Emperor Francis Joseph. But his interests included far more [than only scientific and agricultural matters]. He was well acquainted with all the currents in intellectual and artistic life. He counted among his many friends most of the important musicians, writers, and visual artists. He had the gift of creative achievement for all to understand and appreciate. . . . Strakosch clearly understood the contradiction in the economic and sociopolitical ideas in the agricultural circles. Around the declining old aristocracy were found landowners and peasant farmers who supported a socialist program. Their ideal was a conservative state that would support the principle of the self-sufficient farmer. This is what they had in mind when they spoke about the practice of moral values. But what was not explained was how such [agrarian] independence could be preserved with continued involvement of the state. Strakosch stated quite correctly that every measure to "protect" and "favor" agriculture was a step down the road to socialism. . . . In the years after World War I . . . The vast majority of the electorate [in Austria] opposed the plan of a small band of Marxist firebrands who wanted to follow the Russian example. But the key word "socialization" was the dominating spirit of the time, and the government appointed a socialization commission that was entrusted with the theoretical task of preparing for the transformation of Austria into a socialist society. The resistance of the "bourgeois" parties was primarily directed against the general political and cultural program of the socialists. They were less against the attempts to bring about socialization through step-by-step interventionist methods. Inflation had ruined the state budget, but all of the resulting consequences were wrongly interpreted by

possible to do today. Those who come later will be able to gather more material and include many more details; but they will not be able to surpass him in his grasp of the deeper connections and his understanding of the basic problem.

Austria is suffering from a fundamental problem: the dominance of socialist ideas in the country. The rule of the Social Democratic Party is unrestrained even though it does not have a majority among the population or in parliament; formally it is in the opposition. "The bourgeois parties stand fragmented and weak against the Social Democrats, unable to draw any advantage from their impressive numerical superiority," Strakosch points out. The Social Democrats rule because they have armed forces behind them, and because at every moment they can impose their will upon the populace by shutting down the transport facilities and the power stations. As long as their unbroken dominance continues, every attempt to put the country back on its feet must fail.

The national budget cannot be balanced if the numerous public enterprises are not closed; with their billions in deficits, they frustrate every attempt to put the public budget in order. Yet the Social Democrats do not allow the railroads, the tobacco factories, any of the municipal enterprises, or the cooperative institutions to be handed over to the private sector. The eight-hour day cannot be touched, even though it is clear that Austrian industry cannot become competitive as long as it remains in effect.

All that the economic policy of the socialist parties achieves is the taxing away of capital, which is converted into consumer goods and

---

public opinion as being due to the shortcomings of the market order. This was the state of affairs that was dealt with by Strakosch in his book *The Suicide of a Nation* (1922). In plain words that anyone would understand, he showed that a change in economic policy was inevitable. Balance had to be restored to the public budget, and the currency had to be stabilized. The economy had to adjust to the new circumstances, and the spirit of entrepreneurship had to be set free without bureaucratic obstacles getting in its way. That was the only way that Austria could be reconstructed. . . . In an era of the destruction of old values and institutions, Siegfried von Strakosch was a man of constructive work. He united in his person scientific-technological knowledge and economic understanding; he was a businessman, an industrialist and a farmer; he was a successful writer and an economist; he was a friend, advisor, and colleague to all, in the first third of the twentieth century. At a critical moment in Austrian history, even while some sincere patriots questioned the "viability" of the new Austrian state, he was among that small band of pioneers working for a better future.
—Ed.]

therefore eaten up. The only remedy recommended by the "fiscal policy" of the Social Democrats is the confiscation of physical wealth of all sorts, as well as the confiscation of currency, foreign credits, and securities. Consume and destroy, that is the final end to their wisdom. "We hand out not only the people's income, but far more," says Strakosch. "We consume not only income but wealth. What is falsely represented to us as national income, is only the smaller part of national income; the greater part is destroyed productive capital, the legacy of more industrious and less demanding times."

The demagogue thinks only about today, and not about the future. Almost forty years ago René Stourm, the historian of the French Revolution, masterfully characterized the principles behind the fiscal policy of the Jacobins.

> The attitude of the Jacobins about finances can be quite simply stated as an utter exhaustion of the present at the expense of the future. They never worried about the morrow, handling all their affairs as though each day were the last. That approach distinguished all actions undertaken during the Revolution. What permitted it to survive as long as it did was the fact that the day-to-day depletion of the resources accumulated by a rich and powerful nation allowed unexpected large resources to come to the surface. The *assignats*, as long as they had any value at all, little as it might be, flooded the country in ever increasing quantities. The prospects of impending bankruptcy never stopped their being issued even for a moment. Only when the public absolutely refused to accept paper money of any kind, at no matter how low a value, did the issue of new notes come to a halt.[3]

One cannot read Stourm's description of capital levies and forced loans, of measures against the stock market and against currency speculation, of regulations concerning profiteering and food rationing without thinking of the policy that Austria has been practicing to its own detriment for ten years now. The dismal picture that Strakosch sketches is, unfortunately, only too true.

---

3. [René Stourm, *Les Finances de l'Ancien Régime et de la Révolution* [The Finances of the Old Regime and the Revolution], 2 vols. (Paris: Guillaumin et Cie, 1885).—Ed.]

CHAPTER 22

The Gold-Exchange Standard[1]

The Bismarck-Bamberger coinage reform of 1871–73 put an end to the fragmentation of the German currency and at the same time shifted the German currency system from one based on silver to one based on gold. The idea behind it was the view that in everyday commercial transactions wider scope needed to be assigned to the use of gold coins.

The practice in England served as a model. In Germany things were never carried as far as in England, where all banknote denominations under five pounds were suppressed. Nevertheless, all regulations concerning banknote denominations and German Imperial Treasury certificates were clearly based on the idea that paper-money substitutes did not belong in the hands of the farmer, the worker, the craftsman, and the subordinate. It was considered an important task of the new German imperial monetary policy to "satisfy" the demand for gold, for which a not inconsiderable material sacrifice was made.

German sales of silver [to buy the gold needed to back the currency under the reform] were the impetus if not the primary cause for the decline in the price of silver. This, and the fact that the action of Imperial Germany decided the controversy over the currency question in favor of gold, compelled India also to shift from the silver standard to the gold standard in the last decade of the nineteenth century.

The Indian government was not inclined to follow the German example in the technical details of carrying out the currency reform. Neither did the Indian government want to bear the great financial sacrifice that supplying the economy with a large stock of gold would entail, including the selling off of a large amount of silver at what likely would be a falling price. It did not want to force the Indian population

1. [This article was originally published in German in the *Deutsche allgemeine Zeitung. Ausgabe Grosse* (February 24, 1925).—Ed.]

to give up the ancient, inherited use of silver money and accept unaccustomed gold money.

But above all else, it feared the reaction that such policy measures would have on the movement of international gold prices. Such large purchases of gold to cover Indian financial requirements would have driven the price of gold significantly higher and exacerbated the general decline in the prices of goods. In the first half of the 1890s, this decline in prices was still, at this time, the leading concern of statesmen in all the countries of the world.

Instead, India seized upon the expedient of having a gold standard without creating a circulation of gold in domestic transactions. The free coinage of silver was suspended; and after the accumulation of a currency reserve fund, the silver rupee was converted into a sort of silver banknote. Rupees were exchanged for gold and gold for rupees at a fixed rate. Thus the rupee was brought into a fixed relation to gold; if previously it had been the unit of a silver currency system, it now became a money substitute for a gold standard. The monetary policy goal behind the Indian currency reform was achieved.[2]

In the last decades before the war, the currency question was resolved in a whole series of Asian and American silver- and paper-currency countries in a way similar to the reform in India. This new system also found its way into Europe. For example, Austria-Hungary began to create a gold standard following the German model without the actual circulation of gold. What was finally achieved—from around 1900—was a gold standard without gold in circulation.

David Ricardo[3] was the intellectual father of this new system, which bears the name "the gold-exchange standard," or the gold-"core" currency. In a paper that was published in 1816 under the title "Proposals for an Economical and Secure Currency," he recommended a metal-

2. [On the history of Indian monetary reform in the late nineteenth and early twentieth centuries, see Edwin W. Kemmerer, *Modern Currency Reforms: A History and Discussion of Recent Currency Reforms in India, Porto Rico, Philippine Islands, Straits Settlements, and Mexico* (New York: Macmillan, 1916), pp. 3–154.—Ed.]

3. [David Ricardo (1772–1823) spent his formative years in his family's brokerage business, until he retired at the age of forty-two after accumulating a large fortune. He devoted his time to the study of political economy, writing several influential essays on inflation, gold, and monetary reform in the early nineteenth century during Britain's wars with France. In 1817, he published his most famous work, *The Principles of Political Economy and Taxation*, which became a cornerstone of the Classical system. Among his contributions was the development of the theory of comparative advantage. He served as a Member of Parliament in the House of Commons from 1819 until his death.—Ed.]

lic currency as the best and least costly currency system—a currency based on a noble metal (gold or silver)—but without the noble metal in actual circulation.[4] In a conscious imitation of Ricardo's forgotten proposals, Lindsey and Probyn recommended the gold-core standard as the best way out of India's currency difficulty.

The advantage offered by the gold-core standard, and what has made it attractive to finance ministers, is to be exclusively found in the fact that it reduces the higher costs connected with the actual use of gold in daily monetary transactions. Since this reduces the need for gold, the gold-core currency must be considered responsible for the fall in the price of gold, that is, for the general increase in the prices of goods.

As was mentioned earlier, the economizing on the use of gold was considered a singular advantage to the system. Perhaps if this causal connection between the lower demand for gold and the general rise in prices was clearly recognized, people would be more inclined to see it as a disadvantage.

The gold-core currency, however, is now practiced in such a way that a part of the currency reserve, and in many countries the entire reserve, is held as claims to gold in a gold-standard country in the form of gold-backed foreign exchange—and not in the form of actual gold (ingot or coins) in the domestic economy. The benefit from investing the reserve currency in this way is clear: the gold-backed foreign exchange earns interest, while the stock of gold lies "unproductively" in the vaults of the national central bank.

The gold-core standard, however, has reached a critical turning point with this arrangement. It is clear, of course, that the investment of currency reserve funds in gold-backed foreign exchange cannot become the general norm for all the countries of the world. At least one country must remain on an actual gold standard of the old type, or at least retain a gold-core standard with real metal, otherwise there would remain no place in the world where gold was used as a monetary metal.

After the great inflationary episode of the last several years, all the countries of the world have or are trying to put their monetary systems back in order on the basis of a gold-core standard with currency reserves invested in gold-backed foreign exchange. This can happen only for as long as a few countries are willing to absorb all this gold, espe-

4. [David Ricardo, "Proposals for an Economical and Secure Currency," (1816) in Piero Sraffa, ed., *The Works and Correspondence of David Ricardo*, vol. 4, *Pamphlets and Papers*, 1815–1823 (Cambridge: Cambridge University Press, 1951), pp. 41–141.—Ed.]

cially the United States of America. It is doubtful, however, that in the long run the United States will be willing to bear this heavy burden.

It is highly unlikely that the United States will seriously give a hearing to the proposals recommending that country "break away" from gold and shift to an Indian-type currency. The serious drawbacks that speak against the occasional proposals of Irving Fisher and John Maynard Keynes are too great.[5] However, the demand might be made that at least the richer and economically more powerful states of the world should either move back from the gold-core standard to the gold standard with actual gold in circulation, or at least commit themselves to the holding of a certain actual gold reserve.

The problems brought about by the recent development of the gold-core standard so far have been treated in a stepmother-like fashion in the economics literature. Up to now, and especially in Germany and Austria, the gold-core standard has not been given the attention which it deserves; probably there are many for whom it is not clear that Germany's new currency is also a gold-core currency. There still prevail in public opinion many misunderstandings about the gold-core standard that have been spread through the writings of Heyn and Knapp.[6]

For this reason, we welcome with particular satisfaction the fact that Dr. Fritz Machlup[7] has undertaken to explain the gold-core standard in a monograph.[8] Especially to be appreciated is an appendix with Ri-

---

5. [See Ludwig von Mises, "The Return to the Gold Standard," (1924) in Richard M. Ebeling, ed., *Selected Writings of Ludwig von Mises*, vol. 2, *Between the Two World Wars: Monetary Disorder, Intervention, Socialism, and the Great Depression* (Indianapolis: Liberty Fund, 2002), pp. 136–53, for Mises's analysis and criticisms of Irving Fisher's and John Maynard Keynes's proposals.—Ed.]

6. [See Chapter 2, "The Problem of Legal Resumption of Specie Payments in Austria-Hungary," footnote 10.—Ed.]

7. [Fritz Machlup (1902–83) was an internationally recognized economist for his writings on international trade, finance, and currency; methodology of the social sciences; and market structures in his two major works, *The Political Economy of Monopoly* (1952) and *The Economics of Sellers' Competition* (1952). He is also considered a pioneer in the development of the theory of the economics of knowledge in the three-volume work he completed before his death, *Knowledge: Its Creation, Distribution, and Economic Significance* (1980, 1982, 1984). He studied at the University of Vienna under Friedrich von Wieser, and Ludwig von Mises was his dissertation advisor for the book reviewed in this chapter. In Mises's copy of the book, Fritz Machlup wrote the inscription "To my spiritual father." Machlup also contributed to literature on the Austrian monetary and business cycle in *The Stock Market, Credit, and Capital Formation* (1940) and defended the Austrian theory of capital in his article "Professor Knight and the 'Period of Production,'" *Journal of Political Economy* (October 1935).—Ed.]

8. *Die Goldkernwährung. Eine währungsgeschichtliche und währungstheoretische Untersuchung* [The Gold-Core Standard: A Historical and Theoretical Monetary Investigation] by Dr. Fritz Machlup. With an appendix: translation of Ricardo's currency plans from the year

cardo's currency proposal of 1816 translated and made available for the first time in the German language. In various particulars and even in many fundamental questions one may be of a different opinion than those of the thoroughly expert and well-read author of this monograph.

One cannot contest, however, that we have here a sound work that deals with the whole sphere of problems in a comprehensive way, which covers the core questions with great skill, and seeks intelligently to prepare the way for their solution. Until now, a book of this kind has been lacking from our monetary literature. Everyone who proposes to deal in a serious way with the question of monetary systems—especially the German system–should not merely look over this work but study it thoroughly. It offers the best foundation for the discussion of the further development of the German and the European monetary system.

1816 by Dr. Wilhelm Frontowitz and Dr. Fritz Machlup (Halberstadt: H. Meyers Publisher, Abteilung Verlag, 1925).

CHAPTER 23

The Social Democratic Agrarian Program[1]

In spite of the collapse of the ideology of socialism, and the failure of its prescriptions for universal happiness, the Social Democratic Party has not disappeared from the scene. It continues to exist, even after renouncing its original program. And although it will not admit it, its new program now means: devour the wealth that has been accumulated by capitalism.

In the Austrian Social Democratic Party's agrarian program, this goal is presented to us in a more unmasked and open way than in the past. Large-scale agricultural enterprises operate far more efficiently than the individual farmer on a small plot of land. The Social Democrat's agricultural program cannot deny this. But its program demands the expropriation of the large agricultural estates, and their transfer to government ownership—even though everyone knows that all such federal undertakings end up operating at a loss.

Twelve percent of the forest land in Austria is administered by the federal government, and its annual deficit swallows up a million schillings in tax money. In comparison, private owners of forest lands all operate at a profit. Nevertheless, the Social Democrat's agricultural program insists on the expropriation and nationalization of all large forest lands that are held in private hands.

These socialist forests, the program says, should be administered "not as capitalist for-profit forests, but as socialist welfare woods." This last phrase was certainly superfluous, since all nationalized enterprises that we have had the "opportunity" to experience have freed us from

1. [This was originally written in German as a foreword to Siegfried Strakosch's *Das sozialdemokratische Agrarprogramm in seiner politischen und volkswirtschaftlichen Bedeutung* [The Political and Economic Meaning of the Social Democratic Agricultural Program] (1926). The foreword was dated January 5, 1926.—Ed.]

any fear that operations managed by government, or by cooperative enterprises, could ever yield a profit!

In essence, the goal of the Social Democratic agricultural program is the transformation of a large part of the farming and forestry economy into a government-subsidized undertaking. Forests and products produced on the land would no longer be expected to yield any net profits. Those assigned to oversee the management of these lands are to be supported by funds supplied from other sources. Almost every paragraph in this agrarian program speaks of expenditures from the public coffers for the benefit of agriculture.

For example, combined associations of cottagers and small farmers are to be "promoted from public means." Expenditures from federal and regional funds also will be required to facilitate the provisioning of quality seeds, chemical fertilizers, good breeding stock, and for the setting up of agricultural machine stations and so on.

Where the financial means to cover these expenditures are supposed to come from is, of course, never explained in this Social Democratic program. On the other hand, it is proposed to eliminate various presently existing taxes, for example, the taxes on sugar and wine. Doing away with the tax on wine would promote alcoholism! But such factual considerations seem not to have bothered the authors of this new Social Democratic agricultural program. There is precisely only one motive that has guided the composition of this program: its effect on the voters.

Up until now the Social Democratic Party, in all questions relating to agriculture, has exclusively "represented" the viewpoint of urban consumers. Right now, however, the party also needs the votes of the rural constituencies if it is to achieve political power; it therefore offers an agricultural program full of enticing promises. Will the farmers let themselves be deceived by this program? Will they realize that in the long run it will not be possible for the Social Democrats to impose financial burdens on the urban population for the benefit of agriculture? Won't this sudden awakening of "interest" in agricultural matters by the Social Democratic Party seem suspicious?

Dr. Siegfried Strakosch, our most successful agriculturalist, who is at the same time a prominent natural scientist and a writer on economics, has undertaken the task of examining the Social Democratic agricultural program in detail. When Dr. Strakosch speaks about agricultural policy, everyone in Austria can learn something, even if one may not completely agree with him on many economic issues.[2]

The sober objectivity of his analysis will not fail to have its effect. Let us hope that it will open the eyes of many about the magnitude of the danger that carrying out of any part of the Social Democratic agricultural program would create in our country.

2. [See Chapter 21, "The Austrian Problem," footnote 2.—Ed.]

CHAPTER 24

America and the Reconstruction of the European Economy[1]

Politically, Europe can expect no help from America for the solving of its own problems. Even in purely economic policy matters it is a fantasy to expect a remedy from the United States for the plight of Europe.

Until the final decade of the last century the United States was principally a supplier of raw materials and an importer of manufactured goods. For decades Europe constantly invested capital in the United States. The big factories that developed the wealth of the American economy had been financed by European capital. A generation ago three-fifths of all American railroads were controlled by London.

Although in the last years of the nineteenth century America had already begun to buy back occasional parcels of American securities from Europe, the debt of the United States to Europe rose constantly until the outbreak of the World War. Even conservative estimates calculated that at the outbreak of the World War the debt of the United States to Europe amounted to more than five billion dollars.[2] While England and the capitalist states of the West were in first place among the securities holders, even Austria participated, although with modest amounts. The United States paid the interest on these debts by its enormous, yearly rising balance-of-trade surplus, which no longer only

1. [This article originally was published in German in *Mitteilungen des Hauptverbandes der Industrie* [Reports of the Chief Association of German Industry], vol. 8 (1927). It was first delivered as a lecture at a meeting of the Austrian Industrial Association. During the three months from March 9 to May 31, 1926, Mises had toured the United States under the financial auspices of the Laura Spelman (the Rockefeller) Foundation, visiting and lecturing in a dozen cities.—Ed.]
2. [This would be approximately $109.4 billion in 2010 dollars. In 1913, U.S. Gross Domestic Product (GDP) was 39.1 billion, or $855.8 billion in 2010 dollars. Thus, U.S. debt to European creditors was about 12.8 percent of GDP.—Ed.]

resulted from the export of raw materials but also, now, in large part from the export of staple commodities and manufactured goods.

Even if the World War had not intervened, no doubt in the course of a number of years the rising surplus of the American balance of trade would have enabled the United States to pay off its debt to Europe and to change from the role of a capital-importing to that of a capital-exporting country. The war enormously accelerated this development. Within a few years—almost overnight, one could say—America became the great banker of the world.

At the end of 1925 American capital investment abroad was estimated by the Department of Commerce to be $10.5 billion, in comparison to about $3 billion of foreign capital investments in the United States. This does not include, however, the debts among the Allies. The trade balance from interest and capital gains is put at $355 million by the U.S. Commerce Department, to which $160 million in interest on debt owed by the Allies must be added. If one includes the surplus trade balance of $660 million plus film rental charges of $75 million, it comes to a total of $1.424 billion on the credit side of the ledger. The counter-entries in the American balance of payments are the expenditures of travelers in the amount of $560 million, $310 million sent back home by immigrants, and some smaller items coming to $63 million, adding up to a total of $922 million. The difference of about a half billion dollars is covered by the surplus of new investments of American capital abroad beyond the sum of the repayments of debts and the purchase of American securities by foreigners.

It is estimated that in recent years new capital formation in the United States has amounted to about $10 billion, of which one to two billion are available for investment abroad. These are large amounts; they cannot, however, be fully counted upon. Against them one must put the mentioned repayments and purchases by foreigners. One must further consider that the limitation on immigration into America will finally bring about a reduction in the remittances of immigrants, since naturally the immigrants who have already been living in the United States for a long time and who have established families there hardly come into consideration in regard to money sent back home. The immigrants who go to America only for a short time and then return to Europe with their savings are basically not worth considering in the present circumstances.

With the rising standard of living in the United States and the organization of transoceanic steamship traffic, the number of Americans traveling abroad will grow, as will the sums they spend while visiting abroad. On the other hand—and this is perhaps most important—it is to be expected that America's trade balance surplus will decrease. The assumption that the American balance of trade must soon become negative is no doubt exaggerated. It is, of course, true that in the first eight months of 1926 there occurred an excess of $84 million in imports over exports; but that the inferences drawn from this were too hasty is shown by the fact that in September the American balance of trade had a surplus of $105 million.

Moreover, it would only be natural for America, as a creditor nation, to have a negative trade balance. The debtors to America really have no way to pay the interest and dividends they owe other than by the supplying of goods. American economic policy, which seeks to keep out foreign goods by an extremely high tariff system, must, in the end, collide with its investment activities abroad.[3] All reasonable Americans admit that its high-protective-tariff policy is inconsistent with the desire of the United States for the Allies to be able to pay the interest on and amortize their debts.

Nevertheless, the idea of a protective tariff is still extraordinarily popular in the United States today. It has support in those industries that demand duties to compensate for the difference in costs of production between the United States and other countries. The literal fulfilling of this desire would make any importation to the United States impossible, since, logically, only those goods can be imported into the United States for which the costs of production are lower abroad. The same goes for the demand by labor that all those goods be excluded from being imported into the United States that are produced abroad at lower wages. Since, as a consequence of the ban on immigration,

---

3. [In 1922, the U.S. Congress passed the Fordney-McCumber Tariff Act, which increased the average ad valorem tariff rate to 38.5 percent, as a protectionist measure against foreign imports. It soon resulted in retaliatory trade restrictions against American goods in France, Spain, Italy, and Germany. Three years after Mises wrote this article, the U.S. Congress passed the Hawley-Smoot Tariff in 1930, which imposed an effective tax rate of about 60 percent on foreign imports into the United States, which again soon resulted in trade retaliation on the part of many other nations. The Hawley-Smoot Tariff is usually credited with exacerbating the intensity of the Great Depression, with international trade declining by around 30 percent during 1930–33.—Ed.]

wages are necessarily higher in America than anywhere else (with the exception of Australia), this too would mean a complete prohibition of imports. Essentially even the demand for allegedly more "reasonable" tariffs amounts to the same thing, because a "reasonable" tariff is generally understood to mean one that makes it possible for domestic goods to compete successfully against foreign goods.

Even the farmers are partly in the camp of the protectionists insofar as they produce products that are in competition with foreign goods exported to the United States. The majority of American farmers realize, of course, that as an interest group concerned with exporting a part of their produce, they cannot benefit from a protective tariff. They suffer from the fact that labor is made more expensive by the laws restricting immigration. At the same time, the prices for industrial products are raised due to the high protective tariff,[4] while the farmers have been seriously affected by the fact that agricultural products have suffered a severe decline in price. It is the farmers who insist that the United States work toward a solution of the political conditions in Europe in order to strengthen European consumption demand for American goods.

In terms of America's domestic economic policy, it is becoming a more and more prevalent idea that the government should control the economy.[5] As a capital-exporting country, the United States understandably—but not logically—disapproves when other countries follow the same foreign economic policy that it practices toward other nations. The United States forcefully opposes efforts by Mexico to bring production under the controls of the state. As a creditor nation, America must act against the attempts to nationalize and expropriate foreign-

---

4. [American farm groups attributed the rise in the prices of many manufactured goods used in agriculture to the reduction in foreign competition due to tariff restrictions on imports. For example, it was estimated that between 1918 and 1926, a fourteen-inch plow had doubled in price from $14 to $28; mowing machines from $45 to $95; and farm wagons from $85 to $150. On the other hand, by the mid-1920s, much of European agriculture had either normally recovered from the destruction and disorganization of the First World War, or had been artificially stimulated by government protectionist measures; as a consequence, American food exports to Europe had significantly decreased and, therefore, lowered American farming revenues from export sales.—Ed.]

5. [See Ludwig von Mises, "Changes in American Economic Policy," (1926) in Richard M. Ebeling, ed., *Selected Writings of Ludwig von Mises*, vol. 2, *Between the Two World Wars: Monetary Disorder, Interventionism, Socialism, and the Great Depression* (Indianapolis: Liberty Fund, 2002), pp. 160–62.—Ed.]

owned property; and in the case of Mexico, U.S. resistance goes so far that bellicose developments are not beyond the realm of possibility.[6]

America's bad experiences with debtors' unwillingness to pay, on the one hand, and the reduction in its balance of payments surplus, on the other hand, could result in the United States economically withdrawing into its own territory to a far greater degree than is the case today. American industries that have enormously increased their production capacity, partly in the expectation of finding more favorable opportunities for the sale of mass-produced articles on the world market, will have to make adjustments. This will mean the United States will both import less and export less, and especially invest less capital abroad.

Only an end to the general opposition to international trade can prevent such a development. There would have to be a general elimination of tariff restrictions, as well as debtor nations renouncing, under whatever name, those policies that threaten foreign capital invested within their borders and therefore limit new capital investments.

Nevertheless, the United States is still rich enough to make significant financial sums available for the economic reconstruction of Europe. But America is not prepared to furnish the political, economic, or ideological leadership for this reconstruction. It is a mistake to assume that the United States can contribute anything for the economic rebuilding of Europe other than financial capital, for which profitable investment possibilities should be exploited.

---

6. [The Mexican Constitution of 1917 declared that the private ownership of land was no longer a right but a privilege, and that the state possessed the authority to seize land and redistribute it in the national interest. This included restrictions on foreign ownership and use of land and resources in Mexico. It finally culminated in the Mexican government's nationalization of American and other foreign-owned oil companies in 1938. See Ludwig von Mises, "Mexico's Economic Problems," (1943) in Richard M. Ebeling, ed., Selected Writings of Ludwig von Mises, vol. 3, The Political Economy of International Reform and Reconstruction (Indianapolis: Liberty Fund, 2000), pp. 203–54.—Ed.]

CHAPTER 25

The Currency and Finances of the Federal State of Austria[1]

The basic ideas of the reconstruction plan that federal Chancellor Dr. Seipel decided to carry out when he assumed his duties in summer 1922 were extremely clear and simple: the rejection of any further use of the printing press to fund state finances, restoration of a balanced budget, and fixing the gold value of the crown.[2] It was a complete repudiation of the inflationary and capital-consuming policies that were implemented in the first days of the war, and which the postwar government—being dependent as it was on the destructionist mood of the masses—had carried to an extreme.

The difference between Seipel's policies and the policies inaugurated by the Social Democratic Chancellor Renner[3] in 1918 is seen most clearly with the use they respectively made of foreign loans. The relief credits that foreign governments granted to Renner and his successors, and against which they pledged Austria's national property, were in the form of foodstuffs; their price was debited against the Austrian state. The government sold these provisions to the populace at prices below their cost of production. The proceeds from their sale were used to finance current government expenditures, not to repay

---

1. [This article was originally published in German in *Deutsche Wirtschaftszeitung*, vol. 25 (September 20, 1928).—Ed.]

2. [Ignaz Seipel (1876–1932) was a Roman Catholic prelate and head of the Christian Social Party in Austria. He twice served as chancellor of Austria (1922–24 and 1926–29). In general he followed a policy of social welfarism and interventionism, but he opposed the more directly socialist policies advocated by the Austrian Social Democratic Party during this time. He most especially opposed the inflationary policies of the immediate post–World War I period in Austria, and was able to bring the inflation to an end in 1922–23 with the financial and supervising assistance of the League of Nations.—Ed.]

3. [See Chapter 10, "On the Goals of Trade Policy," footnote 23.—Ed.]

the debt. The state loans received by Seipel, by contrast, were used for investments.[4]

The stabilization of the gold value of the Austrian crown was completely successful. The rate of exchange was stabilized at 14,400 paper crowns = 1 gold crown. Under the law of December 20, 1924, the official designation *schilling* was introduced for 10,000 paper crowns and the designation *groschen* for the hundredth part of a schilling. The Austrian National Bank is holding strictly to the regulations of the Bank Law. There is absolutely no use of the Bank, indirectly or directly, for the purposes of fiscal management.

The Austrian National Bank, which began its activity in January 1923, is obligated to cover the entire quantity of banknotes in circulation and those liabilities immediately payable on demand (minus the debt of the federal government) with its specie reserves; both currency and foreign exchange may be included for this purpose, at the rate of 20 percent during the first five years, 24 percent during the following five years, and at one-third thereafter. At the end of 1927, in fact, there were quantities of precious metals and foreign exchange worth about 830 million schillings at the discretionary possession of the Austrian National Bank, meaning that 80 percent of the notes in circulation and giro obligations were fully covered.

The Austrian National Bank actually is not required to redeem its notes in specie. It has the obligation to make sure, by all means at its command, that until the redemption of the banknotes in metal becomes legally required, there should be no decline in the gold value of its notes. Obviously, it can fulfill this obligation in no other way than by actually exchanging its banknotes for foreign exchange at the legal, stabilized rate of exchange (one dollar = 7.10 schillings or one kilogram of fine gold = 4723.20 schillings), and from which parity it does not deviate by more than the gold points beyond which it would be profitable to import or export gold. In order to fulfill this obligation the Austrian National Bank follows the policy that, decades ago, Wilhelm

---

4. [See Ludwig von Mises, "The Direction of Austrian Financial Policy: A Retrospective and Prospective View," (1935) in Richard M. Ebeling, ed., *Selected Writings of Ludwig von Mises*, vol. 2, *Between the Two World Wars: Monetary Disorder, Interventionism, Socialism, and the Great Depression* (Indianapolis: Liberty Fund, 2002), pp. 286–93, for Mises's more detailed summary of the consequences of what he, there, calls the "Renner System" of fiscal mismanagement and inflation, and what followed in the 1920s.—Ed.]

von Lucam[5] called the fundamental rule for the conduct of a note-issuing bank that does not redeem in specie, but which is determined to maintain the stability of the metal value of its notes: Do everything that a specie-paying bank would do and not do anything that a specie-paying bank would not do.

The success of this stabilization policy can be seen in the fact that no one any longer talks about an Austrian currency problem.

As has already been mentioned, the precondition for this currency policy was the government's renunciation of any further indirect or direct use of the note press for the purposes of fiscal management.

The federal budget estimated for 1928 is given below:

The current budget, therefore, shows surpluses. A deficit arises only because of investments.

The total income of the federal government from public taxes is estimated at 934.8 million schillings. Of that amount only 698.4 million is left for the federation since 236.4 million is transferred to the provinces and municipalities. The proceeds from direct taxes are estimated at 285 million schillings, of which 147 million schillings are attributable to the income tax, 52 million schillings to the general profit tax (i.e., the profit tax of those enterprises that are not obligated to tender public accounts), and 58 million schillings due to the corporate tax (i.e., the profit tax of enterprises that are obliged to render public accounts). The proceeds from customs duties are estimated at 227 million schillings, and the proceeds from excise taxes at 85.7 million schillings. These direct taxes are clearly excessively oppressive, and it will be necessary to reduce them as soon as possible.

Compensation could easily be found in an increase in excise taxes since these have not yet reached their prewar level. This is especially blatant in the case of sugar. Sugar is taxed at 14.40 schillings per 100 kg as against 38 crowns before the war; hence the prewar tax was 3.8 times as high as the present tax. The proceeds from the stamp taxes and legal fees (including inheritance and gift taxes) are estimated at 102.3 million schillings. Of very special importance is the sales tax on goods, the proceeds of which are estimated to come to 215 million schillings. The tobacco monopoly is calculated to produce a net profit of 183.1 million

---

5. [See Chapter 19, "The Austrian Currency Problem Thirty Years Ago and Today," footnote 6.—Ed.]

Estimated Expenditures	Current Budget			Investment		Total Budget	
	Expenses	Receipts	Surplus Schillings	Deficit	(Expenses)	Surplus	Deficit
Ntl. Administration	1,132,968,092	986,236,122	—	146,731,970	36,944,000	—	183,675,970
Monopolies	202,225,073	409,858,386	207,633,313		5,970,000	201,663,313	
Federal Operations	265,928,341	262,805,773	—	3,122,568	78,463,985	—	81,586,553
Railroads	22,263,400	5,010	—	22,258,390	69,730,000	—	91,988,390
Totals	1,623,348,906	1,658,905,291	207,633,313	172,112,928	191,107,985	201,663,313	357,250,913
			35,520,385				155,587,600

schillings, the salt monopoly some 13.3 million schillings, the national lottery some 10.3 million schillings, and the monopoly for gunpowder and explosives about 0.8 million schillings.

The conditions of federal public enterprises are hardly satisfactory. It is true that the post-and-telegraph office is calculated to have a cash surplus of 0.6 million schillings, but the facilities have not been appropriately depreciated, and no doubt a considerable depreciation needs to be recorded; there is also an excess in personnel and inefficient management, which is characteristic of public enterprises. Similarly unfavorable are the conditions of the federation's abundant possession of forests; and even more unfavorable is the situation of the (fortunately not very extensive) national coal and steel enterprises.

The situation of the federal railroads is also extraordinarily unfavorable. The federal railroads were established as an "independent economic body," so that their activities do not appear in the national budget. The figures concerning the railroads and the postal system given in the above summary of the federal pre-estimate include only the part of the departments which the tangled and artificial structure allows to go through in the national general accounts.

Whoever wants to be informed about the condition of the railroads must examine the business report of the "Austrian Federal Railroads" for the year 1927. The details of this report cannot be gone into within the framework of a short article. Anyone who evaluates the condition of the federal railroads from the viewpoint of national finances will be less interested in confirmation of the universally known fact of their unprofitability; the real problem is how, or even whether, there can be any improvement in this situation as long as they remain public enterprises. The great expectations over the electrification of the federal railroads seem not to have been fulfilled, even though there are still differences of opinion among the experts; moreover, it should be pointed out that the financial condition of the federal railroads will become even more unfavorable to the extent to which the highway network (which today is no longer adequate to meet modern demands) will be organized in such a way that motor transportation in Austria will acquire the same place in the modern system of transportation that it has elsewhere.

Let just one fact be highlighted from the federal railway report. The total business expenses of the federal rail system came to 550.5 million schillings in 1927. Of this amount 57 percent went to pay the wages of the current personnel and 17.4 percent to cover retirement pensions;

hence the combined outlays for personnel constitute three-quarters of total business expenses.

The financial condition of the Austrian Federation would be far more favorable if the federation were not burdened with the ownership and operation of the railroads, the post and telegraph system, the national forests, and the mines.

Moreover, the national administration is much too expensive. Austria consists of nine federal states. Five of these have fewer than 400,000 inhabitants and seven have fewer than 1,000,000. The smallest federal state, Vorarlberg, numbers only 140,000. The constitutional right of autonomy that was granted to the provinces has led to their setting up an excessively large administrative apparatus, which not only is exorbitantly expensive but does not even work very well and, above all, only puts impediments in the way of economic activity. But the worst is that in the provinces and in the towns those who must raise the revenues do not decide on the expenditures.

We have already spoken about the remittances of the federation to the provinces, which represents more than a quarter of the provincial revenues. In the provincial diets there predominates among the elected representatives a rural or petty bourgeois mentality, which sees industrial enterprises and especially banks as objects for unlimited taxation. It is even worse in the municipal chambers. The situation here is basically no different than in Germany; but it must be kept in mind that the Austrian economy is even less in a position to afford the luxury of a costly administration, along with superfluous provincial and local socialistic experiments. The leading fiscal policy problem in Austria is the financial regulation of the autonomous entities. The extent of the fiscal problem is clearly seen by the fact that the provincial and municipal budgets account for about six-tenths of the total budget of the federation.

Vienna, which constitutionally is both a province and a municipality at the same time, is in a far more favorable situation than the one prevailing in the other provinces. In the period before the war the Christian Social Party developed a vigorous municipal socialistic system that monopolized the streetcars and the provision of electricity and gas, and set up various other economic operations. All these investments were financed through loans, the burden of which was reduced to almost zero by the inflation. The Social Democratic Party, which rules Vienna today, consequently has taken over a rich inheritance. Moreover,

Vienna succeeded in coming out extraordinarily well in its financial arrangement with the federation.

Finally, the Social Democratic municipal administration exploits its taxing authority without any regard for the city's economic capacity to pay.[6] The municipal socialistic activity of the Vienna government very severely harms the development of the city. Vienna's most important means of urban transportation is still the streetcar. The municipal government thwarts the development of modern autobus traffic in order not to endanger its revenues from the streetcars and the metropolitan railway (the latter was turned over to the municipality gratis by the federal government and was electrified in a way that was far too expensive). Vienna has no subway since the municipality shrinks from this sort of enterprise, which might well make no profit under city management; on the other hand, private entrepreneurs are not allowed to set up a subway system due to the reigning socialistic bent of the city.

The development of an urban transportation system would be a far more beneficial influence on the housing situation in Vienna than the construction of rental apartments. The Social Democratic thesis is that the housing shortage (in a city whose population of 2.2 million in 1914 declined by 335,000 to 1.86 million in 1923) is not due to rent controls but merely the scarcity of housing.[7] The municipal government in Vienna undertook a brisk construction activity in the last few years. The city government spent on these projects 117 million schillings in 1926; for 1927, 118 million schillings are projected for the same purpose and 76 million schillings for 1928.

To pay for these expenditures a special-purpose tax was imposed, but it covered only a part of the outlays. For 1927 the yield from this special tax is estimated to be 35.3 million schillings, not even a third of the amount spent on housing construction. In reality it is financial transfers from the federation that make building activity possible for the

6. [In the mid-1920s, one Vienna newspaper referred to the fiscal policy of the Social Democratic government in control of the city as "the success of the tax vampires." See Richard M. Ebeling, "The Economist as the Historian of Decline: Ludwig von Mises and Austria Between the Two World Wars," in *Political Economy, Public Policy, and Monetary Economics: Ludwig von Mises and the Austrian Tradition* (London: Routledge, 2010), pp. 88–140, especially pp. 96–98.—Ed.]

7. [On the negative impact of rent controls imposed on residential housing in Vienna during this time, see F. A. Hayek, "The Repercussions of Rent Restrictions," (1928) in Walter Block and Edgar O. Olsen, eds., *Rent Control: Myths and Realities* (Vancouver: The Fraser Institute, 1981), pp. 87–103.—Ed.]

municipalities. In 1926, the last year for which the figures have already been published, the proportion of general federal revenue transferred from the federation to Vienna amounted to 118.2 million schillings, which approximately equaled the expenditure by the City of Vienna for residential building and housing-project construction.

Austria's future fiscal policy, first of all, must be directed toward cutting back on the direct taxes that impose a heavy burden on industry. This is necessary in order to stimulate investment activity, attract foreign capital, and strengthen the competitiveness of our industry on the world market. It must be acknowledged that much has been done in this area in recent years. The corporate tax rate has been lowered from 36 percent to 25 percent; some oppressive regulations connected with the pension tax have been eliminated; some tax encouragements for investment have been created; and the regulations relating to the personal tax law have been moderated.

All this, however, is still far from enough. It will not be possible to avoid radical reforms in the area of provincial and local taxes, especially in Vienna. This is true in the first place in reference to the hotel tax, which hampers the development of the tourist industry and has far more importance for Austria than it has for Germany. To carry out these reforms it will be necessary to simplify the administrative apparatus, especially in the provinces and municipalities, and to eliminate superfluous expenses. The crucial problem, however, relates to the public enterprises, above all the national railways.

One can see, then, that the financial problems that Austrian fiscal policy is confronted with are basically the same fiscal policy problems that other European states have to solve. For the present, Austria's financial situation is by no means disadvantageous; the treasury holdings of the federal finance administration are very considerable, the balance of the federal budget is not endangered, and the financial difficulties of a number of provinces and municipalities could be sorted out with a bit of good will. Hence the task of reconstruction that Seipel tackled in 1922 has unquestionably succeeded.

Today, Austria's fiscal policy problem is a problem of production. Not all the factors affecting costs of production in the Austrian economy can be influenced by domestic economic policy measures. The raw materials and semimanufactured goods that Austria has to import from abroad must be paid for at world-market prices. As a capital-poor country, Austria must have recourse to foreign capital; it follows that profit and interest rates have to be higher in Austria than in the majority of the industrial states that compete with her. The labor unions use all the means at their disposal to resist a lowering of wages.

A reduction in costs of production, which is an unavoidable precondition for an increase in Austrian exports and a decrease in imports, therefore, must be attempted, first of all, through a reduction in the taxes that burden industry.

CHAPTER 26

The Economic Crisis and Lessons for Banking Policy[1]

The events of the last few weeks have made obvious to everyone the defects in the German and Austrian banking systems, which previously were recognized by only a few.

At least until very recently, English and American banks have acted, in principle, purely as bankers in the classical sense of the term. That is, they have viewed their primary business to be the lending of money. The development of German banking activity made them not merely banks but also put them in the business of being industrial holding companies and investment trusts. This development did not occur through any logical process. In the beginning, German banks also limited themselves to the granting of credit. They ended up becoming partners in the businesses to which they had granted credit because they lent too much to these enterprises in proportion to their own capital. These banks were plunged into difficulties when there were attempts for immediate conversion of those enterprises' stocks and debentures into cash.

---

1. [This article originally appeared in German in the *Allgemeiner Tarifanzeiger* (August 1, 1931). For Mises's general analysis of the causes, consequences, and cures for the Great Depression, see Ludwig von Mises, "The Causes of the Economic Crisis," (1931) in *The Causes of the Economic Crisis, and Other Essays Before and After the Great Depression* (Auburn, Ala.: Ludwig von Mises Institute, 2006), pp. 155–181; also, Mises, "The Economic Crisis and Capitalism," (1931) in Richard M. Ebeling, ed., *Selected Writings of Ludwig von Mises*, vol. 2, *Between the Two World Wars: Monetary Disorder, Interventionism, Socialism, and the Great Depression* (Indianapolis: Liberty Fund, 2002), pp. 169–73; and for a general exposition of the Austrian theory of the trade cycle in the context of an analysis of the causes of and policy cures for the Great Depression in comparison to the Keynesian approach, see Richard M. Ebeling, "The Austrian Economists and the Keynesian Revolution: The Great Depression and the Economics of the Short Run," in *Political Economy, Public Policy, and Monetary Economics: Ludwig von Mises and the Austrian Tradition* (London: Routledge, 2010), pp. 203–72.—Ed.]

Gradually, banks were pushed out of the role of creditor into the role of the chief interested party. As a result, these banks no longer faced those enterprises with the critical eye of a banker who carefully judges the businesses' prospects as debtors, and who constantly evaluates the borrower's creditworthiness in order to limit or withdraw lines of credit if changing circumstances warrant it. These banks no longer looked at businesses' activities from the standpoint of a lender but from the viewpoint of the borrower. When the monitoring function that the lending institution normally exercises over businesses fell by the wayside, an essential regulator of the money market disappeared in fact if not in name.

The news media would appropriately offer strong criticisms of any combination of the banking business with production and trading activities, when individual enterprises and business firms made attempts to publicly raise investment money. But it was overlooked that at many respected banks that had readily put money into risky ventures (including three major banks in Vienna and Berlin that have recently failed) conditions were no better.[2] The independence of these banks from industrial enterprises was in many cases purely formal in the legal sense.

The representatives of the banks who had to decide on the granting of credit were, unfortunately, in many instances, identical with the representatives of the debtors who appealed for loans and credit expansion. When writers on the economy spoke out against this combining of banking and industry, those in banking labeled them ivory-tower theoreticians. Modern conditions, it was said, absolutely demand the amalgamation of banking and industry. The failure of this system clearly proves who was right. The more cautious the bank was in the establishment of its associations, the better off it is today.

The most pressing reform that must be pushed for is the elimination of the existing close ties between the banks and industrial combinations. Everyone agrees with this. Of course, this goal can be only slowly achieved. It will be years before it will be possible to transfer the

---

2. [A leading Austrian bank, Credit-Anstaldt, declared bankruptcy on May 11, 1931, when under Austrian banking law it had reached the threshold of losing more than half of its capital, due to demands from foreign and domestic depositors and lenders for withdrawals of sums owed to them. In May 1931, as well, the prominent German Danot-Bank fell into bankruptcy due to demands by depositors. The same happened to a series of other German banks in the weeks after Danot-Bank's collapse.—Ed.]

large debts of many enterprises from the banks to the public through the issuing of stocks and bonds. Recent experience has caused severe mistrust of stocks and bonds issued by industry, and this mistrust will not be quickly overcome. But the distrust is even stronger against stocks issued by banks, due to the serious doubts about their connections with industry.

This situation will necessarily lead these banks to loosen their ties with industry, or in any case to structure them so transparently that, at least to some extent, an outsider will be able to evaluate the relationship. Banks will, no doubt, be pushed in this direction due to the greater carefulness that American, English, and Dutch banks will practice in extending credit in the future. It may be expected that bankers in these foreign countries will want to see their debtors carry out that highly valued system of division of labor in the banking industry.

The intimate connection between banking and industry resulted in banks investing in industrial undertakings from which it was impossible to quickly withdraw the money invested, while they were committed to pay back money in the short term to their depositors. The well-known golden rule of banking, that a bank should never extend credit in the form of gold-backed banknotes and checkable deposits for a period longer than it receives funds from its depositors, is, of course, not possible for banks that issue currency and fiduciary media. But it should be strictly followed in all other banking matters. It is unnecessary to emphasize that it is not very wise to take in hundreds of millions under the obligation to pay on demand or at short notice, and to use an equivalent sum of money to buy industrial stocks or lend to enterprises that use the borrowed funds for longer-term capital investments.

Concerning interest rates, a clearer distinction will have to be made than in the past between deposits that are payable on demand or on short notice and deposits that are left on deposit for longer periods of time. Particular care must be taken that the savings of the general public are deposited only on a long-term basis to minimize the danger of bank runs. But it must also be insisted that in their regular reports banks should provide precise information about the dates when money they have lent will be repaid in relation to their outstanding deposit obligations.[3]

3. [See Ludwig von Mises, "Senior's Lectures on Monetary Problems," (1933) in Richard M. Ebeling, ed., *Money, Method, and the Market Process: Essays by Ludwig von Mises* (Norwell, Mass.: Kluwer Academic Press, 1990), pp. 104–9, especially pp. 107–8:

Secret dealings have turned out to be especially harmful for the banks. It has been discovered that often there were reasons for the taciturnity in bank reports as a means of covering up the losses being suffered. Oversight by the general public is an indispensible element in maintaining the soundness of our banking institutions.

Deposits subject to cheques and savings deposits are two entirely different things. The saver wishes to entrust his money for a longer period; he wishes to get interest. The bank that receives his money has to lend it to business. A withdrawal of the money entrusted to it by the saver can only take place in the same measure as the bank is able to get back the money it has lent. As the total amount of the saving deposits is working in the country's business, a total withdrawal is not possible. The individual saver can get back his money from the bank, but not all savers at the same time. That does not mean that the bank is unsound. It does not become unsound until the banks explicitly or tacitly promise what they cannot perform: to pay back the savings at call or at short notice.

The deposits subject to cheques have a different purpose. They are the businessman's cash like coins and banknotes. The depositor intends to dispose of them day by day. He does not demand interest, or at least he would entrust the money to the bank even without interest. The bank, to be sure, could not earn anything if it were to hold the whole amount of these deposits available. It has to lend the money at short notice to business. If all depositors simultaneously were to ask for their deposits back, it could not meet the demand. This fact that a bank which issues notes or receives deposits subject to cheque cannot hold the total amount corresponding to the notes in circulation and to the deposits in its vaults, and therefore can never redeem at once the total amount of its liabilities of this kind, is the knotty problem of banking policy. It is the consideration of this difficulty that has to govern the credit policy of the banks that issue notes or receive deposits subject to cheque. It is this consideration that led to the legislation that limits the issue of banknotes and imposes on the central banks the retention of a reserve fund of a certain magnitude.

But the case of the savings deposits is different. Since the saver does not need the deposited sum at call or short notice it is not necessary that the savings bank and the other banks that take over such deposits should promise repayment at call or short notice. Nevertheless, this is what they did. And so they became exposed to the dangers of a panic. They would not have run this danger, if they had accepted saving deposits only on condition that withdrawal must be notified some months ahead.
—Ed.]

PART 4

Interventionism, Collectivism, and Their Ideological Roots

CHAPTER 27

The Economic System of Interventionism[1]

Two economic systems are struggling for supremacy. On the one hand there is the capitalist system—that is, private ownership of the means of production—advocated by liberalism; on the other hand, there is the socialist or communist system—that is, collective ownership of the means of production supported by socialists of all shades.[2] Between these two systems, however, there is a third system, interventionism, which its adherents and supporters claim is neither socialism nor capitalism, and avoids the drawbacks of both while combining the advantages of each. It is applied today by almost all governments, and virtually all political parties advocate it in one or another form.[3]

1. [This article originally appeared in German in *Mitteilungen des Deutschen Hauptverbandes der Industrie*, vol. 11, no. 31 (July 31, 1930).—Ed.]
2. [On Mises's general critique of the "impossibility" of comprehensive socialist central planning in replacing a functioning, competitive market economy due to the former's inability to undertake efficient "economic calculation" for allocating scarce factors of production among competing uses in a complex system of division of labor, see Ludwig von Mises, "Economic Calculation in the Socialist Commonwealth," (1920) in F. A. von Hayek, *Collectivist Economic Planning: Critical Studies on the Possibilities of Socialism* (London: George Routledge, 1935), pp. 87–130, and *Socialism: An Economic and Sociological Analysis* (Indianapolis: Liberty Fund, [1951] 1981), especially pp. 95–194, also, *Bureaucracy* (Indianapolis: Liberty Fund, [1944] 2007), especially pp. 17–46, and *Human Action: A Treatise on Economics* (Irvington-on-Hudson, N.Y.: Foundation for Economic Education, 4th rev. ed., 1996), pp. 689–715. In addition, see Richard M. Ebeling, "Economic Calculation Under Socialism: Ludwig von Mises and His Predecessors," in *Austrian Economics and the Political Economy of Freedom* (Northampton, Mass.: Edward Elgar, 2003), pp. 101–35, and "Why Socialism is 'Impossible,'" *The Freeman: Ideas on Liberty* (October 2004), pp. 8–12.—Ed.]
3. [On the "Austrian" theory on the nature, workings, and limits of interventionism as an economic system in place of the competitive market economy, also see Ludwig von Mises, *Liberalism: The Classical Tradition* (Indianapolis: Liberty Fund, [1927] 2005), pp. 37–75, *Critique of Interventionism* (Irvington-on-Hudson, N.Y.: Foundation for Economic Education, [1929] 1996), *Interventionism: An Economic Analysis* (Irvington-on-Hudson, N.Y.: Foundation for Economic Education, [1940] 1998), *Human Action*, pp. 716–79, and *Planning for Freedom: How the Market System Works* (Indianapolis: Liberty Fund, [1980] 2008). Also, Murray N. Rothbard, *Power and*

Interventionism does not want to abolish private ownership of the means of production but only to restrict it. It declares, on the one hand, that unlimited private ownership of the means of production is harmful to society; but it maintains, on the other hand, that public ownership of the means of production—socialism—is, either in general or at least for the time being, impractical. Thus it wants to create some third way: a state of society that is midway between private ownership of the means of production, on the one hand, and collective ownership of the means of production, on the other hand. In this way the "excesses" and damages of capitalism are supposed to be prevented, while the advantages of free initiative and vitality, which socialism cannot provide, are preserved.

The method that is used is "interventions" in economic life. By such interventions we mean isolated commands of social control (through the regulation of the state) that force the owners of the means of production and the entrepreneurs to use the means of production at their disposal in a way different than they otherwise would. "Isolated commands" means that the commands do not form a part of a system of interventions that regulates all production and distribution, and would thereby eliminate private ownership of the means of production and put collective ownership (socialism) in its place. The commands that we have in mind, no matter how much they may pile up, are to be regarded as isolated commands as long as they are not issued as a plan to direct the whole economy in place of the individuals' pursuit of profit guided by the forces of the market. The term "means of production" is to be understood to mean all goods of a higher order, that is, all goods that are not yet ready for use or consumption by the consumers; this includes all those goods that retailers have in stock and are designated as "ready for use" in the commercial sense.

The interventions can be of two kinds: they can be either production-restricting interventions, that is, orders that directly obstruct or impede production, or price-restricting interventions, which amount to

Market: The Government and the Economy (Menlo Park, Calif.: Institute for Humane Studies, 1970); Israel M. Kirzner, "The Perils of Regulation: A Market-Process Approach," in *Discovery and the Capitalist Process* (Chicago: University of Chicago Press, 1985), pp. 119–49; Sanford Ikeda, *Dynamics of the Mixed Economy: Toward a Theory of Interventionism* (London: Routledge, 1997); and Richard M. Ebeling, "The Free Market and the Interventionist State: The Political Economy of Public Policy," in *Austrian Economics and the Political Economy of Freedom*, pp. 203–30.—Ed.]

the same thing as setting the prices of goods and services other than as they would be formed on the unhampered market.

Production-restricting interventions, by their very nature, can have no other effect than to reduce the productivity of economic activity. No more will be said about them here. We will limit ourselves exclusively to the treatment of price-restricting interventions; for this purpose we will investigate price controls ordered by the authorities that legally specify a maximum price.

At the price that is formed on the unhampered market, or would have been formed if the government had not prevented the free formation of prices, the costs of production are covered by revenues. If a lower price is ordered by the authorities, the revenues fall below costs. If it is not a question of nondurable goods that can undergo a rapid loss of value if kept in storage, the dealers and producers will refrain from selling them in order to hold on to their goods in the hope of more favorable times, for instance, in the expectation that the official order will soon be rescinded. If the authorities do not want their command to result in the product in question completely disappearing from the market, they cannot limit themselves to fixing the price; at the same time, they must also order that all existing stocks be sold at the prescribed price.

But even that does not suffice; at the ideal market price, supply and demand would have matched each other. Now, since the price has been set lower by official decree, the quantity demanded has increased while the supply remains unchanged. The available supplies are not enough to satisfy fully all who are ready to pay the prescribed price. The market mechanism that normally brings supply and demand into balance by changes in price no longer operates. Now people who would be ready to pay the price prescribed by the authorities must leave the market without having achieved what they want. Those who got there earlier or who know how to exploit some personal relationship with the sellers have already acquired the entire supply; the others are left empty-handed. If the authorities want to avoid this consequence of their intervention, which goes directly counter to their intentions, they must go further and add rationing to the price controls and the mandatory selling of the existing stock. An official regulation determines how much of the product can be allotted to each applicant at the prescribed price.

But once the supply is used up that was on hand at the time the intervention was introduced, a very difficult problem then arises. Since selling at the price prescribed by the authorities is no longer profitable, its production is either cut back or completely stopped. If the authorities want to have production continued, they must oblige the producers to produce, and for this purpose they must also set the prices of raw materials and semifinished goods, as well as workers' wages. These commands, however, cannot be limited to the one or the few branches of production that the authorities want to regulate because they consider these products to be especially important. They must extend the commands to encompass all branches of production; they must regulate the prices of all goods and every labor cost, and the conduct of all entrepreneurs, capitalists, landowners, and workers.

If they were to leave some branches of production free, then capital and labor would flow into them, and the goal that the authorities wanted to reach with their first intervention would completely fail. But the authorities imposed price controls on this particular line of production precisely because of the importance they attached to there being an ample supply of this particular good. It runs completely against their intention if precisely because of the intervention there is now less of this good than before.

Thus, one sees that the isolated intervention—in our case the maximum price—imposed on the working of an economic order based on private ownership of the means of production fails to achieve the purpose that its advocates want to attain; it is—from the point of view of its advocates—not merely useless but really counterproductive, because it dramatically makes worse the "evil" that the intervention was supposed to fight. Before the price control was enacted, the commodity was—in the opinion of the authorities—too expensive; now it disappears from the market. But this was not the intention of the authorities, who wanted to make the item available to the consumer at a lower price. From their own viewpoint, the impossibility, now, of obtaining the article must appear as the greater, the far greater evil. In this sense, one can say that isolated interventions are useless and counterproductive, and such an interventionist economic system is unworkable and inconceivable, in that it contradicts economic logic.

If the authorities do not want to get things back on track by reversing the first isolated intervention—revoking the price control—then they must follow this first intervention with others. The command to sell at no price higher than the one prescribed must be followed not only by the command to sell existing stocks at this price and to introduce rationing; it is also necessary to impose price controls for higher-order goods and wage rates, and finally to impose compulsory labor on both entrepreneurs and workers. Furthermore, these regulations cannot be limited to one or a few branches of production, but must include all branches of production. There is simply no other choice: either desist from isolated interventions in the workings of the market or instead turn over the entire management of production and distribution to the authorities. Either capitalism or socialism; there is no middle way.

It is the recognition of this fact that leads liberalism to reject interventionist intrusions in the arena of economics. Liberalism opposes authoritarian interventions not out of hostility to the state, not because of any insistence on natural law, but out of a sober recognition of the facts. It rejects direct commands by the state and the municipalities in economic affairs because it is convinced that unhampered entrepreneurial activity leads to greater productivity, that is, to a better provision of the consumers; and it rejects governmental interventions into the activities of entrepreneurs because it is of the opinion that the authorities cannot reach the goals that they wish to attain through this method.

CHAPTER 28

Economic Order and the Political System[1]

Economic and political liberalism go hand in hand, and appeared in history at the same time. Only in the second half of the nineteenth century did political parties begin to believe that in the long run it was possible to successfully combine liberalism and democracy with interventionist, statist, and socialist economic policies. This view is still firmly held in Western Europe and the United States. It is the source of the prevailing confusion that surrounds all political and economic policy ideas and concepts. In recent decades—and this can hardly be contested—the abandonment of economic liberalism has gone hand in hand with the retreat from parliamentarianism and with imposed restrictions on the political freedom of the citizenry.

Soviet Russia, which leads in the flight from economic liberalism, has been the first to proclaim dictatorship, to declare parliamentary government and freedom to be "bourgeois prejudices," and to eliminate all the institutions that ought to protect the individual against the arbitrary power of government.[2] No other state has gone so far in either

1. [This article originally appeared in German in *Wiener Wirtschaftswoche*, vol. 5 (1936) as a review of William E. Rappard, *L'individu et l'état dans l'évolution constitutionnelle de la Suisse* [The Individual and the State in the Constitutional Evolution of Switzerland] (Zurich, 1936).—Ed.]
2. [The Russian Czar, Nicolas II, abdicated in March 1917 during the First World War. A provisional government was formed of Left-oriented political parties. This government was overthrown in the Bolshevik coup d'état of November 7, 1917. A free election for a Constituent Assembly was held on November 25, 1917, which resulted in the Socialist-Revolutionary Party winning 40.1 percent of the vote, the Bolsheviks 24 percent, and a variety of other parties, including the Constitutional Democratic Party (4.7 percent) and the Mensheviks (1.5 percent), winning the rest. The Constituent Assembly met once on January 5–6, 1918. Vladimir Lenin, the leader of the Bolsheviks, declared that his party would not accept any decisions of the Assembly, and the Assembly was prevented from meeting again by Red Guard units under Bolshevik command. A three-year civil war soon broke out that resulted in the victory of Lenin's Bolshevik (Communist) Party, which then dictatorially ruled over what became the Soviet Union until December 1991. Marxists argued that the liberal idea of freedom—including freedom of

abolishing private ownership or in establishing the unrestrained despotism of the political authorities.

But the Russian example has been followed by many other countries, even if less radically and especially with less cruelty and bloodshed. Year by year dictatorship advances and parliamentary government and democracy lose ground.[3] Only yesterday many Englishmen expressed

speech, the press, religion, association, the voting franchise, and freedom of enterprise and trade—was a "bourgeois" illusion to make "the masses" believe they were free when in fact they were the victims of "wage slavery" and exploitation by the ruling capitalist class, who used the power of the state to maintain their private control over the means of production. Only socialism would provide "real freedom" for people through collective ownership of the means of production, along with central planning that would assure "production for use" rather than "production for profit."—Ed.]

3. [When Mises wrote this article in 1936, virtually the only functioning democracy in Central and Eastern Europe was Czechoslovakia. All the other nations in this part of Europe had totalitarian political regimes (Fascist Italy and Nazi Germany) or authoritarian regimes with political dictatorship, restrictions on civil liberties, and economic systems of control and intervention. See William E. Rappard, "Nationalism and the League of Nations Today," in *Problems of Peace, Eighth Series: Lectures Delivered at the Geneva Institute of International Relations* (Freeport, N.Y.: Books for Libraries, [1934] 1968), pp. 17–19:

For generations and, in some cases, for centuries, all nations within the orbit of our Western civilization have, through wars and revolutions, been striving to secure for all their members, greater physical and moral security, greater political equality, greater individual freedom. Greater security, that is, more assured protection against the violence of their fellow-citizens and against the arbitrary oppression of their Governments. Greater equality, that is, less discrimination on grounds of race, or sex, or religious and philosophical creed, and social position. Greater freedom, that is, more latitude for the self-expression and self-assertion of the individual in the face of the authority of tradition, and of the State. Guarantees for the protection of the fundamental rights of man; the abolition of arrest without trial and imprisonment for debt; the suppression of slavery; the extension of the suffrage to all and thereby the subordination of the Government to the will of the people, that is, of the majority of the people; parliamentary control of the budget, that is, no taxation without representation; the recognition of the freedom of thought, of speech, of assembly, of the Press, the independence of the Judiciary, and the autonomy of the university; such are some of the ideals for which our fathers, grandfathers, and great-grandfathers fought, bled, and died. Such are some of the conquests of human dignity over barbarism, of knowledge over ignorance, of right over might, which they triumphantly achieved and which they proudly bequeathed to us.

And such are some of the ideals which, after the greatest struggles in human history, we, their children of the twentieth century, through stupidity and cowardice are, sometimes with the blind enthusiasm of mad fanaticism and sometimes with the dull resignation of impotence, disavowing, renouncing, abandoning. The individual, the family, the local or regional community, everything and everybody are being sacrificed to the State. The State, itself, once held to be the protector and the servant of the people, is in several countries of our Western civilization being turned into a weapon for oppressing its own citizens and threatening its neighbors, according to the capricious will of one or of a few self-appointed individuals. These individuals, whether they style themselves chiefs, leaders, or dictators, are all what free men of all times, under all climes, have combated as

the idea that Western Europe and the states founded by Western Europeans around the world were immune from all dictatorial ventures. The nations that had created modern culture, they thought, would never abandon such essential elements of their culture as representative government and the citizens' right to political freedom. Today the parliamentary constitution of France is already seriously threatened; in England itself, the land of habeas corpus, a party advocating dictatorship is raising its head;[4] and in the United States a great writer believes he must warn his countrymen about the danger of losing their freedoms.[5]

Especially in the last few years there has been an uninterrupted and triumphant advance of interventionism on the one hand and of dictatorship on the other. Is this an accidental coincidence, or is there a real connection between the two?

The democratic system rests on the market economy with private ownership of the means of production. Each penny represents a ballot. Consumers, by their conduct in buying and abstaining from buying, control the market system. Entrepreneurs and capitalists are forced to follow the instructions that the consumers give them on the market. If they are unable to fulfill the desires of the market in the best and least expensive way, they experience losses; finally, if they do not change their conduct in time, they are removed from their favored position into other roles where they no longer have control over some of the means of production, and therefore can no longer do harm.

The market selects the entrepreneurs and capitalists—it makes them rich; the market can also make them poor again and remove them from their position, if they fail to satisfy consumer wants. It is true that

---

tyrants. They are today acclaimed as heroes by hundreds of thousands of European youths, welcomed as saviors by millions of European bourgeois, and accepted by tens of millions of European senile cowards of all ages.
—Ed.]

4. [Mises is referring to the British Union of Fascists (BUF), founded by Sir Oswald Mosley (1896–1980), who had served in the Labor Party government in 1929, but broke away in 1931. After visiting Italy, he was inspired to form the BUF in 1932 on the model and ideology of Mussolini's Italian fascist movement. The BUF was banned in 1940 and Mosley was first interned and then placed under house arrest for the remainder of the Second World War.—Ed.]

5. [Mises is referring to an article by American journalist and political analyst Walter Lippmann, "The Permanent New Deals," *Yale Review* (June 1935); Lippmann extended the core elements of his argument in his book *An Inquiry into the Principles of the Good Society* (Boston: Little, Brown, 1937), which in its critique of the planned society and the regulated economy relies heavily on Mises's and Friedrich A. Hayek's analyses of the economic unworkability of the state-managed economy and the dangers to political and personal freedom with the elimination of the market order.—Ed.]

on the market there are universal but not equal voting rights. Voting power increases with the size of income. But this greater voting power is itself the result of the voting of the market. It can be won and held only by the test of the market, by the successful use of the means of production that is in compliance with the wishes of consumers. In a capitalist economy that is not restrained by government intervention, ownership is the result of a daily plebiscite of the consumers, who have a sovereign and revocable mandate. Even though landownership has its origin in precapitalist times, the wealth of the landowners must meet this test if it is to be preserved; therefore, real estate, too, is subject to the law of the market.

The structure of political democracy corresponds to the democratic structure of the market. The citizen as well as the consumer decides who should direct production according to his desires; just as he replaces the entrepreneur and the capitalist who does not satisfy his consumption wants with other men, so it is granted to the hands of the electorate to replace political leaders who do not lead where the voter wants to go. Just as the market sees to it that production is directed according to the desires of the consumers, so a democratic constitution makes sure that governmental power is exercised in agreement with the political ideals of the electorate.

Now political democracy has decided against the economic democracy of the market. Whether one welcomes this or deplores it, it is an incontestable fact that public opinion today wants to replace the capitalist economy with a system in which it is the government that manages production and distribution rather than the market. No longer will people put up with, as a universally employed slogan coined by the Marxists says, the "anarchy of production"—that is, the absence of coercion and the freedom of the market. People want interventionism, statism, the planned economy, and socialism. The outcome of every election confirms anew that the masses do not want capitalism but want a controlled economy. Even in the dictatorial states where there are no elections, this, too, is the will of the masses.

One may argue that if there were free elections in Germany they would produce a different outcome than those that resulted in the last several votes.[6] But no one supposes that any German opposition to the

6. [In the German national election of July 1932, the National Socialist German Workers (Nazi) Party won 37.8 percent of the vote, the Social Democratic Party won 21.9 percent, and the Communist Party won 14.6 percent. In the national election of November 1932, the Nazis lost votes, winning 33.1 percent, the Social Democrats, 20.4 percent, and the Communists, 16.9

current government is striving for the return to capitalism. It, too, wants a planned and controlled economy, although under the direction of a different leader and for other foreign and domestic purposes. The insoluble conflict in the policies of the "Left parties" of England, France, and the United States is that they advocate a planned economy while refusing to realize that they are preparing the way for dictatorship and the abolition of civil liberties.[7] Their conceptual confusion is so great that they wish to fight for the preservation of democracy in cooperation with Soviet Russia.[8]

The adherents of those dictatorships that are called "fascist" have clearly acknowledged and expressed the fact that in a state in which the economy is directed by the government it is meaningless to talk about democratic constitutions and the freedom of the individual. The National Socialists argue as follows: if the farmer is no longer free to cultivate his field as he wishes and to dispose of the produce of his soil, and if the entrepreneur is no longer allowed to manage his company

---

percent. The German president, Paul von Hindenburg, appointed Adolf Hitler as chancellor on January 30, 1933. Following the Reichstag fire in March 1933, Hitler consolidated powers in a way that shortly resulted in his becoming absolute dictator—the *Führer*—in Germany until the Allied victory over Nazi Germany in May 1945.—Ed.]

7. [This general theme on the relationship between economic liberty and political freedom was one developed by a number of writers in the 1930s, along the lines of Mises's argument. Of note among them were Gustav Cassel, *From Protectionism Through Planned Economy to Dictatorship*, the sixth Richard Cobden Lecture (London: Cobden-Sanderson, 1934); Francis W. Hirst, *Liberty and Tyranny* (London: Duckworth, 1935) and *Economic Freedom and Private Property* (London: Duckworth, 1935); William Henry Chamberlin, *Collectivism: A False Utopia* (New York: Macmillan, 1936); Walter Lippmann, *An Inquiry into the Principles of the Good Society*. This was also the central theme of F. A. Hayek, *The Road to Serfdom* (Chicago: University of Chicago Press, [1944] 2007). See also Ludwig von Mises, *Omnipotent Government: The Rise of the Total State and Total War* (New Haven: Yale University Press, 1944) and "Socialism Versus European Democracy," *The American Scholar* (Spring 1943), pp. 220–31.—Ed.]

8. [Mises is referring to the "popular front" movement of the mid and late 1930s. In May 1934, the Communist Party of the Soviet Union inaugurated what became called the "popular front" of all those parties united in their opposition to fascist governments and ideas. This replaced Soviet opposition to all cooperation with socialist parties and movements not controlled by Moscow. In June 1934, the socialist government in France made an alliance with the French Communist Party, and the French government entered into a defense treaty with the Soviet Union in 1935. The Soviet government also used the popular front movement to violently gain control of the antifascist movement in Spain during the Spanish Civil War (1936–39). The popular front movement collapsed in August 1939, with the Soviet-Nazi nonaggression pact, which included a secret protocol between Moscow and Berlin to divide Poland between Nazi Germany and the Soviet Union in case of war, and for the Baltic Republics to be recognized as part of the Soviet sphere of influence.—Ed.]

according to his own ideas, then writers, artists, and scholars will not be allowed to create as they wish, either.[9]

If the economy rests entirely in the hands of the authorities, then those authorities can prevent the publication of all unacceptable intellectual writings and suppress the activities of all groups of which they disapprove. Even any claimed right to freedom of conscience, freedom of inquiry, and of expression of opinion will not help. The power of the totalitarian state is so great that it can take control over every conceivable activity without arousing resistance. Schiller was able to evade the tyranny of the twelve dukes of Württemberg by fleeing to the nearby "abroad."[10] Where will a sanctuary be open for a persecuted genius if all states become totalitarian?

The paradox of modern times is the fact that the democratic era that was created by liberalism led to the rise of both economic freedom and political democracy. William E. Rappard presents this development in a masterly way based on the example of his native Switzerland. No other man could have created such a work. Originally from the French-speaking part of Switzerland, culturally a citizen of all three ethnic regions of his homeland, and connected with the Anglo-Saxon tradition by scholarship at the oldest and most eminent university of the New World, Rappard has been active not only as a researcher and teacher.[11]

9. [On the structure and workings of the Nazi planned economy, see Gunter Reimann, *The Vampire Economy: Doing Business Under Fascism* (Auburn, Ala.: Ludwig von Mises Institute, [1939] 2007); and Walter Eucken, "On the Theory of the Centrally Administered Economy: An Analysis of the German Experiment," *Economica*, Part I (May 1948), pp. 79–100, and Part II (August 1948), pp. 173–93.—Ed.]

10. [Friedrich von Schiller (1759–1805) was one of Germany's most famous poets and playwrights. He fell out of favor with the Duke of Württemberg in 1782 due to the Duke's displeasure over the themes in several of his plays. After being placed under a fortnight's arrest, and an order written by the duke commanding him to write no more comedies and not to interact with anyone outside the principality of Württemberg, Schiller escaped during the dead of night. After first living in Mannheim and then Leipzig, he finally settled in Weimar in 1787, where he soon formed an enduring and close friendship with Johann Wolfgang von Goethe.—Ed.]

11. [William E. Rappard (1883–1958) was the cofounder of the Graduate Institute of International Studies in Geneva, Switzerland, and one of the leading classical liberals in Europe in the interwar period. Born in New York of Swiss parents, he studied economics at Harvard University and at the University of Vienna before the First World War. He supposedly influenced Woodrow Wilson in arranging for the League of Nations to have its headquarters in Geneva, and was an active advocate of international peace and free trade; he served on the League of Nations Mandates Committee, and was a member of the Swiss delegation at League of Nations Assembly meetings. Rappard developed the themes discussed in this review in his University of Chicago Harris Lectures, *The Crisis of Democracy* (Chicago: University of Chicago Press,

As a Swiss statesman and a brilliant representative of that Geneva internationalism that is working for the pacification of our weapons-choked world, he has experienced the history of our times as an active participant. Succinctly and factually, Rappard sketches out in his new book *L'individu et l'état dans l'évolution constitutionnelle de la Suisse* [The Individual and the State in the Constitutional Evolution of Switzerland] the path that Switzerland has followed from the patriciate of the eighteenth century through wars, revolutions, and party struggle to the liberalism and democracy of the constitutions of 1848 and 1874.

His analysis clearly shows how the mobilization of the citizenry in exercise of their political rights was the outgrowth of the development of political democracy; it was also the starting point for the new economic interventionism, which has now become a threat to political democracy.[12] Rappard always speaks only as a historian who follows Ranke's principle of simply presenting things as they were. Only in the final chapter does he articulate the problem with which Switzerland today is confronted. It is necessary to choose. "Should our liberal and democratic achievements be sacrificed to our statism?" Rappard asks. "Or do we wish to sacrifice our statism for our love of liberty and our desire for self-government?"

1938). For a brief biography of Rappard's life and work, see Richard M. Ebeling, "William E. Rappard: An International Man in an Age of Nationalism," *Ideas on Liberty* (January 2000), pp. 33–41.—Ed.]

12. [See William E. Rappard, "The Relation of the Individual to the State," *Annals of the American Academy of Political and Social Science* (January 1937), pp. 215–18:

The revolutions at the end of the eighteenth century . . . were essentially revolts of the individual against the traditional state—expressions of his desire to emancipate himself from the ties and inhibitions which the traditional state had imposed on him. . . . After the rise of individualism, which one may define as the emancipation of the individual from the state, we had the rise of democracy, which one may define as the subjection of the state to the will of the individual. In the latter half of the nineteenth century and up to the present, the individual, having emancipated himself from the state and having subjected the state to his will, has furthermore demanded of the state that it serve his material needs. Thereby he has complicated the machinery of the state to such a degree that he has again fallen under the subjection of it and he has been threatened with losing control over it. . . . The individual has increasingly demanded of the state services which the state is willing to render. Thereby, however, he has been led to return to the state an authority over himself which it was the main purpose of the revolutions in the beginning of the nineteenth century to shake and break. . . . The individual demanding that the state provide him with every security has thereby jeopardized his possession of that freedom for which his ancestors fought and bled.
—Ed.]

Switzerland, Rappard thinks, cannot evade the need to make this decision. The direction of current policies cannot be continued. Statism, today, lives by consuming the wealth created by the capitalist economy. Statism has extraordinarily raised the cost of living, created an extravagant administrative apparatus, pursued a protective tariff policy, practiced deficit spending in funding federal highways, and used its alcohol monopoly to lavishly distribute subsidies to now one and then another special interest, but always to agriculture. Either statism must be given up due to its financial shortcomings, or the economy must be restructured along the lines of the example of Russia, Germany, and Italy. That, however, cannot be done without some sort of dictatorship, Rappard says, since the Swiss people will not be inclined to freely choose to have their standard of living decreased.

No one has previously formulated the political and economic policy problems of our time so clearly and with such relentless consistency as Rappard. In the face of this formulation the dogmas and illusions collapse that for decades have ruled the politics of the civilized nations. The conditions in England, France, and the United States are not unlike those in Switzerland. Thus Rappard's book acquires universal significance beyond the geographic, historical, and material borders of the country in question. It will direct the political thinking of all those who in the current generation possess a mature sense of civic responsibility.

CHAPTER 29

Remarks Concerning the Ideological Roots of the Monetary Catastrophe of 1923[1]

The ideas that shape the policies of nations do not drop from the sky. They are conceived by thinkers. Whoever wants to write the history of an age must first study the writings that have shaped public opinion. The ideas that guided German policies in the twentieth century were those created by German political philosophy and economists during the Second Reich.[2] That is no less true of monetary policy. In the writings of Lexis,[3] Knapp,[4] and Bendixen[5] one finds all the ideas whose practical application led to the collapse of 1923.

The future historian of these events will be forced to ask a question for which he will not easily find an answer. The age of Gustav Schmoller,[6]

1. [This essay was originally published in German in *Freundesgabe zum 12. Oktober 1959 für Albert Hahn* [Homage by Friends for Albert Hahn on October 12, 1959] (Frankfurt am Main: Fritz Knapp, 1959).—Ed.]
2. [The "Second Reich" refers to the German Empire from its formal founding in 1871, under Prussian leadership during the Franco-Prussian War (1870–71), until the abdication of Kaiser Wilhelm II at the end of the First World War in 1918.—Ed.]
3. [Wilhelm Lexis (1837–1914) was a German statistician, economist, and social scientist, as well as a founder of the interdisciplinary study of insurance. He is primarily known today as a statistician due to his creation of the Lexis ratio.—Ed.]
4. [See Chapter 2, "The Problem of Legal Resumption of Specie Payments in Austria-Hungary," footnote 10.—Ed.]
5. [Friedrich Bendixen (1864–1920) was a leading follower of Knapp's state theory of money. He served as director of the Hythekenbank in Hamburg until his death in 1920.—Ed.]
6. [Gustav von Schmoller (1838–1917) was a prominent University of Berlin economist in Imperial Germany who led the "Socialists of the Chair" and who defended and glorified Prussian military power. He was a leading member of the German Historical School, which rejected abstract deductive theorizing in economics in favor of detailed historical studies from which it was hoped empirical laws of economics might be discovered. He was also a strong advocate of the German welfare state and regulation of industry and trade in the name of the national interest. He was a founding member of the *Verein für Sozialpolitik*.—Ed.]

Adolf Wagner,[7] and Lujo Brentano[8] was also the age of Helmholtz,[9] Hertz,[10] Frege,[11] Georg Cantor,[12] and Planck.[13] How can we explain the fact that the flourishing of mathematics and physics coincided with a nadir in the sciences of human action? How was it that out of a population of seventy million people no one came forward to oppose the dogmas that reigned over monetary policy?

To understand this we must refer back to that "ethical pathos" out of which there emerged the exhortations leading to the founding of the *Verein für Sozialpolitik* (Society for Social Policy) in 1872.[14] Economic questions were to be treated as moral problems, and not as logical ones. It was all a matter of good intentions, not of knowledge and ability. The pursuit of truth was not considered to be of ethical or practical value in and of itself. It was morally suspect to deviate from the doctrines espoused by the state-appointed university professors. It was considered unnecessary to go into the philosophical foundations of their ideas or to make any attempt to refute them. In this regard Imperial Germany already contained the ideas to which not much later communism and nationalism tried to give international respectability.

7. [Adolph Wagner (1859–1917) was another well-known University of Berlin economist in Imperial Germany. He was an advocate of "state socialism," which called for the transformation of liberal capitalism into a state interventionist welfare state.—Ed.]

8. [See Chapter 8, "On Rising Prices and Purchasing Power Policies," footnote 8.—Ed.]

9. [Hermann Ludwig Ferdinand von Helmholtz (1821–94) was a prominent German medical doctor and physicist known for his theory of the eye and vision, and his work on electrodynamics and thermodynamics.—Ed.]

10. [Heinrich Rudolf Hertz (1857–94) was well known for his work on the electromagnetic theory of light, and for demonstrating the existence of electromagnetic waves in the form of VHF and UHF radio waves.—Ed.]

11. [Gottlob Frege (1848–1925) was a German mathematician who is often called the father of analytical philosophy. He attempted to develop a formally exact and unambiguous logic.—Ed.]

12. [Georg Ferdinand Ludwig Philipp Cantor (1845–1918) was a famous German mathematician best known for his development of set theory.—Ed.]

13. [Max Planck (1858–1947) was a leading German physicist who is considered to be the founder of quantum theory. He was awarded the Nobel Prize in Physics in 1918.—Ed.]

14. [The *Verein für Sozialpolitik* was founded in 1872 as an association of historians, economists, political scientists, and sociologists devoted to the reconstruction of the social sciences on historical-empirical lines, in opposition to the logical, deductive methods of the British Classical economists, and then later the Austrian School of economics. The society was also dedicated to an active governmental role in the areas of social welfare and regulation of private enterprise. It was the inspiration for like-minded American economists who established the American Economic Association in 1885. See Eugen von Philippovich, "The Verein für Sozialpolitik," *Quarterly Journal of Economics* (January 1891), pp. 220–37, and "The Infusion of Socio-Political Ideas into the Literature of German Economics," *The American Journal of Sociology* (September 1912), pp. 145–99.—Ed.]

It was to Max Weber's[15] credit that he took up the fight against the politically biased dogmas that at that time passed for economics and sociology in Germany. The *Verein für Sozialpolitik* was certainly not the most appropriate place for discussing the problems of "value free-dom." However, in the German-speaking world, there was no other organization at whose meetings questions of economics could be discussed. Since what Schmoller and his friends talked about they called "science," they could not object when the question was raised whether or not science was expected to make value judgments.[16]

In those years I did not yet belong to the board of directors of the *Verein für Sozialpolitik*, and therefore I did not participate in the closed board meeting of January 5, 1914, at which the question of value judgments was discussed, but from which the public was excluded. However, I did have exhaustive discussions with several prominent members of the society about this issue.

Before the publication of my book *The Theory of Money and Credit*

15. [Max Weber (1864–1920) is considered one of the greatest contributors to sociological theory in the last one hundred years. He developed the concept of the "ideal type" for sociological and historical analysis, and emphasized the importance of subjective meaning—the meaning of an action from the individual actor's point of view—in social theory. He also argued that professors in the social fields, including economics, history, and political science, should not take advantage of the influence that an academic position gave to their lectures and writings to infuse their normative values and beliefs in discussions of theory and fact. Weber's essays on the importance of a value-free social science are contained in Max Weber, *The Methodology of the Social Sciences* (New York: The Free Press, 1949).—Ed.]

16. [See Ludwig von Mises, *Critique of Interventionism* (Irvington-on-Hudson, N.Y.: Foundation for Economic Education, [1929] 1996), pp. 19, 43–70, and *Memoirs* (Auburn, Ala.: Ludwig von Mises Institute, [1940] 2009), pp. 85–89, for Mises's impressions of the political and economic ideas expressed at the professional associations in Germany during this time, and a discussion of Max Weber's role in defending "value-freedom" in the social sciences. Mises adamantly insisted that economics was and should be a "value-free" science whose primary task at any policy level was to demonstrate whether the means chosen were or were not appropriate for attaining the end in mind. He once forcefully expressed this point about his own role as an economist; see Ludwig von Mises, "Interventionism as the Cause of the Economic Crisis," (1932) in Richard M. Ebeling, ed., *Selected Writings of Ludwig von Mises*, vol. 2, *Between the Two World Wars: Monetary Disorder, Interventionism, Socialism, and the Great Depression* (Indianapolis: Liberty Fund, 2002) p. 201:

I am an economist, not a preacher of morality who wishes to judge, avenge, and punish. I do not look for guilty parties but for causal connections. And if I speak of interventionism, I am not making accusations against the "state" or against "labor." I only attempt to point out to what consequences a system, a policy, an ideology must necessarily lead.

Also see Ludwig von Mises, "The Treatment of 'Irrationality' in the Social Sciences," (1944) in Richard M. Ebeling, ed., *Money, Method, and the Market Process: Essays by Ludwig von Mises* (Norwell, Mass.: Kluwer Academic Press, 1990), pp. 16–36.—Ed.]

in the spring of 1912,[17] the discussions were mainly about the theories of Carl Menger and Böhm-Bawerk,[18] as well as my own contributions. I was in the habit of taking notes about these conversations, in which I tried to record the ideas of my conversation partners. I preserved these notes in my Vienna apartment, which I kept after my move to Geneva (1934). In March 1938 they disappeared with everything else in my apartment when the National Socialists plundered it.[19] What I have on hand is only a summary of the objections raised against Böhm-Bawerk and myself, which I wrote down at Böhm-Bawerk's request in the spring of 1914. Since in this manuscript I omitted the names of the individuals who made specific comments, and my memory could easily deceive me after more than 45 years, I will also omit mentioning any names in what follows.

Böhm-Bawerk, my conversation partners remarked, is without a doubt an honorable man searching after truth. Nevertheless, his dreadful mistakes resulted in an unacceptable justification of the worst form of unearned income—interest on capital. According to them, it was the moral duty of the state to use governmental measures to bring down any high market rates of interest. The most absurd book in economic literature, they said, is Bentham's *Defense of Usury*.[20] An unbiased scholar, Wilhelm Lexis, they said, had clearly proven that the employers' income should be viewed as being in the same economic category as the income received by a slave owner.[21] They claimed that Böhm-Bawerk's arguments against Marx's exploitation theory were foolish.[22]

17. [Ludwig von Mises, *The Theory of Money and Credit* (Indianapolis: Liberty Fund, 3rd rev. ed., [1924; 1951] 1981).—Ed.]
18. [See "On Carl Menger's Eightieth Birthday," Chapter 16 in the present volume, especially footnote 6 (on Menger) and footnote 11 (on Böhm-Bawerk).—Ed.]
19. [Mises's papers were captured by the Soviet Army at the end of the Second World War from a Nazi repository of looted documents in Czechoslovakia, and kept in a secret Soviet archive in Moscow. For an account of how they were discovered in the 1990s, see Richard M. Ebeling, "Mission to Moscow: The Mystery of the 'Lost Papers' of Ludwig von Mises," *Notes from FEE* (Irvington-on-Hudson, N.Y.: Foundation for Economic Education, July 2004), http://www.fee.org/pdf/notes/NFF_0704.pdf. Also see my introduction to *Selected Writings of Ludwig von Mises*, vol. 2, pp. xvi–xx, for an account of Mises's "lost papers" and their recovery.—Ed.]
20. [Jeremy Bentham, "Defense of Usury," (1797) in Werner Stark, ed., *Jeremy Bentham's Economic Writings*, vol. 1 (London: George Allan & Unwin, 1952), pp. 121–207. Bentham called for the end to all restrictions on market-determined rates of interest.—Ed.]
21. For a criticism of Lexis's theory, see my *Socialism: An Economic and Sociological Analysis* (Indianapolis: Liberty Fund, [1951] 1981), pp. 298–99.
22. [Eugen von Böhm-Bawerk, *Capital and Interest*, vol. 1, *History and Critique of Interest Theories* (South Holland, Ill.: Libertarian Press, [1884] 1959), pp. 241–321, and "Unresolved Contra-

No matter how much Marx may have been mistaken in his criticisms of modern society, he nevertheless had the merit of having revealed the motives behind the ideas of the British economists. Compared with the contributions of the German Historical School, Böhm-Bawerk was a stubborn reactionary.

The same thing was claimed to be true about my theory of money. The regular appearance of economic crises was a phenomenon inherent in the nature of capitalism, they said. Marx was, of course, wrong when he assumed that only the destruction of capitalism and the establishment of socialism could prevent the recurrence of these crises. Strict oversight and skillful regulation of market activities by a super-party government would free the economy from economic crises. It was pointless, they thought, to try to explain economic fluctuations on the basis of monetary and credit policies. The real causes had to be found at a deeper level, they said.

What was especially and violently attacked was what I said about the development of "fiduciary media" and the efforts to concentrate the entire gold reserves of the country in the central bank. The monetary system, they said, is not an end in itself. Its purpose is to serve the state and the people. Financial preparations for war must continue to be the ultimate and highest goal of monetary policy, as of all policy. How could the state conduct war, after all, if every self-interested citizen possessed the right to demand redemption of banknotes into gold? It was blindness not to recognize that only full preparedness for war—not only in the military sense but also with regard to the economy—could ensure the maintenance of peace. It was admitted that the Historical School has long neglected the treatment of monetary problems. Yet with Knapp's *State Theory of Money*, they said, the German spirit has finally rejected the destructive theories of the English economists.

The gold standard, they alleged, made Germany permanently dependent on the gold-producing countries. The merit of having first recognized this belonged to the German Agrarians. It was a vital necessity for the German nation to have a monetary system independent of foreign powers, they claimed.

There was only one excuse for my "errors," namely, that they were the logical outcome of the subversive ideas that the "Austrian School" had taken over from the doctrines of the Manchester men. Thinking

diction in the Marxian Economic System" (1896) in *Shorter Classics of Böhm-Bawerk* (South Holland, Ill.: Libertarian Press, 1962), pp. 201–302; see also H. W. B. Joseph, *The Labour Theory of Value in Karl Marx* (London: Oxford University Press, 1923).—Ed.]

in a vacuum was characteristic of Menger, Wieser, and Böhm-Bawerk, and this was my mistake, too. What would the monetary system be like if the state did not put all of its power behind it? It was fortunate, they alleged, that even in Austria only a small group of naïve authors shared the views of the "Austrian School."

Such were the opinions of my interlocutors during the five years that preceded the outbreak of the First World War. They were willing to grant me that I wrote in good faith. But they were convinced that my book only served the interests of unpatriotic and subversive speculators. They never entered into any kind of theoretical discussion. The quantity theory of money and the theories of the Currency School[23] were, in their eyes, nothing but curiosities in the historical literature. One of these gentlemen remarked that a colleague of his had asked whether I was not also an adherent of the phlogiston theory.[24] Another gentleman suggested that he considered my "Austrianness" to be a mitigating circumstance; with a citizen of Germany he wouldn't even discuss such questions.

Much later, at the time of the Regensburg meeting of the *Verein für Sozialpolitik* (1919), several of the participants said in conversation that they considered "simply ridiculous" and "not discussible" the view that the increase in the quantity of banknotes had brought about the devaluation of the mark.[25]

23. [In the 1820s through the 1860s, there was a heated and highly sophisticated debate between two groups of British monetary theorists known as the Currency School and the Banking School. The Currency School argued: (a) note currency should vary precisely with changes in the specie currency on deposit in the banking system; (b) the note currency should be fully convertible into specie; (c) the rate of interest was a significant influence on the volume of notes in circulation; (d) the foreign exchange rate was a good guide for controlling the volume of notes in circulation. The Banking School argued that (a) the "needs of business" should regulate the quantity of banknotes issued, and the banks should not "force" notes into circulation in excess of the needs of business; (b) the Currency School was correct that banknotes should be fully convertible; but (c) any drain of specie on the banking system might be counteracted by a decrease in the "hoards" of money held by the public, and an increase in specie or notes put into circulation might have no influence on spending and prices, because it might be absorbed into people's "hoards." On the controversy between the Currency and Banking schools, see Jacob Viner, *Studies in the Theory of International Trade* (New York: Augustus M. Kelly, [1937] 1965), pp. 218–89; Charles Rist, *History of Monetary and Credit Theory: From John Law to the Present* (New York: Augustus M. Kelly, [1940] 1966), pp. 202–36; and Lloyd Mints, *A History of Banking Theory, in Great Britain and the United States* (Chicago: University of Chicago Press, 1945), pp. 74–114.—Ed.]

24. [The phlogiston theory originated in 1667 with Johann Joachim Becher; it posited that inside flammable substances was a special element without odor, color, taste, or mass that is freed by the burning process, and is what caused the burning process. It was refuted in the eighteenth century through a variety of quantitative experiments.—Ed.]

25. [For Mises's analysis of the Great Inflation in Germany during and then after the First World War, see Ludwig von Mises, "Stabilization of the Monetary Unit—from the Viewpoint

Errors have always been made and also will be made in the future. Men are not infallible. The historian's task is not to point out errors, an undertaking that in retrospect is never difficult. It is his duty to identify the causal connections between things. Perhaps the foregoing remarks will be of some use in this regard.

When Max Weber was teaching at the University of Vienna in the summer of 1918, he said to me one day, "You do not like the *Verein für Sozialpolitik*; I don't like it much either. But the only remedy is for us to take an active part in the work of the society." I followed his advice. Beginning in 1919, I was on the board of directors, and from 1930 I also served on the board of governors. I promoted the discussion of problems relating to the theory of value; in cooperation with Arthur Spiethoff, I prepared and published the volume of the society's writings devoted to this topic; and I opened the discussion of this subject at the Dresden meeting (autumn 1932),[26] which the old guard of the society allowed to be called only a working committee report, an "epilog"[27] of the meeting. As was soon to be seen, it was the "epilog" of the *Verein für Sozialpolitik*, its last report.[28] A new age containing the worst economic policies had begun.

---

of Theory," (1923) in *The Causes of the Economic Crisis, and Other Essays Before and After the Great Depression* (Auburn, Ala.: Ludwig von Mises Institute, 2006), pp. 1–51; also, Richard M. Ebeling, "The Great German Inflation," *The Freeman: Ideas on Liberty* (November 2003), pp. 2–3, and "The Lasting Legacies of World War I: Big Government, Paper Money, and Inflation," *Economic Education Bulletin*, vol. 58, no. 11, 8 pp.

26. [See Ludwig von Mises, "The Controversy over the Theory of Value," (1932) reprinted in *Epistemological Problems of Economics* (New York: New York University Press, [1933] 1981), pp. 204–16.—Ed.]

27. See Franz Boese, *Geschichte des Verein für Sozialpolitik, 1872–1932* [History of the Society for Social Policy, 1872–1932] (Berlin: Duncker & Humblot, 1939), p. 236.

28. [The 1932 meeting of the *Verein für Sozialpolitik* in Dresden was the last meeting of the society until after the Second World War. See Peter G. Klein, ed., *The Collected Works of F. A. Hayek*, vol. 4, *The Fortunes of Liberalism: Essays on Austrian Economics and the Ideal of Freedom* (Chicago: University of Chicago Press, 1992), pp. 145–46, where Hayek says that

in September 1932, during a committee meeting of the *Verein für Sozialpolitik* in Bad Kissingen, a rather large group of professional colleagues was sitting together at tea in a garden, when Mises suddenly asked whether we were aware that we were sitting together for the last time. The remark at first aroused only astonishment and later laughter, when Mises explained that after twelve months Hitler would be in power. That appeared to the other members too improbable, but more than anything they asked why the *Verein für Sozialpolitik* should not meet again after Hitler had come to power. Of course, it did not meet again until after the end of the Second World War!

—Ed.]

Appendixes

Maxims for the Discussion of Methodological Problems in the Social Sciences: Paper Delivered at the Private Seminar[1]

1. It is inadmissible to make the a priori assumption that physics, along with the empirical sciences that are based on it, and the science of human action utilize the same methodology (methodological monism, physicalism). Such commonality of methods might be main-

---

1. [Ludwig von Mises delivered this paper at his "private seminar" on March 9, 1934, in his office at the Vienna Chamber of Commerce. From 1920 until the spring of 1934, Mises organized and chaired a private seminar of interested scholars in the fields of economics, history, sociology, political science, and philosophy. It met twice a month between October and June on Fridays at 7 p.m. The private seminar came to an end when Mises accepted a full-time teaching position at the Graduate Institute of International Studies in Geneva, Switzerland, as professor of international economic relations beginning in the autumn of 1934. Many of those who participated in the seminar recalled in later years that they considered it to be one of the most rewarding and challenging intellectual experiences of their lives because of the consistent quality of the papers delivered and the discussions that followed. For accounts of the seminar by some of the participants, see Ludwig von Mises, *Memoirs* (Auburn, Ala.: Ludwig von Mises Institute, [1940] 2009), pp. 81–83, and the recollections of other members of the seminar in the appendix to Margit von Mises, *My Years with Ludwig von Mises*, 2nd ed. (Cedar Falls, Iowa: Center for Futures Education, 1984), pp. 201–10.

In 1933, the year before delivering this paper at his private seminar, Mises published a collection of essays on various aspects of the methodology of the social sciences, *Grundprobleme der Nationalökonomie*, which in English has been published under the title *Epistemological Problems of Economics* (New York: New York University Press, [1933] 1981). Mises attempted to define and explain what he considered to be the unique and distinct qualities and characteristics that delineate the logical structure of and the methods for theory-formation in economics from both the methods of history and the methods of the natural sciences (physics, biology, chemistry). He developed what he came to refer to as *praxeology*, or the logical science of human action, as distinct from the interpretive method of "understanding" (*Verstehen*) in historical analysis and

tained only a posteriori, that is, after investigating the logic of both branches of science.

2. An investigation into the logic of the science of human action leads to the conclusion that there is an unbridgeable difference in the methods used in physics and in the science of human action, a difference that is produced by the different situations in which the researcher finds himself when confronted with natural phenomena versus the phenomena of human action. In physics, experiments permit the verification or falsification of hypotheses. It is experiments, alone, that permit us to draw a posteriori inferences from experience. If we were not able to experimentally investigate the dependence or independence of elements or variables from each other, we could not describe the relations inherent in natural processes by formulating empirical laws.

3. The experience that is the subject of the science of human action is history. (All empirical economic research, economic statistics, etc., are also history, because it refers to the past, even if the most immediate past.) We observe the complex phenomena that result from the interaction of many unknown components. We cannot conduct experiments; we therefore can neither verify nor falsify hypotheses, and thus cannot derive empirical laws. We could assert anything and disprove nothing if we had no other avenue than that of simply interpreting the experience.

4. This other avenue is that of the praxeological a priori. We understand action because we are, ourselves, acting humans. This understanding enables us to develop a closed system of the categories of and conditions for human action.

5. By relying on our understanding of the universally valid (theoretical) science of human action (pure sociology, particularly its thus far most developed part, namely pure economics) and by using logic and mathematics together with the empirical sciences of nature, we are in a position to analyze the historical facts contained in the documents of the past, such that we may finally attempt to show the qualitative and quantitative forces that have led to a particular outcome. Insofar as

the "hypothesis-experimental" methods of the natural sciences. He also argued strongly against what he considered to be the often antitheoretical approach of the German Historical School, which believed that period-specific economic relationships were discoverable through a primarily inductivist study of historical facts through time. It was, clearly, the controversial nature of many aspects of his argument in this book that led him to present a paper on this theme at the private seminar.—Ed.]

this insight into the historical factors, in terms of their qualitative and quantitative importance, is not uniquely determined by the results of scientific research and pure praxeology, and insofar as it does not comprehend the significance of these factors by conception (*begreift*) but uses, instead, the understanding (*Verstehen*) specific to the human sciences (*Geisteswissenschaften*), it is subjectively influenced by the character of the researcher. Conception (*Begreifen*) alone affords general objective knowledge, the formulation of which may very well be influenced by the perspective of the observer while remaining independent of his character and subjective point of view. With understanding (*Verstehen*) there cannot be any such independent knowledge in the historical sciences. The sphere of understanding excludes the use of the terms "true" and "false," "correct" and "incorrect" in the same sense in which they are used in discussing the empirical sciences or the theory of human action.[2]

(Addendum: "An interpretation determined by the viewpoint of the observer" does not imply a concession to the sociology of knowledge, which fundamentally errs in admitting within the human sciences nothing but understanding [*Verstehen*] and its subjective limitations,

---

2. [On the meaning and distinction between "conception" and "understanding" developed in more detail, see Mises, "Conception and Understanding" (1930) in *Epistemological Problems of Economics*, pp. 130–45, and *Human Action: A Treatise on Economics* (Irvington-on-Hudson, N.Y.: Foundation for Economic Education [3rd rev. ed., 1966] pp. 51–58. In essence, "conception" refers to those general or universal propositions in economic theory that are logically correct and valid within the context in which they are formulated. Thus, insofar as individuals have goals or ends that they desire to attain, and insofar as they discover that the means available to achieve them are scarce, they will, by necessity, have to rank the ends in order of importance and assign the means to achieve those ends ranked more highly before others ranked less highly; and in this process they will have to weigh the "costs" and "benefits" of pursuing one goal rather than another, and decide on the trade-offs (at the margin) that they consider the relatively more "profitable" ones in the context of the given circumstances. This would be universally and "objectively" true of any person, and therefore of all people, in which the means are found to be insufficient in relation to the ends that they can serve. "Understanding" refers to those unique and individual historical events that may be interpreted with the assistance of the logic of human action and the theorems of economics, but which are open to different "subjective" ("intuitive") interpretations as to their meaning and the relative importance of the factors that have brought about the observed outcome. Thus, historians may study the same historical event, say, the Battle of Waterloo, but they may differ concerning the "weight" or relevance of the various factors that brought about the historically unique outcome, the defeat of Napoleon. See also Kurt R. Laube, "Begreifen und Verstehen: Some Remarks on the Methodological Position of the Austrian School," in Kurt R. Laube, Angelo M. Petroni and James S. Sadowsky, eds., *An Austrian in France: Festschrift in Honor of Jacques Garello* (Torino: La Rosa, 1997), pp. 267–79.—Ed.]

while ignoring the conception [*Begreifen*] of facts and their general objectivity. Rather, it implies that the use of such terms as "success" and "failure," "favorable" and "unfavorable" depends, as a matter of course, on the observer's viewpoint. What are imports for one are exports for the other. For the sake of illustration, a comparison with a natural science that is otherwise inappropriate may for once be used by pointing out that classical physics understands the laws of physics to be invariant with respect to a rotation of the coordinate system. If a bacillus were to write a textbook of bacteriology, it would hardly say that using disinfecting agents yields "favorable" results. But this extends only to the interpretation, not to the content of the knowledge.)

6. The thinking that involves understanding (*Verstehen*) in the human sciences may be conceived of as dialectical thinking in Hegel's sense, as a thinking of things in their totality, or with Lasson as "cognition of everything particular from the concept of organic context, which posits it at that moment."[3] The thinking that involves praxeological conception (*Begreifen*), on the other hand, is founded on Kant's sharp rejection of dialectics.[4]

7. Einstein's often-repeated dictum, "As far as the laws of mathematics refer to reality, they are not certain; and as far as they are certain, they do not refer to reality," has no bearing on praxeological knowledge. The verdicts of conception are certain, but the assertions of understanding are not; and yet both refer to reality. What Einstein regards as a conundrum, how "human reason can through pure thought

3. [Adolf Lasson (1832–1917) was a German philosopher and served as professor at the University of Berlin. He was a Hegelian who emphasized the idea of the organic unity of the universe.—Ed.]

4. [Immanuel Kant (1724–1804) was one of the leading German philosophers of the Enlightenment. What Mises interpreted as Kant's insight for the grounding of a universally valid science of human action was Kant's idea in his *Critique of Pure Reason* (1781) that the mind operates in terms of certain categories outside of which thought and reasoning are impossible, for those categories are the context in which the mind can reflect on anything, including itself. Or in the words of Ernst Cassirer, *The Philosophy of the Enlightenment* (Princeton, N.J.: Princeton University Press, [1932] 1951), p. 94: "The nature of human knowledge can only be explained in terms of the ideas which the mind finds within itself." These a priori categories, for Mises, are the ones in which both human reasoning and human action occur, and are the only ones in the context of which man can reflect upon, through introspection, to understand the logic of his own conscious conduct. Since man's reasoning and ability to act are both conditioned by these same categories of thought, they are "prior to" experience and yet explain the reality of how men must and do act. Hence they are both logically valid and empirically true.—Ed.]

and without experience fathom properties of real things," praxeology answers by pointing out that both thinking and action have their origin in the same human mind.

8. One may say that the path of physics is one of increasing abstraction: it leads from less abstract and more intuitive concepts to more abstract and less intuitive ones. The path of praxeological conception is one of decreasing abstraction: it leads from highly abstract and unintuitive concepts to those of less abstraction and greater intuitiveness (Wieser).[5] This formulation may give rise to misgivings from a logical point of view, but rightly understood, it may pass as an approximate characterization of the difference.

9. The historical-realist school of opponents of economics has made the following claims:

a. There is no a priori science of human action: the historian approaches data—historical evidence—equipped only with knowledge provided by logic and the sciences and seeks to determine how something has happened, without any reference to an a priori science of human action. Today few will adhere to this viewpoint of consequential historicism. Even Sombart[6] admits that in the domain of culture, particularly in human society, there is something like "conceptually necessary relations." These constitute "what we call conceptual regularity, and the propositions we derive from it on a priori grounds are referred to as its laws." Thus Sombart has, albeit without wishing to do so and without noticing it, conceded everything that is required for justifying the neces-

5. [See Friedrich von Wieser, *Social Economics* (New York: Augustus M. Kelley, [1914] 1967), p. 6: "The theorist starts from the most abstract isolating and idealizing assumptions. . . . However, if he would accomplish his task he must not stop with these extreme abstractions. Should he do so, he would fail to convey an understanding of reality. Step by step by a system of decreasing abstraction, he must render his assumptions more concrete and more multiform."—Ed.]

6. [Werner Sombart (1863–1941) was professor of political economy at the University of Breslau and, beginning in 1917, at the University of Berlin. While never labeling himself a Marxist, in the 1890s and 1910s he strongly sympathized with Marx's critique of capitalist society. However, beginning in the 1920s, he became highly critical of Marx, and of Marxism for its positive outlook on the progress to industrial society. Sombart came to oppose what he considered to be the uniformity and ugliness of modern civilization. Instead, he looked back to the world before industrial development as a more desirable one of social hierarchy and stable order. By 1934, he had become a supporter of German National Socialism, endorsing the corporativist state, the führer (or leader) principle for Germany, state intervention and planning of the economy, national autarky, and partial reagrarianization of German society.—Ed.]

sity of a universal science of human action, which is fundamentally different from the historical disciplines of human action. If there are indeed such propositions and laws, there must also be a science that encompasses them, and this science must logically precede any other treatment of these problems. It is inconceivable to accept these propositions merely in the way they would appear in the nonscientific conception of everyday life. It is absurd to keep scientific thinking from penetrating any domain and to request toleration for traditional errors and imprecise, contradictory thinking.

b. There are empirical laws of human action that can be deduced, on an a posteriori basis, from historical experience: but such laws can typically be postulated only with the proviso that they are valid for human action within certain historical periods. These periods are demarcated either by chronology or by the race, class, ethnicity, culture, or the country of residence of the protagonists, or else by the predominance of particular historical, cultural, or economic characteristics. Only a part of the opponents of apriorism hold to this viewpoint, which one might call empiricism. Marx, the Marxists, and Gustav von Schmoller count among this number. The majority of historians reject this position and instead cling to historicism, without establishing any connection with empiricism. The empiricist view is untenable since the impossibility of experiments in the science of human action denies the human mind the ability to derive a posteriori, empirical laws from experiential data.

10. From the above, it follows that it is inadmissible to refer to the propositions of the theoretical science of human action as conventions in the sense in which this is done for the propositions of physics.[7] It is inadmissible to say that the propositions of this theory might not correspond to facts, since the impossibility of experiments does not enable us to determine their conformity or incompatibility with the facts.

11. It is inaccurate to make the assertion that whenever there is an inconsistency between the propositions of economics and the facts, that

---

7. [See Felix Kaufmann, *Methodology of the Social Sciences* (London: Oxford University Press, 1944), pp. 46–47.

economists simply give the reply that this is due to "interfering factors" without being able to clarify the nature of these factors. It has already been demonstrated that the sciences of human action do not admit of any contradiction between theory and the facts in the way it may exist in physics. Nor are the propositions of economics undermined by not corresponding to the facts. Economists tried to show that other motives also guide human action besides the motives of action investigated by Classical economics, and thus tried to identify those factors that are supposedly left out of the analysis. Modern economics, on the other hand, includes the effects of all those motives that previously were regarded as "non-economic," and therefore finds no inconsistent facts in the form of "interferences" or "resistances" that might serve as challenges to the validity of its laws.[8]

12. The subjective theory of value regards all action as "given," and therefore can never assert that any action was "right" or "wrong." It must not and cannot make any assertion that there is a dichotomy between an actual action and an "economic plan."[9] It is the task of his-

---

8. [See Mises, "Remarks on the Fundamental Problem of the Subjective Theory of Value," (1928) in *Epistemological Problems of Economics*, pp. 167–82, and *Human Action*, p. 3:
Until the late nineteenth century political economy remained a science of the "economic" aspect of human action, a theory of wealth and selfishness. It dealt with human action only to the extent that it is actuated by what was—very unsatisfactorily—described as the profit motive, and it asserted that there is in addition other human action whose treatment is the task of other disciplines. . . . The general theory of choice and preference . . . is much more than merely a theory of the "economic side" of human endeavors and of man's striving for commodities and an improvement in his material well-being. It is the science of every kind of human action. Choosing determines all human decisions. In making his choice man chooses not only between various material things and services. All human values are offered for option. All ends and all means, both material and ideal issues, the sublime and the base, the noble and the ignoble, are ranged in a single row and subjected to a decision which picks out one thing and sets aside another. Nothing that men aim at or want to avoid remains outside of this arrangement into a unique scale of gradation and preference. The modern theory of value widens the scientific horizon and enlarges the field of economic studies. Out of the political economy of the classical school emerges the general theory of human action, *praxeology*.
See also Israel M. Kirzner, *The Economic Point of View: An Essay in the History of Economic Thought* (Kansas City: Sheed and Ward, [1960] 1976), especially pp. 146–85.—Ed.]
9. [See Mises, *Human Action*, p. 21: "In this sense we speak of the subjectivism of the general science of human action. It takes the ultimate ends chosen by acting man as data, it is entirely neutral with regard to them, and it refrains from passing any value judgments. The only standard which it applies is whether or not the means chosen are fit for the attainment of the ends aimed at. . . . At the same time it is in this subjectivism that the objectivity of our science lies."—Ed.]

tory to investigate if a particular action was able to attain the desired ends; and in determining whether, indeed, the action did attain those goals, history must avail itself of the methods of analysis provided by economic theory. If one applies the insights of economic theory to the problems of economic policy, one may say in reference to particular policy measures whether, from the actor's point of view, they are appropriate and consistent or, instead, inappropriate and inconsistent, depending on whether or not they seem appropriate to attain the desired end aimed through a particular political action.[10]

10. [Mises developed more fully his conception of the methods of the social sciences in comparison to the methods of the natural sciences, and his theory of the logical character of human action; see the following works by Mises: "The Logical Character of the Science of Human Action," (1937) in Richard M. Ebeling, ed., Selected Writings of Ludwig von Mises, vol. 2, Between the Two World Wars: Monetary Disorder, Intervention, Socialism, and the Great Depression (Indianapolis: Liberty Fund, 2002), pp. 341–47; "Social Sciences and Natural Sciences," (1942) in Richard M. Ebeling, ed., Money, Method, and the Market Process: Essays by Ludwig von Mises (Norwell, Mass.: Kluwer Academic Press, 1990), pp. 3–15; Human Action, pp. 1–142; Theory and History: An Interpretation of Social and Economic Evolution (Indianapolis: Liberty Fund, [1957] 2005); The Ultimate Foundation of Economic Science: An Essay on Method (Indianapolis: Liberty Fund, [1962] 2006).—Ed.]

Short Curriculum Vitae of Mayer Rachmiel Mises of Lemberg[1]

I was born on June 23, 1801, in Lemberg, the son of the wholesaler and real estate owner Fischel Mises, who had been awarded, as a distinction, the right of domicile and of conducting business in the so-called "restricted district."[2] In 1819, I married Rosa, daughter of Mr. Hirsch Halberstamm of the town of Brody, who was at the time Brody's most important Russian-German export trader.

In 1832, while still co-owner of my father's business, I was appointed commissioner at the commercial court, a function I was to exercise for 25 years.

Following my father's death in 1842, I went into the wholesale business on my own, which enabled me to stay in the family home located on Ringplatz.

In 1854 I employed my oldest son, Abraham Oscar, in my company. In 1856 he went on to establish a wholesale business in Vienna and

1. [Mayer Rachmiel Mises (1801–91) was the great-grandfather of Ludwig von Mises. In June 1881 he prepared this short curriculum vitae to submit to the office of the Austrian emperor, Francis Joseph, as part of the legal process for ennoblement and the bestowing of the honorific and hereditary title of "Edler von." He was ennobled on April 30, 1881, with the ennoblement document issued on July 13, 1881. Ludwig von Mises is not mentioned at the end of the document among Mayer Rachmiel Mises's great-grandchildren because Ludwig was not born until September.—Ed.]
2. [The "restricted area" referred to that part of Lemberg, the capital of the Austrian province of Galicia, which was reserved as a residence and place of business for non-Jews. For a brief history of the Jews of Austria and Vienna in the second half of the nineteenth and the first half of the twentieth centuries, and in the context of Ludwig von Mises's life and work, including his own critique of anti-Semitism, see Richard M. Ebeling, "Ludwig von Mises and the Vienna of His Time," in *Political Economy, Public Policy, and Monetary Economics: Ludwig von Mises and the Austrian Tradition* (London: Routledge, 2010), pp. 36–56.—Ed.]

played a prominent role in the foundation of the Galician Carl-Ludwig Railroad, on whose board of directors he then served.

In 1859, under my said son's leadership, the Viennese branch of my company was commissioned with the purchase of Galician corn for the Austrian army in Italy. The business was conducted to the full satisfaction of Creditanstalt, the bank responsible for all monetary transactions in the contract. In 1860, Creditanstalt made my son director of its new Lemberg branch office, which resulted in the liquidation of my Viennese company.

Fifteen years later I also liquidated my Lemberg wholesale business and eventually retired from active business.

For nearly a half century I have been in public life in various positions and capacities.

I have already mentioned that for a period of 25 years I served as commissioner at the commercial court while also repeatedly serving on the city council and as a full member of the Chamber of Commerce.

Already in 1831 I became president of the Lemberg Jewish Community and have remained in this position ever since, with only a brief interruption in the years 1843–1845.

At the beginning of 1840, I was cofounder of the Lemberg Savings Bank, and for a period of nearly 16 years I was its internal auditor. I only resigned in 1857 when the Austrian National Bank appointed me to the board of its Lemberg branch; I served in this capacity for 22 years until this institution was transformed into the Austro-Hungarian Bank.

In 1848 I was a member of the "Confidential Committee" appointed by Governor Count Stadion,[3] and also a member of the committee for the integration of émigrés returning from exile, which in the following year had to facilitate the reemigration of those among them who had not found gainful employment within the country.[4]

I have been substantially involved in the foundation of an orphanage, a reform school, a secondary Jewish school, a charitable institution

---

3. [Franz Stadion, Graf von Warthausen (1806–53), was a prominent Austrian statesman who served as Austrian governor of the Littoral (the capital of which was the Adriatic port city of Trieste) during 1841–46, and governor of Galicia (1847–48), during which time he freed the peasants from compulsory labor duties; he also served as Austrian minister of education. He was a supporter of constitutional government within Austria and other liberal reforms.—Ed.]

4. [Many who had been part of the failed revolution of 1848 in Austria, including the uprising in Hungary and the rebellion of Poles in Russia and Austria, had left the Austrian Empire. Some began to return shortly afterward to resettle in their own homelands, found it difficult to reintegrate into their communities, and departed to live abroad once again.—Ed.]

for infant orphans, a Jewish library, and several other charitable and educational foundations, some of which I endowed out of my own financial means.

I dedicated myself no less to the administration of the Jewish Hospital in Lemberg, which owes its existence largely to one of my father's foundations.

And last, I may add that my marriage has produced five children. Only my two daughters, Mrs. Esther Klärmann and Mrs. Elise Bernstein, are still alive. My two older sons, Abraham Oscar Mises, director of the Galician Carl-Ludwig Railroad and director of the Lemberg branch of Creditanstalt, and Hirsch Mises, partner and director of the Halberstamm and Nirenstein banking institutions, and my youngest daughter, Clara Bodek, are no longer alive.

My male grandchildren are:

Hermann Mises, publisher and deputy to the Reichsrat in the years 1873–1879, and an honorary citizen of the city of Drohobycz;

Max Mises, privatier;[5]

Dr. Felix Mises, medical director emeritus of the Imperial-Royal General Hospital;

Emil Mises, engineer at the Galician Carl-Ludwig Railroad;

Arthur Mises, engineer at the Lemberg-Czernowitz Railroad Company.[6]

Lastly, my great-grandson is Heinrich Mises, son of Dr. Felix Mises.

Lemberg, June 1881

---

5. [A "privatier" is a financially independent individual, either through former business success or inheritance or marriage.—Ed.]

6. [Arthur Mises (1854–1903) was Ludwig von Mises's father.—Ed.]

Austro-Hungarian/Austrian monetary
and economic policy issues
(*continued*)
empire, xix–xx; independent state,
postwar viability of Austria as, 265;
Mises's writings on, before the Great
War, xxxv–xlv; Mises's writings on,
during the Great War, xlv–xlix; nationalist movements, xxi–xxv, xl–xli, xlix,
lxi, lxv–lxvi, 78; postwar breakup of
Austro-Hungarian Empire, xlix–l, 242;
Prussia, 1866 war with, xxiii, xxxi–
xxxii, lix, 12, 98*n*6, 252*n*2; reformist
movements of mid-nineteenth century,
xxi–xxiv; territory and population,
xx–xxi; turn-of-the-century society and
culture of, xxvi–xxix. *See also* specific
issues, e.g. gold standard, inflation
Austro-Hungarian Bank: claims of note
holders on liquidation of, 252–58; constitution of, effect of legal resumption
of specie payment on, 75–78; creation
of, xxxi; de facto specie redemption
by, xxxiv–xxxv, xxxviii–xl, 49–54,
86–87; Hungary, bank feud between
Austria and, 78–83; interest/discount
rate and specie payment policy, 54–
66, 71, 88–91, 93–94; interest/discount
rate, foreign rates compared to, 66–71,
88; Lemberg Savings Bank and, 334;
right to petition for legal resumption
of specie payment, 110–12; successor
state claims on assets of, li, 258; war
financing through banknote issuance
by, 209, 213, 252–53. *See also* foreign
exchange policy of Austro-Hungarian
Bank; fourth privilege or note-issuing
right of Austro-Hungarian Bank;
specie payments
Austro-Hungarian Export Association, 13
Austro-Prussian war of 1866, xxiii, xxxi–
xxxii, lix, 12, 98*n*6, 252*n*2
authoritarian tendencies, German, 205
automobile gasoline, proposal to abolish
tax-exempt status of, 124

Baernreither, Dr. (Minister of Trade), 91
balance of trade: in Austria-Hungary/
Austria, 10–11, 17, 53, 79, 170–71, 181,
237; in United States, 283, 285, 286
Balkans Conflict and financial crisis of
1912–13, 169
Bamberger, Ludwig, 27, 34, 262, 274
Bank of England, 15*n*28, 17, 36, 45*n*18,
60, 88, 90
Bank of France, 17, 34, 40, 60, 85
Bank Statute of 1887 (Austria-Hungary),
44
Bank Statute of 1899 (Austria-Hungary),
44, 46
Banking School, 321*n*23
banks and banking: Great Depression,
banking crisis of, liv, 296–99; pre-
war banking business in Austria, 19;
reform of Austrian currency, views of
financial institutions on, 18–20
Baring Crisis of 1890, 15
Battle of Valmy (1792), 202*n*20
Becher, Johann Joachim, 321*n*24
Beck, Austrian Minister, 38
beer and wine, excise tax on, 121–22, 124,
125, 127, 128, 129, 266, 280
Bendixen, Friedrich, 316
Benedikt, Moriz, xxxiii, 10*n*15, 21, 81,
259, 261
Bentham, Jeremy, 319
Berger, Wilhelm Freiherr von, 22
Berlin, Congress of (1878), 9
Bertels, Adolf, lxvi*n*78
Bilinski, Leon Ritter von, 42, 47, 99–100,
121, 126
bimetallists, 20–21, 22
birth rate, drop in, and migration issues,
198–99
Bismarck, Otto von, xxiii, xxiv, 9*n*12,
22*n*39, 274
Bland-Allison Act of 1878 (United
States), 11
Böhm-Bawerk, Eugen von, xxxiii,
xl, 144, 147*n*21, 170–71, 245, 259,
319–20

The typeface used in setting this book is Electra, designed in 1935 by the great American typographer William Addison Dwiggins. Dwiggins was a student and associate of Frederic Goudy and served for a time as acting director of Harvard University Press. In his illustrious career as typographer and book designer (he coined the term "graphic designer"), Dwiggins created a number of typefaces, including Metro and Caledonia, and designed as well many of the typographic ornaments or "dingbats" familiar to readers.

Electra is a crisp, elegant, and readable typeface, strongly suggestive of calligraphy. The contrast between its strokes is relatively muted, and it produces an even but still "active" impression in text. Interestingly, the design of the *italic* form—called "cursive" in this typeface—is less calligraphic than the italic form of many faces, and more closely resembles the roman.

This book is printed on paper that is acid-free and meets the requirements of the American National Standard for Permanence of Paper for Printed Library Materials, z39.48-1992. ♾

Book design adapted by Erin Kirk New, Watkinsville, Georgia, after a design by Martin Lubin Graphic Design, Jackson Heights, New York
Typography by Newgen North America
Printed and bound by Edwards Brothers, Ann Arbor, Michigan